Connectedness and Contagion

Connectedness and Contagion

Protecting the Financial System from Panics

Hal S. Scott

The MIT Press
Cambridge, Massachusetts
London, England

This book was set in Palatino LT Std by Toppan Best-set Premedia Limited. Printed and bound in the United States of America.

Library of Congress Cataloging-in-Publication Data

Names: Scott, Hal S., author.
Title: Connectedness and contagion : protecting the financial system from panics / Hal S. Scott.
Description: Cambridge, MA : The MIT Press, 2016. | Includes bibliographical references and index.
Identifiers: LCCN 2015039900 | ISBN 9780262034371 (hardcover : alk. paper)
Subjects: LCSH: Financial crises—History—21st century. | Global Financial Crisis, 2008–2009—Government policy. | Global Financial Crisis, 2008–2009.
Classification: LCC HB3722 .S385 2016 | DDC 339.5/3—dc23 LC record available at http://lccn.loc.gov/2015039900

10   9   8   7   6   5   4   3   2   1

To all of those who so successfully fought the panic created by the financial crisis of 2008

Contents

Acknowledgments

This book has been made possible through the efforts of many individuals. C. Wallace DeWitt, Eric M. Fraser, John Gulliver, Brian A. Johnson, Jacqueline C. McCabe, each a former Research Director of the Committee on Capital Markets Regulation, and Jacob Weinstein, Senior Advisor to the Committee, worked on early drafts of a paper from which this book evolved. Matthew Judell and Megan Vasios, each a Research Fellow at the Committee on Capital Markets Regulation, also contributed to this book.

I particularly appreciate the significant support and outstanding work provided by the following research assistants, each of whom assisted in drafting significant portions of earlier versions of this book: Ledina Gocaj, Adam Jenkins, Conor Tochilin, Yuli Wang, and Peter Zuckerman. In addition, research assistants Pam Chan, Weiwei Chen, Elaine Choi, Joseph Costa, Michael DiRoma, Katrina Flanagan, Brent Herlihy, Carys Johnson, Paul Jun, Tsz hin Kwok, Hye Kyoung Lee, Steven Li, Brice Lipman, Sai Rao, Jeffrey Scharfstein, and David Willard provided general assistance. Also thanks to Roel Theissen for his work on the European Union.

This study arose from a broader review of issues in financial regulatory reform conducted by the Committee on Capital Markets Regulation in the wake of the 2008 financial crisis, the first stage of which resulted in a report (The Global Financial Crisis: A Plan for Regulatory Reform) released in May 2009. The views expressed in this book are my own and do not necessarily represent the views of the Committee on Capital Markets Regulation or any of its individual members. Any errors are, of course, mine.

Connected	Contagion

Connected

* FIs directly overexposed
Shadowy FI. Fails to Big FI2
Chain reaction failures

* DFA/PRA address this
issue OFC due to contagion

Contagion

* indiscriminate run
on FIs by SR creditors
led to fire sale
to give pay SR creditor
∴ FI assets
being sold

* systemic risk

* runnable uninsured
SR liabs
↳ > 1 yr

* US gvt bailed contagion
GFC 2008 ex F Lehman

* how rules don't
PRU
address contagion

Introduction

This book is concerned with the fundamental stability of our financial system upon which the viability of our economy, and ultimately our polity, rests. In the 2008 financial crisis we witnessed a severe plunge in real estate prices—the Case Shiller National Home Price Index stood at 184.62 in July 2006, but by September 2008 it had fallen to 161.95. It eventually fell as low as 134.03 in 2012.[1] This decline in housing prices was unprecedented; before 2006, the index had never declined by more than five points over a three-year period.[2] The Moody's/RCA Commercial Property Price Index for US commercial real estate experienced a similar fall, peaking at 173 in the fourth quarter of 2007 and declining to 104 in the fourth quarter of 2009.[3] These declines led to significant losses for financial institutions exposed to residential mortgages and commercial real estate. Five of the twenty largest US financial institutions either became insolvent—Washington Mutual, Lehman Brothers, and AIG (at least the holding company)—or were acquired with government assistance—Bear Stearns and Wachovia.[4] The IMF estimated total losses to be $4.1 trillion.[5] GDP growth fell from positive 5.12 percent in 2006 to negative 0.92 percent in 2008 and negative 0.11 percent in 2009, putting the US economy into recession.[6]

This book demonstrates that "contagion," not "connectedness," was the most potentially destructive feature of the 2008 financial crisis. Connectedness occurs when financial institutions are directly overexposed to one another and the failure of one institution would therefore directly bankrupt other institutions, resulting in a chain reaction of failures. Contagion is a different phenomenon. It is an indiscriminate run by short-term creditors of financial institutions that can render otherwise solvent institutions insolvent due to the fire sale of assets that are necessary to fund withdrawals and the resulting decline in asset prices triggered by such sales.

Contagion indeed remains the most virulent and important part of systemic risk still facing the financial system today. This is because, as set forth throughout this book, our financial system still depends on approximately $7.4 to $8.2 trillion of runnable and uninsured short-term liabilities—defined as liabilities with a maturity of less than one month, with about 60 percent of these liabilities held by nonbanks. The losses and the impact on our economy and country in September 2008 would have been much worse but for the response of our government to halting the contagion that broke loose following the bankruptcy of Lehman Brothers. However, since then the Congress has dramatically weakened the Federal Reserve, FDIC, and Treasury's ability to respond to contagion, leaving our financial system sharply exposed to another contagion.

The Federal Reserve was created in 1913 to stem such panics, which were rife in the nineteenth century and culminated in the panic of 1907, by acting as a lender of last resort. After the bank runs experienced in the Depression of 1933, Congress created the Federal Deposit Insurance Corporation (FDIC) to guarantee deposits. These two powers were used extensively during the 2008 crisis. The Fed supplied liquidity to the banking and nonbanking financial sector, the latter through its authority under Section 13(3) of the Federal Reserve Act. The FDIC expanded the scope and amount of deposit insurance. In addition, the US Treasury offered temporary guarantees to money market funds. And finally, TARP was enacted to infuse public capital into the banking system, beginning with the nine largest banks. In the aftermath of the crisis, the use of these powers has been called into question as contributing to moral hazard—giving institutions the incentive to take on risk—and as constituting undesirable public bailouts of insolvent institutions. In fact some members of Congress believe that public funds in any form should not be used to support the private sector, including financial institutions.

As a result of these concerns, the Fed's and FDIC's powers were pared back by the Dodd–Frank Act of 2010, and in the case of the Treasury's temporary guarantee to money market funds, by TARP. The Fed's powers to loan to nonbanks under 13(3) can now only be used with the approval of the Secretary of Treasury, the Fed can only loan to nonbanks under a broad program (not to one institution as it did in the case of AIG), and nonbanks must meet heightened collateral requirements. The Fed now ranks fourth to its central bank peers—the Bank of England, the European Central Bank, and the Bank of

Japan—in its powers to act as lender of last resort. The FDIC and the Treasury cannot on their own, without prior congressional approval or new authority, expand guarantees. The authority to make public capital injections, even to address widespread insolvency that could seize up the banking system and real economy, has expired with the expiration of TARP.

The contraction of powers, which former Secretary Timothy Geithner calls barely adequate in his book *Stress Test*, puts us at severe risk in dealing with the next financial crisis. Secretary Geithner states: "We went into our crisis with a toolbox that wasn't exactly empty, but also wasn't remotely adequate for our complicated and sprawling modern financial system. … What should be in the toolbox? The vital tools are: an ability to extend the lender-of-last-resort authority to provide liquidity where it's needed in the financial system, resolution authority … and, along with deposit insurance … broader emergency authority to guarantee other financial liabilities."[7]

Or consider this quote from former Secretary of the Treasury Paulson:

Dodd–Frank falls short in other areas …. Congress has also removed some of the most creative and effective tools used to stave off collapse. In order to provide greater Congressional control, Dodd–Frank limits regulator discretion in times of crisis. In one respect, of course, that's all to the good. Congress is responsible to our citizens, so it's encouraging to see the focus on taxpayer protection. The bank rescues were a source of public outrage, so it is understandable that Congress would take steps to ensure that failing institutions not be propped up in their present form. But some of the powers that Congress limited or constrained, such as some Federal Reserve lending authorities or the FDIC guarantee authority, were rarely used, if ever. Emergency measures such as we used to stem the crisis should be employed only when we are facing the economic equivalent of war, and the president and two-thirds of the Fed and the FDIC make a financial emergency declaration to protect the American people. Why give up these tools and disarm when there is no assurance that policy makers will not need such flexibility again?[8]

In significant part, the Dodd–Frank Act is premised on the diagnosis that connectedness not contagion was the major problem in the crisis—this is reflected in the requirement for central clearing of over-the-counter derivatives (swaps), net exposure limits for banks, and the designation of systemically important banks and other financial institutions as systemically important financial institutions (SIFIs) and therefore subject to heightened supervision by the Federal Reserve. The recent Federal Reserve rule calibrating a capital "surcharge" for systemically important banks is also based on a connectedness analysis, which I show has no empirical relation to reducing the risk of contagion. But connectedness was not the major problem, contagion was. Some argue that the old powers to fight contagion are no longer necessary because we have put in place new regulations to prevent future contagion—namely enhanced capital requirements, new liquidity requirements, and new resolution procedures. I call this the two wings and prayer approach. Capital and liquidity requirements, the wings, are ex ante policies designed to prevent contagion, not to deal with it if it does occur. It would be foolhardy to believe we can completely avoid contagion by adopting such policies. Capital requirements only apply to banks and a few specific nonbanks (e.g., the three nonbank SIFIs, for which the requirements have not yet been determined), and could never be at a high enough level to assure short-term creditors that capital would not be seriously eroded by the fire sale of assets in a crisis. For example, according to Warren Buffet's Financial Crisis Inquiry Commission testimony:

> No capital requirements protect you against a real run. I mean, if virtually all of your liabilities are payable that day, you can't run a financial institution and be prepared for that. And that's why we've got the Fed and the FDIC. You could be the most soundly capitalized firm in town, but if there were no FDIC and the Fed and you had a bank capitalized with 10% of capital and I had one with 5% of capital and I hired 50 people to go over and start standing right in front of your bank, you're the guy that's going to fall first. Then when they get through with you they're going to come over to my bank too, that's why we don't do that sort of thing because you can't contain the fire over on the other guy's bank. You just can't stand a run. So you need the Federal Reserve and the FDIC. And even with Northern Rock, the UK government had come and said we guarantee everything and they still had lines. When people are scared they're scared. I mean, if you see its uninsured and you see a line at a bank where you've got your money, then get in line, get your money and put it under your mattress. That's why we've got a Fed and FDIC. I think the FDIC and Social Security were the two most important things that came out of the '30s. I mean the system needed an FDIC.[9]

New liquidity rules, also only applicable to banks, seek to assure that banks have liquid assets to cover withdrawals in a run. But they are based on dubious assumptions about the withdrawal rates of different kinds of bank funding, and ultimately cannot avoid the need of a central bank to act as a lender of last resort. At best, this level of private liquidity can buy some breathing room for the central bank to determine what to do. At worst, they create a hoarding situation where the assurance of each institution of its own liquidity prevents each institution from supplying liquidity to others, thus worsening a weak institution's options during a crisis.

New resolution authority under the Orderly Liquidation Authority in Dodd–Frank is the prayer. First, its use is not assured. It only comes into play if a financial institution on the brink of insolvency is designated by the Treasury, upon the recommendation of a super-majority of the boards of the Fed and FDIC, as a threat to the financial stability of the United States. Second, while procedures are being designed with the objective of making sure no short-term creditors of banks and other subsidiaries of financial institutions, like broker dealers, would lose money in an OLA procedure (as opposed to equity and longer term debt), these procedures may not prove effective or credible enough to stop runs on solvent institutions. Short-term creditors may still flee because they believe it is better to be safe than sorry.

Money market fund reforms are also inadequate to address contagion. As described throughout this book, runs on money market funds were a central feature of the 2008 crisis and were only stopped by the provision of temporary guarantees by the Treasury and indirect lender of last resort support by the Fed (lending to banks to purchase the assets of money market funds). Since 2008 the SEC has implemented new rules that require money market funds to hold more liquid assets, and prime institutional money market funds to have floating rather than fixed asset values. However, these reforms are unlikely to stop runs on such funds in the future, since investors could still fear further declines in the value of assets and the depletion of the most high-quality liquid assets to meet the withdrawals of investors that redeem first. Furthermore new SEC rules that give fund boards the authority to charge fees for withdrawals or suspend redemptions may only accelerate runs of investors fearful of the imposition of such limits.

This book takes the view that we need to restore and strengthen our weapons to fight contagion. Having strong anti-contagion weapons would indeed mean that a very large financial institution could be allowed to fail. This is because such a failure would not spark contagion, as the market would know that the necessary government authorities, including a strong lender of last resort and the provider of guarantees, exist to protect the solvent financial institutions. Having strong contagion fighting powers would therefore allow us to solve the too-big-to-fail problem and reduce moral hazard. At the same time a strong lender of last resort should not be one operating under an ill-defined framework. The legally permissible actions of the Fed should be bounded in a clear framework so that it is politically and legally accountable such specification of actions that might be taken in a contagious panic could well forestall the panic in the first place.

However, this book recognizes that it is impossible for Congress to strengthen these weapons now—anyone proposing such measures would be attacked as trying to bail out Wall Street rather than congratulated for trying to improve the stability of our financial system. This book is meant as a measure to prepare the ground for a more rational and less populist discussion of these issues.

The book is organized as follows.

Part I gives an overview of the three components of systemic risk: (1) connectedness, (2) contagion, and (3) correlation. It is backed up by an appendix with a review of the economic literature on these components.

Part II examines in depth whether asset connectedness, specifically firms with credit exposure to Lehman, proved to be a problem after Lehman's failure. It also considers whether asset connectedness would have been a problem if AIG had not been rescued. It then addresses liability connectedness, which is whether the failure of a major funder of the financial system could trigger the failure of others. It concludes by explaining that important parts of Dodd–Frank are focused on dealing with the systemic risk caused by connectedness. This includes a discussion of SIFI designation, particularly for asset management firms. The conclusion of part II is that connectedness is not the major contributor to systemic risk.

Part III begins with a general review of the problem of contagion, and how it manifested itself in the financial crisis, particularly in the nonbank sector. It then reviews the government response to contagion in the crisis. Part III also discusses potential solutions to contagion, beginning with a focus on the measures used in the crisis, lender of last resort and guarantees. This includes a comparison of the lender-of-last-resort powers of the major central banks. It also details the limitations imposed on the Fed's lender-of-last-resort powers and the FDIC's and Treasury's authorities to guarantee liabilities. It then describes certain reforms to the Fed's lender-of-last-resort authorities and the FDIC's guarantees that could strengthen the financial system.

Part IV turns to the two wings and the prayer approaches to contagion—capital, liquidity, and resolution procedures. This part also sets forth the problems with the recent money market fund reforms. It concludes with an examination of an alternative approach to limiting contagion—by dramatically reducing the dependency of banks and nonbanks on the short-term funding (liabilities with one month or less in maturity) that exposes them to contagion.

Part V looks at TARP and other techniques of capital injection, and compares the US approach of eliminating TARP with the standing TARP policies of the eurozone and Japan, and the ironclad bailout policy of China.

Connectedness

Δstli in 3rd street
cause SN to Hosp'
failure of other
Shs

Lender → Cailure of SN
cause failure of Shs
ed de SN eqty/drawn
→ failure 3SN

Asset C ⇒ Shs dep'
failing SN ten
→ failing SN ten
Credit' i w SN ten
Sw & rish w/ Δdz, collateral
diversifica

Contagion

sudden spread of
SN run from
firms SN and
health Shs

Catastrophe

Shs faild w
de collapse
asset PS
* Q

I   Connectedness, Contagion, and Correlation: Definitions and a Review of the Economic Literature

This part gives an overview of the concepts of connectedness, contagion, and correlation, the three Cs of systemic risk. For a detailed literature review on these concepts, see the appendix. Connectedness describes the concern that the failure of one bank will cause the failure of others through balance sheet links. In asset connectedness, the failure of one bank will destabilize other banks that own its debt or equity, or are exposed through derivatives contracts. In liability connectedness, the failure of a bank that is an important source of short-term credit will destabilize banks that depend on it for funding. Correlation describes the failure of multiple institutions due to a collapse in asset prices. Contagion is the indiscriminate spread of run-like behavior throughout the financial system, including to healthy institutions. There may be important relationships and some degree of overlap between connectedness and contagion. For example, liability connectedness may intensify contagion. Correlated declines in real-estate prices were the spark that ignited the contagious panic observed in the 2008–2009 financial crisis. Nonetheless, the three Cs are distinct concepts. A review of the literature leads to a number of points about the current state of academic research on systemic risk. First, most of the connectedness literature is focused on liabilities rather than assets. Second, the existence of asset connectedness does not necessarily imply an increase in risk, since collateral, hedging, and diversification all serve to reduce risk. Third, the connectedness literature that discusses the concept of "indirect" connectedness is really discussing correlation and not connectedness. Finally, none of the academic literature materially addresses the principal problem of contagion.

1   The Concept of Connectedness

Asset connectedness is the concern that the failure of one financial institution will provoke a chain reaction of failures by other financial institutions with direct credit exposures to the failed institutions. This phenomenon was not observed in the financial crisis. Most important, the losses imposed on firms by Lehman were not large enough to push them into bankruptcy. Liability connectedness refers to the connection between the providers and recipients of short-term funding, whereby if a funding institution fails, the failure of its dependent recipient institutions will also result. Like asset connectedness, liability connectedness defaults were not a problem during the crisis, as Lehman, nor other financial institutions, were an important source of short-term funding for other financial institutions. Most of the connectedness literature is focused on liabilities rather than assets.

Much of the literature on connectedness is theoretical in nature, given the rarity of financial crises and the tendency of governments to intervene when large financial institutions become distressed. Network theory is emerging as a powerful tool to analyze how asset and liability connectedness influence the propagation of shocks throughout the financial system. However, most of the literature that uses network theory to analyze financial stability makes unrealistic assumptions about bank behavior or assumes implausibly large idiosyncratic shocks. Some models do incorporate behavior consistent with the contagious runs witnessed in the 2008–2009 crisis, and may therefore shed light on the relationship between asset connectedness and contagion. Connectedness is tinder that might allow a small spark to ignite contagious runs.

1.1   Asset Connectedness

The economic literature on asset connectedness (or connectedness) supports the conclusion that asset connectedness is not likely to be a major source of systemic risk. A simple theoretical structure of asset connectedness would be the following: Bank B has direct exposure to Bank A (e.g., owning debt extended to Bank A). Bank C has direct exposure to Bank B. If Bank A fails, then the subsequent loss to Bank B through its asset exposure to Bank A causes Bank B to fail. Similarly Bank C fails due to its asset exposure to Bank B. These failures can permeate throughout the financial system via asset connectedness. Such an asset connectedness model of systemic failure has been widely studied and universally rejected as a plausible cause of the financial crisis.[1] In addition these models generally consider just the fixed credit exposures without taking into account how such exposures are reduced in practice through the use of hedging collateral. For example, if Bank B's credit quality declines, Bank A may purchase credit default swaps, which will pay off if Bank B does fail, to reduce its exposure to a Bank B failure. The literature concludes that while it is theoretically possible to have chain reactions of default, there would have to be implausibly large shocks for this to occur. This conclusion is supported by the historical record, as no large bank has ever failed as a result of losses incurred in the interbank lending market.[2] Furthermore, even the existence of asset connectedness does not imply the presence of substantial risk, since much of the risk from asset connectedness exposure can be reduced through collateral, hedging, and diversification. For a detailed overview of the academic literature on asset connectedness, see the appendix.

1.2 Liability Connectedness

Modern financial markets are a highly complex system of financial institutions with a high degree of interdependence and interconnections. Financial institutions are not only connected through exposure on the asset side of the balance sheet, as discussed above, but also on the liability side through funding relationships, referred to herein as "liability connectedness." As part II demonstrates, Lehman's failure did not present liability connectedness issues, primarily because Lehman was not a significant funder of the US financial system. Moreover money market funds, which some have suggested are potential sources of liability connectedness as heavy investors in the short-term liabilities of banks, were not, as shown in part II, a significant source of systemic risk. For a more detailed overview of the academic literature on liability connectedness, see the appendix. Overall, the real story of liability connectedness is contagion.

2   The Concept and History of Contagion

Contagion involves run behavior, whereby fears of widespread financial collapse lead to the withdrawal of funding from banks and other financial institutions. The problem of contagion is of hoary vintage.[1] The term "contagion" denotes the spread of run-like behavior from one financial institution to an expanding number of other institutions, reducing the aggregate amount of funding available to the financial system and in turn to the economy.[2] Contagion can also spread to short-term capital markets that fund the complex and growing assortment of nondepository financial institutions in the financial system. The special feature that distinguishes contagion from other causes of systemic instability is the tendency of contagious runs to propagate *indiscriminately, apart from connectedness*. Contagion is "indiscriminate" when it afflicts healthy markets and solvent institutions.[3]

Financial institutions are vulnerable to contagion due to their dependence on short-term borrowing to fund long-term investment activity. When short-term debt investors suddenly refuse to extend funding, institutions relying on such funding engage in fire sales of assets and ultimately fail. The fire sales may generally decrease asset values of other institutions who may also fail, as well. Runs of short-term creditors may be rational or irrational and need not be indiscriminate. A run by short-term creditors can be targeted to a single or limited number of financial institutions, for example, those known to have incurred significant losses.[4] During a *contagious* and *indiscriminate* run, however, investors may also withdraw funding from multiple institutions or markets that are not themselves facing any objective business distress. In such an environment the decision to exit is made not on the basis of specific information but rather because investors possess insufficient information to differentiate their own risks from those that others are—or appear to be—facing. This dynamic, one former central banker has warned, may "lead to failures of other financial intermediaries, even when [they] have not invested in the same risks and are not subject to the same original shocks."[5] If these intermediaries fund themselves using short-term capital instruments, contagion effects may spread to the markets where these instruments trade. Sudden demand for liquidity by investors in intermediaries that normally hold these instruments or a refusal on the part of interbank lenders to renew their funding can trigger liquidations or freeze-ups in these markets, triggering fire sales, decimating asset prices, and halting lending activity.

Contagion presents risk of a singular nature to financial institutions.[6] Contagion is a structural feature of the financial system that is endogenous to the economics of maturity transformation and, in my judgment, is not likely to be resolved through better risk management or improved prudential oversight. Absent affirmative steps to contain it, the problem of contagion will continue to haunt the financial system.

2.1   History of Contagion

Financial historians disagree as to the extent of contagion's role in the periodic disruptions of the US financial system over the past two centuries. Clearer is the role that contagion has played in the development of the US Federal Reserve System, which was created in reaction to the Panic of 1907, although the notion of a central bank lender of last resort had been contemplated throughout the late nineteenth century in response to successive panics and waves of bank failures.[7] Critical in the creation of the Fed was the belief that private efforts of the clearinghouses to provide liquidity to their members were not sufficient to forestall panics.[8]

Some economic historians trace the frequency of bank failures in US history to an abnormally high level of concentration risk promoted by the decentralized structure of the US banking system. This decentralization was a by-product of the restructuring of the American banking industry during the National Banking Era, stimulated by distinctive legislative changes in the United States that were not duplicated elsewhere.[9] According to this account, branching restrictions embodied in the National Bank Act of 1864 propelled a thirteenfold increase in the total number of US banks over the next fifty years.[10] By 1914 the unprecedented expansion of banking in the United States had culminated in a unit banking system comprising 22,030 institutions nationally.[11]

The massive proliferation of small banks managing localized loan portfolios created a banking system in which each bank's balance sheet was concentrated in a local economy. This lack of diversification left each bank vulnerable to idiosyncratic shocks, and therefore increased the overall failure rate.[12] The small banks might also have suffered from poorer management relative to their larger and more sophisticated peers. This background of "too small to survive" is ironic in view of the current concern with "too big to fail."

Countries whose banking systems did not develop along decentralized lines have not faced repeated waves of financial panic. In Canada, for example, bank failures have been rare, even though the Canadian macroeconomic environment has generally tracked the US experience.[13] Between 1870 and 1913, Canadian banks underwent 23 liquidations, compared with 3,208 recorded in the United States over the same period.[14] No banks failed in Canada between 1923 and 1985, whereas between 1930 and 1933 alone, 9,000 US banks suspended operations.[15] Such discrepancies are not attributable to the variance in the performance of the Canadian and US economies but may reflect dramatic differences in industry consolidation.[16] Then again, the different bank failure rates across the two systems might also be the result of any number of other political, regulatory, and social factors distinguishing the Canadian and US environments from each other during the Great Depression.

In their study of the Chicago Banking Panic of 1932, Charles Calomiris and Joseph Mason conclude that worsening economic conditions can cause depositors to withdraw their money from weak banks in favor of stronger ones, showing that most bank failures resulted from homogeneous balance sheet impairments caused by the collapse in asset prices after the onset of the Great Depression.[17] This finding is striking given the tight geographic focus of the Panic, in which some 40 Chicago-area banks failed, including 26 during a single turbulent week in June 1932.[18] Although these characteristics appear to resemble a classic bank run, the authors reject this interpretation, insisting instead that most of the banks that did succumb were "distinguishable months before the panic,"[19] the evidence of their preexisting mass insolvency "reflected in stock prices, failure probabilities, the opinions of bank examiners, debt composition, and interest rates."[20] The authors find, by contrast, that solvent banks did not fail during the Chicago Panic.[21] Part of the explanation for the sharply differentiated performance of solvent banks may be that the healthy banks were able to supplement lost deposits by coordinating private interbank lending facilities, to which insolvent institutions did not have access.[22]

Some scholars and finance professionals have minimized the role of contagion in the unfolding of the 2008 financial crisis. *Financial Times* columnist Martin Wolf, for example, assigns primary blame for the crisis to asset shocks and macroeconomic instabilities linked to long-term international imbalances in global trade, savings rates, and investment.[23] In another study, Nicolas Dumonteaux and Adrian Pop scrutinize the impact on financial institutions of the Lehman bankruptcy, determining that contagion effects, to the extent any existed at all, were "firm-specific, rational and discriminating rather than industry-wide-specific, 'pure' panic-driven or undifferentiated."[24] Like the Chicago Panic, firms that were most affected by the collapse of Lehman possessed comparable core business characteristics, operating fundamentals, and a performance record that was measurably correlated with Lehman.[25] Appraising the totality of the evidence, Dumonteaux and Pop conclude that the effects of Lehman's failure on financial institutions were neither indiscriminate nor contagious.[26]

Other commentators offer a more persuasive, contrary view. William Sterling has argued that studies finding an absence of indiscriminate contagion are based on an incomplete set of indicators.[27] Using the Bloomberg Financial Conditions Index, which incorporates a broader set of indicators, Sterling showed that the Lehman failure was an immediate and massive shock to an already stressed financial system.[28] Other studies have found that Lehman was a dangerous transmitter of contagion, with Jian Yang and Yinggang Zhou finding, for example, that an increase in the price of a Lehman CDS caused subsequent increases in the CDS prices of other financial institutions.[29] Lehman's effect on other firm's was the largest among global financial institutions.[30] JPMorgan was apparently a prime beneficiary of this kind of funding transfer during the financial crisis, as retail customer deposits[31] and prime brokerage assets[32] flowed out of weakened commercial and investment banking institutions and into JPMorgan's insured deposit and prime brokerage accounts. Writing in his annual letter in 2009, Jamie Dimon, JPMorgan's chief executive officer, advised shareholders that the bank received a net *inflow* of deposits as investors fled lower quality institutions. "As we entered the most tumultuous financial markets since the Great Depression," Dimon wrote, "we experienced the opposite of a 'run on the bank' as deposits flowed in (in a two-month period, $150 billion flowed in—we barely knew what to do with it)."[33]

Several important US financial firms that arguably possessed considerably stronger business models than Lehman, such as Morgan Stanley and Goldman Sachs, do in fact appear to have been affected by some degree of run behavior after the Lehman failure. Although "[s]ignificant bank runs were not a feature of the financial crisis," some large banks did fall prey to runs. Wachovia faced a bank run on its deposits prior to its acquisition by Wells Fargo.[34] Washington Mutual faced a similar fate before its eventual sale to JPMorgan.[35] Importantly, nonbank financial institutions, beginning with Bear Stearns[36] and later spreading to critical segments of the short-term capital markets, as well as the money market funds, also underwent serious runs.[37] Although no significant financial institution sharing Lehman's basic business attributes collapsed as a result of Lehman's failure, this was likely a reflection of the bailout signals transmitted by the Federal Reserve's rescue of AIG as well as by the multifaceted public support programs instituted by the US Treasury and the Federal Reserve.[38] As discussed at greater length below, the evidence shows substantial contagion effects elsewhere in the financial system. These effects were transmitted initially through the Reserve Primary Fund (RPF) to other prime money market funds; certain segments of the asset-backed, financial, and corporate commercial paper markets; and unsecured interbank lending and secured repo borrowing markets. Ultimately, they resulted in serious runs on other investment banks as investor confidence in the vitality of the independent investment banking business model deteriorated.

2.2 Panicked Runs: Multiple Equilibria (Outcomes)

The best-developed theory of systemic risk attributes financial panic to run behavior by short-term creditors that spreads to multiple financial institutions.[39] Depositors, operating under the constraints of asymmetric information, withdraw from all banks indiscriminately. Douglas W. Diamond and Philip H. Dybvig have suggested that the "shift in [creditor] expectations" can "depend on almost anything," whereas others have attributed contagion to a change in the business cycle,[40] as originating from a lack of timely market information,[41] or as one instance of a more general form of crowd behavior documented in nonfinancial contexts.[42] According to the first view, contagion can be triggered by purely random phenomenon, or economic "sunspots." The latter view attributes contagion to "informational cascades" in which individual market participants use the actions of peers as cost-effective surrogates for actual data collection about an underlying reference entity. When peers run, they run too.[43] Each of these explanations shares the recognition that contagion is not conditioned on insolvency. Instead, contagion is a liquidity-driven phenomenon that reflects the maneuvering of short-term creditors in response to informational constraints, rational incentives, and structural vulnerabilities uniquely characteristic of financial intermediaries dependent on short-term borrowing and longer term assets. Such constraints can provoke short-term creditors to withdraw from institutions preemptively, even if they are fundamentally well-capitalized and have no exposure to losses connected to an asset shock, as occurred in money market funds with no exposure to Lehman during the financial crisis.

Contagion theory historically focused on runs by uninsured depositors to explain the wave of bank failures of the 1930s and elsewhere in modern financial history, although the underlying economic explanation for contagious runs applies equally to the behavior of nondeposit short-term creditors.[44] Contagion can spread indiscriminately to solvent institutions, causing "real economic problems because even 'healthy' banks can fail."[45] Financial institutions that succumb to contagion may be solvent immediately beforehand and may not display characteristic warning signs of distress detectable in advance by regulators.[46] Importantly, contagion and runs on individual financial institutions are distinct, albeit related, phenomena. An isolated run by short-term investors on a single financial institution is not an example of contagion. Contagion only occurs when a run at one institution or some other event induces short-term creditors of multiple other institutions to run, including from institutions that are adequately capitalized and have no financial linkage to the same set of problematic risk exposures.[47] Under certain circumstances individual runs can generate systemic contagion effects, provoking further runs. Contagion can therefore develop from a generalized fear of failure on the part of short-term creditors as much as it may represent a reaction to specific cases of real distress.

The Diamond and Dybvig model establishes that banks and other financial intermediaries exist at "multiple equilibria."[48] Because maturity transformation requires an intermediary to finance long-term illiquid assets (e.g., mortgages with maturities spanning multiple decades)[49] with short-term or demand liabilities redeemable at par, one of these equilibria is a run:

> Banks are able to transform illiquid assets by offering liabilities with a different, smoother pattern of returns over time than the illiquid assets offer. These contracts have multiple equilibria. If confidence is maintained, there can be efficient risk sharing, because in that equilibrium a withdrawal will indicate that a depositor should withdraw under optimal risk sharing. If agents panic, there is a bank run and incentives are distorted. In that equilibrium, everyone rushes in to withdraw their deposits before the bank gives out all of its assets. The bank must liquidate all its assets, even if not all depositors withdraw, because liquidated assets are sold at a loss.[50]

The core of this account is what some commentators have labeled a collective action problem.[51] When short-term creditors of a maturity-transforming firm develop suspicions that the firm is verging on insolvency, the creditors have a rational motivation to withdraw funding before the firm's supply of liquid reserves is drained by others responding to the same incentives. Generating enough liquidity to redeem exiting creditors at par forces the firm into monetizing long-term assets at noneconomic valuations. In the ensuing fire sale, the firm incurs actual losses, thus realizing the concern that had caused creditors to panic in the first place. Even though all short-term creditors would collectively be better served by remaining invested and seeking to maximize their recoveries through an orderly disposition of long-term assets, each *individually* has a strong incentive to be the first to exit. A downward spiral at one firm becomes contagious when it induces short-term creditors of other firms to develop similar concerns and incentives, initiating multiple distressed liquidations that ultimately engulf healthy financial institutions, drive down asset prices, and cause systemic balance sheet impairment of otherwise solvent firms through forced sales of assets at fire sale prices and mark-to-market accounting losses, where accounting rules force banks to mark down their assets to the fire sale prices.[52]

Runs can be a self-fulfilling prophecy. Fire sales initiated by affected institutions to (1) fund withdrawals of liquidity, (2) post margin, or (3) cover defaults by counterparties through the liquidation of collateral[53] cause asset prices to fall, impairing institutional balance sheets, depleting capital, and driving institutions into insolvency. Milton Friedman and Anna Schwartz observed that at this point the run may become "self-justifying," since the fire sale "force[s] a decline in the market value of ... the remaining assets" held on institutional balance sheets, which in the worst cases brings about actual insolvency.[54]

Mason (1998) argues that "pure contagion involves changes in expectations that are self-fulfilling, with financial markets subject to equilibria or sunspots," and that "changes in expectation ... are not related to changes in ... fundamentals."[55] One potential weakness of this theory is that it may be challenging to construct empirical tests for the presence of multiple equilibria. However, Hortacsu et al. (2011)[56] constructed a testable model in which companies face a negative feedback loop between their perceived financial health and demand for their products. In this model, financial distress can reduce the demand for a firm's products by, for example, reducing the expected value of the company's warranties. In the banking sector, a warranty corresponds to a bank's promise to convert deposits to cash on demand. The relationship between demand and financial health can generate a vicious cycle: financial distress reduces demand, reduced demand increases financial distress, which further reduces demand. As in the Diamond Dybvig model, perceived distress can be just as pernicious as actual distress, because "if consumers suddenly believe a firm is distressed, even incorrectly, the resulting demand effect could push the firm into distress and even bankruptcy."[57] The potential for multiple outcomes—all dependent on the company's perceived financial health—yields "multiple equilibria."

2.3   Information Economics

According to the widely cited work of Gorton and Metrick (2012), "[t]he 2007–2008 financial crisis was a system wide bank run,"[58] They draw a historical analogy between the recent crisis and nineteenth-century panics, when banks "suspended convertibility [of deposits] and relied on clearinghouses to issue certificates as makeshift currency."[59] In the nineteenth century, evidence of contagion could be found in the discounts at which these certificates traded. In the twenty-first century, contagion is evidenced by "unprecedented[ly] high repo haircuts and even the cessation of repo lending on many forms of collateral." There were additional runs on asset-backed commercial paper and other products. The authors observe that the potential for traditional banking runs, of the type observed in the nineteenth century, was eliminated by the expansion of Fed discount window lending and deposit guarantees. They argue that collateralized lending arose as a private-sector partial substitute for government guarantees. For example, in a repo transaction an investor lends money to a bank (equivalent to a traditional deposit) by purchasing a security and agreeing to sell it back after a fixed period of time. The collateral fills the role of a government guarantee, as the investor can sell it should the bank become unable to repurchase it. In the traditional bank run, investors simply refused to lend to banks through deposits. In the recent bank run, investors refused to lend through repos. The root cause of the modern run was a refusal to accept collateral, because investors decided its value as a guarantee-substitute was diminished. Hence it is important to ask what drove the contagious refusal to accept collateral.

Gorton and Ordonez (2014)[60] and Dang, Gorton, and Holmstrom (2013) offer information economics as an explanation for the run on repo and collateralized lending. They argue that during ordinary periods, short-term collateralized debt is "money-like" in the sense that traders of it are information insensitive. In other words, the prices of these assets are not sensitive to the release of new information, and market participants therefore have limited incentive to generate this information. However, a small idiosyncratic shock can trigger investors to become information sensitive, which creates price drops as negative information is generated. In addition the fact that the assets become information sensitive means that some market participants will have superior information to other market participants ("asymmetric information"). Fearing that their counterparty has superior information, purchasers of these assets will offer prices lower than their expected value to avoid adverse selection (i.e., buying at a price higher than the asset is worth given existing information). According to this model, the sudden shift in information sensitivity, coupled with asymmetric information, is the root cause of contagion. The response to asymmetric information pushes asset prices below their fundamental value. This amplifies the original idiosyncratic shock that caused the market to become information sensitive, and the market plunge can lead to systemic crisis. Because the "adverse selection discount" is rooted in asymmetric information, rather than price-relevant fundamental information, the result is an indiscriminate bank run spreading from asset-to-asset and institution-to-institution. Once adverse selection discounts are recorded in market prices, banks realize losses by marking their balance sheets to market.[61] This may be enough to trigger further contagion.

2.4   Measures of Systemic Risk

In the academic literature, the three leading measures of systemic risk
are Adrian and Brunnermeier's (2010) conditional value at risk (CoVaR),
Acharya et al.'s (2011) systemic expected shortfall (SES), and Billio
et al.'s (2012) measure of interconnectedness.[62] However, each such
measure is really a measure of correlation, and not of connectedness or
contagion. As a result these measures fail to have predictive power for
systemic risk that arises from either connectedness (which I show is
not the primary source of systemic risk) or contagion (which I show is
the primary source of systemic risk). A gap remains in the academic
literature for measuring the risk of contagion. For a detailed discussion
of each systemic risk measure, see the appendix.

3   The Concept of Correlation

Correlation describes the failure of multiple institutions resulting from the collapse of asset prices due to an exogenous event (e.g., the fall of housing prices in the period prior to the 2008–2009 financial crisis). Correlation can also refer to the herding instinct of asset managers that can result in market crashes and instability, or in irrational asset bubbles. In addition the academic literature discussing "indirect" connectedness is really discussing correlation. Although correlation played an important role in the recent crisis, contagion is what transformed $100–200 billion in losses on subprime mortgage products[1] into the destruction of roughly $8 trillion of equity market capitalization between October 2007 and October 2009.[2]

Recently, the risk of the asset management industry's herding behavior has come to the forefront of the discussion about correlation risk, as it may result in market crashes and instability, particularly during periods of distress.[3] Herding behavior involves the tendency of asset managers to move out of a particular security or asset class in a correlated manner. The concern is that if most large asset managers sell at the same time, the market for that security or asset class may collapse, putting stress on all holders of such assets. As a consequence of this herding concern, regulators have considered the idea of designating large asset managers as systemically important financial institutions (SIFIs), though managers may have escaped the spectre of SIFI designation for the time being due to recognition that any risks are industry-wide and not firm specific.[4]

SIFI regulation would likely be unsuccessful in preventing adverse herding behavior. Herding by definition involves a number of firms across the industry acting in a coordinated fashion.[5] SIFI designation and the consequent regulation of the SIFI is firm specific, so would be ineffective in combatting an industry-wide problem. The only potentially effective solution to correlated market declines that result from herding behavior is to impose a temporary form of circuit breaker that may help slow the price drops in an asset class or in particular securities, at least give time for a deep breath. During the market crash of October 1987, specialists halted trading in some of the most severely affected stocks.[6] In addition the Federal Reserve issued a public statement indicating its intent to foster stability by providing liquidity to the market.[7] The Federal Reserve followed through by both increasing the level of reserves in the system through open market operations and by reducing the target federal funds rate by 50 bps.[8] When asset prices plunge, the Federal Reserve could also become the buyer or market maker of last resort.

This book does not focus on correlation risk and herding. Obviously, if the correlated losses in housing had never occurred, contagion would most likely not have occurred either. But the prevention of correlated risks and herding behavior, while important, may be extremely difficult—this is the task for so-called macroprudential regulation. At the very least it involves policies like the detection and prevention of bubbles, which are beyond the scope of this book. For a more detailed discussion of the academic literature on correlation, see the appendix.

The three distinct C's of systemic risk, connectedness, correlation, and contagion, are not mutually exclusive. They overlap to some extent. Thus, for example, a funding connectedness problem may set off a contagion, or fire sales of assets may intensify a contagion due to correlated holdings of assets subject to fire sales. Despite these overlaps, I believe the concepts are distinct enough to be very useful in analysis.

II   Connectedness in the Crisis

This part of the book discusses connectedness. In chapter 4, I examine the 2008 Lehman bankruptcy and conclude that connectedness of other institutions to Lehman did not create systemic risk. In chapter 5, I turn to liability connectedness. I first examine whether the connectedness of money market funding to banks caused a problem in the crisis, concluding that it did not. I then examine a possible future source of connectedness, the tri-party repo market. While this market could cause systemic risk, it has been altered in significant ways to avoid this possibility. In chapter 6, I discuss some key provisions of Dodd–Frank that address connectedness: central clearing, exposure limitations, and SIFI designation.

4   Asset Connectedness: Lehman and AIG

4.1   Lehman Brothers' Collapse and Bankruptcy

It took more than 150 years to build the Lehman Brothers franchise from its humble beginnings as an Alabama general store[1] and only a few weeks for the firm to collapse.

On September 15, 2008, the Lehman group parent holding company, Lehman Brothers Holdings Inc. ("LBHI"), filed for bankruptcy protection,[2] setting into motion the largest corporate failure in US history.[3] As recently as May 31, 2008, the firm had reported itself solvent, with consolidated assets of $639 billion against liabilities of $613 billion.[4] Even as late as the day before filing, the Lehman estate's unaudited balance sheets for LBHI and its affiliates indicated that the entire firm had $626 billion of assets against just $560 billion of liabilities, with LBHI itself holding $209 billion of assets and only $189 billion of liabilities.[5] Nevertheless, LBHI and its affiliates[6] seem to have had little choice but to file for Chapter 11 protection.

Lehman faced a severe liquidity crisis, which regulators and market participants had increasingly feared would befall the firm after the near failure of The Bear Stearns Companies, Inc. ("Bear Stearns") in March 2008, which itself suffered from a run before being acquired by JPMorgan.[7] Lehman's court-appointed bankruptcy examiner (the "Examiner") explained the rationale behind this fear, noting that "[f]inancial institutions such as Lehman ha[d] a relatively greater risk of failure due to a lack of liquidity, as compared to a risk of failure due to the value of their liabilities exceeding the fair value of their assets."[8] Lehman management, however, downplayed the firm's liquidity risk and "told the rating agencies that it was focused on building its 'liquidity fortress.'"[9]

In the end, the fortress was breached. Describing the firm's final days, Lehman's CFO reported that "cash and collateral were being tied up by [its] clearing banks ... [and] cash had drained very quickly over the last three days of the previous week."[10] The market believed that the current value of the firm's liabilities exceeded the value of its assets or soon would. While former Lehman CEO Richard Fuld has argued that fears over Lehman's solvency were unwarranted,[11] the Examiner uncovered evidence to suggest otherwise, concluding that at least some of Lehman's assets might have been unreasonably valued, without regard to fire sale considerations.[12]

Lehman made significant missteps in the years leading up to its bankruptcy, although the firm was not alone in embracing high leverage and risky strategies. "Excessive leverage was a pervasive problem" among financial institutions, according to former Federal Deposit Insurance Corporation ("FDIC") Chairman Sheila Bair.[13] Indeed, in concluding that "[i]n the years leading up to the crisis, too many financial institutions ... borrowed to the hilt," the Financial Crisis Inquiry Commission ("FCIC") emphasized that "as of 2007, the five major investment banks were operating with extraordinarily thin capital," leading to leverage ratios as high as 40:1.[14]

Chief among Lehman's missteps was an overly aggressive growth strategy that, beginning in 2006, led it to commit an increasing amount of capital to commercial real estate, leveraged loans, and illiquid private equity investments.[15] This plan proved exceedingly risky given the firm's high leverage and small equity cushion.[16] When the market for certain assets targeted for increased investment began to show signs of weakness in 2007, Lehman management decided to "double-down" so as to take advantage of "substantial opportunities."[17] The Examiner found that even as its competitors were shedding risk, Lehman saw an "opportunity to pick up ground and improve its competitive position."[18] Seizing this opportunity proved costly, nearly doubling the reported value of Lehman's commercial real estate assets from $28.9 billion at the end of 2006 to $55.2 billion at the end of 2007.[19] Not only did the firm's commercial real estate portfolio account for a large portion of the company's reported losses,[20] but it also fueled concerns among possible suitors over future write-downs.

Lehman explored a number of options to secure at least a partial survival of the firm. By the summer of 2008, management began contemplating a spin-off of the firm's problematic commercial real estate exposure into an entity labeled SpinCo, relieving Lehman's balance sheet of worrisome assets and reducing the need for continued mark-downs.[21] Lehman would need to ensure that SpinCo was a viable standalone entity and infuse it with equity equivalent to at least 20 to 25 percent of the value of the transferred assets.[22] By September 2008, Lehman hoped to obtain this equity by selling 51 percent of its investment management division for $2.5 billion, issuing $3 billion of equity directly and raising over $2 billion from a third-party investor.[23] Lehman was ultimately unable to carry out this plan quickly enough to avoid bankruptcy. Even absent time constraints, Treasury Secretary Henry Paulson, JPMorgan CEO Jamie Dimon, and Berkshire Hathaway CEO Warren Buffett, among others, were highly skeptical of the spin-off.[24] In its final months, Lehman also borrowed from the Fed in order to access needed liquidity. The firm had as much as $18 billion outstanding under the Fed's single-tranche open market operations in June 2008, as well as a $45 billion loan from the Primary Dealer Credit Facility near the time of its bankruptcy.[25]

Lehman also explored the possibility of entering into a strategic partnership or, as its situation grew more dire, selling itself to a competitor. Lehman contacted, among others, (1) Warren Buffett, who demanded better terms than Lehman was willing to offer in March 2008 and dismissed Lehman's SpinCo proposal around September 2008;[26] (2) Korea Development Bank, which had expressed interest in a $6 billion investment in "Clean Lehman" (i.e., Lehman without SpinCo) as late as August 31, 2008, but failed to reach an agreement with Lehman owing to significant valuation differences and rapidly deteriorating market conditions;[27] and (3) MetLife, which passed on an investment on August 20, 2008, because it already had substantial commercial real estate exposure.[28]

Lehman's most promising potential buyers were Bank of America Corporation ("Bank of America") and Barclays PLC ("Barclays"). Lehman held two rounds of discussions with Bank of America, first proposing a merger between the two firms' investment banks that would have given control over the combined entity to Lehman.[29] Then, in early September 2008, fearing "that Lehman could become a serious problem," Secretary Paulson began pressuring Bank of America to buy Lehman.[30] Bank of America ultimately refused, as CEO Ken Lewis believed that the deal would yield little strategic benefit. Bank of America's due diligence team concluded that Lehman's commercial real estate positions were overvalued. It "had uncovered approximately $65–67 billion worth of Lehman assets that ... it did not want at any price," and was unwilling to pursue a deal without government assistance, which was not forthcoming.[31]

Barclays expressed greater interest and, indeed, ultimately purchased Lehman's US and Canadian investment banking and capital markets businesses in bankruptcy.[32] Barclays was unable to consummate a deal prior to the bankruptcy filing because its UK regulator, the Financial Services Authority ("FSA"), refused to waive the requirement that a guaranty by Barclays of Lehman's obligations prior to the closing of the transaction (as demanded by the Federal Reserve Bank of New York, "FRBNY") garner the prior approval of Barclays shareholders.[33] Had the requirement been waived, Barclays would have purchased Lehman's operating subsidiaries for approximately $3 billion and would have guaranteed Lehman's debt.[34] Notably, however, Barclays would not have assumed any of the commercial real estate assets that Lehman planned to transfer to SpinCo.[35] Thus, even had the envisioned transaction been consummated, the remaining Lehman entities would have retained the highly problematic commercial real estate exposure, although they might have succeeded in avoiding a bankruptcy filing. The Fed had great difficulty determining whether or not Lehman was solvent over "Lehman weekend," due to these commercial real estate assets that Lehman valued at $50 billion but a valuation that others disputed.[36] Reportedly, certain staff members at the FRBNY had determined that Lehman *was* solvent, while other senior government officials had reached the opposite conclusion. The fact that these assets could not be valued, contributed to the Fed's unwillingness to lend to Lehman.[37]

As a result LBHI was left with no choice but to file for bankruptcy. Because LBHI was so critical to Lehman's operations and functioned as "the central banker for the Lehman entities,"[38] its filing caused key subsidiaries to seek similar protection. Although apparently solvent, such subsidiaries lacked the liquidity to function without LBHI's support. On the same day as LBHI filed under Chapter 11, its European broker-dealer subsidiary, Lehman Brothers International (Europe) ("LBIE"), was placed into administration.[39] While LBIE's balance sheet then implied that it had nearly $17 billion in equity ($49.5 billion in net assets against only $32.6 billion in net liabilities), it was forced to seek administrative protection because "LBHI managed substantially all of the material cash resources of the Lehman Group centrally," and "LBIE was informed by LBHI that it would no longer be in a position to make payments to or for LBIE."[40] Four days later, LBHI's US broker-dealer,

Lehman Brothers Inc. ("LBI"), was placed into liquidation proceedings under the Securities Investor Protection Act of 1970 ("SIPA").[41] Despite reporting more than $3 billion in excess capital at the end of August 2008 and generally being in compliance with regulatory requirements, LBI was forced to wind down because "it was a foregone conclusion that [it could] not survive as an independent entity."[42] By the beginning of October, fifteen LBHI subsidiaries filed for Chapter 11 in the United States, and in the end, more than twenty would do so.[43]

Lehman's Chapter 11 filings provoked heated dispute,[44] particularly over the contentious issue of whether and to what degree LBHI's affiliated US debtors would be "substantively consolidated" with LBHI. An equitable remedy that recognizes debtors as one combined entity, "substantive consolidation" "pools all assets and liabilities of ... subsidiaries into their parent and treats all claims against the subsidiaries as transferred to the parent."[45] The remedy also "eliminates the intercorporate liabilities of the consolidated entities,"[46] an important aspect of the Lehman case due to the vast array of intercompany and guarantee claims filed.[47] The estate's initial plan in April 2010[48] rejected substantive consolidation and instead "recognize[d] the corporate integrity of each Debtor,"[49] splitting creditors into two opposed groups, those that favored substantive consolidation (the Ad Hoc Group) and those that opposed it (the Non-Consolidation Group), each of which produced its own favored counterplan.[50] After protracted wrangling by the parties over successive plans,[51] a so-called Modified Third Amended Plan[52] was finally confirmed on December 6, 2011, following a creditor vote[53] and became effective on March 6, 2012, enabling Lehman to emerge from bankruptcy.[54] Distributions commenced on April 17, 2012, with a disbursement of approximately $22.5 billion to creditors.[55]

The Modified Third Amended Plan supports the core conclusion of this book: direct exposure to Lehman entities filing for bankruptcy in the United States did not destabilize significant Lehman counterparties, either in the immediate aftermath of the Lehman shock or subsequently. The estimated magnitude of unsecured third-party exposure to LBHI and its US debtor affiliates was between about $150 billion and $250 billion.[56] To be sure, such figures are large. Nevertheless, in light of the fact that such exposures were distributed across a large number of individuals and institutions—only a small fraction of which were of systemic importance—such sums would likely have been manageable in the aftermath of the LBHI filing, even assuming that these parties were to recover nothing of their exposures.

Moreover some creditors believed that they would recover—and in fact did recover—a considerable portion of certain claims well before a plan was even proposed. By September 2009, claims against Lehman Brothers Special Financing Inc. ("LBSF"), guaranteed by LBHI, were trading at roughly forty cents on the dollar, a price around which Morgan Stanley sold a $1.3 billion claim that month.[57] Further, even if unlikely to receive forty cents on the dollar, most other creditors still had good reason to expect nonzero recoveries, given that the estate had substantial assets. The extent of these assets is underscored by the Initial Plan, which indicated that as of the end of 2009, on an undiscounted basis, LBHI and its US affiliates would yield approximately $66 billion to creditors after an orderly liquidation.[58] With the estate then projecting about $370 billion in allowable claims,[59] such a liquidation would have yielded an average recovery of nearly 18 percent. As of March 2014, allowed claims were reduced to $303.6 billion[60] and Lehman's unsecured creditors had received a total of $86.0 billion, representing a realized recovery of more than 28 percent.[61] As of September 2015, distributions totaled $144 billion, amounting to a 35 percent recovery for unsecured general creditors. [62] Given the expectation of substantial recoveries, which were borne out in fact, the exposure of counterparties is further diminished in importance. These findings tend to undermine the "too interconnected to fail" hypothesis.[63]

Other researchers have been unable to find a significant correlation between Lehman's bankruptcy and the failure of other interconnected financial institutions, rejecting the idea that Lehman's downfall led to a cascade of bankruptcies through asset interconnections.[64] Some scholars have argued that connectedness did play an important role during Lehman's bankruptcy.[65] However, the importance of Lehman's connectedness was limited to the internal connectedness among Lehman entities (i.e., Lehman subsidiaries were connected to each other). While the connectedness of Lehman entities potentially played an important role in Lehman's demise, this is entirely separate from the issue of Lehman's connectedness to other firms, which is really the connectedness that would matter for systemic risk.

4.2   Effects of the Lehman Collapse on Different Counterparties

Another way to examine the impact of the Lehman failure is to look at how particular kinds of counterparties, clients or investors, as opposed to creditors as a whole, were affected by the Lehman collapse. This section examines the impact of the Lehman bankruptcy on (1) third parties directly exposed to LBHI and its US affiliates, (2) derivatives counterparties, (3) prime brokerage clients, (4) structured securities investors, and (5) money market funds. The conclusion of each of these separate examinations is that the Lehman failure, while costly, did not prove catastrophic to any of these parties as a result of "asset connectedness."

4.2.1 Third-Party Creditors: Exposures and Expectations

The Lehman bankruptcy implicated a vast number of affiliated and third-party creditors with a dizzying array of connections to the failed firm. The Modified Third Amended Plan dictates how Lehman's assets are to be distributed and thus provides a reasonable baseline for expected losses. Table 4.1 illustrates the Modified Third Amended Plan's projected recoveries and losses for key creditor groups, totaling $135 billion, a modest number especially considering that it was not concentrated in any systemic firm.

The projections in the table are, however, of limited value, as potential recoveries may diverge due to the uncertainty of the realizable values of Lehman's assets.[66] To say claims proved to be modest is less important than gauging how great such claims were estimated to be at

Table 4.1
Projected recoveries of key creditors under modified third amended plan (USD in billions)

Creditor	Allowed claims	Estimated recovery	Recovery	Estimated loss
LBHI secured	$2.5	$2.5	100.0%	$0.0
LBHI senior unsecured (i.e., Lehman bondholders)	83.7	17.7	21.1%	66.1
LBHI third-party guarantee	52.7	6.4	12.2%	46.3
LBHI general unsecured	11.4	2.3	19.9%	9.1
LBSF general unsecured (i.e., OTC derivatives counterparties)	22.7	9.1	40.0%	13.6
Total	**$173.0**	**$38.0**	22.0%	**$135.0**

Note: See Disclosure Statement for Third Amended Plan, *supra* note 190, Exhibit 4. In this table and the text and tables that follow, all claims and recovery data for the Modified Third Amended Plan are based on information from the disclosure statement for the Third Amended Plan.

the time of the Lehman bankruptcy. This subsection therefore focuses on the magnitude and nature of third-party exposures to LBHI and its Chapter 11 affiliates and, to some degree, the recoveries that third parties expected or had reason to expect from the estate, concluding that the potential exposure of $150–250 billion was not destabilizing and that creditors could have reasonably expected to recover on a non-negligible portion of their claims.

The claims data from the Initial and Modified Third Amended Plans provide a clear picture of the magnitude and sources of potential third-party exposure to Lehman. As table 4.2 indicates, $1.162 trillion in claims were initially filed against LBHI and its affiliated US debtors,[67] but, for several reasons, this number is at least around four times higher than the most relevant real exposure figure.

First, only about 50 percent of the initially filed claims—around $570 billion—were actually brought by actual third parties as opposed to Lehman affiliates.[68] The claims of Lehman entities in Chapter 11 against other Lehman entities (the bulk of which were also in Chapter 11)[69]

Table 4.2
Claims filed against LBHI and affiliated Chapter 11 debtors (USD in billions)

Claim type	Filed	Initial plan (Apr. 2010)		Modified Third Amended Plan (Aug./Dec. 2011)[a]	
		Outstanding	Allowed	Outstanding	Allowed
Direct	$210	$183	$102	$110	$110
Intercompany	80	56	43	52	52
Guarantee	570	367	115	156	108
Third-party	255	143	94	97	95
Affiliate	315	224	21	59	13
Total LBHI claims	$860	$605	$260	$320	$273
All other debtors	302	135	135	50	89
	$1,162	$740	$395	$370	$362

Note: Numbers may not add up due to rounding or, in the case of the Third Amended Plan, the exclusion of (a negligible amount of) priority and secured claims. See Alvarez & Marsal, Lehman Brothers Holdings Inc.: The State of the Estate 23 (Sep. 22, 2010) (for the first three columns); Disclosure Statement for Third Amended Plan, *supra* note 190, Annex A-2, A-3 (for the final two columns).

a. Claims data have been made available only for the Third Amended Plan, but the Modified Third Amended Plan is presumably based on the same claims data as the Third Amended Plan. Thus, in the claims context, all references in this report to the Modified Third Amended Plan are based on information from the disclosure statement for the Third Amended Plan.

have no direct impact on the overall recovery of third parties and are thus of limited value in assessing the fallout from LBHI's filing. However, claims of Lehman entities *not* involved in the Chapter 11 proceedings, such as those filed by foreign affiliates, are relevant.

Second, third-party *claims* tend to overstate exposures. Many third-party claims were filed twice—once as a primary claim against an LBHI affiliate and once as a so-called third-party guarantee claim against LBHI pursuant to its guarantee. Underscoring the extent of such double filing, approximately $144 billion in primary third-party claims were initially filed against an LBHI affiliate,[70] and $255 billion in third-party guarantee claims were filed against LBHI.[71] Regardless of the propriety of permitting third-party guarantee claims—an issue that was at the core of the substantive consolidation debate—it is clear that when the same underlying obligation supports multiple claims, total claims overstate total underlying obligations.

Third, invalidly filed claims further contribute to the general over-statement of third-party exposure. In the First Amended Plan filed in January 2011 ("the First Amended Plan")[72], the estate reduced the $775 billion in total then-filed claims to a $367 billion "estimate of claim amounts" on grounds that many filed claims were inappropriate because they were duplicative, overstated, or unrelated to any liability of a Lehman debtor in Chapter 11.[73] Obviously some creditors filed inflated claims to maximize their recovery even though they knew such claims exceeded their actual losses.

Focusing solely on the subset of third-party claims deemed valid by the estate,[74] only $242 billion in unsecured third-party exposure remains.[75] Moreover, as third-party guarantee claims constitute $95 billion of this amount[76] and as most of these claims were also filed as primary claims, the amount of unique third-party claims—and thus the true level of third-party exposure is closer to $150 billion. This relatively low amount of third-party exposure may be attributed to Lehman's capital structure, especially its use of secured financing arrangements. As of August 31, 2008, Lehman had approximately $157 billion of repo obligations and $35 billion of securities lending obligations, which together eclipsed the firm's approximately $136 billion of long-term unsecured debt and $4 billion of commercial paper.[77] Creditors in these transactions had collateral and were thus not significantly exposed to Lehman's failure. Had Lehman financed a greater share of its borrowings with unsecured debt, third-party claims would have been larger. Thus Lehman's capital structure arguably *mitigated* systemic risk. That said, the probability of failure in the first place might have been lower had Lehman been less reliant on short-term secured financing and instead relied more on long-term unsecured funding.

Long-term, unsecured financing, principally in bonds, is neverthe-less the largest source of third-party creditor exposure. The Modified Third Amended Plan estimates that approximately $84 billion in claims were validly filed on account of senior unsecured debt securities issued by LBHI.[78] Not only is this exposure small relative to the firm's repo exposure, but it was also likely spread across a wide variety of parties at the time of LBHI's filing. Standard & Poor's estimates that, as of the filing date, "a broad range of institutions, not just large capital markets players, ... [held] ... this paper."[79]

Relative to bonds, exposure to loans and other debt not classified as securities (accounting for about $20 billion of initially filed claims[80]) appears to have been more concentrated before the filing, with a large amount of such debt seeming to have originated from loans made by major Japanese banks.[81] Japanese banks and insurers announced a com-bined $2.4 billion in potential losses from their holdings during the week following LBHI's filing.[82] The Bank of Japan, however, did not view this sum as sufficiently large to threaten the stability of the Japa-nese financial system.[83]

Aside from senior unsecured debt securities, OTC derivatives accounted for the largest source of third-party exposure. In fact deriva-tives claims were filed in greater amounts than unsecured debt claims, although they have also been reduced to a much greater degree. According to the Initial Plan, about $150 billion in derivatives claims were filed, half as primary claims against an LBHI affiliate and half as guarantee claims against LBHI.[84] Apart from the fact that these claims are duplicative, both the Initial Plan and, to a greater degree, the Amended Plans indicate that the filings significantly overstate expo-sure, because many might have been exaggerated or invalid. The estate significantly reduced estimated primary and guarantee derivatives claims, cutting the former to $30 billion in the Modified Third Amended Plan.[85] More on the significance of derivatives claims below.

Another important class of claims involves instruments with embed-ded derivatives, including structured securities issued in connection with Lehman's European Medium Term Note ("EMTN") Program.[86] According to the estate's estimates, about $30 billion of these securities were issued by Lehman Brothers Treasury Co. N.V. ("LBT"), a Dutch affiliate, and about $5.5 billion were issued directly by LBHI.[87] A large number of third parties filed claims relating to these products in Lehman's US proceedings, either because the instruments were issued by LBHI directly or because they were guaranteed by LBHI.[88] Such claims suggest a substantial level of exposure, but the instruments did not in fact pose systemic risk because of their broad retail investor base and small denominations.

Two other types of third-party claims bear mention, although the estate greatly reduced the estimated amounts of both. First, more than $73 billion in claims were filed in connection with Lehman's obligations either to repurchase residential mortgage loans or to indemnify loan purchasers against losses arising from breaches of loan purchase and sale agreements.[89] The estate asserted, however, that these repurchase and indemnity claims were significantly duplicative, overstated, and unsubstantiated.[90] The Modified Third Amended Plan accordingly estimates that exposure from these claims amounted to only about $10.4 billion.[91] Second, approximately $22 billion in claims were filed against LBHI and its affiliated Chapter 11 debtors in connection with prime brokerage agreements, typically involving LBI or LBIE.[92] The Modified Third Amended Plan does not deem any of these claims to be valid.[93] Unlike mortgage-related claims, however, the estate's main contention is not that parties do not stand to suffer the alleged losses but rather that their claims are not actionable against LBHI and its affiliated Chapter 11 debtors, because these entities were not part of the agreements at issue.[94]

In sum, third-party exposure to LBHI and its US debtor affiliates could not and did not have a systemically significant destabilizing effect. This conclusion does not depend on estimates of the value of the Lehman estate. Even if parties had reason to assume that the estate entirely lacked assets to provide for recoveries, asset connectedness would still not have been a significant problem in the immediate aftermath of LBHI's filing.

Another way to assess the exposure of creditors is based on the expectation of creditor recoveries as reflected in the Lehman bond prices. Figure 4.1 illustrates that even at their lowest point, prices of LBHI bonds and, by extension, LBHI senior unsecured claims were always well above zero in the aftermath of LBHI's filing.

Parties holding claims guaranteed by LBHI had even more reason for optimism. In the months leading up to the September 2009 claims deadline, expected recoveries on LBSF claims backed by LBHI

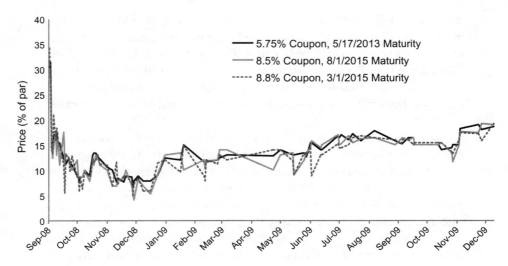

Figure 4.1
Representative LBHI senior unsecured bond trading prices
Sourced from Bloomberg

guarantees rose from approximately twenty cents to forty cents, as market participants believed that they would be able to seek recovery from both entities.[95] The effect of this early optimism was particularly significant, because sellers of LBSF claims during this period were primarily large broker-dealers, while buyers were hedge funds specializing in distressed debt.[96] The buoyant market thus allowed for systemically risky institutions (large broker dealers) to off-load Lehman exposure at meaningful recovery levels and—with transfers of Lehman claims totaling approximately $4.4 billion in 2009, $28.7 billion in 2010, and $32.4 billion in 2011[97]—in substantial amounts. Liquidation would generate about $59 billion and an orderly liquidation would produce about $76 billion in distributable value.[98]

4.2.2 Derivatives Counterparties: Exchange-Traded, CDS, and OTC Portfolios

At the time of LBHI's filing, Lehman's derivatives contracts fueled significant concerns that positions to which Lehman was a counterparty or on credit default swaps ("CDS") for which Lehman was a reference entity—ones that would pay off if Lehman failed—could lead to substantial losses by major financial institutions.[99] First, because Lehman had a large exchange-traded derivatives portfolio—futures and options—its failure could have conceivably imperiled the clearing-houses and clearing firms with which it dealt. Second, because Lehman was a reference entity on a large number of CDS contracts, its default could have triggered a massive payout, potentially bankrupting the sellers of Lehman CDSs. Third, because Lehman was party to a large number of OTC derivatives, its failure to honor its contracts could have left counterparties as unsecured creditors and thereby caused already weak financial institutions to take crippling write-downs. This section demonstrates that none of these issues materialized to the extent that had been feared, if at all.

Exchange-Traded Derivatives Portfolio Lehman's exchange-traded derivatives portfolio was far smaller than its OTC holdings but was far from insignificant: as a clearing member of each of the four Chicago Mercantile Exchange ("CME") designated contract markets, LBI accounted for over 4 percent of the aggregate margin requirements of all CME clearing members and maintained roughly $2 billion in collateral and clearing deposits connected to proprietary positions that it held on behalf of itself and other LBHI affiliates.[100]

The firm's exchange positions, transferred within three days of LBHI's filing, not only were resolved much more quickly than its OTC derivative holdings but also imposed no losses on counterparties. Owing to the size of Lehman's exchange positions, which the CME feared would be difficult for the market to digest in an open market sale,[101] the CME selected six firms from which to solicit bids on LBI's proprietary positions and delivered information to these institutions about LBI's positions on September 14, 2008.[102] Based on this private auction process—the first ever such forced transfer of a clearing member's positions[103]—all of LBI's proprietary derivatives were transferred as of the end of business on September 17. Barclays assumed LBI's energy derivatives portfolio;[104] Goldman Sachs assumed its equity derivatives portfolio;[105] and DRW Trading assumed its foreign exchange, interest rate, and agricultural derivatives portfolios.[106] These institutions did not take on this risk *gratis*, and indeed the Examiner found that LBI could have a colorable claim against these firms and the CME for losses owing to the "steep discount" at which the positions were purchased.[107] Nevertheless, the possible existence of such a claim does not affect the finding that Lehman's exchange-traded portfolio did not impose losses on the firm's exchange counterparties or the CME and thus did not result in a connectedness problem. This was a testimony to how the counterparties and CME managed risk by requiring adequate collateral in the form of margin.

CDS Portfolios Referenced to Lehman   The fear surrounding CDSs referencing Lehman was that *other* parties—with no connection to Lehman whatsoever—would not be able to make good on their obligations. This fear arose because Lehman was a popular reference entity on CDSs, and the aggregate CDS payout on its default was expected to be quite large given the low anticipated recovery on its debt payouts were based on the value of the CDS minus the value of Lehman bonds.[108] Typifying the extent to which CDS notional value in many instances surpassed the notional value of the underlying debt, as much as $400 billion in CDS contracts[109] had been written on only about $72 billion of deliverable Lehman bonds.[110] The payout on the CDS contracts was determined through a bond auction and the auction settled at $0.08625 (implying a payout of $0.91375).[111] With as much as $400 billion in outstanding CDS notional value, the Lehman CDS settlement auction could have therefore produced an aggregate payout—and thus, direct losses for CDS sellers—of over $360 billion, by far the most in the history of the CDS market.[112]

The fallout from such a payout would have been considerable and, indeed, far more significant than the losses suffered by creditors to LBHI and its affiliated debtors. As discussed above, third-party creditor exposure to LBHI and its affiliated debtors was on the order of only $150 billion to $250 billion, spread across a variety of parties. By contrast, it was thought that the $360 billion in CDS losses would be borne by a concentrated group of systemically important financial institutions ("SIFIs") assumed to be net sellers of Lehman CDS. Thus, as the Lehman CDS auction approached, these large institutions suffered double-digit percentage declines in their stock prices. On October 9, 2008, the shares of Morgan Stanley, Barclays, Goldman Sachs, and JPMorgan dropped 44, 18, 16, and 12 percent, respectively.[113]

Although the auction was ominously expected to be a "day of reckoning,"[114] the reckoning proved to be quite small, notwithstanding the lower than expected auction settlement price. For the $72 billion of Lehman CDS registered in the Depository Trust & Clearing Corporation ("DTCC") warehouse, a total of only about $5.2 billion was actually required to be paid after the Lehman auction.[115] There is no evidence that the settlement of CDSs *not* registered through the DTCC proved any more problematic.[116] The low percentage of funds transferred relative to outstanding CDS notional value in Lehman proved to be the rule, not the exception, for other institutions. For example, the Bank of France estimates that the percentage of net funds exchanged relative to total CDS notional value was only 3.4 percent following the Washington Mutual failure and 6.5 percent following the collapse of the major Icelandic banks Landsbanki, Glitnir, and Kaupthing.[117] In the case of payments on CDS contracts related to Greece, $2.89 billion in net funds were exchanged.[118] With $80.1 billion of total CDS value notional outstanding,[119] this amounted to a payout of 3.61 percent.

The generally low ratio of required payments to outstanding notional value can be attributed to the prevalence of offsetting positions,[120] which caused the *net* exposure for institutions on outstanding CDS holdings—and OTC derivatives more generally—to be far lower than notional CDS exposure. Further, while by June 2008 the OTC market had reached a peak of nearly $684 trillion in notional amount of derivatives outstanding,[121] parties would not have suffered anything close to $684 trillion in losses if all contracts were breached, quite apart from netting. The notional of a derivatives contract is merely the face amount of the contract, a sum that provides the basis for the calculation of each party's payments to the other. A more appropriate measure of exposure is the fair market value of a contract, which represents the worth of a derivative at midmarket and is far smaller than aggregate notional. For example, the Bank for International Settlements ("BIS") estimates that in December 2007, at the dawn of the credit crisis, the "gross market value"[122] of all outstanding OTC derivatives was $15.8 trillion.[123] However, gross market value is an overestimate of risk in the derivatives market, as it does not incorporate the risk-reducing effects of netting. BIS also estimates "gross credit exposure," which does incorporate netting effects. The gross credit exposure of the global OTC derivatives market was around $3.3 trillion in December 2007.[124] Even this figure may overstate the risks from derivatives, as it does not incorporate the risk-reducing effects of collateral. The International Swaps and Derivatives Association has estimated that, after adjusting for collateral, gross credit exposure of the global OTC derivatives market was $1.1 trillion in December 2007.[125]

The prevalence of such offsetting positions explains why the net payment demanded after the Lehman auction was relatively small and, ultimately, why the auction did not have destabilizing effects. Also contributing to the auction's muted impact, albeit to a lesser extent, was its price efficiency. In general, implied recoveries from auction

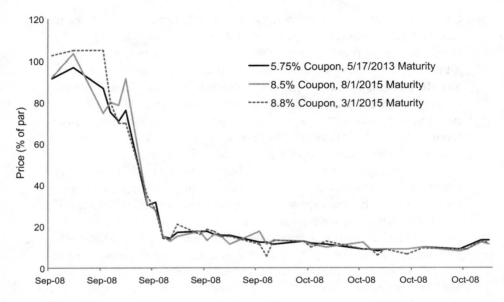

Figure 4.2
LBHI senior unsecured bond trading prices before and after the filing
Sourced from Bloomberg

settlement prices tend to track market expectations as expressed by
bond prices preceding the auction.[126] To be sure, the link between the
settlement price and pre-auction bond prices was smaller for Lehman
than it has been for other defaulting entities, because, as noted above,
the Lehman auction settled several cents below pre-auction expectations.[127] Nevertheless, relative to the fall in bond prices that had already
occurred before and after LBHI's filing, the further decline induced by
the auction was small.

As illustrated by figure 4.2, almost the entire decline in Lehman
bond prices occurred before the October 10 auction. Between early
September and October 9, bond prices declined from around $1.00 to
about $0.13. Against this approximately $0.87 fall, the $0.04 to $0.05
decline following the auction appears *de minimis*. This fact is relevant
because CDS prices reflect recoveries implied by reference bonds, and
CDS sellers are generally required to post collateral if their positions
decline in value. Accordingly, with the bulk of the bond price decline
having occurred before October 10, most of the losses that parties
suffered from Lehman CDSs were likely already taken into account
and collateralized prior to the auction.[128] In other words, the

"reckoning"—which did not prove to be large in any case—had for the most part already happened.

Lehman OTC Derivative Portfolio   Lehman's own positions in CDSs and other OTC derivatives might have been the most significant cause of concern among market participants and regulators.[129] Indeed, given the size of Lehman's derivatives business, many feared that LBHI's filing would produce an "immediate tsunami."[130] As of August 31, 2008, the derivatives assets and liabilities of LBHI-controlled entities were valued at $46.3 billion and $24.2 billion, respectively.[131] Based on BIS estimates, this combined gross market value of approximately $70.5 billion (assets plus liabilities) likely accounted for about 0.3 percent of the gross market value of all outstanding derivatives.[132] Lehman was estimated to have a portfolio of between $3.65 trillion and $5 trillion in total notional value of CDSs alone,[133] accounting for as much as 8 percent of the overall notional CDS market.[134] Moreover, across products, Lehman had a derivatives portfolio at the time of its bankruptcy filing consisting of over one million trades,[135] or perhaps around 2 percent of all outstanding OTC positions.[136]

Simply stated, the market feared that if Lehman were to fail, its OTC derivatives counterparties could themselves be vulnerable to failure, as they would not be able to fully recover or recover at all on Lehman contracts for which they were owed money (i.e., "in-the-money" contracts).[137] This fear proved to be vastly overstated. As noted above, misplaced emphasis on notional value rather than actual market value tended to exaggerate the true risks of these derivatives, and netting further reduced the market's exposure. Moreover the safe harbors for derivatives under Title 11 of the United States Code (the "Bankruptcy Code")[138] served to mitigate the fallout from a default. Specifically, derivatives counterparties to a bankrupt institution can seize collateral posted prior to the default (which would normally violate the automatic stay),[139], including collateral posted on the eve of the institution's bankruptcy filing (which would normally violate preference rules).[140] These special rules—criticized by some—place derivatives counterparties on firmer ground than many other creditors, both before and during bankruptcy.[141]

Nonetheless, the high concentration of the OTC derivatives market raised fears that the default of a major counterparty could prove catastrophic. Before the crisis a small number of institutions accounted for the vast majority of dealer holdings and activity, and this concentration has only intensified since. The Office of the Comptroller of the Currency ("OCC"), for example, reports that in the first quarter of 2012, just five holding companies accounted for almost 96 percent of the OTC derivatives notional value of the top twenty-five holding companies in the United States.[142] Notwithstanding this heavy concentration, the concern that the collapse of Lehman would bring down the entire financial system was nevertheless exaggerated. The risk of Lehman's collapse was significantly mitigated by (1) the positive positioning of Lehman's derivatives portfolio, with assets exceeding liabilities— Lehman was in the money (their counterparties owed them money)— and (2) the frequency with which Lehman's derivatives contracts were collateralized, could be netted, and were centrally cleared (interest rate contracts). Central clearing mutualized the losses on Lehman contracts to all members of the clearinghouse, rather than imposing it just on Lehman counterparties. The value of central clearing in risk reduction played a significant role in the requirements for central clearing imposed by the Dodd–Frank Act. By contrast, AIG had a negatively positioned and noncentrally cleared portfolio of CDS, thereby potentially exposing counterparties to greater losses. The remainder of this subsection discusses the Lehman and AIG OTC derivatives portfolios in turn.

Lehman: "Big Bank" Derivatives Claims and Recoveries On Sunday, September 14, 2008, major market participants moved to net down their Lehman exposure through a special trading session.[143] This effort proved largely ineffective, as some entities could not fully determine the extent of their Lehman exposure and others sought to resolve only contracts for which Lehman owed them money.[144] Nevertheless, despite the failure of this session, Lehman's collapse did not produce a cascade of losses. As burdensome as the effects of Lehman's default might have been on certain derivatives counterparties, they fell well short of the market's worst fears and resulted in no counterparty insolvencies of systemically important institutions.

A starting point for considering the losses on OTC derivatives is the $75 billion in third-party OTC derivatives claims filed against the Lehman estate,[145] with a group of about thirty major financial institutions that the Lehman estate labels "Big Banks"[146] accounting for approximately 50 percent.[147] Practically all of these claims were governed by standard form agreements designed by the International Swaps and Derivatives Association ("ISDA"),[148] in particular, the 1992 and 2002 ISDA Master Agreements. These agreements each classify bankruptcy as an event of default,[149] upon the occurrence of which the nondefaulting party has the right to terminate all transactions under the agreement.[150] Accordingly, the vast majority of Lehman trades had been terminated by January 2009,[151] with the gross derivatives assets and liabilities of LBHI-controlled entities falling to about $26 billion by June 2009.[152]

Counterparties who terminated their derivatives contracts or otherwise had grounds for a derivatives claim against the estate were required to file a special Derivative Questionnaire by October 22, 2009.[153] The questionnaire instructed claimants to provide a valuation statement for any collateral,[154] specify any unpaid amounts,[155] and, most significant, supply their derivatives valuation methodology and supporting quotations.[156] To the extent that a nondefaulting party is owed more than the defaulting party has posted in collateral, it becomes an unsecured creditor to the estate. Under this framework, the Master Agreements enable a nondefaulting party to assert a claim for an amount that, if fully recovered, would place it in the same position absent the default.

The Master Agreements permit parties a choice between three different valuation methodologies,[157] each of which shares two important features. First, the valuation methods premise claims primarily on replacement costs—that is, the value that the nondefaulting party would need to pay or receive to enter into an economically equivalent position, in effect to be made whole. Notably, this amount is likely to depart from fair *market* value, as parties generally must pay an amount above fair market value when they buy (paying the offer price to dealers) and receive an amount below fair market value when they sell (receiving the bid price from dealers). In markets where the bid-offer spread is high, as is typical following a major counterparty default, there can therefore be a considerable difference between what a nondefaulting party would have to pay or receive to reestablish a position and what the market value of the position is worth. Thus, it is not surprising that the Lehman estate has cited "abnormally wide bid-offer spreads and extreme liquidity adjustments resulting from irregular market conditions" as core challenges in the claims and recovery process.[158] Second, calculating replacement costs under each of the methodologies is as much an art as a science. To assert a claim based on replacement costs, the nondefaulting party need not actually enter into a replacement position. Indeed, in the Lehman case, few contracts seem to have been substituted in a manner replicating the exact terms of the trades,[159] and it is unclear to what extent their economic substance was actually replaced. As a result replacement costs need not— and in the Lehman case, likely did not—track actual costs.[160]

The inexact nature of the derivatives claims and valuation process fueled considerable contention between Lehman and the Big Banks. Believing that the Big Banks exaggerated the extent of the damage suffered, the Lehman estate reduced estimated allowable Big Bank derivatives claims by over $11.7 billion in the Third Amended Plan, to $10.3 billion from claims of $22 billion.[161] In May 2011 the Lehman estate proposed a settlement framework to thirteen of the largest Big Banks "with the intent of creating a standardized, uniform and transparent methodology to fix unresolved Derivative Claims ... of the Big Bank Counterparties."[162] This framework called for derivatives contracts facing Lehman to be valued at mid-market (the midpoint between the bid and offer) as of a specific valuation date (between September 15 and September 19, 2008), plus an "additional charge" based on product-specific grids adjusted for the maturity and risk of the contracts.[163] However, if the Big Banks can prove that they actually entered into economically identical and commercially reasonable replacement trades on the date of LBHI's filing, they could substitute the value of these trades for the settlement framework's methodology.[164]

The Lehman estate has contended that derivatives claims against it have been exaggerated. However, even at the outside figure of $75 billion, such claims are far smaller than had originally been feared for three reasons. At the end of Q3 2008, five dealer banks—JPMorgan, Bank of America, Citi, Wachovia, and HSBC—represented more than 95 percent of bank-held derivatives in the United States.[165] At the end of Q4 2008 JPMorgan had $184.7 billion in capital,[166] Bank of America had $171.7 billion in capital,[167] Citi had $156.4 billion in capital,[168] and HSBC had $35.1 billion in capital.[169] Excluding Wachovia, which was placed into receivership in September 2008, these four banks had total capital of roughly $550 billion, or seven times the $75 billion figure.

As it entered bankruptcy, Lehman was owed more by its derivatives counterparties than vice versa, namely Lehman's derivatives portfolio was overall "in the money." As of August 31, 2008, the firm's stated derivatives assets exceeded its liabilities by $22.2 billion.[170] Moreover, consistent with its pre-bankruptcy status, the Lehman's derivatives book has been a positive source of cash during bankruptcy. Although the estate has encountered difficulty monetizing certain transactions,[171] it had already collected $15 billion in cash through July 2013.[172] By April 2014, Lehman had roughly $1 billion in derivatives assets remaining.[173] In short, Lehman made money from its derivatives trades. The losses borne by any derivatives counterparty from Lehman's default were in effect reduced by the extent of the party's derivatives liabilities. If Lehman's derivatives liabilities had exceeded its assets such that Lehman on net owed its counterparties money, one might expect derivatives claims to have been considerably larger.

Despite the fact that Lehman's overall position was in the money, some counterparties did have an in-the-money portfolio against Lehman. Even so, most large financial institutions would not have incurred sizable losses from Lehman derivatives exposure, because their exposure to Lehman was collateralized by collateral provided by Lehman. The vast majority of these parties had entered into Credit Support Annexes ("CSAs") with Lehman, requiring the out-of-the-money party to post collateral based on mark-to-market liability.[174] Indeed, among Lehman's top twenty-five counterparties by number of derivatives transactions, all but one were subject to a CSA.[175] Although these agreements may not have insulated parties from "gap risk"—that is, the risk that mark-to-market value dramatically changes between collateral postings—the evidence suggests that they greatly mitigated the effects of a default. For example, JPMorgan, one of Lehman's largest derivatives counterparties,[176] has sought a comparatively small amount of damages for derivatives exposure, mainly because the bank applied nearly $1.6 billion in cash collateral posted by LBHI against the roughly $2.2 billion owed to its main derivatives affiliate.[177] To be sure, JPMorgan's experience may not be representative, as the bank also served as Lehman's principal clearing agent.

Most significant, JPMorgan provided Lehman with tri-party repo clearing services, functioning as an intermediary between Lehman and the institutions supplying the repo funding that it used to finance its daily operations.[178] In this role JPMorgan held collateral that Lehman posted to obtain repo financing and provided Lehman with intraday cash advances to be repaid with funds that Lehman received from tri-party investors.[179] Lehman thus might have faced greater pressures to submit collateral to JPMorgan than to other derivatives counterparties. These pressures might have been particularly strong in Lehman's final weeks as JPMorgan obtained added protection by executing amended clearing, security, and guaranty agreements with Lehman in both August and, more controversially, September 2008.[180]

It is important to emphasize that JPMorgan and other large Lehman counterparties had put in place protections well before the filing. The prevalence of such protections, in the form of CSAs, suggests that even if Lehman's portfolio had not been as strongly in the money as it ultimately proved to be, the fallout from its failure would still have been manageable for its counterparties. In other words, large derivatives counterparties did not escape calamity from Lehman's collapse merely because Lehman fortuitously held a net in-the-money derivatives portfolio. They escaped because of standard collateral arrangements, which, by 2007, covered 59 percent of all derivatives transactions and an even higher percentage of such transactions among large, systemically important firms.[181]

Clearinghouses also benefited large counterparties. The exact percentage of Lehman's OTC derivatives subject to clearing is difficult to determine, yet it appears that a large portion of its interest rate derivatives (while almost none of its credit derivatives) were cleared.[182] Across products that were cleared, "[t]he comprehensive responses by [central counterparty clearinghouses] enabled the vast majority of Lehman Brothers' proprietary and client positions to be settled as expected, with no substantial losses to central counterparties or the members of the clearinghouse."[183] For example, LCH.Clearnet managed the default of Lehman's interest rate swap portfolio (consisting of 66,000 trades and $9 trillion in notional value) within three weeks and without loss to other market participants.[184] According to the Bank of England, LCH. Clearnet "illustrate[d] the ability of a clearinghouse to protect market participants from bilateral counterparty risk, even in the event of default of a major participant."[185]

In addition to directly protecting counterparties from Lehman's default and thus mitigating any potential connectedness problems, clearinghouses might have helped mitigate *contagion* problems by reducing systemic risk. Some scholars have observed that the opacity of the OTC markets might lead to excessive, inefficient risk-sharing that can be remedied by increasing the transparency of OTC clearinghouses in a manner that reduces the probability of default.[186] Others have found that when default seems likely, "[clearinghouses] ... lower the systemic risk associated with runs by derivatives counterparties," since "[their] contractual obligations to [their] clearing participants prevent [these participants] from novating or terminating positions"[187] and since the guarantees that they provide reduce the incentives for counterparties to run.[188] Runs are potentially destructive not only because they might hasten a large dealer's demise but also because, before and after a default, they might foment general market instability. Thus, even if OTC derivatives did not lead to Lehman's failure and caused only limited connectedness problems in the wake of the failure, more pervasive central clearing might have still been beneficial to market participants. Of course, the requirements of Dodd–Frank for more widespread central clearing will further reduce the potential for destabilizing connectedness from OTC derivatives.

The estate's framework has been relatively successful. Through settlements with 8 of the 13 Big Banks, net of collateral, it reduced approximately $19.2 billion in derivatives claims (about 44 percent of those at issue) to about $12.4 billion.[189] Extrapolating this set of resolutions to the entire pool of Big Bank derivatives claims, the approximately $44 billion in derivatives claims would be reduced to $28 billion. As half of these claims were guarantee claims, this would imply underlying derivatives exposure of only $14 billion in contrast to the $22 billion that the Big Banks initially asserted. Even were the Big Banks to have a full $22 billion in collective derivatives exposure, their losses would be manageable. Had the Big Banks written their entire exposure down to zero in 2008, they would have recorded at most $22 billion in losses, quite small compared to the $1.8 trillion of total losses incurred by financial institutions during the credit crisis[190] and, more significantly, compared to the amount of capital that they held on their balance sheets. At the end of 2008, the five institutions with the largest OTC derivatives portfolios in the United States[191] held over $530 billion in tier I capital.[192] Even the smallest institution among this group held nearly $50 billion in tier I capital,[193] and no bank individually has sought anything close to such a figure for derivatives claims against Lehman.[194]

This limited exposure was no accident, as risk management practices reduced exposure to an acceptable percentage of capital by limiting uncollateralized exposure and using clearinghouses to mitigate bilateral risk. In short, there was no significant connectedness problem flowing from the very substantial OTC derivatives portfolio of Lehman.

Comparison to AIG   It is often asserted that AIG was rescued by the government due to the interconnection of its derivatives positions with other important financial institutions. As such, a comparison of the Lehman and AIG situations is instructive.

While it is clear that derivatives were at the heart of AIG's failure, there is no substantial evidence that its failure would have put its counterparties at risk of insolvency. Unlike Lehman, AIG's derivatives portfolio was overall "out of the money," but direct losses from in-the-money CDS positions held by counterparties were small relative to their capital. AIG also suffered losses from its securities lending practice, which might have endangered the solvency of its insurance subsidiaries. However, prior studies have shown that if AIG had defaulted and failed to pay its securities lending counterparties, then the losses to AIG's securities lending counterparties would not have endangered their solvency.[195] As former Treasury Secretary Timothy Geithner stated, "the risk to the system from AIG's collapse is not particularly reflected in the direct effects on its major counterparties, the banks that bought protection from AIG."[196] Rather, as with Lehman, the real threat of an AIG failure would be the potential spread of contagion through short-term funding markets and through the fire-sale spillovers to the collateral held by AIG's counterparties,[197] particularly when such collapse came so closely on the heels of the Lehman bankruptcy. McDonald and Paulson show that "even for the six banks that were individually owed more than $500 million, in no case did the shortfall exceed 10 percent of their equity capital."[198] However, as these counterparties began to sell assets to stabilize their debt-to-equity ratios, the risk of fire-sale spillovers can also emerge, a matter of contagion and not connectedness.[199]

In sharp contrast to Lehman, the government offered considerable support to AIG, ultimately as much as $182 billion.[200] The support started the day after LBHI's filing, on September 16, when the Federal Reserve Board of Governors exercised its emergency powers under §13(3)[201] of the Federal Reserve Act[202] to authorize the FRBNY to establish a secured credit facility of up to $85 billion in return for a 79.9 percent preferred stock stake in AIG.[203] Further, about a month later, on October 8, 2008, the Board of Governors used its emergency §13(3) powers to supply AIG with up to an additional $37.8 billion of liquidity secured by investment-grade fixed-income securities.[204] This was followed on November 10 by the Treasury's purchase of $40 billion of AIG preferred shares under the Troubled Assets Relief Program ("TARP") as well as the establishment under §13(3) of two additional Fed lending facilities totaling up to $52.5 billion for two portfolios of mortgage-related securities.[205]

Although some believe that AIG's derivatives portfolio might have been a significant factor in the government's decision to bail out the ailing firm, it remains unlikely that a default on AIG's positions would have directly caused destabilizing losses or capital shortfalls for its counterparties. That the failure of one of the derivatives markets' riskiest participants—which "had made the gross error of taking only one side of CDS transactions"[206]—would not have imperiled the solvency of other major financial institutions underscores the thesis that derivatives connectedness was not central to the 2008 crisis.

Table 4.3 summarizes AIG's CDS portfolio. Having used AIG's sterling credit rating to sell credit protection on ostensibly low-risk exposure,[207] AIG Financial Products ("AIGFP") had amassed a $527 billion notional value CDS portfolio insuring "super-senior" risk—a layer of credit risk even senior to AAA[208]—consisting of credit derivatives on corporate loans ($230 billion), prime residential mortgages ($149 billion), multi-sector CDOs ($78 billion), and corporate debt and collateralized loan obligations ("CLOs") ($70 billion).[209] AIGFP also sold CDS on less senior tranches, but as table 4.3 illustrates, this portfolio was relatively inconsequential.[210]

Table 4.3 further reveals that AIG's CDS losses stemmed almost entirely from its CDS on multi-sector collateralized debt obligations

Table 4.3
AIG's CDS portfolio (USD billions)

Type of CDS	Notional of CDS written (end of 2007)	Cumulative unrealized losses (2007 and 2008)
Regulatory capital		
Corporate loans	$229.3	$ 0.0
Prime residential mortgages	149.4	0.0
Total regulatory capital	378.7	0.0
Arbitrage		
Multi-sector CDOs	78.2	36.9
Corporate debt/CLOs	70.4	2.6
Total arbitrage	148.6	39.5
Total super-senior	527.3	39.5
Non–super-senior (mezzanine tranches)	5.8	0.2
Total CDS	$533.1	$39.7

Note: See Am. Int'l Grp., 2008 Annual Report (Form 10-K) 130–31 (2008) [hereinafter AIG 2008 Annual Report].

(CDOs)—namely CDOs backed by a combination of other CDOs, commercial mortgage-backed securities, and prime, Alt-A, and subprime residential mortgage-backed securities.[211] While the CDS on these CDOs accounted for only about 15 percent of AIG's super-senior portfolio by notional, they contributed to more than 93 percent of the firm's super-senior losses from 2007 to 2008, as $61.4 billion of these CDS were exposed to US subprime mortgages.[212]

Counterparty losses on AIG's CDSs on multi-sector CDOs were, however, manageable. First, much of this exposure was collateralized. AIG's multi-sector CDS portfolio accounted for about 96 percent of the $13.8 billion in collateral that the firm had posted as of June 2008,[213] and as table 4.4 illustrates below, at least $5 billion more collateral had been posted by the time of the government bailout. After AIG's long-term debt was downgraded by each of the three rating agencies on the

Table 4.4
Maximum losses on multi-sector CDS relative to equity (USD billions)

Firm	Exposure to Maiden Lane III portfolio	Collateral posted prior to bailout	Max. possible loss	Shareholders' equity (Q2 2008)	Max. possible loss as % of shareholders' equity
Société Générale	$16.5	$5.5	$11.0	$56.1	19.6%
Goldman Sachs	14.0	5.9	8.1	44.8	18.1%
Deutsche Bank	8.5	3.1	5.4	50.3	10.7%
Merrill Lynch	6.2	1.3	4.9	42.2	11.6%
Calyon	4.3	2.0	2.3	56.9	4.0%
UBS	3.8	0.5	3.3	42.2	7.8%
Ten other banks	8.8	0.2	8.6		
Total	$62.1	$18.5	$43.6		

Note: See COP AIG Report, *supra* note 356, at 76; FCIC Report, *supra* note 151, at 376–77. For shareholders' equity information, see Crédit Agricole, *Financial Review at 30 June 2008*, Sept. 11, 2008, http://www.credit-agricole.com/en/Investor-and-shareholder/Financial-reporting/Credit-Agricole-S.A.-financial-results; Deutsche Bank, *Interim Report as of June 30, 2008*, https://www.db.com/ir/en/download/Interim_Report_2Q2008.pdf; Goldman Sachs, *Goldman Sachs Reports Second Quarter Earnings per Common Share of $4.58*, June 17, 2008, http://www.goldmansachs.com/media-relations/press-releases/archived/2008/pdfs/2008-q2-earnings.pdf; Merrill Lynch, *Merrill Lynch Reports Second Quarter 2008 Net Loss from Continuing Operations of $4.6 Billion*, July 17, 2008, http://phx.corporate-ir.net/External.File?item=UGFyZW50SUQ9MTY1MzB8Q2hpbGRGRJRD0tMXxUeXBlPTM=&t=1; Société Générale, *Second Quarter 2008 Press Release*, Aug. 5, 2008; UBS, *Second Quarter 2008*, Aug. 12, 2008, https://www.ubs.com/global/en/about_ubs/investor_relations/quarterly_reporting/archive/2008.html?template=layer&selected=139333&template=layer&selected=139333.

date of LBHI's filing, AIG did not have enough liquidity to meet further collateral demands, absent Fed support. Indeed, the downgrades, coupled with subsequent market movements, caused AIG's collateral posting obligations to soar to more than $32 billion over the following fifteen days,[214] compared to only about $9 billion of cash entering the week.[215]

AIG's potential inability to meet collateral demands would have caused it to go bankrupt (since it could not, due to state regulation, liquidate its solvent insurance companies to cover its losses) and was the proximate cause of its bailout, suggesting that counterparties might have been so significantly undercollateralized as to threaten their solvency had AIG actually defaulted. Yet losses from any collateral shortfalls would have been mitigated by counterparties' own hedging activities. For example, Goldman Sachs, AIG's second largest counterparty, attests that it was not exposed to AIG's credit risk, since it bought CDS on AIG in an amount that covered what it perceived to be its uncollateralized exposure on the CDS that it had purchased from AIG.[216] Moreover losses from multi-sector exposure would have been manageable, since the notional value of the portfolio was relatively small and risk was spread across a number of firms. Table 4.4 underscores this point. The table, which is based on exposure to the $62.1 billion in multi-sector CDSs that AIG fully honored in its Maiden Lane III transaction, suggests that in the extremely unlikely event that counterparties suffered losses equal to the notional value of their CDSs less any collateral posted prior to the government bailout, no firm would have faced losses of more than one-fifth of its equity, around the 25 percent single-counterparty credit limits established by Section 165(e) of Dodd–Frank.[217] Further the firms would still have likely remained above capital adequacy thresholds after bearing these maximum possible losses. In fact, based on its reported 14.2 percent total capital ratio at the end of the second quarter of 2008,[218] even Goldman Sachs— whose exposure-to-equity ratio is among the highest of the firms listed in table 4.4—would have exceeded the 8 percent Basel II total capital minimum if it had absorbed the maximum possible loss.[219]

Some were concerned with another part of AIG's swap portfolio that was devoted to regulatory capital relief. AIG's combined $379 billion notional value of CDS on corporate loans and prime residential mortgages had been sold to provide such relief primarily to European banks subject to Basel I.[220] Under Basel I, counterparties could use CDSs written on their borrowers to reduce the amount of capital required against loans from as much as 8 percent (if the underlying loans had a 100 percent risk weighting) to a level of 1.6 percent.[221] But this regulatory capital portfolio was not a source of write-downs or liquidity strains for AIG, as it consistently had a fair value of around zero,[222] meaning that unlike its other CDSs, AIG could terminate (and indeed, has since terminated) these positions at essentially no cost.

But what about the counterparties who would lose the benefit of these "Basel-friendly" swaps?[223] Regulators were concerned that there was no longer a market for these derivatives to which counterparties could turn, that they could not be replaced and counterparties would then not be adequately capitalized.[224] The FRBNY estimated that counterparties subject to regulatory capital requirements would have to raise approximately $18 billion in equity upon an AIG's default.[225] In the prevailing market climate of late 2008, raising such an amount of capital would have proved challenging.[226]

However, as indicated by table 4.5, no individual firm would have lost more than $3.5 billion in capital relief from AIG's default. Given the size of the banks listed, this suggests that most would have remained above required capital adequacy levels. It is impossible, however, to state with certainty how European bank regulators would have reacted to a decline in capital ratios. As the Congressional Oversight Panel concluded, some countries might have granted forbearance, while others might have taken a tougher approach, perhaps even seizing the

Table 4.5
Regulatory capital relief recipients (USD billions)

Firm	Estimated capital relief
ABN Amro	$ 3.5
Danske	2.1
KFW Bank	1.9
Credit Logement	1.9
Calyon	1.6
BNP Paribas	1.5
Société Générale	1.0
Other	2.4
Total	$16.0[a]

Note: See, for example, COP AIG Report, *supra* note 356, at 92.

a. Based on the Congressional Oversight Panel's estimate of $16 billion in total capital relief.

noncompliant banks.[227] The most likely outcome is that these banks would have stayed afloat.

4.2.3 Prime Brokerage Clients

This section considers an important group of financial institutions that were directly affected by the insolvency of LBIE, which was placed into administration in the United Kingdom on September 15, 2008.[228] In the aftermath of the Lehman failure, certain hedge funds that had used Lehman's prime brokerage unit (part of LBIE), for a variety of bank services, lost access to their assets since LBIE was in bankruptcy.

Serving as prime broker to about 900 hedge funds and asset managers,[229] LBIE held between $40 billion and $65 billion in client assets, an estimated $22 billion of which had been rehypothecated, loaned by Lehman to various borrowers. Through rehypothecation, Lehman was able to use hedge fund assets as security for its own funding purposes.[230] Hedge funds that granted Lehman the right to hypothecate were able to reduce their financing costs by as much as 2.5 percent.[231]

These rehypothecation agreements were governed by UK law, which differed in several important respects from US law. First, UK law enables prime brokers to rehypothecate an unlimited amount of client assets, in contrast to the United States, which limits rehypothecation to 140 percent of funds owed to a customer. The UK framework offered customers little in the way of protection for their rehypothecated assets.[232] Not only did the United Kingdom lack a broker-dealer protection regime akin to the Securities Investor Protection Corporation in the United States,[233] but once assets were rehypothecated, the customer lost title to them.[234] Thus Lehman's rehypothecated prime brokerage assets became part of the LBIE estate and were unavailable for return to customers.[235] Hedge funds that had allowed rehypothecation faced the prospect of becoming unsecured creditors to LBIE and ultimately never seeing their money again.[236] Regardless of whether they stood to recover any of their assets over the long term, the inability to recover funds in the short term undoubtedly caused problems for a limited number of firms. Notably, MKM Longboat Capital Advisors closed its $1.5 billion fund partly because of frozen assets,[237] and the chief operating officer of Olivant Ltd. committed suicide, apparently because the fund had accumulated a $1.4 billion equity stake in UBS that it placed with LBIE and was believed to be unlikely to recover.[238]

The freezing of LBIE's prime brokerage assets did not, however, produce widespread consequences, in part because of the small size of

Lehman's prime brokerage operation. Before the collapse of Bear Stearns, the prime brokerage industry had long been dominated by just three firms, with Goldman Sachs, Morgan Stanley, and Bear Stearns accounting for roughly two-thirds of the market.[239] Lehman had never been a large player in the industry. Moreover, in the wake of Bear Stearns's demise, funds had increasingly used multiple prime brokers to mitigate counterparty risk.[240] In fact, despite the traditionally concentrated structure of the prime brokerage business, as far back as 2006, about 75 percent of hedge funds with at least $1 billion in assets under management relied on the services of more than one prime broker.[241]

The fact that not all of LBIE's prime brokerage assets were, or should have been, commingled with other funds, or rehypothecated, further mitigated the impact of LBIE's insolvency. When it entered administration, LBIE held $2.16 billion in segregated accounts and was believed to have segregated several billions more.[242] In December 2009, a UK High Court judge held that clients whose assets should have been segregated but were instead commingled would not receive the same protections as those entities whose money had actually been segregated.[243] In August 2010, an appeals court reversed the decision and ruled that clients whose money should have been segregated would be treated as if their funds had been.[244] Although the total size of the claims that may be affected by this ruling is unclear, some hedge funds will now obtain higher payouts to the detriment of the pool of general unsecured creditors. Moreover, according to LBIE's administrator, the decision is likely to slow the return of money to clients.[245] However, as of March 2014, the administrators of LBIE expect to have a surplus of £5 billion after repaying unsecured creditors.[246]

The prime brokerage connectedness therefore did adversely affect a few hedge funds, but there is no evidence that they raised any significant systemic risk concerns.

4.2.4 Structured Securities Investors

Lehman guaranteed and issued tens of billions of dollars in face value of structured securities backed by a variety of different assets.[247] Most of the securities were sold through other financial institutions. These securities attracted the interest of retail investors, who viewed the instruments as low-risk investments offering the possibility of high returns.[248] Lehman, on its part, increasingly relied on structured securities as a means of obtaining relatively cheap funding in a market that was growing wary of its credit risk.[249] From 2007 to 2008 alone, Lehman issued approximately $19.2 billion of structured securities,[250] and in total, parties would file about $78 billion in guarantee claims against LBHI on account of such "program securities."[251]

Losses related to these securities have not been and will not be systemically destabilizing. First, although some of Lehman's structured securities were issued to institutions,[252] they tended to be issued mainly to retail investors, whose losses pose little systemic risk.[253] Second, unlike many other Lehman creditors, structured security investors could pursue remedies against the financial institutions that sold them the structured products on behalf of Lehman, and have successfully pursued such settlements.[254] In April 2010, Citigroup, for example, paid approximately $110 million to repurchase Lehman-issued products at fifty-five cents on the dollar from more than 2,700 Spanish investors, and the bank has recently made an analogous offer to Hungarian investors. Similarly Credit Suisse spent over $85 million to buy back Lehman-issued products from Swiss nationals. There is no evidence that the settlements could have been or were problematic for these firms.

Although structured securities come in a variety of forms and tie returns to a variety of different assets, most amount to a hybrid of a vanilla credit instrument—in effect, an unsecured loan—and a derivative. One such variant, principal protected notes, provides investors with exposure to a particular asset (e.g., a stock index) while promising to return their full principal upon maturity.[255] Investors are thereby able to obtain the chance of enhanced returns with no apparent downside to their principal—a seemingly "no-lose" prospect that explains their appeal. The downside comes from the possible failure of the guarantor to honor the guarantee. Even if the guarantor does honor the guarantee, investors tend to pay far more for the instruments than they are worth. For instance, one study examining a representative Lehman principal protected note found that it was worth only about $89 per $100 invested when it was issued in August 2008.[256]

The investors who purchased such products not only paid more than they were worth but also exposed themselves to the issuer's credit risk, the possibility that the issuer-guarantor would not make good on the principal. As Lehman's structured products were primarily by European affiliates,[257] the ultimate recovery on these products depends partly on the resolution of Lehman proceedings outside the United States. However, because these instruments were also subject to a blanket LBHI guarantee,[258] about $78 billion in total third-party guarantee claims were filed against LBHI on account of "program securities."[259] These claims were reduced in the bankruptcy proceeding by $31.5 billion in valid claims due to LBHI-guaranteed securities and by $5.5 billion due to LBHI's own issuance.[260]

Another type of structured security issued by Lehman were "minibonds," and losses on these securities were also manageable. Ironically, these structured products received the most attention in the aftermath of Lehman's collapse, despite the fact that they were not actually issued by Lehman. Minibonds were credit-linked structured notes sold to Asian retail investors subject to certain LBHI guarantees. "Minibonds" were essentially basket credit derivatives that paid a coupon unless a reference entity defaulted, in which case the investor's principal would be reduced and they would continue to earn coupons on undefaulted entities.[261] They attracted the interest of about 43,000 retail investors in Hong Kong and about 10,000 in Singapore, who together invested approximately $2 billion in the products on account of their enhanced fixed coupons.[262] While they aroused considerable concern in the wake of LBHI's filing,[263] like other structured products, the minibonds have not posed any systemic risk due to their small and diffuse retail investor base. Minibond investors ultimately recovered between 85 and 96.5 percent.[264]

4.2.5   Money Market Funds

As will be discussed at greater length in part III, the US money market industry was afflicted by contagion in the aftermath of Lehman's collapse. Asset connectedness, however, was a much less significant problem. While many funds held Lehman debt, only one fund was ultimately forced to "break the buck" on account of its Lehman exposure.

Money market funds, which managed $3.8 trillion in assets in the United States by the end of 2008,[265] were a key part of Lehman's funding model, as they financed Lehman's long-term assets through short-term tri-party repos.[266] Money market funds also invested in unsecured short-term commercial paper issued by Lehman.[267] This paper was supposed to carry negligible credit risk but became increasingly risky. In the years leading up to Lehman's collapse, certain money market funds began to take more risk as they sought higher yields in a quest for more investors, the so-called chase for yield. [268]

On September 16, 2008, one day after the announcement of the LBHI bankruptcy, the Reserve Fund's Primary Fund "broke the buck." The RPF was a prime money market fund, that is, a fund that holds "a variety of taxable short-term obligations issued by corporations and banks, as well as repurchase agreements and asset-backed commercial paper."[269] The RPF was the flagship prime fund of the fastest growing fund family over the preceding several years and had invested $785 million in unsecured Lehman commercial paper, accounting for about 1.25 percent of its assets.[270] While the RPF did not immediately write down the value of its Lehman investment and continued to report a $1.00 net asset value ("NAV") on September 15, 2008, the fund faced redemption requests totaling almost $25 billion.[271] Unlike other funds that had invested in Lehman paper, the RPF could not rely on credit support from a deep-pocketed parent to maintain the fund's NAV.[272] On September 16, the market value of the RPF's assets had fallen below $0.995, legally requiring the fund to "break the buck" and float its NAV. Upon breaking the buck, the RPF also exercised its legal authority to suspend investor redemptions for up to seven days.[273] In order to extend its suspension of investor redemptions beyond seven days, the RPF was required to file an application with the SEC. The RPF promptly did so, and the SEC granted the application shortly thereafter.[274]

During that same week, and prior to the RPF's breaking the buck, a run had begun by institutional investors on prime money market funds in general, including on funds with no significant asset exposure to Lehman. Following the Lehman shock, contagion effects were evident not only among prime money market funds but also in the ABCP market, interbank lending markets (including the market for unsecured LIBOR borrowing and secured repurchase agreement financing), and other areas of the nondepository banking system. However, this severe money market fund run was not a by-product of asset connectedness, for other funds did not incur catastrophic losses on account of their exposure to Lehman but still suffered large withdrawals. Moreover even the RPF's losses from Lehman exposure were quite small, as the fund held only $785 million of Lehman debt. Indeed, even if the RPF had not been able to recover anything for this debt, investors would have received about a 98.75 percent recovery, according to the fund's subsequent projections.[275] In any event, the RPF was able to sell its Lehman holdings for over twenty-one cents on the dollar,[276] providing investors with a recovery of over 99 percent.[277] That investors ulti-mately lost less than 1 percent from the RPF's collapse underscores the insignificance of asset connectedness to the money market run.

~ ~ ~

Whether assessed from the perspective of direct third-party exposures, derivatives counterparties, prime brokerage clients, structured securities investors, or the money market fund industry, the above review demonstrates that asset connectedness was not central to either the Lehman collapse or to that of AIG, and there is no evidence of any other significant asset connectedness problem during the 2008 crisis. Furthermore, those studies that do claim to show high interconnectedness often provide evidence of the *relative* levels of interconnectedness among financial institutions, without demonstrating that *absolute* levels are a problem.[278] There is evidence that some types of direct interconnectedness among banks – such as interbank counterparty exposures – has decreased since the crisis; however, other types of direct interconnectedness have increased (for example, clearinghouse exposures).[279]

This is consistent with the findings of the empirical literature. The relatively small shock of subprime losses could be absorbed by the system, and network externalities due to asset connectedness "did *not* pose a serious threat to the financial system."[280] While sufficiently large enough shocks at implausibly high levels could theoretically lead to systemic collapse,[281] such was not the case in 2008.

5 Liability Connectedness: Money Market Funds and Tri-Party Repo Market

Modern financial markets are a highly complex system of financial institutions with a high degree of interdependence and interconnections. Financial institutions are not only connected through exposure on the asset side of the balance sheet but also on the liability side through funding relationships, referred to herein as "liability connectedness," as discussed earlier.

Lehman's failure did not present liability connectedness issues, primarily because Lehman was not a significant funder of the US financial system. The money market funds, which some have suggested are important sources of liability connectedness, as substantial investors in the short-term liabilities of banks, were not, in my view, a significant source of systemic risk. Liability connectedness becomes a problem when one institution's failure (a funder) and consequent cessation of funding of other financial institutions (borrowers), through a variety of forms, including loans, commercial paper purchases or repos impacts the ability of borrowing institutions' ability to fund their operations. Economic theory has explored the network effects of interbank lending, examining both direct funding links between banks (e.g., Bank A lends directly to Bank B)[1] and indirect liquidity links through common exposure to aggregate funding (e.g., Bank A and Bank B both contribute to and rely on an aggregate liquidity market).[2] In general, in this context, network theory studies the tendency of a decision by a single bank to hoard liquidity to propagate to other connected banks throughout the financial system. A review of the literature was provided earlier in this book.

The Lehman failure did not did not directly lead to failures of other financial institutions via liability connectedness because Lehman was not among the most significant providers of short-term funding to the financial industry. At the time of its fall, Lehman held $4.8 billion of commercial paper and other money market instruments in aggregate,[3] representing only 0.27 percent of all commercial paper in 2008[4] and only 0.61 percent of financial commercial paper.[5] Furthermore, in the repo market, Lehman held $170 billion of repos,[6] which is estimated to be only 1.7 percent of the total repo market.[7]

5.1   Money Market Funds and Liability Connectedness

Prime money market mutual funds invest heavily in the short-term debt of large global banks and thus have been widely considered a potential source of liability connectedness risk. David S. Scharfstein of Harvard Business School testified before the Senate Committee on Banking, Housing, and Urban Affairs that as of May 2012, of the roughly $1.4 trillion in prime money market fund assets, approximately 22 percent was invested in government-backed securities, 3 percent in nonfinancial firm securities, and the remaining 75 percent in the money market instruments of global banks.[8] Indeed, of the top 50 nongovernment issuers whose obligations are held in prime MMF portfolios, 48 are financial institutions.[9] However, while the importance of global banks to the balance sheets of money market funds is indisputable, the role of money market funds as a transmission mechanism for systemic risk via the provision of short-term funding to these banks has been vastly overstated.

Systemically important banks are not dependent on money market funds for funding. Scharfstein has estimated that prime money market funds are responsible for 25 percent of the aggregate short-term wholesale funding of large financial firms, where such funding is defined as uninsured domestic deposits, primary dealer repos, and financial commercial paper.[10] However, this definition excludes insured deposits and any long-term funding. Similarly a FRBNY Staff Report suggests that the money market industry's role as funder of the financial system is a significant source of instability, citing, for example, that prime funds hold 43 percent of the total volume of financial commercial paper in the United States.[11] Then again, the mere fact that money market funds hold a large percentage of the outstanding financial commercial paper does not imply that the funds represent a *significant* funding source from the perspective of a particular recipient financial institution.

The Investment Company Institute has estimated that money market funds provide only approximately 2.4 percent of total funding (including insured deposits and long-term liabilities) to US banks with over

$10 billion in assets.[12] Recent data suggest that individual large US banks' reliance on funding from US prime money market funds is limited. Such funds provided no more than 3.0 percent of funding as a percentage to any of the largest foreign or domestic banking groups as of June 30, 2013.[13] Table 5.1 shows the low level of dependence on money market funds as a percent of total funding for several of the largest US banks as of June 30, 2007, prior to the financial crisis. Baba et al. (2009) find that European banks also relied on US prime money market funds to finance large portfolios of dollar-denominated assets.[14] However, even foreign banks' reliance on US prime money market funds is now limited. As demonstrated in table 5.1, EU banks' reliance on US prime money market funds has declined since US prime money market funds reduced their exposure to European banks following the 2011 eurozone crisis.[15]

Regardless of the importance of money market funding to the financial system *in aggregate*, the liability connectedness concerns that may arise from a sudden loss of this funding depends on the extent to which *individual* significant banks rely on prime funds. If an important financial institution were to draw a substantial portion of its funding from money market funds, then a collapse of the fund industry could theoretically lead that institution to the brink of collapse. The liability connectedness of the fund industry would in such a case become a significant source of systemic risk. Considering that large banks have balance sheets typically exceeding $1 trillion and that Rule 2a-7 permits a given money market fund to invest up to only 5 percent of its assets in the securities of an individual issuer, losing funding from a single institutional prime fund complex alone could not in itself endanger a large bank.

5.2 Tri-Party Repo Market and Liability Connectedness

The tri-party repo market, in which sellers trade securities (collateral) to buyers in exchange for cash with an agreement to return the cash and get back their securities at an agreed date, is a large and important source of short-term funding for securities dealers who need short-term cash to fund their positions; consequently, this market is a potential source of systemic risk through the resultant liability connectedness.[16] As of October 2013, the total value of the tri-party repo market was approximately $1.6 trillion with approximately 81 percent involving treasuries or agency securities.[17] The total value of tri-party repo market

Table 5.1
Select US financial institutions' reliance on US prime money market mutual funds in June 2007

Bank	Dependence on MMFs as % of total funding (June 2007)[a]
Lehman	5.7%
Merrill Lynch	5.0%
Morgan Stanley	5.0%
Goldman Sachs	4.2%
Bank of America	3.9%
JPMorgan	2.4%
Citibank	3.0%

Select European financial institutions' reliance on US Prime Money Market Mutual Funds in June 2013

Bank	Dependence on MMFs as % of total funding (June 2013)[b]
Barclays	3.3%
Deutsche Bank AG	2.2%
Societe Generale	1.9%
Credit Agricole	1.4%
BNP Paribas	1.3%
HSBC	0.9%

a. Methodological note: Aggregate data regarding prime money market funds' asset holdings was not available prior to the financial crisis. In order to determine prime money market fund asset holdings as of June 30, 2007, we searched Form N-CSRs, the semi-annual reports by registered investment companies. This allowed us to review the asset holdings of prime money market funds with total assets of $1.05 trillion. However, based on iMoneyNet, the prime fund industry had aggregate assets of $1.65 trillion as of June 30, 2007. Thus, for the remaining $600 billion in prime fund assets that we were unable to identify, we assumed that these prime funds had invested in each of the largest US banks as much as legally allowed (5 percent of total money market fund assets). We were, however, unable to get data on the investments of European banks as of June 2007.

b. Crane data (Jun. 30, 2013), available at http://cranedata.com.

peaked in 2008 at approximately $2.8 trillion.[18] Repos constitute a significant portion of the funding for large US financial institutions. As a percentage of total assets at the end of 2014, repos accounted for 10.3 percent of Goldman Sachs' funding, 6.5 percent of JPMorgan's, 8.0 percent of Citigroup's, 9.6 percent of Bank of America's, and 8.7 percent of Morgan Stanley's.[19]

In the repo market, the repo seller—the party receiving cash—pays the repo buyer—the supplier of the cash—a return that reflects the low level of risk due to the posting of the securities as collateral.[20] In the tri-party repo market, a clearing bank both supplies cash to the seller and holds the securities on behalf of the buyer. Because it may not receive both cash and securities simultaneously, from the two parties to the transaction, the clearing bank is thus exposed to potential losses in the event that either side of the repo were to default.[21] This phenomenon is referred to as "intraday credit risk." In the United States, two banks, JPMorgan Chase and BNY Mellon, serve as the clearing banks in the tri-party repo market.

In the wake of the financial crisis, the FRBNY has sponsored an industry-led effort to study the problem of the concentration of a dangerous amount of counterparty risk on the two clearing banks.[22] Significantly, in 2009, the FRBNY established the Tri-Party Repo Infrastructure Reform Task Force.[23] Since then, the task force has convened workshops and issued a series of reports recommending ways to reduce intraday credit dependence, and thus the exposure of the clearing banks.[24] The FRBNY also released its own white paper in May 2010, discussing possible reforms.[25] Since the establishment of the task force, several concrete steps have been taken to reduce intraday credit exposures. First, the two clearing banks have implemented various collateral optimization capabilities that reduce intraday credit exposures.[26] The task force has already met its goal of reducing the share of tri-party repo volume that is financed with intraday credit from a clearing bank: today, 3 to 5 percent of tri-party repos are financed with intraday credit, compared to 100 percent in 2012.[27] Second, the daily "unwind" of most tri-party repo transactions has been moved from early morning to midafternoon, reducing the duration of intraday credit extensions.[28] Third, many dealers have undertaken efforts to reduce their reliance on intraday funding in accordance with Basel III liquidity regulations.[29] Finally, both clearing banks are implementing key changes in their respective settlement processes. These changes are expected to reduce

intraday credit risk further while improving the resiliency of the settlement process.[30]

~ ~ ~

While the deeper integration of modern financial markets has been said
to lead to a "robust-yet-fragile" system, neither the Lehman's failure
nor the runs on MMF presented important liability connectedness
risks, primarily because neither Lehman nor money market funds were
significant funders of major banks. However, the tri-party repo market
remains a liability connectedness risk.

6   Dodd–Frank Act Policies to Address Connectedness

The Dodd–Frank Act was the principal response of the United States to the 2008 financial crisis.[1] Despite the fact that the crisis actually had little to do with asset connectedness, many of the most important provisions of the Act are addressed to this form of systemic risk. This is not to say these policies are bad and may not address potential problems in the future, but as we will see, contagion was the major problem in the crisis, and Dodd–Frank made this problem worse, not better.

There are three key provisions of Dodd–Frank addressed to asset connectedness: (1) the requirement for central clearing of over-the-counter derivatives,[2] (2) the imposition of counterparty exposure limits,[3] and (3) the designation of systemically important nonbank financial institutions.[4]

6.1 Central Clearing

Central clearing of derivatives and other financial contracts may reduce the magnitude of asset connectedness. Under central clearing procedures, counterparty exposures are guaranteed by a central clearing counterparty ("CCP"), whose sole business is to stand between parties and assume the credit risk of buyers and sellers. Some scholars have concluded that participants in centrally cleared markets will have reduced incentives to flee from a weak counterparty.[5] By making "counterparty runs" less likely, central clearing may forestall the failure of a weak financial institution,[6] and in the unlikely event of a financial institution's collapse, "[e]ffective clearing mitigates systemic risk by lowering the risk that defaults [will] propagate from counterparty to counterparty."[7] As indicated by the experience of counterparties holding centrally cleared exchange-traded derivatives against Lehman—which suffered no losses from the bank's collapse[8]—central clearing can completely insulate market participants from losses associated with the default of a dealer. Moreover, to the extent that it might have mitigated liquidity pressures on Lehman by reducing the likelihood of derivatives counterparty runs, a greater degree of central clearing might have also benefited Lehman. Given the potential risk-reducing effects of central clearing, it is not surprising that the Dodd–Frank Act mandates central clearing in certain cases. Specifically, swaps and security-based swaps *not* used to hedge commercial risk must be cleared if the relevant regulator so determines.[9] In making this determination, the regulators are instructed to examine, *inter alia*, contract liquidity, operational capacity, and the effect of clearing on the mitigation of systemic risk.[10] The more standardized a contract, the more likely it is to be subject to mandatory clearing.

The efficacy of central clearing is, however, subject to certain limitations. One key limitation of central clearing is that CCPs are ill-suited to handling highly customized derivatives contracts. For example, a CCP would likely be unable or unwilling to clear AIG's notorious CDS portfolio on multi-sector CDOs.[11] Some might argue that the inability of CCPs to clear highly customized derivatives contracts is a rationale for the abolition of such contracts, yet, as the Treasury has recognized, such derivatives can play a "legitimate and valuable role."[12] Nevertheless, even if all contracts were standardized and subject to clearing, systemic risk would not be entirely eliminated and, under certain circumstances, could even increase. As derivatives increasingly head toward central clearing, CCPs themselves may cross the "too-big-to-fail" threshold.[13] As Fed Chairman Bernanke has observed, "[T]he flip side of the centralization of clearing and settlement activities in clearinghouses is the concentration of substantial financial and operational risk in a small number of organizations, a development with potentially important systemic implications."[14] While clearinghouses do minimize the risk of bilateral connectedness, they increase the risk of multilateral connectedness because they connect multiple participants who, but for the clearinghouse, might not be connected at all.

A second limitation of central clearing is that counterparty credit risk transfers to CCPs may not be one for one. The nature of the transfer depends on the extent to which market participants are able to net exposures across asset classes and parties, which in turn depends on the number and nature of CCPs. The introduction of a CCP for a particular asset class will be risk reducing only "if the opportunity for multilateral netting in that class dominates the resulting loss in bilateral netting opportunities across uncleared derivatives from other asset classes."[15] In other words, by using a CCP for a particular asset class, market participants may obtain the benefit of netting in the asset class across parties (multilateral netting) but will lose the benefit of netting against another party outside the asset class (bilateral netting). One might wonder why such a trade-off between multilateral and bilateral netting need exist in the first place. Indeed there would not necessarily be as striking a trade-off if a CCP itself were to net multiple asset classes or CCPs each netting one (different) asset class were linked to one another in a manner allowing netting across asset classes. However, at present, such a "first-best" solution does not exist.[16]

A third and final limitation of central clearing is that derivative participants will lose initial margin as a source of funding, since under central clearing procedures margin is instead posted to a CCP. As a result banks will likely seek alternative sources of short-term funding. At the same time, increased central clearing of derivative products will cause a corresponding increase in demand for safe collateral. Studies have estimated that demand for such collateral could increase by $5 trillion as a result of the migration of swaps to CCPs.[17] Such increased demand will likely lead to rising costs of safe collateral, and hence rising funding costs for financial institutions.[18]

6.2 Exposure Limitations

The single-counterparty credit concentration limits required by the Dodd–Frank Act are also designed to address the systemic risks of asset connectedness.[19] Banks commonly monitor and limit their exposures to individual counterparties and have long been subject to state and federal laws limiting the amount of credit that may be extended to a single borrower. The Dodd–Frank Act requires the Federal Reserve to establish limits to prevent covered companies from having credit exposures to any unaffiliated company in excess of 25 percent of the capital stock and surplus of the covered company.[20] The Federal Reserve is authorized to reduce this limit if "necessary to mitigate risks to the financial stability of the United States."[21] In January 2012 the Federal Reserve proposed rules to implement this provision,[22] and in fact chose to lower the counterparty exposure threshold to 10 percent for entities with greater than $500 billion in consolidated assets.[23]

Implementation of counterparty exposure limitations poses numerous challenges. First, a 25 percent limit may simultaneously be overly generous or overly restrictive, depending on the counterparty in question. Critics of the Federal Reserve's approach have argued that the proposed rules' method of calculating counterparty exposure is extremely narrow and inconsistent with the approach the Fed itself has taken in other contexts.[24] The Federal Reserve has not explained why a 10 percent restriction for large banks is more appropriate than a 25 percent limitation, particularly given the potential increase in connectedness as large banks are required to "spread their exposures across more and smaller, potentially less stable counterparties."[25] The lack of an exemption for a bank's exposure to central clearing parties is also troubling, as it works at cross-purposes to the Dodd–Frank Act's central clearing requirements.[26] But the fact remains that the members of a clearinghouse are all ultimately at risk if clearinghouse losses exceed collateral and clearinghouse capital.

Exposure limitations are also a potential response to problems of liability connectedness. Liability connectedness involves a firm's exposure to the risk of a withdrawal of credit by a significant funding source. In theory, regulators could impose caps on the level of a financial institution's dependence on any single funding source, thus checking the funding domino effect in the event of the failure of a large financial institution. As argued throughout this book, liberal recourse to the central bank's lender-of-last-resort facilities is better approach to addressing funding shortfalls.

6.3   SIFI Designation

Section 113 of Dodd–Frank gives the Financial Stability Oversight Council the power to designate nonbank systemically important financial institutions (SIFIs), with the consequence that such firms shall be regulated by the Federal Reserve and be subject to enhanced supervision and capital requirements. In making such designations the connectedness of potential SIFI designees plays a major role. Section 113 requires the FSOC to consider the "connectedness of the company"[27] and the "extent and nature of the transactions and relationships of the company with other significant nonbank financial companies and significant bank holding companies"[28] In its final rule the FSOC finds that the most important factor for determining the systemic importance of a nonbank financial company is the "exposure of creditors, counterparties, investors, or other market participants to a nonbank financial company."[29] This focus on connectedness is underscored by the fact that three insurance companies, AIG, MetLife, and Prudential, have been designated as nonbank SIFIs despite the fact that none of these nonbanks depends to a significant extent on short-term funding, and is therefore not susceptible to contagion risk.

Although all US banks with assets over $50 billion are designated as systemically important under Dodd–Frank, the additional capital surcharges applicable to global systemically important US banks (G-SIBs) is also premised on the theory of connectedness. This is plainly obvious from the relevant measures in the Federal Reserve's recent rule, which is largely consistent with the Basel Committee standards.[30] For example, the Basel Committee requires the consideration of five

Table 6.1
Federal Reserve: Banking organization systemic risk report

Size indicators	Line items
Total exposure	On-balance sheet items
	Total assets
	Securities financing transactions (SFTs)
	Net value of SFTs
	Gross value of SFTs
	Securities received as collateral in security lending
	Cash collateral received in conduit securities lending transactions
	Derivatives
	Derivative exposure with positive NPV
	Cash collateral netted against exposure in c(i)
	Total on-balance sheet items
	Derivatives and off-balance sheet items
	Counterparty risk exposures
	Counterparty exposure of SFTs
	Potential future exposure of derivatives
	Credit derivatives
	Notional amount credit derivatives sold
	Net credit derivatives sold
	Net credit derivatives sold with maturity adjustment
	Notional amount of off-balance sheet items with 0% credit conversion factor (CCF)
	Cancelable credit card commitments
	Other cancelable commitments
	Notional amount of off-balance sheet items with a 20% CCF
	Notional amount of off-balance sheet items with a 50% CCF
	Notional amount of of-balance sheet items with a 100% CCF
	Total off-balance sheet items

Source: http://www.federalreserve.gov/apps/reportforms/reportdetail.aspx?sOoYJ +5BzDaRHakir9P9vg==

broad categories: (1) size, (2) connectedness, (3) cross-jurisdictional activity, (4) substitutability, and (5) complexity. However, the relevant data inputs for factors other than connectedness frequently relate to connectedness, as demonstrated below for the category of size.[31]

Thus the Dodd–Frank Act has strong measures to combat connectedness despite the lack of evidence that this was a real problem in the crisis. That said, however, it could be a problem in the future. We now turn to the real problem in the crisis, contagion.

III Contagion

Part III begins by describing how contagion principally manifested itself in the nonbank sector during the 2008 financial crisis. It next turns to how the government successfully responded to the problem through the Fed's use of its lender-of-last-resort authority, the expansion of guarantees by the FDIC and the Treasury, and public capital injections under TARP. These powers were attacked after the crisis as undesirable bailouts and were either restricted or eliminated, leaving us vulnerable to future contagion. The book then looks in depth at two of these powers, lender of last resort and guarantees, concluding that they not only need to be restored but strengthened. Although the central bank's lender-of-last-resort capability can play two roles: (1) lender to individual institutions during periods of market stress and (2) general liquidity provider (a market maker of last resort), this book focuses only on the first of these roles because the need for general liquidity is generally a volatility issue, not a contagion or systemic risk issue.

7   Contagion in the 2008 Crisis: The Run on the Nonbank Sector, "Shadow Banks"

7.1 Overview

As discussed earlier, the term "contagion" denotes the spread of run-like behavior from one financial institution to an expanding number of other institutions, reducing the aggregate amount of funding available to the financial system.[1] Contagion can also spread to short-term capital markets that fund the complex and growing assortment of nondepository financial institutions in the financial system. The special feature that distinguishes contagion from other causes of systemic instability is the tendency of contagious runs to propagate *indiscriminately*. Contagion is "indiscriminate" when it afflicts healthy markets and solvent institutions.[2]

Financial institutions are vulnerable to contagion due to their dependence on short-term borrowing to fund long-term investment activity. When short-term debt investors suddenly refuse to extend funding, institutions relying on such funding may fail and lead to destabilizing fire sales. Runs of short-term creditors may be rational or irrational and need not be indiscriminate. A run by short-term creditors can be targeted to a single or limited number of financial institutions, for example, those known to have incurred significant losses.[3] During a *contagious* and *indiscriminate* run, however, investors may also withdraw funding from multiple institutions or markets that are not themselves facing any objective business distress. In such an environment, the decision to exit is made not on the basis of specific information but rather because investors possess insufficient information to differentiate their risks from those that others are—or appear to be—facing. This dynamic, one central banker has warned, may "lead to failures of other financial intermediaries, even when [they] have not invested in the same risks and are not subject to the same original shocks."[4] If these intermediaries fund themselves using short-term capital instruments, contagion effects may spread to the markets where these instruments trade. Sudden demand for liquidity by investors in intermediaries that normally hold these instruments or a refusal on the part of interbank lenders to renew their funding can trigger liquidations or freeze-ups in these markets, triggering fire sales, decimating asset prices, and halting lending activity.

Until recently, studies of contagion focused primarily on its effects upon the depository banking system.[5] The past 30 years have witnessed growing intermediation of financial markets via derivatives, asset securitization, and structured finance products, introducing a new universe of credit intermediaries and suppliers of short-term credit.[6] These nonbank financial institutions perform largely the same economic role as the conventional banking system[7] and are often collectively referred to as the "shadow banking" sector[8] or "securitized banking system,"[9] although such terms are imprecise and must be deployed with caution.[10]

Like traditional depository institutions, many of these "shadow" intermediaries conduct maturity transformation (or intermediate the process of maturity transformation through ownership of short-term liabilities issued by other maturity-transforming firms). Unlike depository institutions, however, they do not accept deposits. Nonbank financial intermediaries fund themselves in a variety of wholesale short-term borrowing markets, including commercial paper, asset-backed commercial paper (ABCP), unsecured interbank lending, and secured repo borrowing. Money market funds, unregulated investment funds, and various securities lenders are particularly significant purchasers of such instruments.[11]

Banking conventionally involves a single intermediary that originates long-term loans and issues short-term deposit accounts or other funds. By contrast, nonbank institutional credit creation often entails multiple layers of intermediation, resulting in greater amounts of short-term liabilities to finance assets held by intermediaries at each layer.[12] For example, one scholar has identified at least seven representative stages in the process of originating, warehousing, and funding long-term assets.[13] In the first stage, loan origination is conducted by nonbank finance companies funded in the commercial paper markets and by longer term notes.[14] Loans are subsequently warehoused in a variety of funding conduits financed using ABCP before undergoing securitization through special purpose vehicles created by broker-dealers.[15]

Next the asset-backed securities are warehoused temporarily on broker-dealer trading books funded with short-term secured repo and structured into asset-backed or synthetic CDOs.[16] They may undergo further intermediation through structured investment vehicles, credit hedge funds, and other conduits funded in the repo and ABCP markets and by longer term bond markets.[17] Finally, the collection of commercial paper, ABCP, and repo funding issued to finance various stages in the intermediation process are absorbed by wholesale funding markets through regulated money market funds, unregulated enhanced cash funds, and direct investors in money markets, among other cash investors.[18] The short-term instruments created as byproducts of this intermediation process are also susceptible to, and can serve as a conduit for, contagion, as they may represent a vital source of funding to originators farther up the intermediation chain. Longer term liabilities created in the process may be purchased by mutual funds, pension funds, and other long-term investors.[19]

Although the actual number of steps in the intermediation of financial assets varies,[20] the economic outcome of the process is virtually identical to the depository banking intermediation process: long-term assets are converted to short-term debt instruments, often with exceptionally short maturities. In 2008, for example, 69 percent of total outstanding commercial paper had maturities of one to four days and 75 percent of nine days or less.[21]

Nonbank credit origination is also distinctive in that it is financed by the capital markets: short-term commercial paper, unsecured and secured repo borrowing, and bonds and other long-term capital instruments. Unlike bank deposits, these liabilities are uninsured, although "some investors seem to believe that implicit guarantees [of money market funds] exist, either from the management company or from the U.S. Government."[22] Due to their role in transforming short-term maturities into long-term capital, such short-term financing sources are subject to the same collective action problems and run risks that have historically plagued uninsured bank deposits.[23] Thus nonbank financial intermediaries, including money market funds, are vulnerable to both runs and contagion. This vulnerability also extends to major commercial and investment banks, which heavily depend on large quantities of uninsured deposits and nondeposit wholesale funding, as exhibited by table 7.1.

Taken together, the size of the nondeposit wholesale funding markets eclipses the sum of insured deposits outstanding in the US financial

Table 7.1
Assets and liabilities of major US commercial and investment banks, 2008 (USD millions)

	JPMorgan	Citigroup	Bank of America	Wells Fargo	Goldman Sachs	Morgan Stanley
Balance sheet date	12/31/2008	12/31/2008	12/31/2008	12/31/2008	11/28/2008	11/30/2008
Total assets	2,175,052	1,945,263	1,817,943	1,309,639	884,547	658,812
Liabilities						
Deposits	1,009,277	774,185	882,997	781,402	27,643	42,755
Secured repo[a]	192,546	205,293	206,598	62,203	118,626	129,749
CP and other short term	37,845	126,691	158,056	45,871	52,658	10,483
Nondeposit short term	230,391	331,984	364,654	108,074	171,284	140,232
Trading account, derivative, brokerage, and other[b]	166,878	238,452	87,996	-	429,815	245,112
Accrued expenses and other[c]	187,978	90,275	36,952	53,921	23,216	16,445
Other[d]	142,961	-	-	-	-	
Long-term debt	270,683	359,593	268,292	267,158	168,220	163,437
Total liabilities	2,008,168	1,794,489	1,640,891	1,210,555	820,178	607,981
Shareholders' equity	166,884	150,774	177,052	99,084	64,369	50,831
Total liabilities and equity	2,175,052	1,945,263	1,817,943	1,309,639	884,547	658,812
Nondeposit short-term debt % assets	10.6%	17.1%	20.1%	8.3%	19.4%	21.3%
% as of year end 2010	14.7%	14.0%	13.5%	4.4%	28.5%	23.6%

Note: See JPMorgan Chase, 2008 Annual Report (Form 10-K); Citigroup Inc., 2008 Annual Report (Form 10-K); Bank of America Corporation, 2008 Annual Report (Form 10-K); Wells Fargo & Co., 2008 Annual Report (Form 10-K); Goldman Sachs, 2008 Annual Report (Form 10-K); Morgan Stanley, 2008 Annual Report (Form 10-K).

a. Includes federal funds purchased and sold, securities borrowed, loaned, or sold under repurchase agreements, plus other collateralized borrowing.

b. Includes trading and derivative liabilities, payables to customers, counterparties, brokers, dealers, and clearing services.

c. Includes reserves for unfunded commitments, allowances for credit losses, and other payables.

d. For JPMorgan includes borrowing associated with the Federal Reserve AML facility.

system. Estimates of the total amount of nondeposit banking liabilities outstanding range from $11 trillion[24] to $16 trillion.[25] At the end of 2008, money market funds alone managed $3.8 trillion in assets,[26] as against $4.8 trillion of deposits insured by the FDIC.[27]

7.2   Contagion after Lehman

Chairman Bernanke succinctly described the influence of panic behavior on nondepository credit intermediaries and money markets in a 2009 speech:

Panics arose in multiple contexts last year. For example, many financial institutions, notably including the independent investment banks, financed a portion of their assets through short-term repo agreements .... As we saw last fall, when a vicious funding spiral of this sort is at work, falling asset prices and the collapse of lender confidence may create financial contagion [in repo markets], even between firms without significant counterparty relationships. In such an environment, the line between insolvency and illiquidity may be quite blurry .... Panic-like phenomena occurred in other contexts as well. Structured investment vehicles and other asset-backed programs that relied heavily on the commercial paper market began to have difficulty rolling over their short-term funding very early in the crisis, forcing them to look to bank sponsors for liquidity or to sell assets. Following the Lehman collapse, panic gripped the money market mutual funds and the commercial paper market .... More generally, during the crisis runs of uninsured creditors have created severe funding problems for a number of financial firms. In some cases, runs by creditors were augmented by other types of "runs"—for example, by prime brokerage customers of investment banks concerned about the funds they held in margin accounts. Overall, the role played by panic helps to explain the remarkably sharp and sudden intensification of the financial crisis last fall, its rapid global spread, and the fact that the abrupt deterioration in financial conditions was largely unforecasted by standard market indicators.[28]

The Lehman bankruptcy and ensuing breaking of the buck by the RPF highlight the centrality of nonbank financial institutions in the contagion context.[29] Contagion effects spread from the money market funds to the ABCP, interbank lending, and secured repo markets as well as to other areas of the nondepository banking system.

7.2.1   Money Market Funds and Commercial Paper Markets
On the day Lehman filed in US bankruptcy court, the RPF received approximately $25 billion in redemption requests.[30] Like in a classic bank run, sudden demand for immediate liquidity from investors forced the RPF into a fire-sale liquidation of assets, crystallizing the

actual losses whose imagination prompted investors to rush to exit in the first place. By September 19, investors demanded redemptions totaling $60 billion from the RPF.[31] The RPF's suspension of redemptions compounded the panic in other funds. Other money market funds in The Reserve Fund family experienced significant withdrawals "even though they had not broken the buck and had no investments in Lehman paper."[32] Unlike the flood of deposits to risk-free accounts issued by JPMorgan, the RPF's safest funds underwent *outflows*. At least 36 of the 100 largest US prime money market funds faced a decline below the $1.00 NAV level and required sponsor support.[33] Investors in prime money market funds generated self-fulfilling contagious runs immediately after the Lehman collapse: investors were more inclined to run on their own fund if another fund in the same fund complex was experiencing a run.[34] Clearly, investors were running as a result of general panic and not concern over a particular fund's fundamentals. As of September 18, 2008, $142 billion of institutional investment money had been withdrawn from prime funds (amounting to 16 percent of prime money market fund holdings).[35] As of the end of the week, a total $300 billion of investment in prime money market funds had been liquidated by investors.[36]

Although prime funds had already begun to reduce their investment in commercial paper prior to Lehman's failure, they continued to hold "about 40 percent of their assets in commercial paper, with about 25 percent of their assets in bank notes and certificates of deposit.[37] As investment continued to shift out of commercial paper instruments and into risk-free government securities, "the flight ... stressed commercial paper ... markets, causing second-tier thirty-day commercial paper rates to double within two days."[38] Appetite for commercial paper contracted severely, with annual average daily issuance volume plummeting from approximately $150 billion per day in 2008 to under $100 billion in 2009.[39] As depicted in figure 7.1, the contraction in commercial paper was sustained across all segments of the market, with the sharpest declines seen in asset-backed and financial commercial paper outstanding.[40]

The scaling back of investment in commercial paper caused overnight spreads to leap to unprecedented highs.[41] The total value of commercial paper outstanding continued to fall even after the US Treasury announced on September 29, 2008, that it would guarantee money market fund investments.[42] The decline in the overall commercial paper market was largely due to financial commercial paper—the corporate

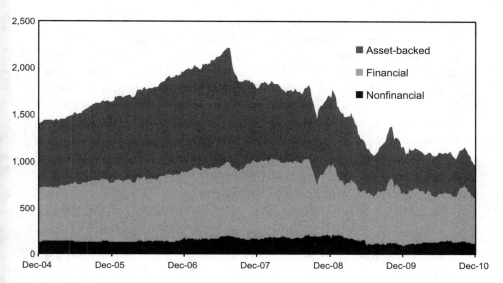

Figure 7.1
Seasonally adjusted commercial paper outstanding (in USD billions) and [Functions: FCPONCS, FCPOFCS, FCPOAB]
Source: Bloomberg Terminal, Bloomberg LP.

commercial paper market suffered much less disruption, although major corporate issuers such as Coca-Cola, General Electric, and Well-Point replaced commercial paper financing with higher yielding long-term debt[43] and also reacted by drawing on balance sheet cash and reducing overhead expenditures.[44] The impact on money market funds and the partial paralysis of commercial paper markets in the aftermath of the RPF debacle thus began to spill directly into the nonfinancial economy as contagion effects were transmitted to capital markets for corporate borrowing. Testifying before the FCIC, bankruptcy attorney Harvey Miller observed that "[w]hen the commercial paper market died, the biggest corporations in America thought they were finished."[45]

7.2.2   Interbank Lending and Repos
The post-Lehman contagion also afflicted short-term interbank lending and the repo market. LIBOR borrowing costs rose sharply and in unison. One-month US dollar LIBOR rose to 3.43 percent by September 24, 2008, its highest level since the beginning of the year.[46] euro and pound LIBOR rates exhibited similar increases.[47] The LIBOR-OIS

spread, a measure of interbank credit risk, rose sharply.[48] The TED spread, another important indicator of the cost of interbank borrowing,[49] widened dramatically, registering an all-time high of 464 basis points on October 10, 2008, thirteen times its level two years earlier on December 31, 2006, and six times its median level through December 31, 2009.[50] The market for unsecured lending vanished.[51] Many banks simply discontinued lending to each other altogether.[52] Inability to obtain financing from crippled interbank borrowing markets exacerbated the decline in bank stock prices that had been underway for over a year.[53] Ordinary depositors of well-known consumer banks, including Wachovia and Washington Mutual, reacted by initiating so-called silent runs, withdrawing funds electronically en masse,[54] compounding the drain on funding. Both institutions ultimately failed and were acquired by Wells Fargo[55] and JPMorgan,[56] respectively.

Repo markets were also seized by contagion, with borrowing rates increasing across the board.[57] The quantity of collateral demanded by lenders in interdealer repo markets skyrocketed.[58] An index of haircuts on interdealer repo borrowing indicates that haircuts on less liquid collateral leapt from an average of 25 to 45 percent during September 2008, after already having risen from 0 percent as of January 2007.[59]

7.2.3   Investment Banks

Contagion in short-term capital markets shook confidence in the ability of the surviving investment banks to continue funding themselves. Hedge funds and other prime brokerage customers of Morgan Stanley, Goldman Sachs, and Merrill Lynch reacted by withdrawing assets on deposit and diverting them to JPMorgan, Credit Suisse, and Deutsche Bank.[60] Morgan Stanley may have sustained $20 to $120 billion in outflows in the weeks surrounding the Lehman bankruptcy filing.[61] Interviews with Morgan Stanley executives by the FCIC indicate that hedge funds requested $10 billion in redemptions on Monday, September 15 and as much as $32 billion on Wednesday, September 17, 2008.[62] Withdrawals of prime brokerage assets by hedge funds were partly driven by investor redemptions underway at hedge funds themselves, which averaged 20 percent of assets in the fourth quarter of 2008.[63] Furthermore hedge funds and other institutional clients began to insist on segregated accounts and refused to allow the rehypothecation of their collateral.[64] As a result prime brokers saw a dramatic decline in their holdings of pledgable collatezral. In particular, from August 2008 to

November 2008, Morgan Stanley's holdings fell from $877 billion to $294 billion, while Goldman Sachs's fell from $832 billion to $579 billion.[65]

The outflows from prime brokerage and mounting skepticism about the future of the independent investment banking business model pushed CDS spreads on Goldman Sachs and Morgan Stanley upward.[66] For example, the cost of insuring $10 million of debt issued by Morgan Stanley rose 88 percent between September 12 and September 15, 2008.[67] The share prices of both banks plummeted, falling 12 and 14 percent, respectively, on September 15, a further 2 and 11 percent on September 16, and 14 and 24 percent on September 17,[68] prompting speculation that Morgan Stanley would seek a merger with a commercial banking partner.[69] The run on both investment banks continued even after the Federal Reserve approved the conversion of each to a bank holding company on September 21,[70] and was finally averted only after the FDIC issued guarantees of new unsecured senior bank debt the next month through the Temporary Liquidity Guarantee Program ("TLGP") program,[71] after which the share price decline at both banks began to stabilize.

7.3   Government Responses to the 2008 Contagion

The unprecedented government response to the financial crisis began even before the contagion triggered by Lehman Brothers. On December 12, 2007, the Federal Reserve announced the term auction facility ("TAF"), which auctioned funds to all banks, to avoid the reluctance of banks in trouble to get conventional loans for fear knowledge of their borrowings would exacerbate their problems.[72] On March 7, 2008, the Fed initiated a series of single-tranche 28-day term repurchase agreements ("ST OMO"), to provide funds to primary dealers in exchange for Treasury securities, agency debt, or agency MBS (collateral accepted in conventional open market operations).[73] On March 11, 2008, the Federal Reserve launched the Term Securities Lending Facility in which primary dealers could temporarily exchange program-eligible collateral, which included nonagency AAA/Aaa-rated private-label residential MBS in addition to agency MBS, for Treasury securities.[74] On March 16, 2008, the Fed then extended access to the discount window to primary dealers including investment banks through the Primary Dealer Credit Facility ("PDCF") in connection with the acquisition of Bear Stearns by JPMorgan.[75]

Following the September 15, 2008 bankruptcy of Lehman Brothers, the number and scale of government programs grew. On September 16, 2008, the Federal Reserve approved an $85 billion secured revolving credit facility for AIG under Section 13(3) of the Federal Reserve Act.[76] According to Secretary Paulson, this was like a temporary "bridge loan,"[77] which can be likened to the Japanese authority to provide bridge financing to insolvent financial institutions, as described in part V of this book. On September 22, 2008, the Federal Reserve launched the Asset-Backed Commercial Paper Money Market Mutual Fund Liquidity Facility ("AMLF"), which lent to banks so they could purchase asset-backed commercial paper from money market funds.[78] On September 29, 2008, the Treasury launched the Temporary Guarantee Program ("TGP"), which was funded by the Exchange Stabilization Fund, and provided approximately $3.2 trillion in guarantees for "liabilities" of money market funds to "address temporary dislocations in credit markets."[79] The Emergency Economic Stabilization Act was enacted on October 3, 2008, and permitted the Treasury, under the Troubled Asset Relief Program ("TARP"), to inject equity into failing financial institutions.[80] It also permited the Treasury, through the Capital Purchase Program ("CPP") to restructure the Federal Reserve's emergency support for AIG.[81] On October 14, 2008, the FDIC instituted the TLGP, which consisted of (1) the Transaction Account Guarantee Program ("TAGP") to provide unlimited guarantees to domestic noninterest-bearing transaction deposits and (2) the Debt Guarantee Program ("DGP") to provide limited guarantees of new senior unsecured debt issued by banks and thrifts.[82] On October 3, 2008, the limit on federal deposit insurance coverage was raised temporarily from $100,000 to $250,000.[83] On October 27, 2008, the Federal Reserve launched the Commercial Paper Funding Facility ("CPFF"), which authorized the New York Federal Reserve Bank to purchase highly rated unsecured and asset-backed commercial paper.[84] On November 25, 2008, the Federal Reserve launched the Term Asset-Backed Securities Loan Facility ("TALF"), which authorized the New York Federal Reserve Bank to lend up to $200 billion to holders of certain ABS, and was intended to encourage lending by promoting the issuance of new ABS.[85]

Finally, the Federal Reserve Bank acted as international lender of last resort through swap lines in which the Fed loaned US dollars to foreign central banks, which were then lent to foreign institutions.[86] Four foreign central banks had unlimited access to these swap lines during the crisis—the Bank of England, the Bank of Japan, the ECB, and the

Table 7.2
Government responses to contagion

Date	Agency	Program name
12/12/2007	Federal Reserve	Term Auction Facility
3/11/2008	Federal Reserve	Term Securities Lending Facility
3/16/2008	Federal Reserve	Primary Dealer Credit Facility
9/16/2008	Federal Reserve	§13(3) Lending to AIG
9/22/2008	Federal Reserve	Asset-Backed Commercial Paper Money Market Fund Liquidity Facility
9/29/2008	Treasury	Temporary Guarantee Program of Money Market Funds
10/3/2008	Congress	Emergency Economic Stabilization Act (enabled TARP programs)
10/3/2014	FDIC	Raise deposit insurance limit to $250,000
10/14/2008	FDIC	Transaction Account Guarantee Program
10/14/2008	FDIC	Debt Guarantee Program
10/27/2008	Federal Reserve	Commercial Paper Funding Facility
11/25/2008	Federal Reserve	Term Asset-Backed Securities Loan Facility

Swiss National Bank.[87] The swap lines reached an aggregate amount of $583 billion in December 2008.[88]

Less well known than the actions of the Fed, FDIC, and the Treasury was the role of the Federal Home Loan Bank system ("FHLBank system") in providing liquidity to depository institutions—commercial banks as well as thrift institutions. The FHLBank System is a government-sponsored enterprise established in 1932 whose public purpose is to provide US thrifts and commercial banks, "with financial products and services, most notably advances i to assist and enhance financing of housing and community lending ... by providing a readily available, competitively priced source of funds for housing and community lenders."[89]

The FHLBank system consists of twelve regional Federal Home Loan banks and a central body that coordinates the issuance of public debt obligations, which funds FHLBank advances.[90] As a government-sponsored enterprise, the FHLBank system can typically issue debt at favorable interest rates due to their implicit government guarantee.

Contrary to popular understanding, recipients of FHLBanks are not required to use loans just for housing. Indeed empirical evidence provided by Frame, Hancock, and Passmore (2007) suggests that FHLB advances are just as likely to fund other types of bank credit as to fund residential mortgages.[91] However, there are several important restrictions on FHLBank advances. First, FHLBanks can only lend to banks that meet minimum capital requirements, as prescribed by their prudential regulator.[92] For example, in order to qualify for an FHLBank advance a commercial bank must have a CAMELS rating of 3 or higher. Additionally FHLBank advances must be fully collateralized by US Treasury and GSE debt or residential mortgage-related assets (whole loans and mortgage-backed securities).[93] As part of each advance, a borrower must also purchase FHLB stock in an amount ranging from 2 to 6 percent of the advance (as dictated by the individual FHLB's capital plan).[94]

Between the third and fourth quarters of 2007, FHLBank advances outstanding grew by $235 billion, a 36.7 percent increase, and continued to grow through most of 2008, peaking at over $1 trillion by the end of the third quarter of 2008.[95] Shockingly, during this time, US commercial banks and thrifts received more in cash from FHLBank advances than from the Fed in discount window loans. This is because from the perspective of US thrifts and commercial banks, there were distinct advantages of using FHLBank advances instead of the discount window, as interest rates on FHLBank advances were lower than the rates on discount window loans and the terms of the FHLBank advances were longer.[96] According to a Federal Reserve study, the cost of an advance from the New York FHLB was between 30 and 80 basis points lower than a comparable discount window loan.[97] Of the $235 billion increase in FHLB advances during the second half of 2007, $205 billion carried an original maturity of greater than one year (87.4 percent).

However, by late 2008 US commercial banks and thrifts demand for FHLB advances waned, as FHLB advances had become more expensive than the Federal Reserve discount window.[98] This occurred for two reasons. First, the Federal Reserve had repeatedly reduced the discount rate in 2008, and implemented liquidity facilities, like the TAF, that lent at market rates instead of penalty rates. Second, there was a negative change in investor attitudes toward FHLB debt issuances, which increased the FHLBank's funding costs thereby requiring the FHLBanks to increase the interest rates on FHLBank advances. As recognized in the Federal Reserve study on the FHLBank's role during the financial crisis, "events in 2008 revealed … [that] relying on market funding using an implicit government guarantee is unlikely to be sufficient for a lender of last resort to be entirely effective during a financial crisis—exactly when you need one most."[99]

8 History of Lender of Last Resort in the United States

While the Federal Reserve took heroic and creative measures during the 2008 crisis to expand its LLR function, particularly to extend credit to the nonbank sector, ideally these LLR powers should be clearly defined and deployed in advance. There should be no doubt that the weapons will be used if necessary. The ex ante credibility of LLR prevents a panic in the first place, thus obviating the need to actually provide liquidity. Much as Mario Draghi, President of the European Central Bank ("ECB"), committed to do "whatever it takes to preserve the euro,"[1] a central bank as lender of last resort can commit to do whatever it takes to provide necessary liquidity to the financial system, subject to the general constraint that it will only loan against good collateral to solvent institutions.[2]

In 1797, Sir Francis Baring classified the Bank of England as the "the dernier resort," constituting the probable first mention of the concept of "lender of last resort."[3] In 1873, Walter Bagehot authored *Lombard Street: A Description of the Money Market*[4] following the failure of Overend, Gurney, and Company, a discount bank.[5] With this crisis as a framework, Bagehot offered his famous dictum for an effective lender of last resort: the central bank should "lend early and freely ... to solvent firms, against good collateral, and at 'high rates.'"[6] Bagehot argued that this policy would allay public concerns and preemptively avoid credit access issues.[7] Bagehot subsequently examined why the Bank of England should and could act as an effective lender of last resort. He asserted that the Bank of England's liquid holdings, gold reserves, and public duties positioned the Bank of England as the prototypical lender of last resort.[8] In the 1800s and early 1900s, Bagehot and his lender-of-last-resort policies were effectively applied not only in England but also in Canada, France, and Germany.[9] However, the Bank of England could never confirm which banks were solvent, as it had no ability to inspect their books. The Bank of England could likely only examine their balances at the Bank of England itself, and observe market prices for their debt instruments in secondary markets. Hence it could not definitively determine bank solvency.[10]

The presence of a strong lender of last resort is paramount to financial stability. As further developed below, the need for such a lender was the reason the Federal Reserve System was created. In my view, a strong and independent LLR is even more important than a strong and independent manager of monetary policy. A bad LLR policy could destroy our country in weeks, forcing huge losses of wealth and strong motives for revolt. Bad monetary policy is to be avoided but it can be corrected over a much longer horizon, as illustrated by Paul Volcker's correction of the bad monetary policy of prior Fed Chairman Miller. It took Volcker at least four years to right the ship.[11] Inflation was around 9 percent when Volcker took office in August 1979. It increased to 11 percent in 1980, before declining to 5 percent in 1983 after Volcker's exceptional measures.[12] While the Bank of England was created in 1694 and the Bank of Japan was created in 1882, the United States did not have a central bank until 1913, following the banking panic of 1907. Part of the reason that it took so long has to do with the history of the First and Second National Banks. Although these two banks were not central banks, they were federal banks that could loan to any borrowers, commercial as well as financial institutions, and they ultimately foundered on the idea that it was improper for the US government to make loans to the private sector. It is important to understand this history not only because it explains why it took so long to create the Fed but also because the populist objections to any kind of government bank (even one that lends only to financial institutions) are still with us today, and indeed are the main factor why the Fed is now such a weak lender of last resort.

8.1 First and Second National Banks

8.1.1 General Background and Powers
The First Bank of the United States, inspired by Alexander Hamilton, was chartered for a twenty-year term in 1791, during the Washington administration.[13] Its term was not renewed in 1811.[14] Shortly thereafter, the Second Bank of the United States was chartered in 1816 during the Madison administration, also for a twenty-year term.[15] Its charter was also not renewed in 1836 when Jackson was President.[16]

The Second Bank was much larger than the First Bank, as it had $35 million in equity capital, whereas the First Bank had only $10 million.[17] However, both the First Bank and Second Bank were very large, as compared to the existing state-chartered banking system: the First Bank's $10 million in equity capital was three times the equity capital of all state banks in the United States combined,[18] and the Second Bank's $35 million in equity capital was ten times the equity capital of the largest state bank.[19] At the time of the First Bank's charter, the United States had $204 million nominal GDP; by the Second Bank's charter, this figure grew to $811 million.[20]

Both the First Bank and the Second Bank played three important roles in the United States economy. First, both Banks bought large amounts of war debt. The First Bank bought state government issued debt from the Revolutionary War and the Second Bank bought debt from the War of 1812. In fact the Banks were initially capitalized by exchanging equity for war debt and specie (i.e., hard money like gold and silver).[21] Purchases of state debt by the First Bank were intended to avoid defaults by the state governments.

Second, both Banks lent substantial sums to private entities, including but not limited to state banks, thereby increasing credit in the US economy.[22] The Banks would do so by lending US bank certified notes to borrowers, which would then use the US bank notes as currency. Both banks were required by law to meet any redemptions of outstanding US bank notes in specie.[23] As a result the First and Second Banks sought to maintain specie reserves one-third the size of their circulation of US bank notes.[24] It is important to note that during this time, state banks would lend to private entities using state bank notes, which were also then used as currency.[25] State banks were regulated by state governments and were also required to meet any withdrawals of state bank notes with specie.[26] State banks had had no required minimum ratio of specie reserves to state bank notes.[27]

Third, the First and Second Banks each exerted indirect control over state banks' ability to extend credit by issuing state bank notes, in effect engaging in monetary policy. The First and Second Banks sought to do so to ensure that these state banks were not issuing too many state bank notes without sufficient specie on hand to pay state bank noteholders. Congress considered this among the most important—and controversial—functions of the First and Second Banks.[28]

The First and Second Banks were able to exert control over state bank note issuance, since the First and Second Banks each held a large amount of state bank notes and could therefore present a state bank with its notes and request redemption from the state bank in specie.[29] Redemption requests would further reduce a state bank's specie reserves, thereby reducing the state bank's ability to legally or credibly issue more notes.[30] The First and Second Banks held such a large stock of state bank notes because they were the US Treasury's depository, and taxpayers would often pay taxes in state bank notes.[31] The First and Second Banks also typically lent to state banks with specie as collateral for the loan, so if they questioned the specie reserves of the state bank they could seize the state bank's specie.[32] Of course, this would further reduce a state bank's specie reserves. For example, the First and Second Banks did this to address "wildcat" banks in the west and south from issuing too many notes without sufficient specie.[33]

The First and Second Banks were also able to effectively expand credit in the US economy. They could do so by treating state bank notes "with forbearance" (i.e., would not call for those notes' redemption), even if the state banks specie reserves were low, while simultaneously increasing the availability of its own credit to businesses and state banks.[34] The Second Bank did this during the crash of 1831–32 in order to mitigate the effects of that crash on the US economy. These actions, in large part, ultimately led to the failure to renew the charter of the Second Bank.[35] Not only did such policies address credit creation, they also allowed the national banks to control the potential insolvency of state banks.

8.1.2   First Bank of the United States (1791–1811)

The legislation establishing the First Bank of the United States provided that for a twenty-year term, renewable at the discretion of Congress and the President, no other national bank could be congressionally authorized. Under its charter, the Bank was a private institution that was permitted to lend to private individuals and businesses. Private speculation on new government bonds and on the United States response to Revolutionary War debt consolidation was at least partially responsible for the impetus behind private backing of the First Bank.[36]

Despite being set up as private enterprise, the First Bank was an instrumentality of the government from its inception. The Bank was both the government's creditor and debtor: its creditor because it held government debt, and its debtor because it held government deposits.[37] At the bank's inception, 60 percent of the First Bank's assets were government securities, either state issued war debt or US government debt.[38] The US government was also a part owner of the First Bank, as the government subscribed to 20 percent of the initial public offering (private investors owned the remaining 80 percent).[39] The Bank was headquartered in Philadelphia but had branches in several states.

When state banks or the First Bank (and Second Bank) received specie deposits from individual investors, it would issue these depositors notes as a form of receipt, which was circulated as money. These banks would also make loans, for which they would issue bank notes, also redeemable in specie, to the borrower. The Bank of the United States was able to issue ordinary demand US bank notes for its loans, with denominations greater than $5; it was also able to issue US bank notes for various amounts and dates of payment, which could be transferred by the original owner's endorsement.[40] These notes were receivable at any First Bank or Second Bank branch; state bank notes were also receivable at First Bank or Second Bank branches.[41]

In its early years, the First Bank's heavy load of government obligations, acquired from the states, limited its capacity to lend privately; however, after government loans were liquidated at the end of 1796, private lending was able to expand.[42] Table 8.1, from Jefferson's letters to Treasury Secretary Gallatin, shows the Bank's balance sheet in 1801.

The controversy that led to Congress' failure to renew the First Bank's charter generally stemmed from two sources. First, state banks were dissatisfied with the effective curtailment of their note issuance by the First Bank. Second, there was the fear that the Bank would become a "government subsidized monopoly designed to benefit only a small part of the population."[43] Populist sentiment evinced fear that centralization of any kind could impair national development and undermine individual rights.[44] Further Thomas Jefferson and James

Table 8.1
First Bank holdings, 1801

Liabilities		Resources	
Capital	$10,000,000	Discounts (government and private debt)	$12,150,000
Undivided profits	$40,000	Interest	$5,460,000
US bank notes	$5,200,000	Due from state banks	$1,450,000
Deposits		Specie	$5,000,000
Individual	$3,560,000		
Government	$5,240,000		
$24,040,000		**$24,060,000**	

Source: Holdsworth, *supra* note 1063, at 138.

Madison feared the Bank's concentration of financial power would disproportionately benefit northern trade and commerce at the expense of farmers across the rest of the country, as its branches (and by extension, their reserves) were concentrated in the north. This imbalance would encourage the Bank to make more loans to northern banks and individuals.[45]

Although some would emphasize the illegitimacy of a government bank lending to the private sector, this was a minor consideration in the failure of the bank to survive. The issue was rather control of state bank notes and federal power. And there was no focus at the time on the power of the bank to lend to other banks, as a protean lender of last resort. But that baby was thrown out with the bathwater.

8.1.3 Second Bank of the United States (1816–1836)

The Second Bank of the United States was established just a few years after the first Bank's charter lapsed. Its establishment was largely due to the stress to the American economy from the War of 1812. Embargoes paired with heavy wartime resource demands had resulted in a considerable government deficit.[46]

Private investors, rather than the government, had purchased government loans taken out in connection with the war; when the value of those government loans fell, these investors lobbied for a new national bank as a means of enhancing the value of their holdings.[47] By August 1816, after the British burned the White House and the Capitol, these investors—including John Jacob Astor, Stephen Girard, and later Treasury Secretary Alexander James Dallas—felt they could wait no longer and formed a plan for recouping their investments.[48] As with the First Bank, speculation and arbitrage opportunities resulting from these private investors' holdings were a driving force behind these wealthy, powerful individuals' backing for the establishment of the central bank.[49]

These investors' plans laid the basis for the Dallas–Calhoun bill that would charter the Second Bank of the United States. The Bank would be chartered for twenty years, with capital of $35 million. As the First Bank before it, the government would own 20 percent of the Bank's stock, and the public would own 80 percent. Bank equity capital was paid for with one-quarter specie, three-quarters in government bonds.[50] Although Madison had vocally opposed the First Bank during its congressional approval hearings twenty years earlier, as President he expressed no similar concerns in the second Bank's ratification process.

Just like the First Bank, it was provided by legislation that the Second Bank must be able to pay its noteholders in specie at all times, although there was no explicit requirement for minimum amounts of specie to notes issued. To allay Democratic-Republican fears that the large capitalization of the Bank would make it a "mammoth machine" working against the best interests of the nation's economy, the institution's equity capital could never be raised above $35 million.[51]

With regard to ensuring that state banks maintained sufficient specie, the Second Bank's approach was not consistent among all state banks.[52] This is because banks located in metropolitan centers, like New York and Philadelphia, generally were much more reliable in their efforts to maintain sufficient specie to state bank note issuance than state banks located in country districts in the far south and west.[53] As a result the Second Bank needed to carefully monitor the specie and note issuance by rural state banks and could take a more hands-off approach to the banks located in metropolitan cities.[54]

The first and second presidents of the Second Bank, William Jones and Langdon Cheves,[55] mismanaged the Second Bank by extending too much credit to state-chartered banks and individuals.[56] By mid-1818 the Second Bank and its branches had issued such a large amount of US bank notes that its specie reserves were comparably low and there was a risk that the Second Bank would not have sufficient specie to meet redemptions by US bank noteholders.[57]

When Langdon Cheves became the second president of the bank at the beginning of 1819,[58] he forbade the branches of the Second Bank to issue any more US bank notes.[59] In order to increase its specie reserves, the Second Bank was required to collect payment of some of their loans. This shifted balance sheet pressure from the Second Bank to state banks in three important ways. First, for state bank notes held by the Second Bank as payment for taxes, the Second Bank simply redeemed such notes for state banks' specie.[60] Second, for Second Bank loans directly to state banks, the Second Bank asked for repayment in specie, further draining the specie reserves of state banks.[61] Third, many of the Second Bank's loans to *other borrowers* were repaid by those borrowers in state bank notes, which the Second Bank would then convert to specie by taking the notes to the state bank for redemption in the state bank's specie.[62]

Of course, state banks reacted negatively to this balance sheet pressure shift. For example, state banks in Georgia and North Carolina loaned extensively to land buyers, farmers, and country merchants during the late 1810s and early 1820s. Although these banks had sufficient specie for otherwise ordinary commercial transactions, they "could not withstand the claims which might be made by the (Bank of the United States) bent on obtaining specie."[63]

The resulting contraction of credit was widely thought to have contributed to, or at least increased the hardship produced by, the recessionary Panic of 1819. Although the effect on the US economy was largely negative, the Second Bank was successful in raising its ratio of specie reserves to US bank notes from a low of 12 percent in 1818 to a high of 61 percent in 1821.[64]

After the specie crisis at the Second Bank was resolved, its third president, Nicholas Biddle, once again expanded the institution's role as a provider of credit and stability beginning in approximately 1822. Under Biddle's direction, the Second Bank was effective in ensuring that state banks had sufficient specie to back note issuance.[65] Jeffersonian Albert Gallatin wrote that the Second Bank had "effectually checked excessive issues" by the state banks, and "that very purpose" for which it had been established had been fulfilled.[66] In 1833, he wrote to Bank of England director Horsley Palmer that "the Bank of the United States must not be considered as affording a complete remedy," for the ills of overexpansion, "but as the best and most practicable which can be applied"; and its action "had been irreproachable" in maintaining a proper specie reserve position "as late as November 1830."[67]

From 1831 to 1832, fluctuation in European exportation caused an unfavorable balance of trade with the United States, which caused a slowdown in the US economy. The Second Bank acted to mitigate the harm to the economy by expanding loans to state banks and other private entities.[68] During this time the Second Bank allowed specie reserve to fall by 41 percent.[69] The Second Bank did so "to relieve the community from the temporary pressure to which it was thus exposed."[70]

During the 1831–32 credit crisis, the Second Bank redeemed notes for specie from banks in Boston, New York, Baltimore, and Philadelphia that had maintained large specie reserves.[71] The specie that the Second Bank received from these efforts enabled the Second Bank to expand loan making to banks in the west and southwest, where loan issuances had expanded beyond state banks' capacity to repay with specie.[72]

The success of the Bank's stabilization efforts during this crisis increased the Bank's popularity even among state bankers that had been previously opposed to the Bank's influence.[73] Of the 394 state banks that existed in 1832, none petitioned Congress to withdraw the Bank's charter; 61 sent memorials in favor of renewal.[74]

Like its predecessor, the Second Bank of the United States was also a controversial entity. Allegations of corruption at the Second Bank's local branches began as early as 1825.[75] Branch officials in South Carolina, Louisiana, New Hampshire, Georgia, and Virginia were accused of "unjustifiable political activity," incurring suspicion that the Bank would engage in political favoritism by lending at disproportionately favorable rates to preferred borrowers.[76] After investigation by Jacksonian officials, these charges were largely found baseless; no charges were ever levied against the parent board.[77]

Andrew Jackson and other Democrat-Republicans, who complained that the Bank posed a threat to states' rights, were the primary source of Bank criticism. When Jackson assumed the presidency in 1829, the Second Bank was thriving under Biddle's leadership. The dollar was in good health; the Supreme Court reaffirmed the Second Bank's constitutionality;[78] and the Treasury continued to use it as an official depository.[79] However, Jackson's first message as President was that "both the constitutionality and the expediency of the law creating the bank were well questioned by a large portion of our fellow-citizens."[80]

In 1832, congressional hearings were called in response to the Second Bank's actions during the 1831–32 crisis. At these hearings Biddle's interaction with the legislature—one wary of the Bank's overreach—exacerbated tensions. Biddle, citing the Bank's 1831–32 specie outflow and loan issuance as a means of ameliorating the economic downturn, asserted that the Bank's decisions to provide credit to the market in times of crisis worked in the best interest of the entire market.[81] Anti-Bank members of Congress viewed this statement as Second Bank management overstepping its mandate and threatening congressional authority.[82] One member of Congress expressed his trepidation at the link between the Bank and Congressional authority: "This vagrant power to erect a bank ... has at length been located by [Secretary of the Treasury Crawford] on that provision to lay and collect taxes."[83] John Quincy Adams similarly remarked, "power for good is power for evil, even in the hands of Omnipotence." He and many others in Congress believed that "the soundest discretion may come to different results in different men." Regardless of the Bank's benevolent intent and, often, similarly benevolent results, Congress feared the Bank's power and discretion in helping shape American markets.[84]

In 1832, Henry Clay, during his presidential campaign against Andrew Jackson (who was running for reelection), introduced a bill to

renew the second Bank's charter four years early.[85] Introducing the bill
during the campaign was intended to minimize the chance that Jackson
would veto it, lest he provide his political opponents with grounds for
criticism.[86] However, Jackson not only vetoed the bill on July 10, 1832,
but he used the veto message to send a strong populist message to his
voters.[87] The message focused on the "exclusive privileges" granted to
the Bank and its stockholders and contrasted them with the experience
of the ordinary American: "when the laws undertake to add to these
natural and just advantages artificial distinctions, to grant titles, gratu-
ities, and exclusive privileges, to make the rich richer and the potent
more powerful, the humble members of society the farmers, mechanics,
and laborers who have neither the time nor the means of securing like
favors to themselves, have a right to complain of the injustice of their
Government."[88] In December 1832, shortly after the veto, President
Jackson, now reelected, ordered the withdrawal of federal deposits
from the Bank, instead moving them to a newly established group of
"pet" banks that would serve as depositaries for federal government
assets. Under President Jackson and newly appointed Treasury Secretary Roger Taney, President Jackson's close ally, all government reve-
nues were placed not with the Second Bank but in certain state banks
they would select. The remaining government assets within the Second
Bank, in the tens of millions at the time, would be drawn upon for all
government expenditures until that amount was exhausted.[89]

Less than a year after the Bank's close, the United States experienced
the Panic of 1837, in which money supply fell 34 percent between 1838
and 1842 and prices decreased 33 percent from 1839 to 1843.[90] There
was no Bank of the United States available to expand credit.

The Second Bank of the United States, much more than the First
Bank, did, in effect, play the role of lender of last resort to the banking
system, by forbearing specie redemptions in weaker banks, and did so
successfully to maintain financial stability. This accounted for its popularity with the states. However, there was a continued fear of the
misuse of federal power. Again, the baby of lender of last resort was
thrown out with the bathwater of such federal power.

8.2   Creation of the Federal Reserve System in 1913 and Its
Authority as Lender of Last Resort to Nonbanks

In the United States, a series of nineteenth-century banking panics led
to the creation of the Federal Reserve System.[91] According to Laeven

and Valencia (2013) the United States experienced major banking crises in 1837, 1839, 1857, 1861, 1873, 1884, 1890, 1893, 1896, and 1907.[92] In each case, liquidity crises suffered by New York banks significantly amplified the initial panic, ultimately leading to a nationwide run on banks.

During these crises the United States did not have a central bank to provide liquidity, so stabilizing the banking system required a private solution. The private solution routinely involved private bank clearinghouses that would act together upon the onset of a crisis and provide the necessary liquidity.[93] In each crisis, clearing houses in large cities such as New York and Chicago primarily acted as private lenders of last resort by providing emergency reserve currency.[94] The effectiveness of such actions was varied.[95] J. P. Morgan (the man) also often played this role by pledging personal funds and organizing top bankers to support illiquid but solvent banks.[96] However, after the numerous crises and the realization that J. P. Morgan would not always be around to save the financial system, public support intensified for a central bank to regulate the banking sector and act as an official lender of last resort.[97] More important, while private institutions had become adept at responding to a crisis, the only way to prevent a panic in the first place was to establish a lender of last resort that is "sufficiently credible such that depositors always believe it can ... purchase the assets of the banking system."[98]

By 1913, leading bankers and government officials increasingly agreed that a single centralized lender of last resort was needed.[99] Congress hence enacted the Federal Reserve Act in 1913, which provided the Federal Reserve with lender-of-last-resort powers.[100] However, weakness of the Federal Reserve's 1913 lender-of-last-resort authorities was exposed during the banking panics of the early 1930s. At that time the Federal Reserve was prohibited from lending to non-member banks, and was only permitted to accept a few types of collateral—primarily short-term commercial and agricultural loans, in addition to Treasury securities.[101] When these legal constraints were in place, 65 percent of commercial banks representing 25 percent of deposits were nonmember banks that had "no direct access to the lender of last resort."[102] History shows that deposits held at nonmember banks were clearly at greater risk than deposits at member banks. For example, between 1930 and 1932, one dollar of deposits held at a nonmember bank was five times more likely to be affected by a bank's suspension of operations than one dollar of deposits held with a member bank.[103]

In 1932, following the chaos in the early years of the Great Depression, Congress adopted two major expansions of Federal Reserve's lender-of-last-resort authorities: Sections 10(b) and 13(3) of the Federal Reserve Act.

First, in February, Congress enacted the Glass–Steagall Act of 1932, which amended the Federal Reserve Act to include Section 10(b).[104] Section 10(b) authorized the Federal Reserve, under "exceptional and exigent circumstances," to lend to member banks against a much broader set of collateral than was previously permitted.[105] Although the provision was initially intended to be temporary, subsequent legislation extended its lifetime indefinitely and removed the requirement that such lending only take place in "exceptional and exigent circumstances."[106] The Monetary Control Act of 1980 required all depository institutions to hold reserves and opened discount window lending to any institution holdings reserves, thus extending this lending to non-member banks.[107]

The Federal Reserve continues to act as a lender of last resort to banking institutions through the discount window under Section 10(b), which was redesignated 10B in 1991.[108] Discount window loans from the Federal Reserve must be "secured to the satisfaction of [the] Federal Reserve bank."[109] Acceptable collateral that can include government and agency securities, ABS, corporate bonds, money market instruments, and residential and commercial real estate loans, among other eligible securities.[110] Fed policy (as distinct from the statute) does not permit unsecured discount window lending, so institutions with no acceptable collateral cannot access it.[111] However, subject to several limitations, including the consent of five members of the Board of Governors, the Federal Reserve can lend to groups of five or more member banks that do *not* have sufficient eligible collateral to borrow through 10B.[112] In such cases, recipient banks must "deposit with a suitable trustee, representing the entire group, their individual notes made in favor of the group protected by such collateral security as may be agreed upon."[113] Lender-of-last-resort liquidity support obviously does not carry the same level of risk to taxpayers as straight (and obviously unsecured) capital injections. A recent paper by Martin Hellwig, for example, notes that central banks may have loaned to insolvent institutions during the crisis but that central bank support to banks of dubious solvency does not hurt taxpayers since the central bank is not in danger of losing any money (though inflation may occur and loss of reputation may be at stake).[114] Even Lehman Brothers', which owed the

Federal Reserve $46 billion on the date of its bankruptcy, paid back its Fed loans only three days later.[115] The lender of last resort does not generally loan to insolvent banks, banks that have lost money due to ineptitude, but there is nothing in Section 10B that prevents it from doing so. The power is designed to protect banks and the financial system as a whole from being victimized by destabilizing contagious panics.

Second, in July 1932, "tucked away in a road construction measure" called the Emergency Relief and Construction Act, Congress amended the Federal Reserve Act to include Section 13(3).[116] Section 13(3) allowed the Federal Reserve, "in unusual and exigent circumstances [and after an] affirmative vote of not less than five members," to lend to "any individual, partnership, or corporation"[117] Prior to 2008, the Fed made few loans under Section 13(3), with most coming between 1932 and 1936 to 123 institutions for an aggregate amount of $1.5 million.[118]

As initially enacted, Section 13(3) lending was required to be "secured to the satisfaction of the Federal Reserve bank"[119] by collateral "eligible for discount for member banks under" Section 10B.[120] This collateral requirement effectively limited the Fed's ability to lend to nonbank financial institutions, including investment banks, that primarily held investment securities that were not eligible as collateral.[121]

Less than two weeks before signing 13(3) into law, President Hoover had vetoed a similar provision that would have enabled the Reconstruction Finance Corporation to lend to individuals.[122] He expressed concern that granting these authorities "would place the Government in private business in such fashion as to violate the very principle[s] … upon which we have builded our nation."[123] Although there is scant legislative history to support the hypothesis, it is plausible that the onerous collateral requirement was a legislative bargain that enabled the provision to escape veto.

The 1987 financial crisis, however, led to an amendment of Section 13 that increased the discretion of the Federal Reserve to lend to nonbanks by removing the heightened collateral requirement. In 1991 the FDIC Improvement Act amended Section 13 of the Federal Reserve Act by striking "of the kinds and maturities made eligible for discount for member banks under other provisions of this Act."[124] This opened the door for all notes, drafts, and bills of exchange to be eligible as collateral and left the adequacy of the collateral to the "satisfaction" of the Fed.[125] Senator Christopher J. Dodd (of the Dodd–Frank Act) ironically authored the 1991 legislation that expanded the LOLR powers of the

Federal Reserve, arguing that the expanded powers gave the Federal Reserve "greater flexibility to respond in instances in which the overall financial system threatens to collapse."[126]

In short, before Dodd–Frank, the main predicates of emergency §13(3) lending were a five-of-seven vote by the Federal Reserve Board members coupled with the inability of the recipient institution "to secure adequate credit accommodations from other banking institutions."[127] Funds were required to be "secured to the satisfaction of the Federal Reserve,"[128] leaving the appraisal of the adequacy of collateral posted by recipients to the Board's discretion. Under these circumstances the Federal Reserve was authorized to act as the lender of last resort to individual *non*banks including "[i]ndividuals, [p]artnerships, and [c]orporations" in "unusual and exigent circumstances" by §13(3) of the Federal Reserve Act.[129] Combined with the discount window, §13(3) enabled central bank liquidity to reach potentially the entire bank and nonbank financial system (to the extent that borrowers could post collateral that the Federal Reserve deemed to be adequate).

As already noted, during the financial crisis of 2007 to 2009 the Federal Reserve exercised its §13(3) liquidity power through the creation of a sweeping series of novel borrowing facilities, several of which were intended to benefit nonbanks. Section 13(3) also formed the statutory basis for the Federal Reserve assistance of selected individual nonbank financial institutions, including Bear Stearns and AIG.[130]

The Federal Reserve also acts as international lender of last resort through swap lines under authority codified in the 1980 amendments to the Federal Reserve Act, specifically Section 14(a) and 14(c).[131] Through the swap lines, the Federal Reserve lends US dollars to foreign central banks, which may then be lent to foreign or US institutions. While the use of swap lines was useful during the financial crisis and the subsequent crisis in the eurozone, a potential critique of swap lines is that they could be used as a "backdoor" use of the Fed's authority to lend to nonbank financial institutions, thus circumventing the limits on such lending established by Section 13(3). However, the Fed's authority to grant swap lines rests on authority separate from 13(3) and is thus not restricted by 13(3). Fortunately, Dodd–Frank prudently did not limit the Federal Reserve's authority to use swap lines. Restrictions would pose major concerns for foreign central banks having dollar liabilities of their own banks.

9   Dodd–Frank Restrictions on the Lender-of-Last-Resort Power

The Dodd–Frank Act placed important restrictions on the Fed's power as lender of last resort to nonbanks under §13(3) as part of the post-crisis reaction that its lending constituted an undesirable bailout of "Wall Street." Interestingly, this anti-bailout sentiment only manifested itself on restrictions on lending to nonbanks, rather than banks themselves. These restrictions, detailed below, have substantially curtailed the Fed's ability to be an effective lender of last resort in a future crisis, and have made our financial system much less stable.

The following restrictions were placed on the Fed: (1) no loans can be made to single institutions—they must be part of a broad program approved by the Secretary of the Treasury; (2) all nonbank loans must be approved by the Secretary of the Treasury; (3) loans can only be made to solvent institutions; (4) discount window loans to banks cannot be used to fund their nonbank affiliates, like broker-dealers—instead loans to those affiliates must be authorized under §13(3); (5) new collateral requirements are imposed; and (6) all loans must be publicly disclosed within one year, and disclosed to congressional leaders in seven days. As noted in chapter 7, the Federal Home Loan Bank system played an important role as lender of last resort during the 2008 financial crisis. This authority was not curtailed by Dodd–Frank.

In another respect, Dodd–Frank's Title VIII potentially broadens the Federal Reserve's lender-of-last-resort capabilities with respect to financial market utilities designated as "systemically important," which clearly covers clearinghouses which have already been designated.[1] The designation process is conducted by FSOC, which has designated eight such firms as of the end of 2015.[2] It could also include broker-dealers engaged in certain activities.[3] Emergency lending under Title VIII would be conducted through discount window loans and not be subjected to the same restrictions that Dodd–Frank placed on §13(3) lending. However, not only is it unlikely that broker-dealers will be designated as financial market utilities, the designation requires the affirmative vote of the chair of FSOC (i.e., the Treasury Secretary), making this arguably just as onerous as emergency lending under §13(3).

The Dodd-Frank restrictions on 13(3) lending are particularly dangerous given the additional liquidity requirements imposed on financial institutions. However, Dodd-Frank's new liquidity rules have shrunk private lending by requiring institutions to maintain their own liquidity, leading to hoarding. Thus, the ability of the Fed to encourage solvent and liquid institutions to lend in a crisis is constrained by their own liquidity regulations. Ironically, the liquidity requirements thus increase the need for Fed lending in a crisis rather than reduce it.

9.1   Broad Program Requirement

Section 1101 of Dodd–Frank requires §13(3) programs to have broad-based eligibility,[4] thus prohibiting assistance to individual nonbank financial institutions undergoing runs or in danger of failing. Depending on the interpretation of "broad-based," this requirement could compromise the ability of the Federal Reserve to prevent an incipient run emanating from a single institution—the run starts somewhere. While a financial crisis involves the run on a number of financial institutions, there will likely be a single institution that experiences the run first. Since that initial run could spark contagion, resulting in the failure of many institutions, it is necessary for the Federal Reserve to solve the problem at the outset. Waiting for multiple institutions to require liquidity support could result in the Fed lending into a run. Preventing the run in the first place would avoid that problem.[5] As Secretary Geithner observed in his book *Stress Test*, when the Fed loans into a run, it is very difficult to make solvency determinations, since asset values are uncertain due to fire sales—one does not know whether the fall in prices can be corrected by the provision of liquidity, whether values would not have fallen but for the fire sales, or whether the losses are more fundamental. Allowing the *possibility* of lending to a single institution may then make it unnecessary to actually lend to a single institution, as the prospect of Fed lending will prevent any runs.

The Federal Reserve's one-off loan to an insolvent AIG no doubt figured prominently in the background of this provision—this issue is raised in the House Financial Service Committee Report on Dodd–Frank.[6] But this concern was separately met by Dodd–Frank's insistence that loans only be made to solvent nonbanks, as discussed directly below. Further the Federal Reserve's AIG acquisition might have been illegal even under the pre-Dodd–Frank §13(3). Recently the US Court of Federal Claims ruled that the Federal Reserve did not have the power to acquire AIG's equity in exchange for a §13(3) loan.[7] While the ruling may still be overturned on appeal, it nonetheless raises the possibility that Dodd–Frank's "broad-based program" restriction was unnecessary if the goal was to prevent another AIG-type acquisition by the Federal Reserve. Rather than generally limiting Federal Reserve's lender-of-last-resort power, §13(3) could instead specify that the Federal Reserve cannot acquire a borrower's equity. However, strict limitations to the Fed's ability to customize lending to financial institutions facing insolvency and lacking adequate collateral could be problematic. Under Dodd–Frank programs cannot be tailored to individual situations, as in the cases of Bear and AIG.

Restoring the power to lend to a single solvent institution that was the first victim of a run would not necessarily require new legislation. The Fed could design a broad program available to any solvent nonbank victims of runs, including the first one, and that program could be approved in advance by the Secretary of the Treasury. But in the anti-bailout environment in Washington, DC, such action would be attacked as an attempt to bail out Wall Street. If the Secretary were to authorize a broad program, it is likely she would only do so when faced with the real prospect of another crisis, which could be too late to forestall a run.

On December 23, 2014, the Federal Reserve Board published a proposed rule to amend Regulation A, which covers Extensions of Credit by Federal Reserve Banks, to implement Section 1101 of the Dodd–Frank Act ("Proposed 1101 Rule"), which was the amendment to Section 13(3).[8] As part of its proposal, which basically tracked the language of Section 1101 so as to preserve maximum flexibility, the Fed defined a broad program as one that is not designed for a single and specific company.[9] On January 13, 2014, Jeb Hensarling, the Chairman of the House Financial Services Committee sent a letter to then Federal Reserve Chairman Bernanke (the "Hensarling letter"), asking for a more precise definition of a broad program and suggested that a maximum borrowing amount be set for an individual firm, going beyond the language of Section 1101.[10] This was followed by a later letter, on August 18, 2014, of several members of the House and Senate to Chair Yellen, including Senator Warren, (the "Warren letter")[11] suggesting the possibility that a broad program require more than two recipients (the Fed's proposal implies that any number greater than one would be broad). These letters are important in two respects. They reflect the hostile political environment facing the Fed's use of its lender of resort power for nonbanks and seek to put even more restrictions on the Fed than did Dodd–Frank itself, by urging the Fed to refrain from even exercising what reduced authority it now has.

The Fed responded to some of the concerns in its final rule approved on November 30, 2015, however, one could argue the changes are merely cosmetic.[12] The final rule defines "broad-based" as a program in which five or more institutions are eligible to participate. The question remains as to how this rule restricts the ability of the Fed to lend to the first nonbank financial institution that experiences a run. Would four other institutions also have to experience a run at the same time or would future risk of a run be sufficient? In the end, the eligibility standard will hinge on the specific conditions of the program. The Fed's final rule also made additional cosmetic restrictions that are not required under the statute. As part of a 13(3) program, the Fed must disclose publicly the market sector targeted by the 13(3) lending and the Fed will review each program every six months.[13]

9.2   Requirement of Approval by the Secretary of the Treasury

Dodd–Frank also requires that all lending to nonbanks be subject to "the prior approval of the Secretary of the Treasury."[14] The Act requires that the "policies and procedures governing emergency lending" be promulgated in consultation with the Secretary of the Treasury and that, as already discussed, no program or facility under Section 13(3) may be established "without the prior approval of the Secretary of the Treasury." This provision effectively withdraws exclusive control over the decision to loan to nonbanks from the Federal Reserve Board, an exclusive power it had during the crisis. It severely limits the ability of the Federal Reserve to respond independently to a crisis. The Dodd–Frank Act's requirements for Treasury approval of Federal Reserve actions will arguably politicize the decision of how to deal with contagion and create significant market uncertainty, thereby accelerating the outbreak and pace of future runs.

In some respects the new requirements recall the early days of the Fed's existence when political interference with all central banking operations was a serious concern. Economist Allan Meltzer has conducted extensive research on the Federal Reserve's early struggles to maintain its independence.[15] The Federal Reserve was formed just one year before the start of World War I, and Meltzer finds that the Federal Reserve's early years were spent providing support to the Treasury's war-financing efforts.[16] This arrangement placed the Federal Reserve in a position of relative subservience to the Treasury, symbolized by the fact that the Federal Reserve originally met in a Treasury Department conference room.[17] "[T]he Secretary of the Treasury was the *ex officio* chairman of the Federal Reserve Board until 1935, who sat at the head of the table whenever he chose to attend meetings."[18] In particular, during World War I Federal Reserve officials explained that they allowed inflation risks to rise and rejected rate increases because such increases were "inadvisable from the point of view of Treasury's plans."[19] The early Federal Reserve was also reluctant to oppose the Treasury in light of the Overman Act, which allowed the President to transfer Federal Reserve responsibilities to another agency (e.g., the Treasury) during the wartime period.[20] Overall, Meltzer notes that throughout this early period, congressional officials blamed the Federal Reserve's missteps on the agency's lack of independence from political pressures.[21] Meltzer concludes that the early Federal Reserve "was too weak politically to slow or stop the postwar inflation and too uncertain about the political consequences of its actions to act decisively when the Treasury allowed it to act."[22] A former vice-chairman of the Federal Reserve, Frederick H. Schultz, has described the period of maximum Treasury involvement with the Federal Reserve's operations as a time of "politicized" decision-making.

After World War I the Federal Reserve attempted to assert its independence. Certain congressional members supported this endeavor and passed the Banking Act of 1935, a law that further centralized monetary decision-making power in the Federal Reserve.[23] The primary objective of the Banking Act was to centralize authority in the Board of Governors and to make permanent some of the temporary exceptional measures discussed above.[24] As previously mentioned, the Banking Act expanded the Federal Reserve's lender-of-last-resort authorities by permitting Section 10(b) lending in other than "exceptional and exigent circumstances."[25] The Act greatly enhanced the Federal Reserve's independence by removing the Secretary of the Treasury and the Comptroller of the Currency from the Board of Governors.[26] Two years prior, the Banking Act of 1933 had established the Federal Open Market Committee ("FOMC").[27] However, the decisions of the FOMC with respect to open market operations were not binding on reserve banks.[28] The Banking Act of 1935 placed control of the FOMC in the Board of Governors, by ensuring that a majority of its members were members of the Board of Governors, and by making its decisions about open market operations binding on reserve banks.[29]

However, Meltzer finds that continued "[s]ubservience to the Treasury during the [post–World War I] recovery ... limited the effect of the legislation for a time."[30] Moreover the Federal Reserve returned to a deferential wartime role in the wake of World War II; during this period then Federal Reserve Chairman Marriner Stoddard Eccles characterized his role as "a routine administrative job ... [t]he Federal Reserve merely executed Treasury decisions."[31] After World War II the Federal Reserve obtained formal independence through the 1951 Accord, an agreement that freed the Federal Reserve from the Treasury-induced ceiling on interest rates.[32] Meltzer notes that subsequent to the 1951 Accord, the Federal Reserve "[f]or the first time since 1934 ... could look forward to conducting monetary actions without approval of the Treasury."[33] Federal Reserve independence was thus achieved only after the early Federal Reserve struggled to accede to Treasury instruction. This initial subservience hindered the Federal Reserve's ability to avoid political concerns and effectively combat shifting market environments.

It is interesting, given the long history of the Fed's struggle to free itself from control of the Treasury, to look into the legislative history of Dodd–Frank's new requirement for Treasury approval of Fed lending to nonbanks. The initial proposal for what amounts to a Treasury veto on the Fed's lender-of-last-resort authority to nonbanks came from the Treasury itself. The Treasury's June 17, 2009, Final Report on Financial Regulatory Reform, proposed to revise the Fed's "emergency lending authority to improve accountability," by requiring Treasury approval.[34] Subsequently the Obama administration, on July 22, 2009, introduced draft legislation containing the requirement that the Fed's emergency lending authority have the "prior written approval of the Secretary of the Treasury."[35] The House Republican bill introduced on July 23, 2009, also contained a requirement for Treasury Secretary approval, as well as a provision to allow for congressional disapproval of §13(3) authority.[36] A November 3, 2009, bill by Democratic Representative Barney Frank also contained a requirement of Treasury approval.[37] By December 11, 2009, the bill that ultimately became the Dodd–Frank Act, House bill (HR 4173), not only contained a requirement of Treasury Secretary approval of lending programs but also added several further limitations to the Fed's power of lender of last resort to nonbanks that were not adopted into the Dodd–Frank Act: certification by the President that an emergency exists, FSOC determination that a liquidity event exists, and congressional power to disapprove of any §13(3) program.[38] HR 4173 ultimately passed the House, but only after two major recorded votes for resolving differences, and only after passing the Senate.[39] The bill that was initially engrossed in the House on December 11, 2009, contained these additional restrictions on the Fed,[40] as did the bill that was referred in the Senate on January 20, 2010.[41] However, the amendment engrossed in the Senate on May 20, 2010, substantially revised the provisions affecting the Federal Reserve, removing these restrictions.[42]

Why would the Treasury, headed by a Secretary who previously served as President of the New York Fed, propose such restrictions on the Fed? It is interesting in this regard to note that Geithner in his book *Stress Test*, while criticizing other restrictions on the Fed imposed by Dodd–Frank, never mentions this one, which arguably is one of the most onerous. The reason is clear: he cannot criticize a provision that he himself sponsored. I asked Secretary Geithner, after he left office, why he did this. He responded that sometimes the Treasury would want the Fed to act as lender of last resort when the Fed was reluctant to do so.[43] And that is surely possible—in the crisis Paulson was urging Bernanke on. But requiring the Treasury to approve the Fed acting as lender of last resort does not accomplish that objective—the Treasury must approve the Fed's request to lend, it cannot order the Fed to lend. As we will see later, the power of Treasury to compel central bank lending does exist, however, in Japan and the United Kingdom.

So what was the real reason that Geithner made this proposal? I believe there are only two plausible reasons. First, this could just be a continuation of the historical battle for supremacy between the Treasury and the Fed. Treasury saw an opportunity to control the Fed and took it. While Geithner had served as president of the New York Fed, he had not been chairman of the Board, and outside his service at the Fed, he was a career Treasury official. A second possibility is that he was trying to forestall even worse outcomes in a Congress that was intent on punishing the Fed for bailing out Wall Street. This is plausible given the congressional proposal to have the power to veto loans to particular nonbanks. In any event, Treasury control of the Fed was not proposed by conservative republicans but by the Obama Treasury itself.

Holders of short-term debt issued by failing financial institutions are extremely unlikely to accept the uncertainty inherent in an ad hoc lending regime that might be canceled at any time or simply never initiated at all,[44] especially when the arbiter of the decision is the Secretary of the Treasury, a political appointee, not a an independent agency like the Fed. The risk that the Secretary will withhold lender-of-last-resort assistance from a distressed financial institution at a critical moment prevents this assistance from serving its function as a guarantee, or even a near guarantee.[45]

In 2008, Secretary Paulson readily gave his support of Federal Reserve lending under 13(3), and would no doubt have given his formal approval if required. Some believe that in the future faced with the extreme consequences of not lending, the Secretary of Treasury, staring over the precipice, will have to give approval. Former Fed Chairman Ben Bernanke, for example, pointed out that "the approval of the Treasury Secretary ... is basically okay, for Democratic reasons and because, generally speaking, the Treasury Secretary and the Fed chairman see pretty much eye to eye at trying to prevent the financial system from collapsing."[46] In his recent book, Bernanke further added: "[§13(3)'s ability to lend to individual institutions] was one authority I was happy to lose. We would still be able to use 13(3) to create emergency lending programs with broad eligibility such as our lending program for securities dealers or the facility to support money market funds, although we'd have to obtain the Treasury secretary's permission first. I didn't consider that much of a concession, since I couldn't imagine a major financial crisis in which the Fed and the Treasury would not work closely." [47] But in the new post-crisis political environment, it is far from *certain* that Treasury approval will be given at all, or on a timely basis—most important, the market will think it is uncertain, and thus start to run before such a decision is even made. I read Bernanke's comments as accepting bad restrictions on the Fed in order to fend off even worse ones.

Even if a particular Fed action might be approved by the Treasury Secretary under 13(3), or could be taken for banks without Treasury approval through the discount window, the political environment for the Fed acting as lender-of-last-resort has changed, making it less likely the Fed would even exercise its lender of last resort authority in a crisis. After all, it has been widely criticized for "bailing out Wall Street" in the last crisis. A cornerstone to the Fed's authority as lender of last resort is its independence from political forces; it is thus worrisome that Ben Bernanke believes Treasury approval may be required in a democracy—would he say the same for monetary policy? Fundamentally, Bernanke's concession reflects the strong political attack on the power of the Fed as lender of last resort. Arguably, the Fed's role as a lender of last resort is even more important than its role in conducting monetary policy, so the independence of the Fed as lender of last resort should be a top priority.

9.3   Loans Only to "Solvent" Institutions

Section 13(3) of Dodd–Frank also prohibits the Federal Reserve from providing emergency lending to nonbank financial institutions that are insolvent.[48] A borrower is deemed insolvent if the borrower is in bankruptcy, under Orderly Liquidation Authority (OLA) or any other Federal or State insolvency proceeding.[49] This, of course, is a central tenet of Bagheot's rule. However, the rescue of AIG as well as the loan assisting JP Morgan's acquisition of Bear Stearns seemingly violated this basic principle. In my view, a major consideration in the case of AIG was the fear of compounding the contagion unknowingly unleashed by the decision not to loan to Lehman.

The Fed's own policy and procedures are set up to take solvency into account in making loans to banks. Discount window lending to depository institutions is governed by Regulation A.[50] While the policies and procedures that govern Fed lending decisions depend on the type of discount window lending (i.e., primary credit vs. secondary credit), all decisions involve an inquiry into the solvency of the bank.[51] The availability of primary or secondary credit depends on the financial condition of the bank, as described below.

Primary credit is only available to banks that are in "generally sound financial condition in the judgment of the Federal Reserve Bank."[52] To make this determination, Federal Reserve Banks evaluate criteria set forth in the Board of Governors' Payment System Risk Policy.[53] According to these criteria, a bank will be eligible for primary credit provided it has a strong CAMELS rating of one to three (with one being the highest possible rating), it is adequately capitalized, and there is no "supplementary information [that] indicates the institution is not generally sound."[54] The Federal Reserve Banks do not provide public information as to how they determine whether such supplementary information exists. The CAMELS (Capital adequacy, Assets, Management capability, Earnings, Liquidity, Sensitivity to market risks) rating is a score assigned to a bank by its prudential supervisor, and depends on quantitative factors from the bank's balance sheet and supervisory assessments. A bank with a lower CAMELS rating of four can become eligible for primary credit, provided "supplementary information indicates that the institutions is at least adequately capitalized and that its condition has improved sufficiently to be deemed generally sound by its Reserve Bank."[55] The FDIC Improvement Act sets the legislative framework for bank lending via the secondary credit facility.[56] The secondary credit facility is designed for banks that are not "adequately capitalized" and therefore have a CAMELS rating of five. The secondary credit facility can also be used for banks that are "critically undercapitalized." A bank is critically undercapitalized if it is undercapitalized and does not meet leverage and other requirements set forth by the FDIC.[57] Most important, a Reserve Bank can only lend to these banks if "in the judgment of the Reserve Bank, such a credit extension would be consistent with a timely return to reliance on market funding sources."[58] Additional rules also govern Fed lending to undercapitalized and critically undercapitalized banks that generaly limit the timing of discount window loans. For example, a Federal Reserve Bank can only lend to a critically undercapitalized bank within five days of its classification as critically undercapitalized, or after consultation with the Board of Governors.[59] These procedures depend critically on supervisory information, which would not generally be available for nonbanks, since only nonbank SIFIs are supervised by the Fed.

But while it may be the policy of the Fed to only loan to solvent institutions (banks as well as nonbanks), until Dodd–Frank there was no statutory prohibition on lending to an insolvent nonbank, and there is still no statutory prohibition on lending to an insolvent bank through the discount window. It is hard to see why there should be a double standard on this issue. It is important to note that a statutory prohibition on lending to an insolvent nonbank is likely to act as a political deterrent against the Fed lending to nonbanks because if the borrower turns out to be insolvent, then Congress will have grounds to be highly critical of the Fed's decision to lend. The saving grace of the Dodd–Frank prohibition may be the very limited definition of insolvency—a borrower "shall be considered insolvent" under Dodd–Frank §1101(a) (6) if it is in an insolvency proceeding (e.g., bankruptcy). Thus the Fed could take the position in the future that there would no statutory prohibition on lending to an insolvent institution not in such a proceeding.

Indeed both the Hensarling and Warren letters suggest that the term "insolvency" not be limited to firms that are in an insolvency proceeding. And the Hensarling letter asks the Fed to "create a financial metric to determine whether a firm is insolvent," a demand interestingly not joined in by the Warren letter.[60]

This revision would deprive the Fed of the latitude that the Dodd–Frank Congress may have granted it. But it should be understood that the Congress after the fact might assert that other institutions are not *excluded* from the definition of insolvency and that the policy of the statute is broader. Indeed, the Fed's final November 2015 rule includes a broader definition of insolvency under 13(3); the Fed's updated insolvency definition includes "potential borrowers that are generally not paying their undisputed debts as they become due during the 90 days preceding borrowing from the program, and potential borrowers that are otherwise determined by the Board or the lending Federal Reserve Banks to be insolvent ... [and] any person in a resolution or bankruptcy proceeding."[61] This possibility could still constrain the Fed and the Secretary of the Treasury in taking any significant risk that a borrower could be determined after the fact to be insolvent. It should be understood that while the prohibition of lending to insolvent borrowers is sound, the distinction between merely illiquid and truly insolvent borrowers, in the midst of financial crises, is difficult to determine, in particular because "liquidity problems rarely if ever hit an isolated intermediary unless there is good reason for lenders to attach at least some probability to insolvency."[62] Moreover, in the midst of a run, it is particularly difficult to value an institution's assets. Nonetheless, this is a good prohibition, if it is understood that room for judgment exists. While it is possible to lay out general principles regarding solvency requirements, it is impossible to outline specific metrics. The question of Lehman's solvency at the time of its failure illustrates the problem with specific metrics. Some considering an acquisition, like Bank of America, who inspected Lehman's balance sheet on Lehman weekend, thought there was a "hole" of substantial size. Yet a reported study of the staff of the Federal Reserve Bank of New York, which then President Geithner of the New York Fed said he never saw, thought Lehman was solvent.[63] The valuation of Lehman's assets was debatable, leaving no clear distinction between solvency problems and liquidity problems at the firm.[64] In general, as former Deputy Governor of the Bank of England Paul Tucker has said, a "solvency judgment is inherently probabilistic."[65] I would add that it is also more art than science, particularly when made in real and limited time. Paul Tucker has also suggested that central banks should outline a procedure for making this determination, which might be possible, though it may be difficult to follow a procedure set in advance in cases posing different complexities and time constraints.[66]

9.4 Banks Cannot Use the Proceeds of Discount Window Loans to Make Loans to Their Nonbank Affiliates

Prior to Dodd–Frank, banks could, without limitation, channel discount window loans to nonbank affiliates (including broker-dealers) through repo transactions or other securities financing transactions. For example, repo transactions were not considered "covered transactions," so did not fall under the limitations restricting banks from engaging in such transactions with an affiliate to the extent of more than 10 percent of the bank's capital. However, Dodd–Frank's revision to Section 23A of the Federal Reserve Act has now subjected such affiliate loans to the normal 10 percent limit. Furthermore, while Section 23A does allow the Federal Reserve to exempt transactions from the 23A restrictions by regulation, Dodd–Frank imposed the requirement that the FDIC not object to the exemption on the grounds that it would pose an unacceptable risk to the Deposit Insurance Fund. The combination of the 10 percent limit, a lack of exception for repo transactions, and an extra hurdle for a possible exemption would pose a significant problem during a contagious run. Affiliates will now have to go to the Fed directly as nonbanks for loans under §13(3), subject to all the new restrictions placed on the Fed.

The impairment of the Federal Reserve's lender-of-last-resort capabilities is most concerning with regard to broker-dealers.[67] A key regulatory concern for broker-dealers and the financial system, in general, is the potential lack of access for large broker-dealers to the Fed discount window, which includes the largest broker-dealers in the United States, as they are affiliates of banks and subsidiaries of bank holding companies. For example, at the end of 2012, based on FDIC and SEC filings, Goldman's US bank subsidiary had total assets of just $120 billion while Goldman's US broker-dealer subsidiary had $500 billion in assets. Since the vast majority of Goldman's assets are not held by a US bank, they cannot be pledged in exchange for a traditional discount window loan from the Fed. Creditors of the broker-dealer are thus subject to the vagaries of the new §13(3) of Dodd–Frank.

The FSOC highlighted the lack of public liquidity for large broker-dealers (even those that are a part of a bank holding company) as a potential emerging threat to the US financial system in its 2013 annual report.[68] The report states that "[t]he absence of direct and pre-specified sources of public liquidity and credit backstops makes broker-dealers, as compared to banks, more exposed to vulnerabilities in their funding sources."[69]

9.5 New Collateral Policies Imposed on the Fed

Collateral policy is at the heart of an effective lender-of-last-resort regime. Under old Section 13(3), as used in the crisis, loans only had to be secured "to the satisfaction" of the Fed. This broad authority was used by the Fed to lend to unsecured commercial paper issuers with high credit ratings but with no collateral. Under the revisions to Section 13(3), "security for emergency loans [must be] sufficient to protect taxpayers from losses" and the "policies and procedures established by the Board shall require that a Federal reserve bank assign consistent with sound risk management practices and to ensure protection for the taxpayer, a lendable value to all collateral for a loan executed by a Federal reserve bank under this paragraph in determining whether the loan is secured satisfactorily for purposes of this paragraph."[70] The 13(3) revisions disallow future Fed use of unsecured commercial paper loans.[71] These revisions must be read in conjunction with the power of the Secretary of the Treasury to approve all policies and procedures for lending to nonbanks, so Treasury would also have the ultimate approval over collateral policies.

According to Paul Tucker, it is crucially important that central banks stand ready to lend against a broad range of collateral.[72] Despite these changes, there is still significant discretion that can be exercised by the Fed, if approved by the Treasury, to define the types and amounts of acceptable collateral. A broad interpretation might include cases in which the Federal Reserve deems it unnecessary or inexpedient to require collateral from borrowers at all, as in the 2008 financial crisis, during which the Federal Reserve purchased unsecured commercial paper. In addition to determining the types of acceptable collateral, an optimal collateral policy would ensure that appropriate haircuts are applied to discount all forms of collateral, so as to protect the Fed and ultimately taxpayers from loss.

It is not immediately obvious why Fed losses expose taxpayers to loss, since the Fed's power to create money means it can operate even with negative capital.[73] However, losses do mean that the Fed would have fewer profits to send to the Treasury to support the general revenue of the United States, and these profits have been very substantial. Remittances in 2014 were $99.7 billion,[74] around 3.3 percent of total US revenue that year.[75] Lower contributions to US revenue by the Fed could mean higher taxes or higher US debt. Loans could also impair the Fed's reputation.

9.6   Disclosure Requirements

Section 1103 of Dodd–Frank requires that the Fed disclose any §13(3) lending within one year of the effective date of the termination by the Federal Reserve of the authorization of the lending.[76] Section 1103 has also revised the disclosure rules related to discount window lending to banks. Under Dodd–Frank, the Federal Reserve is now required to publish the names of all banks that borrow from the discount window and how much they borrowed two years after they access the discount window.[77]

In addition Section 1101 of Dodd–Frank requires the Fed to provide to the two congressional banking committees the names of nonbank borrowers and the amount and terms of their loans, within seven days of Fed authorization of such loans.[78] The Fed can request such information be kept confidential in which case the information will only be given to the chairperson or ranking member of the committees.

As we saw in the crisis, the stigma attached to discount window borrowing (which was not disclosed) motivated banks not to use the window during the crisis even when they needed it.[79] Publicly announcing the names and amounts of borrowers might exacerbate the stigma concerns and could increase the likelihood of avoidance, even if such disclosure comes two years later in the case of banks, or one year in the case of nonbanks. A recent paper provides empirical support for the stigma effect, showing that depositors during the Great Depression withdrew more from banks included on a disclosed list compared to those left off of the list.[80] Further the requirement of a seven day reporting of nonbank loans to Congress, even to chairpersons and ranking members, carries with it a risk of leaking, which might further dissuade nonbanks from borrowing.

In my view, a one or two year lag is reasonable, balancing the needs of transparency against the risk of nonborrowing for stigma, but the requirement of a seven-day reporting to Congress puts Congress into micromanaging such loans, which might not only dissuade nonbanks for asking for such loans but make the Fed less willing to make them or to force the Fed to adopt more stringent requirements than they might otherwise do.

~ ~ ~

All of these new requirements make the Fed a weaker lender of last resort to nonbanks that play an increasingly important role in our financial system. Nondeposit short-term liabilities represented around 75 percent of total uninsured short-term liabilities at the end of 2014. In 1970 they only represented around 17 percent. Nondeposit liabilities include money market mutual fund shares, commercial paper, repurchase agreements, and securities lending. Because these nonbanks rely on short-term funding, they are exposed to contagious runs.

10 Comparison of LLR Powers of Fed with Bank of England, European Central Bank, and Bank of Japan

The Fed's three major peers are the Bank of England, the European Central Bank, and the Bank of Japan. This chapter concludes that the Federal Reserve is currently the weakest of the four. The chapter begins with a description of the powers of the three peer central banks and then compares their powers with those of the Fed.[1]

10.1 Bank of England

The Bank of England ("BOE") was originally formed as a private corporation in 1694 by Royal Charter, pursuant to the Bank of England Act 1694.[2] As Mark Carney, the Bank of England Governor, recently noted, the Bank's assumption of the lender-of-last-resort role was gradual, but by the end of the nineteenth century, the "promotion of financial stability through its role as the effective lender of last resort" was among the BOE's *informal* responsibilities.[3] Thus the BOE's role as lender of last resort was established informally early in its history, although it was not effectively codified into law until 2009.

In 1946 the BOE was nationalized and its capital stock was transferred to HM Treasury ("the Treasury").[4] However, according to Governor Carney, "the BOE's responsibilities remained broad and largely informal until 1997."[5] The BOE's independent responsibility for monetary policy was then codified by the Bank of England Act in 1998, which established that the Treasury may not give direction on matters of monetary policy.[6] According to Governor Carney, the BOE's lender-of-last-resort authority is derivative from its monetary policy authorities. "Central banks have a primordial responsibility to act as guarantors of trust and confidence in money because of their status as monopoly issuers of currency. This naturally gives them control over the quantity of money and interest rates—monetary policy. It also means that a core part of financial stability policy—acting as lender of last resort to private financial institutions at times of financial stress—falls naturally to central banks."[7] This conception of a subsidiary role for lender of last resort is different than the experience in the United States, where the Federal Reserve was created in 1913 to deal with financial panics which the private sector proved unable to deal with—only later came its role in monetary policy.

The formulation of the BOE's role further changed with the Banking Act of 2009, which established that "[a]n objective of the Bank shall be to contribute to protecting and enhancing the stability of the financial systems of the United Kingdom."[8] The BOE now identifies its mission as being "to promote the good of the people of the United Kingdom by maintaining monetary and financial stability."[9] Moreover the BOE expressly acknowledges that "financial stability requires an efficient flow of funds in the economy and confidence in financial institutions. This is pursued through … the Bank's financial operations, including as lender of last resort."[10] Furthermore Deputy Governor of the Bank of England, Minouche Shafik, has recently pointed out that "[s]ince the onset of the financial crisis, to keep the financial system open for business, central banks have used their balance sheets as never before."[11]

10.1.1 Sterling Monetary Framework

The BOE's Sterling Monetary Framework ("SMF") is the BOE's set of publicly available guidelines governing its money market operations to implement monetary policy.[12] The BOE publishes a summary of the programs in the "Red Book."[13] The events of the global financial crisis gave rise to the review and reform of the SMF. Although the SMF had historically focused on monetary policy operations, the 2008 consultative paper issued by the BOE "for the first time recognised that it should be an explicit objective of the SMF to provide liquidity insurance to the banking system to 'reduce the cost of disruption to the liquidity and payment services supplied by banks to the UK economy.'"[14] The Red Book was formally revised in its 2010 publication to incorporate the findings and recommendations of both internal BOE review and the House of Commons Treasury Committee.[15] The most recent version of the Red Book was published in June 2015.[16] Under the current SMF, the BOE provides details regarding its discount window facility ("DWF"). This is the type of lending that is identified with the lender-of-last-resort role, outside a liquidity crisis.[17] The Red Book also provides for a "contingency liquidity facility" that the Bank can activate in times of extreme market-wide stress, called the Contingent Term Repo Facility ("CTRF").[18]

10.1.2   Participation in the Sterling Monetary Framework and Acceptable Collateral

Participation in the SMF is generally voluntary, and banks and building societies are eligible to apply for access at any time by submitting an application form and supporting documents to the BOE.[19] A building society is a financial institution that provides banking services and is owned by its members, with the primary purpose of providing loans that are secured by residential property.[20] Although SMF participants are required to submit extensive data filings clarifying that they are in compliance with all other prudential regulatory requirements (e.g., capital), they are not required to meet any additional prudential requirements for SMF membership. However, the terms for participation in the SMF clarify that "the BOE may, in its absolute discretion, waive, add to, or vary any or all of the criteria" for eligibility to participate in the SMF.[21]

In November 2014 the BOE opened SMF access to broker-dealers and central counterparties ("CCPs"), so they can now apply to use the discount window; this is similar to the expansion of access to the Fed's discount window that took place in 2008 with the creation of the Primary Dealer Facility.[22] The BOE expanded this access without approval from the Treasury. It is therefore possible that they could further expand access to these facilities to other nonbanks without consent of Treasury. Banks, building societies, broker-dealers, and CCPs make up the current group of institutions the BOE has deemed eligible for that facility.[23] Broker-dealers, banks, and building societies are also eligible for CTRF use (when activated), while CCPs are not eligible.[24] In order to be eligible for SMF participation, broker-dealers must be supervised by the Prudential Regulatory Authority and CCPs operating in the United Kingdom must be authorized under the European Market Infrastructure Regulation and subject to regulations approved by the European Securities and Markets Authority.[25]

The change in institutions eligible for the SMF followed June 2014 remarks by Governor Carney, that "in the coming year, the BOE will widen access to our facilities to include the largest broker-dealers regulated in the United Kingdom and to those central counterparties authorized to operate in UK markets.[26] The change in policy reflects an understanding that these other financial institutions "provide critical financial services to the UK economy which expose them to liquidity risk."[27] In particular, the Red Book acknowledges that broker-dealers are key intermediaries in the capital markets and CCPs play an important role in managing credit risk.[28] There is not a publicly available list of banks, broker-dealers, or CCPs that have registered as SMF participants.

SMF participants may borrow against a wide range of collateral, classified by the BOE into levels A, B, and C. The BOE's acceptance of an expanded list of collateral is consistent with Governor Carney's October 2013 announcement that "[t]he range of assets we will accept in exchange will be wider, extending to raw loans and, in fact, any asset of which we are capable of assessing the risks."[29] Level A collateral consists of high-quality, liquid sovereign securities.[30] Level B collateral is also high quality and liquid, and includes supranational, mortgage, sovereign, and corporate bonds.[31] Level C collateral includes loan portfolios and less liquid securitizations.[32] Loan prices depend on the level(s) of collateral provided, and haircuts similarly vary according to the risk characteristics associated with certain types and classes of securities.[33] The Bank provides detailed guidance on acceptable collateral and applicable haircuts on its website, as well as a fee calculator for prospective DWF borrowers to use.[34] Recent indications are that the Bank may also accept equities as collateral from banks.[35]

10.1.3   Discount Window Lending

The DWF is available on demand to address financial instability at both individual institutions and in the markets generally, with certain limitations.[36] Prospective DWF borrowers are asked to deliver eligible collateral a day or more before drawing.[37] They are then required to initiate the request by phone and submit a "DWF Transaction Notice."[38] The Transaction Notice sets forth the proposed terms of the transaction and certifies that no event of default or *potential event of default exists* or will result from the DWF drawing.[39] If the borrower cannot make such a certification then ELA would apply, as discussed below.

The DWF typically provides funding by lending gilts in exchange for less liquid collateral. Borrowers can then use these gilts to obtain cash at their discretion. The DWF does not lend cash directly, in order to control the facility's impact on money supply and consequently on interest rates.[40] The BOE may lend sterling cash directly in the event of that there are issues with the market for gilts.[41] DWF loans have 30-day maturities for banks, broker-dealers, and building societies, and 5-day maturities for CCPs. DWF borrowers may apply to roll over the draw-ings, when needed over a longer period.[42]

As mentioned above, loan prices depend on the quality of posted collateral banks and building societies are charged a flat interest rate for borrowing up to an amount equal to 5 percent of their liabilities (25 bps above market rates for level A collateral, 50 bps above market rates for level B collateral, and 75 bps above market rates for level C collat-eral). The interest rate charged then increases linearly as the size of borrowing goes up between 5 and 15 percent of their liabilities. The terms of any borrowing greater than that must be discussed with the Bank.[43] The cost for a broker-dealer is negotiated at the time of drawing, and depends on the quality of collateral and total size of that partici-pant's borrowing.[44] CCPs also negotiate their loan price, which depends on collateral quality, at the time of drawing.[45]

The cost to access the DWF is designed to reflect "a premium to the market in routine circumstances but should offer SMF participants affordable liquidity in less normal conditions."[46] This is consistent with the traditional idea that borrowing from a central bank should be at a penalty rate, although this was not technically part of Bagehot's classic formulation of the powers of lender of last resort.[47] As Governor Carney noted, "[b]ecause we are both the supervisor and the central bank, the strong presumption is now that, if a bank meets the supervisory thresh-old conditions to operate and has signed up to our framework, it will be able to use our facilities. Our Discount Window will be open every day for those firms requiring a bespoke facility with lagged disclosure … [and] [i]ts price will be lower."[48] The BOE manages the impact of the potential stigma of DWF borrowing by not disclosing the borrowing activity of individual institutions, instead publishing the borrowing activity only as averaged across borrowers over the period of a quarter.[49] And that information is itself published with a lag of over five quarters after the drawing is initiated.[50]

10.1.4 Contingent Term Repo Facility Lending

The Contingent Term Repo Facility, originally announced in December 2011, is another SMF lending option.[51] The purpose of the CTRF is to supply cash in periods of "actual or prospective *market-wide* stress of an exceptional nature."[52] Accordingly, it is active only when the BOE implements it to respond to such market conditions.[53] CTRF lending is also designed to accept the "full range of eligible collateral": each of levels A, B, and C.[54] The Bank determines the operational details of the

CTRF (e.g., term, size, and price) each time the facility is activated.[55] Distributions via the CTRF occur via a "uniform price" auction procedure.[56] No CTRF operations have been initiated since late 2012.[57] The CTRF is available to all SMF participants, except for CCPs. This includes banks, building societies, and broker-dealers.

10.1.5   Emergency Liquidity Assistance

Pursuant to Section 58 through 66 of the Financial Services Act 2012, the Bank of England, the Treasury, and the Prudential Regulation Authority are required to establish a memorandum of understanding (MOU) on financial crisis management that would provide the financial system with Emergency Liquidity Assistance (ELA) that goes beyond the BOE's SMF.[58] The need for the MOU, and overall clarification of the policies of emergency liquidity assistance, arose due to confusion over how such determinations were to be made during the 2008 crisis, particularly as it related to Northern Rock.[59] The MOU on financial crisis management between the Bank, the Treasury, and the Prudential Regulation Authority sets forth the framework by which the Treasury and the BOE coordinate to provide this aid. Neither the Financial Services Act nor the MOU limits the types of financial institutions that may obtain ELA. Thus nonbanks as well as banks could use ELA.

The BOE's current ELA disclosure policies reflect the need to provide this assistance confidentially, where premature disclosure could exacerbate market uncertainty and compromise the aid's effectiveness. Until recently the Bank Charter Act of 1844 required the BOE to publish a weekly "Bank Return," which provided a summary of the Bank's balance sheet.[60] Publication of the Bank Return could also result in the inadvertent disclosure of the Bank's liquidity operations.[61] During the financial crisis, the need for covert ELA was prominently highlighted by the 2007 run on Northern Rock.[62] In response to the crisis, Section 245 of the Banking Act of 2009 removed the legal requirement to publish the Bank Return.[63] On June 30, 2014, the BOE announced that it would replace the Bank Return with a new Weekly Report, and the first Weekly Report was published on October 2 of that year.[64] The Weekly Report publishes balance sheet information pertaining to the Bank's monetary policy operations, but excludes line items that could result in the disclosure of covert ELA.[65] Sample publications are not available because the BOE has not extended ELA to any borrowers since the new Weekly Reports were instituted. However, the Weekly Reports are only required to disclose aggregate lending on a quarterly basis, with a five-quarter lag.[66] Specific borrowers are not required to be disclosed.

10.1.6   ELA Assistance to Solvent Banks and Nonbanks

According to the MOU, the BOE may provide ELA, comprised of "support operations outside the Bank's published frameworks" to solvent but "at risk" firms.[67] This would include SMF participants where a potential event of default exists, as described in the discount window lending section above. The BOE may initiate the proposal to offer ELA to solvent firms, but it must notify and obtain approval of the Treasury before executing the aid.[68] There is no public guidance or rules establishing the terms of these loans, including whether ELA borrowing must be collateralized.[69] There is also no published guidance as to when ELA initiated by the Bank will be indemnified by the Treasury (i.e., the Treasury will cover any losses the BOE might incur as a result of its lending). Given that the Bank must obtain Treasury permission to extend ELA, it would seem consistent with the breakdown of roles for the BOE to seek such an indemnity before providing the aid.[70] The idea of a Treasury indemnity is premised on the idea that emergency lending is as much a fiscal policy decision, normally reserved to the government, as much as a lender-of-last-resort function of a central bank. Even without a formal indemnity, the government in effect absorbs losses experienced by the central bank, since the losses erode the profits of the bank that would otherwise be remitted to the Treasury to support the general revenue.[71] There is no direct threat to the viability of a central bank from operating at a loss, or even without capital, as it can create money.[72] But there is a threat to its reputation. An indemnity insures that the central bank's capital will not be eroded by ELA losses, so puts the Treasury at risk for erosions of central bank capital as well as lost central bank profits.

10.1.7   Lending at Treasury Direction

The MOU also provides that the Chancellor of the Treasury may direct the BOE to provide ELA to firms that the BOE does *not* judge to be solvent and viable or on terms that diverge from those the BOE proposes.[73] A more general directive to "conduct special support operations for the financial system as a whole" with means that are not set forth in the Red Book may be issued by the Chancellor as well.[74] These directions may only be made after the BOE has notified the Treasury of a material risk to public funds, and either (1) there is a serious threat to financial stability or (2) the Treasury has already committed public funds to reduce or resolve such a threat, and it would be in the public interest to do so.[75] In the event of such direction from the Chancellor, the BOE is considered to be acting as the Treasury's agent.[76] As a result the funds are placed into an special purpose vehicle (SPV) that is segregated from the BOE's balance sheet.[77] In addition the SPV and the BOE are indemnified by the Treasury to cover any risks arising from actions so directed.[78] The execution of a Treasury direction requires Parliamentary oversight. Under Section 63 of the Financial Services Act of 2012 and Section 32 of the MOU, the Treasury direction and the Bank's proposed response must be "laid immediately before Parliament."[79] However, disclosure to the Parliament may be postponed in situations where confidentiality is crucial to financial stability (at the Treasury's determination).[80] Once the Treasury, in consultation with the BOE, has decided confidentiality is no longer necessary, the ELA assistance must then be laid before Parliament.[81]

10.2   European Central Bank

The European Central Bank (ECB) was established in 1998 pursuant to the Treaty on European Union and the Statute of the European System of Central Banks and of the European Central Bank ("ESCB Statute").[82] This makes the ECB extremely independent because its existence is protected by the equivalent of what would be a Constitution in a single country. The ECB is responsible for developing and implementing monetary policy for the European Union, through the primary objective of maintaining the stability of prices.[83] The ECB is also responsible for assuring the stability of the financial system.[84] To conduct these policies, the ECB coordinates with national central banks ("NCBs") in the 28 EU countries (together, the "European System of Central Banks" or "ESCB"), particularly the 19 NCBs in the countries that have adopted the euro as currency (the "eurosystem").[85] The ECB's tasks and authorities relating to the performance of central bank functions for the eurosystem are prescribed in the Treaty on the Functioning of the European Union (TFEU), as well as the ESCB Statute.[86] Because the ECB functions as a central bank for the 19 members of the eurozone and shares powers with the NCBs, its role as lender of last resort is distinctive.

10.2.1   Emergency Liquidity Assistance
The treaties and ESCB Statute do not directly address lender-of-last-resort authority, and indeed there has been a lack of clarity about this

role of the ECB.[87] However, in its 2000 annual report, the ECB set forth that "Emergency Liquidity Assistance" (ELA), which is described below and is analogous to the traditional lender-of-last-resort role to financial institutions, is the province of the NCBs. More specifically, the ECB determined that ELA, which is "the support given by central banks in exceptional circumstances and on a case-by-case basis to *temporarily illiquid institutions*" was "the responsibility and cost of the NCBs."[88] Under this interpretation, ELA is treated as a "national task," as contemplated by Article 14.4 of the ESCB Statute, pursuant to which NCBs "may perform functions other than those specified in this Statute ... on the responsibility and liability of national central banks."[89] Accordingly, the NCB is generally responsible for determining the material terms of ELA. For example, a decision to exclude a particular type of financial institution from ELA eligibility would be set at the national level. The ECB also does not establish restrictions on borrowers' use of ELA, so long as they are commercial purposes. In 2013 the ECB issued a statement on "ELA Procedures," in which it effectively confirmed that traditional LLR should be provided by NCBs.[90] One important consequence of leaving the basic authority with NCBs is that the loans are on their books (albeit consolidated for reporting purposes with the ECB), and losses from such loans are at the risk of the NCBs.

ELA becomes necessary when a solvent financial institution (or a group of solvent financial institutions) faces a liquidity shortage but does not possess sufficient collateral or does not meet the counterparty eligibility criteria to borrow via the ECB's monetary policy open market operations and standing facilities.[91] ECB policy does not permit an insolvent institution to borrow from it or a NCB and this appears to be the case whether or not the member state of the NCB would indemnify the NCB from loss.

Although ELA is technically available to "financial institutions" only banks have ever received ELA and there are no formal guidelines specifying whether nonbanks can also receive ELA funding. Thus it is not clear whether the ECB would allow NCBs to use ELA to lend to nonbanks, particularly if they were not supervised by the ECB or NCBs; as of now, this issue has not arisen. Although the ECB provides updated details regarding eligible collateral for use of its monetary policy facilities on its website, it does not specify what collateral is sufficient for ELA.[92] Since 2007 the ECB has used a single framework for all of its credit operations across the eurosystem.[93] The uniform framework makes no distinction between marketable and nonmarketable assets with respect to their eligibility as collateral, except that nonmarketable collateral cannot be used for outright transactions (where the Bank buys or sells in the market, resulting in a complete transfer of ownership).[94] According to the new ECB guideline that went into effect on May 1, 2015, marketable assets are debt instruments admitted to trading on a market (e.g., government bonds, corporate debt instruments, and asset-backed securities), which meet certain specified criteria, and non-marketable assets are fixed-term deposits, credit claims and retail mortgage-backed debt instruments.[95]

Eligible counterparties for participation in the ECB's open market operations and standing facilities must meet certain baseline criteria separate from the collateral requirements. Notably, they must be "financially sound" and meet certain minimum reserve requirements set by the ECB.[96] They must also be subject to supervision applicable to credit institutions and investment firms regarding compliance with Basel III requirements, as introduced in the EU in the form of the so-called CRD-IV.[97] Banks' compliance with CRD-IV's capital requirements also appears to serve as a proxy to satisfy the "solvency" requirement for ELA recipients.[98] The reliability of these data assumes that Basel capital is "real" capital. This is put in doubt by the fact that CRD-IV permits certain deferred tax assets to be counted as capital: in 2015 up to 57 percent of Greek banks' common equity tier 1 capital was attributable to such assets.[99]

When an institution cannot produce collateral accepted by the ECB, an NCB may decide to bear the risk of lending to the institution via ELA.[100] Although collateral posted for ELA may be of a lower quality than that used in eurosystem monetary policy operations, the ECB has stated that "adequate collateral" is necessary to receive ELA from an NCB.[101] Otherwise, acceptable collateral is set by the NCB, and the ECB will intervene only on an ex post basis, if it considers the collateral to be insufficient. Indeed the ECB states that "NCBs can in principle autonomously design their own collateral framework for ELA, including the applicable risk control measures."[102] The ECB has also clarified that "central bank liquidity support should not be seen as a primary means of managing financial crises, since it is limited to the temporary provision of liquidity in very exceptional circumstances."[103]

The lending NCB discloses certain details of the ELA loan to the ECB such as the interest rate, counterparty, maturity, collateral, and amount of the loan, but the ECB does not make these terms public.[104] The NCB must also report to the ECB "the prudential supervisor's assessment, over the short and medium term, of the liquidity position and solvency of the institution receiving the ELA, including the criteria used to come to a positive conclusion with respect to solvency."[105] In the case of a significant banking group now directly supervised by the ECB, this information supplements the data relating to solvency that the borrower has otherwise provided to the ECB. Although institutions "have to be considered solvent to be eligible ... the exact terms and conditions for ELA are shrouded in even more secrecy than those of the ECB's regular operations. So much so that Richard Barwell, economist at Royal Bank of Scotland, compares the rules of ELA with the rules of 'Fight Club.'"[106] If the ELA is expected to exceed €500 million, the NCB must notify the ECB in advance.[107] ELA at a penalty interest rate was provided by certain NCBs during the eurozone crisis.[108] Cyprus, Ireland, and Greece are among the countries whose financial institutions received such aid.[109]

Certain experts believe that the ECB itself, not just the NCBs, should provide ELA.[110] Charles Goodhart and Dick Schoenmaker, for instance, argue that the ECB should be responsible for lender-of-last-resort functions for the significant banks in the EU banking union.[111] Rosa Lastra argues that there is a statutory basis for this authority. Article 18 of the ESCB specifically empowers the Bank "to conduct credit operations with credit institutions and other market participants, with lending being based on adequate collateral."[112] The ECB could use this authority to lend to a financial institution experiencing a liquidity crisis, thereby acting as a traditional lender of last resort.

10.2.2   ECB and European Commission Authority to Restrict NCB LLR

The ECB has the authority to "restrict ELA operations if it considers that these operations interfere with the objectives and tasks of the eurosystem."[113] An example of such a restriction would be the imposition of a cap on the amount of ELA that a particular NCB can provide, such as the cap on ELA established for Greece in early 2015.[114] Under Article 14.4 of the ESCB Statute, such a determination can only be made with a two-thirds vote of the ECB Governing Council.[115] Moreover an NCB must provide the ECB with details regarding any ELA loan within two days after extension, but the ECB does not make those details public. An NCB must also provide advance notice to the ECB if the funds will exceed €500 million.[116] If the volume of funds is expected to be greater than €2 billion, the ECB Governing Council "will consider whether there is a risk that the ELA involved may interfere with the

objectives and tasks of the eurosystem."[117] This requirement flows from
the oversight role of the ECB regarding ELA as it relates to "the implementation of ... single monetary policy."[118] The recently instituted
Single Supervisory Mechanism, under which the ECB, in cooperation
with the NCBs, oversees the banking sector and the implementation of
banking rules across the euro area, represents an additional mechanism
through which the ECB can supervise the provision of ELA.[119]

The provision of ELA by NCBs is also indirectly constrained by the
European Commission's policies regarding *state aid*. Under these policies, any assistance from a member state that is "incompatible with the
common market" is not permitted; the European Commission must
approve of state aid to confirm that it would not fall into this anticom-
petitive category.[120] Such approval was given, for instance, in the case
of the Bank of England's loan to Northern Rock in September 2007, as
the loan "was secured by sufficient collateral and was interest-
bearing."[121] State aid clearance usually requires prior notice to the European Commission, but temporary rescue aid may be extended in
advance of formal notice to the European Commission in certain circumstances.[122] The Bank of England was therefore able to supply emergency assistance to Northern Rock without obtaining the European
Commission's pre-approval.[123]

In August 2013 the European Commission issued guidance on the
application of state aid rules to the provision of ELA to financial institutions. ELA provided by NCBs could be implicated by the state aid rules,
as "[d]edicated support to a specific credit institution ... may constitute
aid unless ... [certain] cumulative conditions are met."[124] These conditions include (1) that the institution be temporarily illiquid but solvent,
(2) that the facility be fully secured by collateral with the appropriate
haircuts, (3) that a "penal interest rate" be applied, and (4) that the
central bank act on its own initiative, and not be backed by a counter-
guarantee of the state.[125] It is unclear as to what impact these Commission rules on state aid actually have on the ECB or NCBs in supplying
ELA.

10.2.3   Liquidity via ECB Monetary Policy Operations

Although the ECB delegates ELA to NCBs, the Bank does provide
market-level liquidity in crises through its monetary operations. During
the recent financial crises, "[t]he broad range of collateral and counterparties in normal operations limited the need to adjust the framework
and facilitated the supply of central bank liquidity, effectively allowing

the eurosystem to become the main intermediary in the interbank market at the height of the crisis."[126] It is therefore difficult to draw a clear line between lender-of-last-resort activity and the provision of liquidity via monetary operations in the eurosystem. At a recent Bank for International Settlements conference on lender of last resort, it was noted that "an elastic currency supply [may be] a more useful concept than LOLR in the eurosystem context as measures there reflected responses to fluctuations in liquidity demand."[127]

Importantly, Article 123 of the Treaty on the Functioning of the European Union (TFEU) prevents the ECB from purchasing sovereign debt instruments "directly from" EU governments or other public authorities.[128] However, this provision can be circumvented by the authority the ECB does have to purchase sovereign bonds in secondary markets.[129] Under Article 18 of the ESCB Statute, "in order to achieve the objectives of the ESCB and to carry out its tasks, the ECB ... may ... operate in the financial markets by buying and selling outright ... and by lending or borrowing claims and marketable instruments ... conduct credit operations with credit institutions and other market participants, with lending being based on adequate collateral."[130] Section 18.2 provides that "the ECB shall establish general principles for open market and credit operations ... including for the announcement of conditions under which they stand ready to enter into such transactions."[131]

Thus Article 18 of the ESCB Statute empowers the ECB to conduct open market and credit operations, which can be used to supply liquidity to the market generally during a financial crisis.[132] The ECB has implemented a number of unconventional monetary policies using its Article 18 authorities to respond to the 2008 global financial crisis and 2010 to 2012 euro crisis. These policies provided financial institutions with an important source of liquidity during these crises.

10.2.4   Long-Term Refinancing Operations

One major operation pursuant to its Article 18 authorities is the ECB's long-term refinancing operations (LTROs), which it made use of in the 2008 and 2010–2012 financial crises.[133] Through the LTRO program the ECB provides cash loans in euros to credit institutions at low interest rates (1 percent) in exchange for EU member state sovereign debt collateral. LTROs are considered to be open market operations, aimed at supplying liquidity to the financial sector.[134] Although banks obtain loans through LTROs, the program is conducted as an unconventional monetary policy instead of the traditional lender-of-last-resort function; yet the purpose of the program is to provide liquidity assistance to the financial sector rather than to control the money supply. The size of the LTRO program peaked in December 2011 through February 2012, when the ECB used LTROs to inject approximately €1 trillion in cash into the European banking system.[135] These funds were distributed via three-year LTROs to 523 banks in December and 800 banks in February.[136]

10.2.5   Purchasing Programs

In 2009, under its Article 18 authorities, the ECB undertook a €60 billion covered bond purchase program to restore the market in those instruments. This also provided banks with liquidity, as covered bonds are important sources of funding for financial institutions across Europe.[137] In 2010, the ECB instituted the Securities Market Programme (SMP), whereby the ECB and NCBs purchased government bonds in the secondary markets.[138] This policy falls within the letter of Article 123 of the TFEU, discussed above, since the transactions occurred in the secondary marketplace rather than via direct issuance.[139] But the purchase of such bonds from the financial institutions has the effect of providing them with liquidity and was indeed undertaken for this purpose rather than as a means of controlling the money supply. In 2012, the Bank announced the implementation of a new program, Outright Monetary Transactions (OMT), to replace the SMP.[140] Under OMT, the ECB would "address severe distortions in government bond markets" based on investors' "unfounded fears" by purchasing government bonds in the secondary markets.[141] The program resonates with Mario Draghi's declaration shortly before OMT was announced that "[w]ithin our mandate, the ECB is ready to do whatever it takes to preserve the euro."[142] The OMT has not yet been implemented, but market conditions in the EU improved after its announcement.[143] This program would seem to have more to do with supporting government bond markets than providing liquidity to financial institutions, but the willingness of the ECB to purchase these instruments from credit institutions, particularly at par, does provide them with liquidity they could not obtain in the private markets.

10.3   Bank of Japan

The Bank of Japan (BOJ) was originally founded in 1882 under the Bank of Japan Act.[144] Its role as lender of last resort was highlighted during the depression in the 1920s, when the Bank extended special loans to banks in order to stem contagion throughout the financial system.[145] The Bank was later reorganized under the Bank of Japan Act of 1942 (the "old Act") and its lender-of-last-resort authority set forth in Article 25 thereof.[146] The Bank exercised this authority liberally during a period of extreme financial turmoil in Japan during the 1990s.[147] Following this period of instability, the Bank of Japan Act ("BOJ Act") was enacted in 1997, creating the present day Bank of Japan.[148] According to the BOJ, "independence" and "transparency" are the two primary principles underlying the Act.[149] The 1997 amendment also organized the lender-of-last-resort procedures into three provisions: Article 33 (collateralized loans), Article 38 (special loans), and Article 37 (temporary uncollateralized loans).[150] Although each type of loan is designed to address a different lending scenario, there are no express restrictions on borrowers' use of funds under any of these provisions.

10.3.1   Article 33

The primary provision governing the BOJ's lender-of-last-resort authority is Article 33 of the BOJ Act. Article 33 contemplates the flexible provision of collateralized loans by the BOJ, at the Bank's sole discretion.[151] Under Article 33, the BOJ may "make loans against collateral in the form of negotiable instruments, national government securities and other securities, or electronically recorded claims."[152] The BOJ provides further detail on eligible collateral and applicable haircuts on its website.[153] The text of Article 33 does not limit this type of borrowing to banks, so a nonbank financial institution that is a BOJ account holder (e.g., a securities company or money market dealer that holds a current account at the Bank) could be eligible for an Article 33 loan, if they provide adequate collateral.[154] Moreover there are no legal constraints regarding which types of institutions are eligible to hold BOJ accounts, although the Bank restricts certain cooperative institutions (e.g., credit unions) from holding accounts in order to efficiently allocate its resources.

The Bank extends Article 33 loans to institutions it deems solvent, based on the Bank's on-site and off-site monitoring practices (discussed below). The loans do not require an indemnity from the Ministry of Finance, nor are indemnities sought. Two types of Article 33 loans exist: (1) loans for money market operations, to which a low policy interest rate applies, and (2) loans at the request of financial institutions under the Complementary Lending Facility, which are charged a slightly higher interest rate.[155] The BOJ discloses only the aggregate value of loans extended under Article 33, not individual institutions' borrowing activity.[156]

10.3.2 Article 38

The BOJ is authorized to extend special loans under Article 38 of the Act, which BOJ account holders and non-BOJ account holders may receive in certain circumstances.[157] These Article 38 loans or *toku-yu* are intended to be undertaken only when "necessary for the maintenance of stability of the financial system."[158] The BOJ has made it clear that Article 38 loans may be uncollateralized, although this is not expressly stated in the legislation.[159] In addition the text of the Act does not prohibit nonbanks or non-BOJ account holders from receiving such aid.[160] Under Article 25 of the old BOJ Act, the BOJ initiated this lending process but had to obtain the prior approval of the Minister of Finance before extending such loans.[161] The current Article 38 lending process must now begin with a request from the Prime Minster and the Minister of Finance for the BOJ to "conduct the business necessary to maintain stability of the financial system."[162] Thus, as a formal matter, BOJ cannot initiate such loans but it can still ask that the Minister of Finance request it to do so. The Policy Board of the BOJ then assesses in its sole discretion if special operations are necessary, including whether the extension of Article 38 loans is appropriate according to four principles.[163] So, ultimately, loans requested by the Ministry of Finance can be rejected by the BOJ, unlike in the United Kingdom where loans requested by the Treasury must be made by the BOE if there is an indemnification.

The first, and most important, principle is that "there must be a strong likelihood that systemic risk will materialize."[164] The goal of a special loan to an individual firm must be to prevent systemic risk, not to rescue or protect that firm.[165] Presumably this would be the case where the failure of the firm would have a significant impact on the rest of the financial system. The "Financial Crisis Response Council," which includes the governor of the BOJ along with certain government officials (including the Prime Minister, Chief Cabinet Secretary, and Minister of Finance) typically makes the determination as to whether such risk exists. The second principle is that the Article 38 loans must be necessary for the borrower to obtain the funds—Article 38 loans should be available only when there are no other options.[166] Third, the recipients must be penalized and held responsible to avoid moral hazard.[167] This is different from a penalty rate. Such penalties might include replacing management and removing existing shareholders. These types of consequences are unique to lending by the BOJ as compared with its peers. Fourth, the BOJ's financial soundness must not be jeopardized by the loan, so as to preserve public confidence.[168] Considerations relating to the fourth principle include (1) that liquidity, not risk capital be provided, (2) that there be reason to believe that special loans are collectable, and (3) that provisions be set aside for each individual case, to prepare for potential losses.[169]

If the Policy Board of the BOJ finds that special loans are necessary, it determines details of the loans (e.g., costs or procedures for their extension) on a case-by-case basis, but a penalty interest rate is applied to uncollateralized loans.[170] The Bank sets the terms at its own discretion and does not need or require an indemnity from the Ministry of Finance or government approval with respect to the loan terms.[171] Interestingly, the extension of special loans and details regarding their terms are disclosed by press release shortly after these decisions are made.[172] This is quite different than the case for other types of lending by BOJ or by the other peer central banks where the stigma following disclosure is thought to discourage borrowers from coming forward in the first place.

Importantly, the BOJ may also extend special loans under Article 38 to insolvent institutions "in exceptional cases, as measures to prevent a financial crisis from materializing."[173] These loans take the form of bridge loans to facilitate the resolution of failed institutions in situations where the Bank can rely on the government or Deposit Insurance Corporation of Japan (DICJ) to ensure funds will be available for the BOJ to collect on its loans.[174] "For example, [they may be extended] when the government decides to fully guarantee all liabilities of failed institutions."[175] The Bank has only decided to provide special loans to insolvent institutions twice, but the loans were never actually extended because the DICJ's resolution process rendered them unnecessary.[176]

10.3.3 Article 37

The Bank of Japan may also offer uncollateralized loans to financial institutions including non-BOJ account holders under Article 37 of the BOJ Act, in order to address temporary liquidity shortages.[177] These loans are intended for "unexpected" shortages "due to accidental causes" (e.g., technological failures), where the funds are "necessary to secure smooth settlement of funds."[178] Uncollateralized Article 37 loans are provided for a maximum period of one month.[179] The Bank may provide Article 37 loans at its own discretion and may determine their terms on a case-by-case basis, but must report any lending thereunder to the Prime Minister and Minister of Finance "without delay."[180] However, an indemnity from the Ministry of Finance is not required. The BOJ has not yet extended any loans pursuant to Article 37.

10.3.4   Article 44

The Bank of Japan conducts on-site examinations and off-site monitoring "to grasp the business and financial conditions of individual financial institutions" in connection with the exercise of its lender-of-last-resort authorities.[181] On-site examinations of financial institutions that receive loans under Article 37 or Article 38 are contemplated under Article 44 of the BOJ Act.[182] These examinations include visits to the institutions and an assessment of their business operations and property.[183] Off-site monitoring includes "the analysis of financial data collected from banks and information obtained from bank management through interviews."[184] These procedures "ensure that the Bank prepares or adequately conducts ... (1) temporary loans to financial institutions (Article 37 of the Act) [and] (2) business contributing to maintaining the stability of the financial system (Article 38 of the Act)."[185]

10.4   Comparison of LLR Powers of the Four Central Banks

The matrix in table 10.1 summarizes the lender-of-last-resort comparison presented above. The bottom line of this comparison is that the overall changes that Dodd–Frank made to the Fed's lender-of-last-resort power has left the Fed with relatively weak authority as compared to its three foreign peers: BOE, ECB, and BOJ. This is not just a matter of concern to the United States but also to the world, given the economic importance of the United States and the fact that the dollar is the reserve currency. What are the key features of the comparison?

10.4.1   Independence

First, consider the overall independence of the four central banks (here unless specifically noted, ECB includes the NCBs). In a very real sense the most independent is the European Central Bank, which was created by Treaty among EU countries, almost the equivalent of a Constitution in a single member state. The other three banks were created by statute

Table 10.1

	Federal Reserve (Fed)	Bank of England (BOE)	European Central Bank (ECB)	Bank of Japan (BOJ)
Year Bank established	1913	1694	1998	1882
Independence	Statutory	Statutory	Treaty	Statutory
Years of / events giving rise to significant LLR changes	2010 Dodd–Frank, in response to global financial crisis	Consultative paper in 2008 and revised; Red Book in 2010 in response to financial crisis	ELA procedures clarified in 2013, after ELA extended during eurozone crisis	1997 BOJ Act, following 1990s financial instability
Eligible borrowers	DW depository institutions, with reserves at Fed 13(3) Participants in programs with "broad-based eligibility"	SMF banks, building societies, CCPs, broker-dealers; ELA no express exclusions	Monetary policy instruments; credit institutions; ELA "Financial institutions" and "credit institutions"	Article 33 account holders (incl. nonbanks); Article 37 non-account holders eligible; Article 38 non-account holders eligible
Primary liquidity support instruments	DW and 13(3)	SMF and ELA	Monetary policy instruments and ELA	DW; temporary uncollateralized loans extended if a liquidity shortage; special loans, initiated by government request
Collateral policies	DW wide range; 13(3) "Security for emergency loans sufficient to protect taxpayers from losses"; policies approved by Secretary of the Treasury	SMF wide range; ELA not specified	Monetary policy instruments wide range; ELA determined by NCBs, but must be "adequate collateral"	Article 33 Wide range. Article 37 uncollateralized; Article 38 may be uncollateralized
Collateral policies published	DW yes; 13(3) yes (after facilities established)	SMF yes; ELA no	Monetary policy instruments yes; ELA determined by NCBs	Article 33 yes; Article 37 uncollateralized; Article 38 No

Table 10.1 (continued)

	Federal Reserve (Fed)	Bank of England (BOE)	European Central Bank (ECB)	Bank of Japan (BOJ)
Solvency requirement	DW primary credit available if in "generally sound financial condition"; secondary credit available if not "adequately capitalized" if consistent with "timely return" to market funding or to facilitate orderly resolution; 13(3) solvency required, as restrictively defined	SMF borrowers must certify no event of default; ELA to solvent firms requires HMT authorization; to firms BOE does not judge to be solvent requires HMT direction	Monetary policy instruments counterparties must be "financially sound" and meet certain capital requirements; ELA recipients must be solvent; NCBs must report solvency assessment to ECB	Article 33 solvent account holders; Article 37 only for *temporary liquidity* shortages Article 38 Insolvent institutions eligible "in exceptional cases"
Restrictions on use of discount window loans	Yes-limits on transfer of funds to nonbank affiliates	No	No	No
Treasury approval to exercise LLR?	DW no; 13(3) yes	SMF no; ELA yes	N/A	Article 33 no; Article 37 no, but must notify Treasury; Article 38 Treasury must initiate
Can central bank loans be initiated by Treasury?	No	SMF no; ELA yes	N/A	Article 33 no; Article 37 no; Article 38 yes (mandatory)
Treasury indemnity	No	SMF no; ELA available	N/A	No

Table 10.1 (continued)

	Federal Reserve (Fed)	Bank of England (BOE)	European Central Bank (ECB)	Bank of Japan (BOJ)
Limits on emergency lending to individual institutions	Broad program required	No	No	Must be to prevent systemic risk, not to rescue firm
Disclosure rules	DW published quarterly, with 2 year lag; includes borrower identity and loan details; 13(3) to Congress within 7 days; to public within 2 years of termination	SMF Average (not individual) DW use published quarterly with 5 Q lag; ELA published quarterly, with 5 Q lag; immediately disclosed to Parliament (unless confidentiality crucial)	ELA NCBs must disclose to ECB within 2 business days; advance notice if > €500 million; public disclosure determined by NCBs	Article 33 aggregate (not individual) lending disclosed; Article 37 must report to government "without delay"; Article 38 announced with press release
Pricing	DW penalty rate, but none under Term Auction Facility; 13(3) no published guidelines	SMF penalty rate; ELA no published pricing guidelines, but penalty rate is expected	ELA no published ECB pricing guidelines, but NCBs expected to charge penalty rate	Article 33 penalty rate; Article 37 no published guidelines; Article 38 no published guidelines, but penalty rate expected
Express examination authority for LLR	No	No	No	Yes

Key to abbreviations	
Abbreviation	Term
DW	Discount window
ELA	Emergency liquidity assistance
HMT	Her Majesty's Treasury
NCBs	National central banks
SMF	Sterling Monetary Framework

and can be limited or abolished by Congress in the case of the Fed or Parliament in the case of the BOE and BOJ. But it is important to recognize the different threat to the Fed from the Congress as opposed to the threat from the Parliaments of England and Japan. In parliamentary democracies, the parliaments are controlled by the government, indeed they form the government—this means they are more protected from their legislatures than the Fed, where the Congress is not part of the administration and indeed may be controlled by the opposite party from the President. Central bank independence has traditionally been thought of as independence from the government—is the Fed independent of the Secretary of the Treasury? But equally, and perhaps more important today, is the independence of the Fed from the Congress. It was the Congress that limited the Fed in Dodd–Frank and is increasingly attacking the Fed today for bailing out Wall Street. From the perspective of independence from a legislature, I would rank the Fed last.

10.4.2 Ability to Lend to Nonbanks and Supervisory Authority

Second, all four central banks have the power to be a lender of last resort to nonbanks, but none of the four central banks supervise all nonbanks to which they can lend. Thus they are faced with making lending decisions based, at best, on information from other regulators, such as the SEC or state insurance regulators in the United States. However, the BOJ does have the express statutory right to examine any institution to which it makes a loan, an idea that should be more widely adopted. Despite the fact that the Fed, BOE, and ECB lack such express authority, it is possible that they could require such supervision as a condition of granting a loan. This would be a prudent approach.

10.4.3 Regime Structure

While all four central banks have the power to be a lender of last resort to nonbanks, the Fed is the only central bank which has a different regime for banks and nonbanks: the discount window for banks versus Section 13(3) for nonbanks. These two regimes were made much more dissimilar by Dodd–Frank's limitations on lending to nonbanks. With respect to banks, the Fed can lend, under Section 10B of the Federal Reserve Act, to a single bank, with whatever collateral it determines is sufficient, without the approval of the Secretary of the Treasury, and with no requirement that the bank be solvent. While the Dodd–Frank Act did not change Section 10B of the Federal Reserve Act, which is the main authority used to lend to banks, nonbanks are an increasingly important component of the financial sector, accounting for $25.1 trillion of the $37.9 trillion of credit market assets.[186] With respect to nonbanks, under the terms of Dodd–Frank's amendments to Section 13(3) of the Federal Reserve Act, the Fed must loan to nonbanks as part of a broad program, with adequate collateral as effectively approved by the Secretary of the Treasury, only with the approval of the Secretary of the Treasury, and with a requirement that the nonbank be solvent. In contrast, the other central banks have different regimes for normal liquidity and emergency liquidity, while the Fed does not differentiate between normal and emergency liquidity for banks, lending through the discount window in each case. For non-banks, though, the Federal Reserve only supplies liquidity during emergencies through 13(3).

10.4.4 Collateral

All four central banks accept a wide range of collateral for loans to banks and nonbanks, but only the US Treasury controls collateral policy for nonbanks—the three other central banks determine collateral policies on their own. While Dodd–Frank as a technical matter only requires the Fed to consult with the Secretary of the Treasury as to the adequacy of collateral, the power of the Secretary over whether to lend at all to a nonbank effectively gives the Secretary control of collateral policy as well—unlike the case with the BOJ and BOE where the right of the Treasury to approve loans explicitly does not extend to collateral policy.

Japan stands alone in permitting some emergency loans, those under Articles 37 and 38, to be uncollateralized. Recall in the crisis, that the Fed made uncollateralized loans to commercial paper issuers, but that authority appears to be taken away by Dodd–Frank. Whether or not collateral standards are published differs among different facilities and among different countries.

10.4.5 Requirement of Solvency

Fifth, the ECB requires borrowers from all of its facilities, including ELA facilities of NCBs, to be solvent. While the ECB may police NCBs' compliance with this requirement, the "constitutional" independence of the ECB itself ensures that neither its control of the NCBs nor its own lending policies can be effectively policed. The political environment for exercise of lender-of-last-resort powers in the eurozone is also less hostile than in the United States. In this light, the solvency requirement could easily be diluted.

While in the United Kingdom, discount window borrowers must be solvent, and ELA initiated by the BOE also requires a solvency determination, the UK Treasury can order BOE to lend to an institution the BOE does not judge to be solvent, assuming that the Treasury supplies an indemnity. And the BOJ explicitly permits, under Article 38, some borrowers to be insolvent where its loans are a bridge to more permanent government funding. This is similar to what happened in the United States in the case of AIG, where a large part of the Fed's initial exposure was later refinanced by the Treasury as part of TARP.

In the United States, while the Fed may have a general expectation that borrowers will be solvent (but again see AIG), such a requirement was not imposed by statute for banks or nonbanks before the crisis. Post–Dodd–Frank there is a requirement that nonbank recipient of loans must be solvent. The text of Dodd–Frank *deems* any borrower in bankruptcy, any federal or state insolvency proceeding, or resolution under Dodd–Frank's Orderly Liquidation Authority, to be insolvent but does not *exclude* any other entities from the definition of insolvency.[187] Accordingly, borrowers that are not subject to these formal proceedings could also be insolvent. It is hard to see why there should be a double-standard on solvency as between banks and nonbanks—lending to both can result in public losses and induce moral hazard. Solvency determinations are inherently difficult, particularly during a crisis and panic where asset values may represent fire-sale prices that could bounce back through the very provision of liquidity. This reality likely explains the flexibility built into the solvency policies in the United Kingdom and Japan. In contrast, the new nonbank express solvency requirement in the United States discourages the Fed from lending to nonbanks, given the prospect of congressional inquiries, particularly if a borrower later becomes insolvent.

Things could get worse for the Fed under the Federal Reserve Oversight Modernization and Reform (FORM) Act, which was passed by the House of Representatives in November 2015.[188] The FORM Act would limit the Federal Reserve's lending ability in a crisis situation.[189] Per the bill's provisions, the Federal Reserve could lend to non-banks only after 9 of 12 presidents of the Federal Reserve banks vote in favor of the action and after all Federal banking regulators with jurisdiction over the borrower, which would include agencies like the Consumer Financial Protection Bureau or even the SEC, certify that the borrower is solvent.[190] Finally, the bill disallows lending to entities that are not "financial institutions."[191] While the bill is unlikely to pass in the Senate, the very introduction of more stringent solvency restrictions could well make the Fed gun shy to lend under its existing framework. Fed Chair Janet Yellen has spoken out strongly against the FORM Act, noting that the "FORM Act would essentially repeal the Federal Reserve's remaining ability to act in a crisis."[192] Former Fed Chair Ben Bernanke has also warned of the dangers of limiting the Fed's emergency lending powers. In his recent book, Bernanke notes that "still further restrictions on the Fed's ability to create broad-based lending programs and to serve as a lender of last resort, could prove extremely costly in a future crisis."[193] As previously noted, this may be why he appears to accept the limitations of Dodd–Frank.

10.4.6 Treasury Approval or Direction

The relationship between the central bank and the Treasury also differs among the four countries. There are two key dimensions of this relationship. The first question is whether central bank loans can be initiated by the Treasury. This possibility exists in two countries, in the United Kingdom for BOE use of ELA, and in Japan for Article 38 emergency loans. Such a power is not applicable to the European Union, since there is no EU Treasury. No such power exists in the United States. Actually giving the Treasury the power to order such loans could strengthen the lender-of-last-resort powers where the central bank is reluctant to act. In the 2008 crisis, Secretary Paulson did not think he could obtain general funding authority from Congress,[194] which likely contributed to his urging Chairman Bernanke to lend. Treasury orders to lend should probably be accompanied by indemnity as provided in the United Kingdom but not in Japan.

The second question is whether the Treasury must approve the lending of the central bank. Again, this is a moot point in the eurozone. In Japan, the BOJ can make Article 33 and Article 37 loans without Treasury approval, but the Treasury must itself initiate Article 38 loans. In the United Kingdom, the BOE can lend to banks and nonbanks through the discount window or CTRF without Treasury approval, but all emergency loans must be approved or directed by the Treasury. In the United States, only loans to nonbanks must be approved by the Treasury, and no indemnity goes with the approval. The requirement of Treasury approval in the US democracy, where such approval could be widely attacked by the Congress, and even in principle nullified,

would seem much more important than in the context of the UK parliamentary democracy where the government generally controls both
the Treasury and the Parliament. The requirement of US Treasury
approval carries with it a significant enough degree of uncertainty to
risk spooking the markets and accelerating panics. Some say any
responsible Secretary of Treasury will have to approve Fed lending in
a crisis due to the dire consequences of the failure to lend. But any
Secretary of Treasury that approves such lending may be signing a
future political death warrant, much like the many Democrats who
voted for TARP. The irony is that if the lending is successful it is always
easy to come back later and say it was unnecessary and bad to bail out
Wall Street. One does not have the counterfactual of economic collapse
to lay at the doorstep of critics.

The provision of liquidity to financial firms in difficulty always
introduces a level of moral hazard, but requiring Treasury approval of
loans does not eliminate the moral hazard—it merely shifts the source
to the Treasury from the Fed. In addition, moral hazard concerns are
limited in the case of lender-of-last-resort loans to solvent institutions
that are victims of financial panic. These borrowers require assistance
not because they took on too much risk but, rather, because of indiscriminate withdrawals by short-term creditors.

10.4.7 Need for a "Broad Program"

Only the United States prevents loans to single nonbanks, insisting
instead on a broad program approved by the Secretary of the Treasury.
This means that programs cannot be tailored to individual situations,
as in the cases of Bear and AIG. Further, since runs often start somewhere, it makes it hard to stop the first run, and thus avoid the initial
outbreak of contagion. Japan says emergency lending must be to
prevent systemic risk, not to rescue a firm. But the US policy prevents
loaning to a single nonbank for any reason, including that it may be
the first nonbank subject to a run or that the loan needs to be customized, as was the case with AIG.

10.4.8 Disclosure Requirements

In Japan, Article 33 loans are disclosed only in the aggregate, and
Article 38 special loans are disclosed by press release. The United
Kingdom publishes only aggregate DWF and ELA information (with a
five-quarter lag). And while ELA loans must, in principle, be immediately reported to the Parliament, this need not happen if confidentiality

is crucial. In the ECB, disclosure policy on ELA loans is left to NCBs; I have not investigated the practices of different countries.

The United States has the most demanding disclosure policies, requiring discount window loans, including the borrower, to be disclosed publicly after two years and Section 13(3) loans to be disclosed publicly, including the borrower, after one year.[195] Dodd–Frank also requires 13(3) loans to be reported to Congress with seven days.[196] Such public disclosure raises the prospect of stigmatizing the borrower with the undesirable effect that needy borrowers will risk riding out withdrawals rather than borrowing from the Fed. This may lead to their collapse and to the broader collapse of the financial system.

10.4.9 Using Discount Window Proceeds to Lend to Affiliates
Finally, the United States is the only country that prohibits banks from using discount window loans to support their affiliates (e.g., broker-dealers). This requirement forces such affiliates to seek Fed funding independently as nonbanks, with the added conditions of nonbank funding. Even the UK "Vickers report" does not prohibit a bank from funneling central bank liquidity to a nonbank affiliate.[197]

In summary, the Fed is by far the weakest lender of last resort relative to its foreign counterparts and the Fed's lender-of-last-resort powers are under political attack in the United States from both sides of the political spectrum. Even President Jeff Lacker of the Richmond Federal Reserve considers LLR as being part of the government safety net that is contributing to moral hazard, and argues for a weakening of such powers.[198] While all four central banks reviewed above impose strict institutional constraints on lender-of-last-resort authority, the political unpopularity of this traditional function is heaviest in the United States. Just look at the ECB, which is not supposed to loan to insolvent banks, in principle, yet has lent amply to Greek banks. This is not only due to the ECB's structural "constitutional" independence but also due to the fact that the general concept of lender-of-last-resort authority does not face the level of hostility in Europe that it does in the United States.

Apart from the political environment, institutionally the United States grants by far the weakest lender-of-last-resort powers to its central bank, particularly with respect to nonbanks: (1) its independence is more fragile; (2) it is the only country with special limitations on lending to nonbanks as compared with banks; (3) it is the only country, outside the eurozone, that makes no provision for loans to institutions the central bank does not judge as solvent (and as noted the eurozone requirement could be toothless); (4) while the BOE and BOJ require Treasury approval or direction for emergency lending, such requirements are likely to be much less politicized than the US Treasury approval of loans to nonbanks; (5) it is the only country that places restrictions on banks using discount window loans to support affiliates; (6) it is the only country requiring that there be a broad program for borrowing by nonbanks; and (7) it is the most aggressive country in requiring disclosure, thereby possibly inhibiting borrowers from borrowing due to the associated stigma. All but the first point results from changes by Dodd–Frank.

This US weakness is not likely to be rectified in the near future given the politics surrounding bailouts. Indeed, as the FORM Act demonstrates, the situation could get worse not better.

11 Strengthening the LLR Powers of the Fed

Any attempt to strengthen the role of the Fed as lender of last resort is untenable in the current political environment. That is a fact of life. But apart from politics, what *should* one do to strengthen the Fed's role? The beauty of the power of a strong lender of last resort is the power would never have to be used because runs would be deterred by the knowledge that the Fed would do what it took. Stopping runs before they occur avoids the serious problems of lending into a run. At the same time, a strong lender of last resort should not be one operating under an ill-defined framework. It is important to establish a detailed LLR framework, so that the legally permissible actions of the Fed are not unbounded. Further, a clear framework, which includes specification of actions that might be taken in a contagious panic could well forestall the panic in the first place—this is the essence of the "do what it takes" approach of the ECB.

It should also be noted that some have raised the question of whether the Federal Reserve's large balance sheet may impede its lender-of-last-resort capabilities in the future. This is unlikely to be an issue since the Federal Reserve's balance sheet expansion is temporary and it could offset any new LLR lending (which would further increase the balance sheet) by selling other assets, thereby keeping the LLR activities balance-sheet neutral.

The obvious first step for reform would be to restore the Dodd–Frank changes to Section 13(3), including the Fed's independence from the Treasury. But as former Secretary Geithner has written, these powers were barely sufficient to deal with the crisis. What more could be done?

First, we should follow the lead of other central banks by dividing LLR powers between normal times through the discount window and special times through emergency procedures, rather than dividing our lending authority up between banks and nonbanks. In the modern financial world lending to banks and nonbanks should generally be treated the same, while recognizing the need for accurate solvency information will be more difficult to obtain for unsupervised nonbanks.

Second, there should be a more flexible and clearer policy about collateral for emergency assistance. The effectiveness of lender-of-last-resort liquidity in stemming risks of contagion hinges on two key factors: (1) financial institutions must have adequate collateral to access central bank liquidity and (2) short-term creditors must have confidence in the collateral adequacy of the financial institution and certainty that the central bank will indeed lend against it. With respect to collateral, it is important that the central bank accept a broad range of securities as adequate collateral. More risky and less liquid collateral can be subject to haircuts that reflect their riskiness. Requiring that banks publicly disclose their levels of adequate collateral would serve to increase the confidence of short-term creditors that their borrowers could get access to Fed liquidity. The Committee on Global Financial Stability advocates for a requirement that banks provide regular, standardized disclosures on the quality and amount of their collateral as well as the extent to which any assets are encumbered.[1] Disclosures related to asset encumbrance and collateral adequacy should serve to improve market discipline, since unsecured short-term creditors would be in a better position to evaluate the riskiness of the bank's short-term debt.[2]

A crucial issue, however, in collateral adequacy is the dynamic nature of the valuation of collateral; that is, an asset's value or riskiness may change dramatically, thus compromising its usefulness as collateral. As noted by Federal Reserve Bank of Boston President Eric Rosengren, "widespread questions about the appropriate valuation of collateral during the crisis made it apparent that collateral solutions in and of itself was not sufficient to avoid runs."[3] Ultimately the valuation of collateral will be determined by the Fed, likely with help from an outside contractor (e.g., BlackRock's role during the prior financial crisis). Given that Fed lending is likely to restore asset prices to their ex ante value, the Fed should make it clear in advance that collateral should be valued under "normal" market conditions without taking into account the effect of fire sales.

A third reform would be to abandon the ad hoc nature of decision making about when to lend by adopting an advance commitment approach. Solutions focused solely on the collateral of financial institutions do not address the ad hoc nature of central bank lending and the uncertainty of creditors as to whether the Fed will actually lend to their institution. As an alternative, the Federal Reserve could provide an explicit advanced commitment to lend against adequate collateral. Under an explicit contract, short-term creditors can have confidence in the availability of central bank lending in the face of liquidity problems. An advanced commitment by the Fed would specify the relevant details of lender-of-last-resort support, such as adequate collateral, penalty rates, and term, *before* the onset of a crisis. By removing most of the uncertainty of whether a financial institution will receive liquidity from the Fed (it might still fail to come up with agreed collateral), short-term creditors would be able to rely on advanced commitments. This is akin to the approach of the ECB in laying out the conditions for its assistance under its September 2012 Outright Monetary Transactions Policy, the "do what it takes" policy.[4] The power of the Fed to stop contagion would thus be greatly strengthened. This approach would, of course, clash with the doctrine of "creative ambiguity."[5] The main idea behind the "creative ambiguity" concept is that to mitigate moral hazard concerns the central bank should be ambiguous in regards to its liquidity provisions, so that a financial institution cannot always expect that the central bank to provide liquidity when it is needed. However, while "creative ambiguity" may serve to limit moral hazard by introducing uncertainty, it is precisely the uncertainty that exacerbates the problem of contagion. A BIS workshop discussing the lender of last resort with representatives from the world's major central banks concluded that "ambiguity had impaired the effectiveness of LOLR actions during the crisis," by making it harder for central banks to respond and making banks and markets more pessimistic about the central bank's ability to lend.[6] However, some participants suggested that ambiguity in lender-of-last-resort policies was desirable for nonbanks, but not for banks. It is unclear why ambiguity would hinder a central bank's actions for banks but not for nonbanks, particularly given that some major "banks" today are bank holding companies in name but broker-dealers in practice.

In general, academic theory suggests that while "creative ambiguity" does have merits in certain cases due to the reduction of moral hazard, the systemic risks associated with contagion of large financial institutions outweigh the systemic risks associated with moral hazard.[7] While "creative ambiguity" may have a limited role during normal times, there is no place for such a policy during a crisis. However, given that regulators will likely not identify a crisis until it has already occurred, waiting to provide clarity may be too late to combat contagion. A summary of the September 2014 BIS conference on lender of last resort found that "many participants expressed the view that ambiguity with respect to provision of emergency liquidity to banks was not always constructive. Given the scale of liquidity stress, there were doubts that ambiguity had helped reduce moral hazard before the crisis."[8] Further it is hard to see how moral hazard is created by lending to victims of panic runs, as compared to financial institutions that have become insolvent due to their own bad decisions.

A program of advanced commitments to lend by the Federal Reserve does have historical precedent. In 1999, concerns of Y2K computer glitches led many financial institutions to limit exposure to these potential Y2K risks by planning to reduce trading volume. Foreseeing the liquidity problems that would be created by a reduction of trading activity the Federal Reserve created the Standby Financing Facility that "would provide securities dealers with a form of backup funding and ease market anxieties about year-end credit conditions."[9] This liquidity facility allowed primary dealers in government securities to buy options on temporary repos, which gave the contract holder the right to arrange a one-day repo with the Fed for $50 million at a price of 150 basis points over the federal funds target rate (a price determined through an auction).[10] Secondary trading of the liquidity options was not permitted.[11] The Fed's auction of the options was successful as demand surpassed expectations. Even though a disruptive trading event never materialized as a result of Y2K and no dealer exercised their option, an argument can be made that the introduction of the Standby Financing Facility averted market disruptions.[12] Not only did market repo rates decline substantially after the Fed announced the details of the facility and the strong results of the auction, but according to members of the New York Fed's Markets Group, "many dealers indicated that the options program helped ease their anxieties about prospective market conditions around year-end."[13] This result again underscores a central point about lender of last resort—strong powers may never have to be used because they will deter runs in the first place.

While the Fed's Standby Financing Facility does provide a framework for considering advanced commitments, most potential liquidity crises will not be as easily foreseen. Therefore it is crucial that a lending policy be outlined in advance. A policy paper released by the Center for Financial Stability proposes an implementation of advance commitments that is very similar to the liquidity options created through the Y2K Standby Financing Facility. In the paper, Bruce Tuckman introduces Federal Liquidity Options ("FLOs") as an advanced commitment mechanism.[14] Under this proposal, the Federal Reserve would auction off a limited number of FLOs to nonbank financial institutions at market-determined prices.[15] The FLO would give the holder an option to borrow money from the Fed "on a secured basis at a predetermined rate and under prearranged collateral terms."[16] This proposal to use FLOs as the exclusive means of providing liquidity to nonbank financial institutions has several advantages. First, moral hazard should be minimized, since an effective FLO program would allow the Federal Reserve to credibly dismiss the possibility of further liquidity provisions or bailouts in the event of a crisis.[17] In addition financial institutions that borrow from the Fed through an FLO would be required to pay for this privilege through market-determined prices, thus "forcing market participants to internalize the cost of lending of last resort ...."[18]

Three main issues arise regarding the potential effectiveness of the FLO proposal in stemming contagion. First, it is unclear why such a policy should only be adopted for nonbanks, given that contagion in the banking system is an increasing concern given the rising proportion of short-term uninsured liabilities, a point covered in more depth in the next chapter of the book on deposit insurance and guarantees. Second, an appropriate amount of FLOs may not be held by institutions that are experiencing a run, thus limiting their effectiveness in protecting against contagion. Purchase of the liquidity options would not be mandatory as they are sold at auction and completely discretionary. Seen in this light, such options should be additive to ad hoc powers, and not be the exclusive means of lending. The third issue of concern with FLOs is the collateral management. Since FLOs can only be exercised with adequate collateral, FLOs are only valuable, and hence effective in stemming contagion, if the holder of the FLO also has a sufficient amount of collateral. In terms of providing a solution to contagion, the question remains whether collateral management should be left to the individual FLO holders or if the Fed should impose collateral adequacy policies in conjunction with the FLOs. Proponents of the FLO program firmly believe that collateral adequacy will not be a major concern since financial institutions will likely exercise FLOs to replace lost funding that already required the same collateral. In fact the FLO proposal recommends that adequate collateral for the FLO should be the same as the collateral used in the tri-party repo market.[19] The lack of adequate collateral could be further addressed generally by the enhanced collateral policies suggested above.

A fourth reform of LLR could be consideration of opening lender-of-last resort facilities to MMFs, given the dangers of MMF runs. Central bank injection of liquidity can, of course, be provided indirectly using banks as a third party to facilitate the lending. In this manner banks borrow directly from the Fed and pass the liquidity on to money market funds, using the MMF assets as collateral for the Fed loans, as was done in the 2008 crisis through AMLF, in which the Federal Reserve extended indirect access to the discount window to money market funds through a $150 billion facility.[20] But money market funds could also potentially borrow directly from the Fed. Former Chairman Bernanke indicated a possible willingness to provide central bank loans to money market funds during a future crisis.[21] However, any lending to money market funds faces an initial obstacle in the 1940 Investment Company Act, which limits the amount of leverage an MMF can incur.[22] An SEC exception would be necessary to exempt loans from the central bank in regards to any leverage limits on money market funds for lender-of-last-resort liquidity to be a viable solution to MMF contagion. Another potential obstacle that must be overcome is the ownership structure of money market funds. Since MMF investors technically own the MMF assets, the MMF does not have ownership of the collateral that must be used to borrow from the Fed. A solution to this obstacle could be as simple as a requirement that investors agree to subordinate their claims to the Federal Reserve loans.

One reason that broadening lender-of-last-resort facilities to include MMFs may work is that MMFs are regulated by SEC, thus subjecting funds to regulatory oversight, much like the Federal Reserve regulates banks in conjunction with the discount window. In the unlikely case that a MMF needs liquidity support the reporting requirements of MMFs will allow regulators to determine whether the fund is insolvent; indeed, given the nature of money market fund assets, such determination will be easier than for banks. Insolvent funds would not be permitted access to lender-of-last-resort liquidity and would be allowed to fail, similar to insolvent banks. However, a concern arises with the SEC's MMF reforms discussed later, in particular, the imposition of a floating NAV requirement, which could result in regulatory arbitrage. The potential flight of MMF funds to unregulated investment alternatives, including the "enhanced cash fund" market and separately managed accounts, or to private unregulated funds, as contemplated by BlackRock,[23] would make it much more difficult to deploy lender-of-last-resort liquidity to where it is needed most.

This raises a fifth point of reform. A significant problem in the Fed lending responsibly to nonbanks is that it is not the supervisor of its potential borrowers and thus is not able to make an informed decision about their solvency. In Japan the BOJ has examination authority over any borrower. This ensures that it may examine potential borrowers that come for loans. While other central banks may not have the same statutory power, they could impose an examination requirement as a condition for making loans. But in Japan and elsewhere last minute examinations of unsupervised institutions would be problematic. This could be remedied by giving the central bank supervisory authority over any significant financial institution, but this is impractical, particularly with respect to firms that are generally unregulated for solvency, like hedge funds. At least the Fed should have free and complete access to supervisory information collected by other regulators that bears on solvency. Our fragmented regulatory structure contributes to Fed's incomplete picture of the financial system.[24] The lender-of-last-resort capabilities of the Fed would be strengthened by better regulatory coordination and collection of information, without necessarily increasing the regulatory authority of the Fed.

Additionally we should give the Treasury the power to direct the Fed to make loans to certain financial institutions, again whether banks or nonbanks, as is the case in the United Kingdom and Japan. Former Secretary Geithner does have a valid concern over whether the Fed will always want to loan in all cases it should. Consideration could be given to whether such direction should come with indemnity for losses as is the case in the United Kingdom but not in Japan.

Finally, it would be a good idea for the Fed to set forth a general policy of how it would conduct its lender-of-last-resort policy. The more the market knows about what its policy is—albeit that any policy can be altered under unanticipated circumstances—the less it will run out of ignorance. Elements of such a policy could well include setting forth the facilities that may be used to fight contagion (basically those used in the crisis), indicating that, in principle, it should only loan to solvent institutions, with due recognition that determination of insolvency is difficult, and that fire-sale prices of collateral will be disregarded in determining the value of collateral. Such policies would be similar to those contained in the current UK framework.

As is repeatedly pointed out in this book, none of these recommendations are politically feasible—all that can be done for now is to foster discussion.

12 Liability Insurance and Guarantees

Dodd–Frank not only cut back on the Fed's ability to serve as lender of last resort, it also cut back on the FDIC's ability to expand deposit insurance or create other guarantees during a crisis. A strong guarantee system is an important complement to a strong lender of last resort, and indeed even more important when the power of the lender of last resort has been seriously weakened. Nonetheless, increasingly short-term liabilities have moved out of the banking system and uninsured short-term liabilities of nonbanks have increased. So we need not only to restore the powers of the government to insure bank funding, we need to give serious thought to expanding such funding to the shadow banking sector, particularly money market funds. The expansion of guarantees outside the banking sector raises significant challenges.

Dodd–Frank §1105 limits the FDIC's ability to provide the guarantees that helped stabilize the financial system during the financial crisis, such as (1) the Transaction Account Guarantee Program ("TAGP") to provide temporary unlimited guarantees or increases in insurance limits to domestic non–interest-bearing transaction deposits and (2) the Debt Guarantee Program ("DGP") to temporarily guarantee the issuance of senior debt. The FDIC implemented the TAGP and DGP by invoking a general authority to mitigate instability in the financial system once the Treasury Secretary made a systemic risk determination under section 13(c)(4)(G) of the Federal Deposit Insurance Act, an authority now removed.

Dodd–Frank §1106 further diminishes the FDIC's powers to protect bank creditors by eliminating the open bank assistance that had allowed the FDIC to provide loans, purchase assets, assume liabilities, and provide cash contributions to prevent an insured bank from failing. Now, a bank subsidiary must enter an FDIC receivership for the FDIC to have the authority to guarantee the short-term liabilities of the bank subsidiary. The FDIC may only do so if the Secretary of the Treasury (in consultation with the President and upon the recommendation of two-thirds of the Board of Directors of the FDIC and the Board of Governors of the Federal Reserve,) determines that doing so is necessary to avoid or mitigate "serious adverse effects on financial stability."

Finally, new Section 131 of the Emergency Stabilization Act, as a result of the TARP legislation, prevents the Treasury from enacting the same temporary guarantee program that it used successfully to stabilize the money market mutual fund industry during the financial crisis. Congress has barred the Treasury from using the Economic Stabilization Fund to establish any future guarantee program for the industry.

Again, a starting point for reform would be to eliminate the changes made to the guarantee system by Dodd–Frank. But more needs to be done to further strengthen the system. The objective of this chapter is to explore the various problems in designing a better and broader insurance regime but take no position on the best approach. The problems are complicated and deserve much further study.

Insurance for customer deposits administered by the FDIC has formed an integral element of depository banking regulation in the United States since 1934.[1] Deposit insurance is credited with stabilizing the depository banking system after it collapsed in the early 1930s.[2] Indeed its application has not been confined to the United States: explicit deposit insurance is a recurring worldwide feature of modern banking regulation utilized in more than 88 countries (excluding countries that employ an "implicit" guarantee of bank deposits that is not formalized through the provision of a discrete insurance fund).[3] The economic efficiencies of deposit insurance have been demonstrated by Diamond and Dybvig[4] and Carnell, Macey, and Miller (2009),[5] among others.

The federal deposit insurance system arose as a consequence of the Great Depression, with federal officials recognizing the efficacy of using deposit insurance to assure depositors and preemptively forestall bank runs.[6] The leading supporter for federal deposit insurance was Representative Henry Steagall.[7] Throughout the Depression, Representative Steagall indicated that deposit insurance would dissuade depositors from running on a potentially distressed bank, thereby resulting in durable "stability" for the United States' banking system.[8] Opponents, including Senator Carter Glass, countered that the failures of prior state deposit insurance regimes showed the probable ineffectiveness of this approach.[9] Strong public support for the proposal ultimately persuaded those opponents to accept the establishment of federal deposit insurance.[10] In June 1933, the Banking Act of 1933 was accordingly enacted; Section 8 of the Banking Act stipulated the creation of the Federal Deposit Insurance Corporation ("FDIC").[11]

For deposit-taking banks, the role of liability insurer is filled by the FDIC, but only in the context of depository borrowing under a limit (currently $250,000); it does not cover nonbanks.[12] Although depository insurance is rightly regarded as a critical stabilizing attribute of financial regulation, innovation in financial technology over the past three decades and increasing nonbank intermediation in the modern financial system have now rendered the coverage it provides highly incomplete. This was proven most dramatically during the financial crisis. At the beginning of the crisis, short-term creditors of financial institutions assumed the existence of an implicit government guarantee of all short-term liabilities and appeared to be largely justified in doing so. The government's assisted rescue of Bear Stearns in March 2008 in partnership with JPMorgan Chase and its subsequent effective nationalization of the government-sponsored enterprises ("GSEs") Freddie Mac and Fannie Mae in July of the same year are likely to have reinforced belief among market participants (including short-term creditors) in the existence of an unlimited implied public guarantee of large US financial institutions. But then by allowing Lehman Brothers to fail in September 2008, the government was seen as canceling or at least weakening the guarantee. According to this interpretation, the anti-bailout signal transmitted by the failure of Lehman, not the failure itself, triggered the spread of contagion effects in markets for short-term institutional borrowing by withdrawing protection that market participants had assumed they would receive.[13]

Based on this lesson from the financial crisis, an important part of a solution to contagion may be a more complete public guarantee of short-term nondeposit financial liabilities, whether held by banks or by nonbank financial institutions.[14] Such a system of more universal insurance for short-term financial liabilities would assure short-term creditors automatic protection through assessments on issuers,[15] removing the element of uncertainty tied to discretionary emergency lending or politically contingent (and unpopular) bailouts. The costs of supplying a public guarantee could be internalized through the use of insurance premiums or through some other form of assessment, either before or after they are triggered.

Of course, the concern with short-term liability insurance arises from the same moral hazard problem created in all insurance regimes (or actual bailouts as discussed later in this book): insured creditors, like any policyholders protected from loss, have little incentive to monitor risk-taking by issuers.[16] Short-term creditors that are insured against losses will also require a lower interest rate on the credit provided to financial institutions. The resulting lower cost of short-term debt will give financial institutions further incentive to increase short-term funding by taking advantage of the cheaper funding. More short-term funding corresponds with a higher likelihood of failure, and therefore a higher expected payout by the insurance provider. This economic cost of moral hazard can in theory be internalized by optimizing the premiums extracted from policyholders, but it is questionable whether the pricing of insurance on short-term liabilities can be perfected.

12.1   Amount of Liabilities to Insure

Given the current levels of insured liabilities in the financial system, a very challenging question for an insurance regime is what caps, if any, to apply to guarantees of covered liabilities. To estimate the size of short-term liabilities, we include money market mutual fund shares, repurchase agreements, commercial paper, and securities lending. This is consistent with the scope of "shadow liabilities," as defined by Pozsar et al. (2012).[17]

Cumulatively, as shown in table 12.1, nondeposit uninsured short-term liabilities totaled $8 trillion at the end of 2014. While this represents a reduction from their peak level in 2008 of about $9.9 trillion, these nondeposit liabilities (all uninsured) are comparable to total deposits of about $10.4 trillion, and greater than insured deposits of $6.1 trillion.

While uninsured deposits hit a low of $1.6 trillion in 2010, this was caused in large part by the extension of unlimited insurance to all bank transaction accounts from 2008 to 2012. With the end of such unlimited insurance in December 2012, there has been a substantial growth in uninsured bank deposits, standing at $4.2 trillion in 2014, more than two-thirds the size of insured deposits. In 2014 only 59.1 percent of domestic bank deposits were insured, compared with roughly 80 percent from 2010 to 2012. So the level of uninsured bank deposits is significant, and represents a substantial exposure to a run. As illustrated in the final row of table 12.1, the total of uninsured short-term

Deposit and nondeposit US financial system liabilities, 1950 to 2014

Year	1950	1960	1970	1980	1990	2000	2008	2009	2010	2011	2012	2013	2014
MMMF shares	$—	$—	$—	$76	$493	$1,812	$3,757	$3,258	$2,755	$2,643	$2,650	$2,678	$2,688
Open market paper	1	7	40	164	610	1,614	1,599	1,137	1,057	969	952	952	930
Federal funds and repos	(1)	(2)	1	103	336	1,001	3,662	3,251	3,666	3,922	4,173	3,670	3,697
Securites loaned, net	—	—	—	1	71	508	887	857	733	658	580	674	721
Short term (est.)	0	4	41	345	1,511	4,935	9,905	8,504	8,212	8,192	8,354	7,974	8,036
GSE liabilities	3	11	45	190	468	1,923	3,390	2,977	6,589	6,378	6,217	6,315	6,387
Agency/GSE backed pools	0	0	5	114	1,020	2,493	4,961	5,377	1,139	1,305	1,437	1,569	1,645
ABS issuer liabilities	—	—	—	—	269	1,504	4,103	3,291	2,235	1,989	1,769	1,615	1,382
Nondeposit liabilities	$3	$16	$91	$649	$3,268	$10,855	$22,360	$20,149	$18,176	$17,863	$17,777	$17,473	$17,450
Comparison: domestic bank deposits													
Insured	$91	$150	$350	$949	$2,785	$3,055	$4,751	$5,408	$6,315	$6,975	$7,407	$6,010	$6,204
Uninsured	76	111	196	376	631	1,157	2,755	2,298	1,572	1,807	2,068	3,816	4,205
Total deposits	$168	$260	$545	$1,324	$3,415	$4,212	$7,505	$7,705	$7,888	$8,782	$9,475	$9,825	$10,408
Insured	54.4%	57.5%	64.1%	71.6%	81.5%	72.5%	63.3%	70.2%	80.1%	79.4%	78.2%	61.2%	59.6%
Memo: cap (000s)	$10	$10	$10	$100	$100	$100	$100	$250	$250	$250	$250	$250	$250
Estimated uninsured short-term liabilities													
Nondeposit uninsured	$—	$4	$41	$345	$1,511	$4,935	$9,905	$8,504	$8,212	$8,192	$8,354	$7,974	$8,036
Deposit uninsured	76	111	196	376	631	1,157	2,755	2,298	1,572	1,807	2,068	3,816	4,205
Total uninsured	$77	$115	$236	$720	$2,141	$6,092	$12,660	$10,801	$9,785	$10,000	$10,422	$11,789	$12,241
Total short term	45.6%	43.5%	40.4%	43.2%	43.5%	66.6%	72.7%	66.6%	60.8%	58.9%	58.5%	66.2%	66.4%

Note: Bd. of Governors of the Fed. Reserve Sys., Flow of Funds Accounts of the United States, (June 6, 2013), http://www.federalreserve.gov/releases/z1/. The tabulation is based on the convention in Pozsar et al., *supra* note 17, at 5 n.4 (defining "shadow bank liabilities" as sum of MMMF shares outstanding [line 13, L.121119], open market paper [line 1, L.208], federal funds and repo liabilities [line 1, L.207], net securities loaned [line 20, L.130129], GSE liabilities [line 2125, L.124123], agency- and GSE-backed pool securities [line 6, L.125123], and ABS issuer liabilities [line 11, L.126].124): *Quarterly Banking Profile: First Quarter 2013*, 7 FDIC Quarterly 2 (2013) (2012 data found in table I-B).

funding was around $12.3 trillion in 2014, almost triple the $4.2 trillion in insured deposits. This implies that only around 33 percent of short-term liabilities are insured, around half of the fraction that was insured in 1970. So, not only do we have substantial contagion risk at banks, such risk also exists outside banks, as we witnessed during the crisis.

It should be noted that this methodology produces some double counting. This is because the our estimate includes money market funds and commercial paper, repos, and uninsured depositors, even though money market funds are large investors in commercial paper, repos, and uninsured deposits (e.g., CDs). This means that the fraction of these short-term debt instruments held by money market funds would be double counted. However, government MMFs also invest directly in Treasuries and GSE securities, so all MMMF shares ($2.688 trillion) are not double counted. According to Crane Data, government MMFs hold approximately $1.024 trillion in such government securities directly.[18] Thus, to most accurately eliminate double-counting through the inclusion of money market funds, $1.664 trillion in MMMF shares ($2.688 trillion − $1.024 trillion) should be subtracted from the $12.273 trillion total of uninsured short-term liabilities. Total uninsured short-term liabilities would therefore stand at $10.61 trillion at the end of 2014. By this measure, 63.4 percent of all short-term liabilities are uninsured.

Does this mean we need to insure all short-term liabilities to prevent runs on the financial system? According to Crane Data, all money market funds hold approximately $630 billion in repos (or 17.5 percent of outstanding repo), $369 billion in commercial paper (40 percent of outstanding commercial paper), and $511 billion in CDs,[19] so that insuring *only* MMF investments might be sufficient to deter runs in those markets. However, doing so would still leave at least $9.1 trillion in uninsured short-term liabilities. This includes repos, commercial paper, and uninsured deposits not held by money market funds.

The Financial Stability Board and the International Organization of Securities Commissions have suggested that investment funds such as ordinary mutual funds, may also pose run risks.[20] At the end of 2013, the US mutual fund industry had around $15 trillion in assets.[21] Including mutual funds would therefore increase the level of short-term "liabilities" to approximately $25 trillion. Large-scale redemption by mutual fund shareholders could force a fund to liquidate assets, depressing the market price of those assets. However, this "fire-sale" scenario is unlikely to impose losses on significant financial institutions that do not hold the long-term bonds and equities that are typically held by mutual funds.

12.2 Insurance Pricing

One core principle of a nondeposit liability insurance system is that covered institutions should internalize their costs by making payments to the insurance provider (the government and/or private sector) that reflect the cost of providing the guarantee. There are several different timing mechanisms by which these insurance fees may be collected; specifically, institutions could pay for coverage before, during, or after the guarantee is used.

12.3 Ex ante Pricing

Under a system funded ex ante, covered institutions pay a periodic risk-based fee, or insurance premium, in exchange for receiving nondeposit short-term liability insurance. The main reason for this approach is that it provides a private fund from which insurance payments could be made, when necessary, thus avoiding public expenditures.[22] Recurring and risk-based fees also help mitigate the moral hazard that can arise from guaranteed liabilities. By pricing insurance to reflect the risk of covered institutions' activities, regulators can attempt to control moral hazard.

While some of the challenges of pricing insurance for nondepository liabilities are new, many of these issues have been addressed for decades in the analogous case of pricing FDIC deposit insurance. Examining how FDIC insurance is priced is therefore an instructive place to begin the analysis.

When the Banking Act of 1933 established the FDIC, insured institutions were covered for $2,500 for each depositor (a limit that was subsequently raised) and paid premiums as a fixed percentage of insurable deposits.[23] While the basic assessment rates were adjusted over the initial years of the FDIC, under the permanent system, rates settled out at 1/12th of 1 percent (8.33 basis points) of total deposits below the insurance ceiling, some portion of which was credited back to covered banks if the insurance fund's anticipated losses were covered beyond a specified percentage.[24] Despite the lack of sensitivity in this insurance pricing system to risk, it is credited with largely preventing banking panics for over 50 years after its implementation.[25]

Bank failures related to the late 1980s savings and loan crisis caused the FDIC Bank Insurance Fund to become insolvent by $7 billion. This shortfall, and the recognition that the FDIC had likely underpriced its insurance coverage for large institutions, prompted Congress to make key changes to the structure and insurance policies of the FDIC in what became the Federal Deposit Insurance Corporation Improvement Act of 1991 ("FDICIA").[26] FDICIA required the FDIC to set deposit insurance premiums in relation to the risk the bank poses to the insurance fund.[27] The assessment base was still set at banks' insurable deposit base but now assessment rates depended on (1) banks' capital ratings (classified in three groups), and (2) banks' "Supervisory Group," a determination based on a bank's score under the CAMELS rating system (a composite score of different bank health metrics).[28] Premium payments ranged from a low of 2 bps for the most well-capitalized banks to 43 bps for undercapitalized banks with low CAMELS ratings.[29] While this system sensibly reflected an attempt to have the cost of insurance reflect banks' risk to the BIF, it had several problems. Carnell et al. note that the risk-based pricing arguably still did not account for the degree of failure risk for the riskiest banks,[30] perhaps reflected by the fact that the large banks paid the lowest possible rates under this scheme.[31] Moreover, when the BIF reached the target designated reserve ratio (1.25 percent of insured deposits) in 1995, most banks stopped paying premiums altogether; in 1999, for example, 93 percent of FDIC-insured institutions paid no premiums at all.[32]

The Dodd–Frank Act mandated a third wave of changes to the FDIC insurance pricing system,[33] largely prompted by the incurred and expected losses in the DIF (the Deposit Insurance Fund, successor to the BIF) related to the financial crisis. In February 2011 the FDIC promulgated its new rules implementing these Dodd–Frank requirements.[34] These rules affected both of the primary inputs for deposit insurance pricing. First, the assessment base for all banks was changed "from [a system] based on domestic deposits to one based on assets."[35] This new assessment base highlights a fundamental change in the FDIC's definition of risk: while historic approaches had been focused on an institution's covered deposits (which directly represent the maximum potential loss to the DIF), the new approach recognizes that an increase in balance sheet risk—even if it is not funded by additional insured deposits—could increase risk to the DIF from an increase in the probability of losses.

The new rule has modified assessment rates as well, although these rates still depend on similar key inputs, namely capital adequacy and supervisory ratings. The assessment rate system is bifurcated: institutions defined as "small insured depository institutions" (those having less than $10 billion in assets) pay one set of premiums based on risk classifications. These risk classifications are a function of their risk level (which depends on tangible equity and a supervisory evaluation) and the level of reserves in the DIF, as set out in table 12.2.

In contrast, "large" and/or "highly complex"[36] financial institutions pay another set of premiums, which, under the new rule, are not based on risk categories but instead rely on the use of a new risk-based "scorecard" that determines an institution's "performance score" and "loss severity score."[37] The combined scores produce an assessment rate. An institution's performance score is a "weighted average of … three components: the weighted average CAMELS rating score; the ability to withstand asset-related stress score; and the ability to withstand funding-related stress score."[38] Its loss severity score "measures the relative magnitude of potential loss to the FDIC in the event of the insured depository institution's failure."[39] These combine to determine an institution's new risk-adjusted score.

Table 12.2
DIF assessment rates

	Risk category I	Risk category II	Risk category III	Risk category IV
DIF reserve ratio below 1.15 percent	2.5–9 basis points	9–24 basis points	18–33 basis points	30–45 basis points
DIF reserve ratio between 1.15 percent and below 2 percent	1.5–7 basis points	7–22 basis points	14–29 basis points	25–40 basis points
DIF reserve ratio between 2 percent and below 2.5 percent	1–6 basis points	5–20 basis points	12–27 basis points	23–38 basis points
DIF reserve ratio 2.5 percent and higher	0.5–5 basis points	4.5–19 basis points	10–25 basis points	20–35 basis points

Note: Assessments, Large Bank Pricing, 76 *Fed. Reg.* 10,717–20 (Feb. 25, 2011); Barbara R. Mendelson and Marc-Alain Galeazzi, Morrison Foerster, Client Alert: FDIC approves final rule of assessments, dividends, assessment base and large bank pricing, at 2 (Feb. 10, 2011) [hereinafter Morrison Foerster LLP, Summary of New FDIC Rules].

This new FDIC approach to pricing has an important implication for insuring nondeposit liabilities. The FDIC now correctly recognizes that expected loss exposure to the DIF depends on the total net assets of the bank, and not just on insured deposits. This suggests that any scheme insuring nondeposit liabilities should similarly take into account the overall riskiness of the asset side of a financial institution's balance sheet, and not simply the size or particular types of instrument on the liability side of the ledger.[40] This type of pricing exercise could be implemented by performing historical credit analysis on portfolios, as the Basel capital adequacy system does, although one must recognize as well the limitations of that system.[41]

12.4   Option Pricing

The FDIC's approach to pricing insurance starts from the premise (familiar to credit analysts) that the expected cost to the government of providing insurance is equal to the expected losses the insurance fund will incur by providing insurance over time.[42] This expected loss to the insurance fund is contingent on two factors: the probability of loss (failure of the insured institution) and the magnitude of loss given the failure of the institution.[43] However, both of these factors are difficult to quantify accurately. First, the probability of an individual financial institution failing is a complex function of what is going on in the broader financial system; the loss given default will also be affected by such institutional interdependencies. While one might think that looking at the historical default performance of financial institutions would be instructive in this regard, models designed to predict the frequency of such "tail-risk" events often suffer from having insufficient historical data for back-testing (particularly in the case of new financial instruments)[44] and their over-reliance on assumptions about the normality of outcome distributions.[45] Second, both the probability of failure and the expected loss given failure are affected by the very existence of insurance itself; estimating these variables in a system with insurance versus one without insurance is a particularly difficult task.[46]

While this credit analysis framework may provide a conceptually useful way of thinking about the insurer's loss exposure, it is not particularly helpful in quantifying precise prices for the insurance itself. In this regard it may be more helpful to draw on options-pricing theory. From the insurers' perspective, providing a guarantee is analogous to writing a put option on the asset value of the bank, struck at the value of the firm's nonequity liabilities. Indeed Robert Merton has made this argument for a long time, and suggested a quantitative model for pricing deposit insurance based on the same readily observable inputs widely used in contemporary options pricing theory.[47] The essential insight from Merton's analysis is that the option price (i.e., the actuarially fair insurance price) is a function of the volatility of the underlying asset owned by the financial institution; the degree of "moneyness" of the option accordingly corresponds to the equity position of the owners of the firm—when the option, which is owned by the short-term creditors of the institution, is extremely "out of the money," the equity has positive value, and vice versa.[48]

While this option-pricing approach to insurance pricing is elegant and has intuitive appeal, there are some theoretical and practical difficulties with it, which may explain why the FDIC has never adopted this approach to risk-based pricing. On the theoretical front, the option-pricing formula requires an assumption about the shape of the distribution of returns for bank asset valuations.[49] On the practical front, since most banks in the United States, and smaller institutions in particular, do not have publicly traded equity, obtaining accurate asset-pricing information could be difficult, although this problem is mitigated if the insurance coverage is limited to larger institutions.[50]

12.5   Ex post Pricing[51]

A different approach than the one currently used would be for the government to issue a guarantee of the short-term nondeposit liabilities of financial institutions above the designated asset threshold, and to fund this guarantee on an ex post basis, by levying a charge on covered institutions (or their stakeholders) after the crisis has passed. From the perspective of short-term creditors who would benefit from the guarantee, these two approaches would provide the same protection; the difference is that there would be no permanent "insurance fund" under the ex post system, so the payout to short-term creditors of a failed covered institution would first be covered by the government, which would then later recoup the cost of the guarantee through assessments on covered institutions. On the one hand, an advantage of the ex post funded system is that the guarantee does not cost anything unless a covered institution actually fails and the guarantee is used. On the other hand, institutions would not pay for the benefit of avoiding contagious runs through the availability of the guarantee. The mechanics of how an ex post charge would work presents challenges in terms of who would pay the charge and what the size of the charge would be.

Determining who would pay the charge requires two levels of analysis: which institutions would pay the charge and which stakeholders of those institutions would be liable.[52] One might start from the principle that those who benefit from the insurance system should bear the cost of it; on this view, short-term creditors of the failed institution would appear to be the obvious beneficiaries and thus the responsible parties. However, there are two reasons to favor applying the charge more broadly, with respect to both institutions and stakeholders. First, the potential benefits of a guarantee are much broader than any particular troubled institution or its own stakeholders; other stakeholders (besides short-term creditors) in the covered institution benefit because they do not have the value of their investments impaired by contagious run behavior during crises. Short-term creditors and longer term stakeholders in other covered financial institutions also benefit because of the reduced likelihood of contagious runs. Second, if the charge were focused only on short-term creditors of particular troubled institutions, this could actually cause these creditors to run in anticipation of a levy on that institution, thereby exacerbating rather than mitigating the problem of contagious panic. Both of these arguments suggest that the charge should be broadly based with respect to both institutions and stakeholders. Additionally, imposing small charges on a wider range of stakeholders would reduce the risk of distorting the markets for short- or long-term capital (compared with imposing larger, more concentrated charges on particular groups of stakeholders).

Determining the size of the charge under an ex post system would also pose challenges. Perhaps the most obvious way to size the ex post charge would be to simply assess a charge equivalent to the realized cost of guarantee (which would be known after resolving a failed covered institution). Under this approach, charges would only be assessed in the (hopefully) relatively rare event that covered institutions actually fail. While this is arguably attractive, because payments to cover the cost of the short-term liability guarantee would only be required in the rare case that they have been paid out, it is not clear that the magnitude of the necessary ex post assessments can optimally reduce ex ante moral hazard for covered institutions and their stakeholders.

12.6 During a Crisis

Still another option for an insurance scheme would be to implement a guarantee program for short-term nondeposit creditors of financial institutions only when it becomes apparent that there is a crisis involving heightened systemic risk. Under such a system there would be no standing guarantee for nondeposit creditors (as in either of the previous two approaches) or standing insurance fund (as in the ex ante funded approach). Rather, the government (perhaps led by FSOC) would monitor systemic risk and issue a guarantee to a relevant set of short-term nondeposit creditors[53] when it is perceived to be necessary. The guarantee itself would be mandatory for all institutions determined to be within the scope of coverage; this would ensure maximum protection against contagious panic. By contrast, Treasury's guarantee of money market funds during the financial crisis was voluntary; money market funds (and not their shareholders) could opt to join by paying a fee (discussed in the next paragraph). While the practical impact of Treasury's guarantee was ultimately quite similar to a mandatory guarantee—nearly all major money market funds, representing over $3 trillion in industry assets under management, opted to join—it seems reasonable to expect that a mandatory guarantee would be even more effective at minimizing the possibility of systemic contagion, particularly as applied to a potentially broader set of institutions than just money market funds and depository institutions. Such a system could be funded through assessments on covered institutions at the time the guarantee is furnished; to the extent such assessments were insufficient to cover the cost of the guarantee, the government would have to employ an ex post approach as discussed above, but the size of such an assessment would be less given the charges to those covered in the crisis.

A major problem with this approach, as with the ex post approach, is the cost of the insurance would not take into account the benefit of the option to have such insurance in a crisis, when the option never has to be used because of its very presence.

12.7 International Challenges

A potential challenge for an expanded insurance regime is achieving international participation. This is important in order to prevent short-term creditors from transferring funding out of financial institutions in risky and nonguaranteed jurisdictions into safer insured institutions in jurisdictions with public guarantees during a financial crisis. Without coordination, uneven implementation of insurance will exert a destabilizing effect on nonguaranteed institutions as investor funds flow elsewhere or into risk-free instruments backed by the government. This danger is illustrated by the effect on deposit flows of the Irish government's public guarantee of all deposits and debt instruments at six major Irish financial institutions, including Allied Irish Banks, Bank of Ireland, and Anglo Irish Bank in September 2008.[54] The Irish guarantee caused deposit outflows from banking institutions elsewhere in Europe, including the United Kingdom, into Ireland as investors sought to shield themselves from rising credit risk.[55] One straightforward response to this problem is to coordinate to exclude creditors who transfer into a jurisdiction during a crisis from the protection of that jurisdiction's insurance. This would deter outflows seeking to take advantage of a more favorable insurance regime located elsewhere in a moment of panic. But such coordination would be difficult to achieve. In the financial crisis of 2007 to 2009, the US Treasury and FDIC limited foreign access to its stabilization programs to some extent (see table 12.3): foreign subsidiaries and branches were ineligible for the Capital Purchase Program, and foreign branches also were restricted from accessing the FDIC's TLGP debt guarantee. Other Treasury and FDIC protections, including the PPIF, Transaction Account Guarantee, and various Federal Reserve facilities including the TALF and CPFF were, however, made available to foreign subsidiaries and branches.

Table 12.3
Eligibility of branches and subsidiaries of foreign banks in selected US stabilization programs

Program	Program management	Foreign eligibility subsidiaries?	Foreign eligibility branches?	Foreign asset screening?
Capital Purchase Program (CPP)[a] (1)	Treasury	No	No	n/a
Legacy Securities Program (PPIP)[b] (2)	Treasury	Yes	Yes	Yes
Term Asset-Backed Securities Loan Facility (TALF)[c] (3)	Fed	Yes	Yes (must hold Fed reserves)	Yes
Commercial Paper Funding Facility (CPFF)[d] (4)	Fed	Yes	Yes	Yes
TLGP Debt Guarantee Program[e] (5)	FDIC	Yes	No	No
TLGP Transaction Account Guarantee Program[f] (6)	FDIC	Yes	Yes (only grandfathered)	n/a
Depository Insurance Increase to $250,000[g] (7)	FDIC	Yes	Yes (only grandfathered)	n/a
Asset Guarantee Program (AGP) for Citigroup[h] (8)	Treasury	n/a	n/a	Yes

a. See Investment Programs, *supra* note 675.

b. Master agreement among Citigroup Inc. et al. (Jan. 15, 2009), http://www.treasury.gov/initiatives/financial-stability/programs/investment-programs/agp/Documents/Citigroup_01152009.pdf.

c. See Term Asset-Backed Securities Loan Facility: Frequently Asked Questions, *supra* note 670.

d. See Press Release, Bd. of Governors of the Fed. Res. Sys. (Oct. 7, 2008), *supra* note 663.

e. See Temporary Liquidity Guarantee Program, *supra* note 672.

f. Id.

g. 12 CFR pt. 330.

h. Press Release, US Department of the Treasury, Treasury Dep't releases details on public private partnership investment program (Mar. 23, 2009), http://www.treasury.gov/press-center/press-releases/Pages/tg65.aspx.

13 Insuring Money Market Funds

The possible need for insurance of money market mutual funds is of particular concern given the vulnerability of those funds, in particular, prime institutional funds, to contagious runs due to the money-like nature of their liabilities. Totaling $2.6 trillion in liabilities in the second quarter of 2015[1] compared to bank liabilities of $13.6 trillion,[2] money market funds are major buyers of short-term capital markets instruments including short-term Treasury debt, ABCP and secured repo, primarily those issued by global banks.[3] However, institutional prime funds make up a minority of this total, or around $910 billion.[4] In its 2010 report on money market fund reform, the President's Working Group on Financial Markets (PWG) suggested insurance as a reform option for money market funds.[5] Discussion of this option has largely laid moribund since that time due to the unclear case for its need, the complexity and cost of providing insurance, and a political environment hostile to any further support for "Wall Street."

At the outset, however, one must ask whether there is a current need for insurance. First, runs in the crisis were focused on prime institutional funds. Total prime funds now stand at approximately $1.4 trillion[6] compared to $2.18 trillion[7] before the crisis—they are shrinking in value. Additionally institutional prime funds—with assets of $910 billion in the fourth quarter of 2015[8]—are only a fraction of total prime funds. Institutional prime funds are expected to shrink even further after the SEC's requirement that these funds have a floating NAV comes into effect. Fidelity has already announced that it will move its investors in prime institutional funds into fixed NAV government funds where there is virtually no risk of failure.[9] The case could be made for insurance for retail prime funds even though they did not run in the crisis, because retail investors might run in a future one; perhaps the quick provision of the Treasury guarantee, only three days after the Reserve Primary Fund "broke the buck," explains why retail funds did not run.[10] In principle if we think there is a need for deposit insurance for retail deposits to avoid bank runs, one would think one needed the same insurance for retail money market fund investments. One might also argue that the floating NAV and authorization of redemption fees and gates will stop contagion in money market funds—but this is not well founded, as we discuss in part IV. The centrality of money market funds to modern financial intermediation and the powerful influence that investor confidence in the integrity of MMF investments exerts on the stability of financial markets was displayed during the financial crisis of 2007 to 2009, when serious runs on money market funds impaired the orderly operation of the commercial paper markets and propelled contagious knock-on runs up the chain of intermediation. Whatever risk does remain of runs in the money market funds post-crisis might be reduced by insurance. Birdthistle (2010) suggests that, alongside other reforms, MMF insurance organized privately or publicly would help to offset this risk.[11] Private insurance might be impractical, however, because, owing to contagion, loss-causing events are unlikely to be small, isolated occurrences that insurers can comfortably manage. Instead, in the event that one fund breaks the buck, contagion-induced outflows might cause countless other funds to do so, leading to losses that are too large for insurers to bear.[12] Given the potentially extreme losses that private insurers could face, some kind of public insurance may be a more feasible option, at least for the tail risk of large losses.

However, there are serious countervailing arguments against providing any insurance to money market funds. For example, ICI contends that the size and complexity of contemporary MMF portfolios would make a comprehensive insurance system impracticable, drive outflows from depository banking, and create moral hazard.[13] In the ICI's view, providing federal insurance to MMF investments would siphon cash from traditional bank deposits, causing "disintermediation [and] significant disruption to the banking system."[14] Capping the guarantee, as in the depository insurance context, would leave room for runs by investors with uninsured exposures in excess of the cap.[15] On the other hand, exempting money market funds from explicit insurance, as they are today, may encourage investors to shift short-term funding from deposits into money market funds because those investments will continue to benefit from an implied public guarantee (as we saw in the crisis) without internalizing its costs. And clearly industry would prefer an implicit guarantee that they need not pay for since any explicit insurance fees would be passed onto investors. The 2010 PWG report noted several critical issues that would need to be addressed about the provision of insurance to MMFs.[16] These issues included moral hazard concerns, the dramatic expansion of the role of regulators with limited bandwidth, and insurance pricing difficulties.[17]

Considering the issues regarding pure private or pure public insurance, MMF insurance could be provided by a hybrid system that combines private insurance with a public backstop. This approach, also discussed by the ICI, could entail three levels of loss absorption.[18] For example, the MMF would be responsible for losses on the first 0.5 percent of fund assets, while a private insurer covers the next 2.5 percent. The public backstop would kick in after losses exceed 3 percent of fund assets, hence limiting government exposure to extremely high losses and capping potential losses to private insurers. Such a system of government support would resemble the federal backstop created by the Terrorism Risk Insurance Act ("TRIA"), which provides public reinsurance coverage to insurance companies facing claims related to declared acts of terrorism. While private insurance companies may have concern about heightened federal regulation (insurance companies are primarily state regulated) under such a hybrid system, the TRIA model suggests additional regulatory burdens may not be a necessary component. TRIA explicitly preserves the jurisdiction and regulatory authority of the States with only minor exceptions.[19] While an original version of the bill in the House of Representatives included a provision to impose increased capital requirements through tax deductions, ultimately this provision was removed from the final TRIA legislation.[20] However, despite the potential for a hybrid system modeled after TRIA, insurance companies may not have the capacity or desire to allocate sufficient capital for the private portion, even with the capped exposure.[21]

Another strand of criticism urges that insurance of money market funds would confront traditional depository banking institutions with burdensome competition. Since MMF portfolios contain generally high-quality, liquid, readily marketable securities, insurance premiums charged to MMF institutions would presumably be lower than the rates applied to conventional banks, which often transform deposits into longer term, illiquid, and thus riskier loans. Insured MMF instruments would then pass through a portion of this cost advantage to investors in the form of higher yields relative to traditional deposits, encouraging customers to migrate out from depository banking institutions into lower cost (but equally secure) MMF shares. This could decrease bank lending in favor of more direct finance through the markets in which the money market funds invest. Indeed the PWG notes, "Limits on insurance coverage (perhaps similar to those for deposit insurance) would be needed to avoid giving money market funds an advantage over banks."[22] Indeed this is a fundamental problem—having caps on deposit insurance with no caps on MMF account insurance. One could solve this problem by capping MMF insurance levels or providing unlimited insurance to bank deposits. We would tend to favor the first alternative recognizing that insurance is only part of the answer to contagion. Given a strong lender of last resort, partial insurance should be sufficient.

Despite the potential competitive advantage that liability insurance might confer upon the money market industry, many in the industry continue to oppose it, believing that it would represent the first step toward full capital-based regulation of the money market funds.[23] For example, Hanson, Sharfstein, and Sunderam (2014) have proposed adopting money market fund capital requirements as a way to mitigate run risks.[24] It is hard to see, however, why capital regulation would necessarily follow from insurance. Money market funds will not become insolvent like banks—their assets are more liquid and less risky—and thus do not really require capital. At most, liabilities may not be worth par. The purpose of insurance for money market funds is only to prevent runs not to insure solvency.

Recent consideration of the designation of asset management companies as SIFIs,[25] which would be regulated by the Fed and be subject to enhanced supervision and capital requirements, is clearly not the answer. First, it is hard to see why asset management companies themselves pose any systemic risk or how the designation of asset management companies could prevent runs on the money market funds they manage. Second, the risk of runs on money market funds cannot be countered by SIFI designation of particular funds, if there is a problem it is one that is industry wide. A 2013 report by the Office of Financial Research ("OFR") suggests that operational or risk-management failures at a particular asset management firm (including valuation problems, fraud, or even reputational damage[26] could potentially trigger a run on *that firm's funds*. Whatever the likelihood of such an event, the OFR fails to demonstrate the transmission mechanism whereby the idiosyncratic failure of a single fund or manager could spill over into the broader market.

The true competitive impact of expanded insurance on the banking and money market industries requires more detailed study of the appropriate cost and pricing of insurance, before any firm conclusions can be drawn. Given all of the difficulties of extending an insurance regime to money market funds, a more practical approach might be to make clear funds are eligible for lender-of-last-resort support either directly or indirectly through the banks. Liquidity support may be sufficient by itself to stop runs.

Conclusion to Part III

Contagion is an extremely serious problem that has endangered our financial system, economy, and, ultimately, our polity in the crisis. Before the Federal Reserve and FDIC were created to contain financial crises, contagion wreaked havoc on the US economy. For example, the panic of 1893 and the panic of 1907 both resulted in economic output reductions of over 15 percent.[27] Contagion during the most recent crisis was successfully halted by a combination of the traditional remedies, LLR (as extended to nonbanks), and deposit insurance. But in the aftermath of the crisis, in an anti-Wall Street and bailout frenzy, these powers were significantly curtailed. The Federal Reserve is now a weaker LLR, as can be seen in a comparison with its peer central banks. Calls for additional weakening of the Federal Reserve's power continue from both political parties.[28] According to Federal Reserve Vice Chair Stanley Fischer, such restrictions are "a very high price" to pay for hypothetical concerns about moral hazard.[29] We need to not only restore the Fed powers taken away by Dodd–Frank, we need to strengthen the Fed's power so its strength as lender of last resort will insure its powers may never have to be used.

Given the increased presence of short-term liabilities outside the banking system, we must also consider expanding insurance to deal with the increasing risk of runs outside the banking system. But the scope and pricing of such insurance pose great difficulty. It may be the case that in the future we may have to rely even more heavily on the LLR power to nonbanks, without insurance and guarantees, to stop contagion.

IV Ex ante Policies to Avoid Contagion: Capital, Liquidity, Resolution, Money Market Mutual Fund Reform, and Limits on Short-Term Funding

Following the crisis, three strategies have been deployed to make the financial system safer from systemic risk: (1) capital requirements designed to enable banks to incur losses without failing; (2) "private" bank liquidity requirements designed to ensure that banks have sufficient high-quality assets that can be sold or pledged as collateral to meet sudden withdrawals, allowing institutions to survive without public liquidity support; and (3) resolution procedures that impose losses on the debt and equity holders of financial holding companies without impacting the short-term creditors of their banks or other operating subsidiaries like broker-dealers. Some claim these policies alone or in combination will sufficiently insulate the financial system from contagion ex ante so as to obviate the need for a strong LLR and guarantee system. As developed below, I disagree and have called this the two wings and a prayer approach, the resolution being the prayer. While special policies, as we have already discussed, have been developed to avoid runs on money market funds, these policies will not achieve this objective. The problem with these policies is that they are so internally flawed that they are unlikely to achieve their own defined objectives, and even if they did, could not work well enough to stop contagion. Furthermore liquidity provision in the United States has suffered as a result of Dodd–Frank: public provision of liquidity has been limited by the restrictions on the Fed, while private provision of liquidity has also been limited through the combination of the new leverage ratio requirements, the liquidity coverage ratio and the Volcker rule.

That said, this part will look at another approach to stopping contagion, one that has been subject to much discussion but is not close to being adopted—at least in any direct form—to sharply reduce the amount of short-term funding in the financial system as a whole.

Indeed the best that any or all of these policies can do is to reduce the probability of contagion ex ante. Given the destructive nature of contagion, however, we will still need ex post responses, lender of last resort, and guarantees.

14 Capital Requirements: Basel III Framework

Capital requirements may reduce the chance of a financial institution's failure—in theory, the more capital that an institution has, the better it may withstand a run. While capital requirements do serve a necessary function vis-à-vis certain exogenous correlation risks affecting the industry generally, contagious runs are likely to overwhelm any plausible capital requirement, due to the staggering losses that inevitably follow from asset fire sales. Indeed capital requirements at any plausible level will be insufficient to prevent contagion, as it is unlikely that short-term debt-holders even take an institution's solvency into account (which in any event will be difficult for them to determine) during a run—better safe than sorry. Further, and crucially, capital requirements only apply to banking organizations and a few specific nonbanks (e.g., the three nonbank SIFIs, for which the requirements have not yet been determined). So they cannot stop contagion in the nonbanking sector, an important feature of the 2008 crisis. Capital requirements may even increase contagion risk in the nonbank sector as they force activities with high capital requirements out of banks into the nonbank sector.

Government-imposed capital requirements are generally thought necessary to mitigate the ex ante effects of regulatory safety nets, particularly deposit insurance, on banks' risk taking and leverage. A significant unintended effect of deposit insurance is to transform deposits from "*de jure* overnight debt financing," which imposes a high degree of market credit discipline, into "*de facto* patient debt financing," which is much less sensitive to the bank's riskiness.[1] As a result the cost of short-term bank debt from deposits is relatively insensitive to the bank's leverage even as this leverage increases. While banks clearly have an incentive to pile on this relatively "cheap" debt, the cost of the bank's increased risk of default is borne by the deposit insurance fund, effectively allowing banks to extract rent from the insurer. The imposition of capital requirements stems this moral hazard based on the proposition that "capital reduces incentives for incurring risks."[2] Another justification for government-imposed capital requirements is the belief that "capital serves as a buffer against unexpected losses."[3] Unexpected losses and consequent deleveraging can result in fire sales, causing negative knock-on effects on otherwise healthy banks that hold the same or similar assets.[4] Capital requirements potentially mitigate these negative externalities, which can arise regardless of deposit insurance or even the presumption of public bailouts. A third justification for capital requirements is that "a capital requirement provides the supervisor with room for intervention before the bank becomes insolvent."[5] Even if capital requirements could achieve these objectives, they cannot eliminate, or even significantly reduce, the risk of contagion. They are no substitute for strong weapons to fight contagion.

14.1 Higher Basel III Capital Requirements

Following the financial crisis, the Basel Committee on Banking Supervision, the international body entrusted since 1988 with bank capital requirements, issued a reform proposal for capital regulation, entitled "Basel III," as part of a series of initiatives sponsored by the Group of 20 ("G20") nations.[6] US regulators issued a notice of proposed rulemaking in June 2012 implementing key provisions of Basel III, which was adopted in a final rulemaking in July 2, 2013.[7] The centerpiece of Basel III is a series of amendments to the capital adequacy standards embodied in the worldwide framework for capital regulation created by Basel I and extensively revised and expanded under Basel II.[8] These amendments specify three broad revisions to the Basel I and II architecture: (1) increases in minimum mandatory bank capital requirements, (2) new measures to control countercyclicality in capital regulation, and (3) new restrictions on what instruments qualify as capital and adjustments to risk-weightings. Besides proposing the Basel III amendments, the Basel Committee has expanded the stress testing requirements established under Basel II.

Basel III establishes minimum capital ratios for different definitions of capital, set forth in tabular form in table 14.1. A new requirement for a minimum common equity (almost equivalent to tangible equity) provides for a capital ratio expressed as a percentage of risk-weighted assets (RWA). It mandates an increase from 2 percent to a base level of 4.5 percent by 2015.[9] Basel III further provides for a cumulative increase

Table 14.1
Basel III capital requirements provisional phase-in schedule

Phase-in year	Basel II current	2013	2015	2017	January 1, 2019
Common equity (CET1)[a]	2.00%	3.50%	4.50%	4.50%	4.50%
Common equity capital	—	0.00%	0.00%	1.25%	2.50%
Add: Capital conservation buffer	2.00%	3.50%	4.50%	5.75%	7.00%
Common equity + buffer					9.50%
Including maximum 2.5% countercyclicality buffer					
Tier I and total capital					
Minimum tier I capital	4.00%	4.50%	6.00%	6.00%	6.00%
Add: capital conservation buffer	-	0.00%	0.00%	1.25%	2.50%
Tier I capital + buffer	4.00%	4.50%	6.00%	7.25%	8.50%
Minimum total capital	8.00%	8.00%	8.00%	8.00%	8.00%
Add: capital conservation buffer	-	0.00%	0.00%	1.25%	2.50%
Total capital + buffer	8.00%	8.00%	8.00%	9.25%	10.50%
Including maximum 2.5% countercyclicality buffer					13.00%

Note: Press Release, Minimum Capital Standards, *supra* note 1160, at 7.

a. CET1 is common equity tier I capital. http://www.bis.org/publ/bcbs198.pdf at 5.

of 2 percent in minimum tier I capital (the old Basel I definition of capital), raising the minimum tier I ratio from 4 percent currently to 6 percent by the start of 2015. Minimum tier II capital (again an old Basel I measure containing weaker elements of capital) will be reduced from a minimum of 4 to 2 percent of RWA, thus providing that total tier I plus tier II capital ratio stay at its present 8 percent level—this is expressed as minimum total capital in table 14.1. In addition to imposing higher "basic" equity and tier I capital ratios, Basel III requires financial institutions to institute a supplementary common equity capital "conservation buffer" equivalent to an additional 2.5 percent of RWA, to both measures of capital, to be fully implemented by the start of 2019.[10] Thus, in total, the minimum common equity capital requirement imposed under Basel III at the conclusion of the phase-in period will amount to 7 percent of RWA, inclusive of the capital conservation buffer (4.5 percent plus 2.5 percent).[11] Once phase-in of the regime is completed by the end of 2018, minimum tier I capital and total capital under Basel III will amount to 8.5 percent (6 percent plus 2.5 percent) and total capital, tier I = tier II to 10.5 percent (8 percent plus 2.5 percent) of RWA.

Basel III also prescribes a new discretionary "countercyclical buffer" ranging from 0 percent to a maximum 2.5 percent of common equity (or "fully loss absorbing" equivalents; i.e., tier I capital) for banks located in countries where "excess credit growth ... is resulting in a systemwide buildup of risk."[12] It ties the countercyclical buffer to supervisory discretion, prescribing it for use in overheated credit markets that promote rising asset values with an accompanying pro-cyclical increase in bank leverage. The decision to implement this buffer and the assessment of its magnitude would be made by a designated national authority identified by the member jurisdiction.[13] Both the countercyclical and conservation buffers are analogous to forms of loan loss reserves intended to be drawn down to absorb unanticipated credit losses.[14]

These basic capital requirements will apply to all banks in the United States, except those banks with less than $500 million in consolidated assets and certain savings and loan companies.[15] In July 2011, the Basel Committee released a consultative document outlining a proposed methodology for determining which banks were systemically important, called "G-SIBs."[16] In November 2013, the FSB released an updated list of twenty-nine banks designated as G-SIBs, which included eight US banks and replaced four of the original G-SIBs with four new banks.[17] In November 2014, the FSB released an updated list, which contained the same institutions as the 2013 list and added one more bank, bringing the total number of G-SIBs to 30.[18] Based primarily on cross-jurisdictional activity, size, connectedness, substitutability, and complexity, G-SIBs are thus required to hold an additional common equity buffer ranging from 1 percent to 2.5 percent of RWA.[19]

14.2   Surcharges for Globally Systemically Important US Banks

The Federal Reserve proposed in December 2014 to implement surcharges for its G-SIBs by proposing a somewhat different methodology than adopted by the FSB.[20] The proposed rule differs from the Basel requirements, as it includes reliance on wholesale funding in its calculation of the risk-based capital surcharge applied to G-SIBs. According to the proposed rule, the increased capital charge for reliance on wholesale funding would "help the resiliency of the firm against runs on its short-term wholesale funding," thereby reducing the risk of the firm's failure, and help internalize the cost of using wholesale funding."[21] The proposed rule specifically cites the systemic risk arising from reliance on wholesale funding, noting that under difficult market conditions, institutions may be forced to conduct fire sales of assets to meet the withdrawals of short-term creditors. The resulting contagion from these fire sales is the source of systemic risk.[22] Thus it is clear that the Fed sees capital as a key bulwark against contagion.

The proposed rule would double a G-SIB's capital surcharge as compared to the Basel Committee's approach.[23] Table 14.2 displays the Federal Reserve estimates, with effective capital surcharges projected between 1 and 4.5 percent for each G-SIB.[24] Method 1 is the Basel method and method II is the method proposed by the Fed. The total G-SIB capital surcharge for all eight banks will be $209.3 billion. This represents a capital surcharge increase of $94.6 billion as compared to the aggregate surcharge under the Basel standard.[25] A fundamental flaw with this rule, and with a recent Federal Reserve calibration of the G-SIB surcharge, is that each bases the surcharge on an interconnectedness analysis, increasing the surcharge for more interconnected entities.[26] As shown in this book, there is no empirical evidence that interconnectedness in its own right is a significant problem or that decreasing interconnectedness would reduce the risk of contagion.

Table 14.2
Estimated scores and surcharges

GSIB	Score 1	Score 2	Capital surcharge: method 1	Capital surcharge: method 2	Binding method	Effective capital surcharge
BofA	305	555	1.5	3.0	2	3.0
BoNY	157	189	1.0	1.0	Both	1.0
C	426	727	2.0	3.5	2	3.5
GS	247	526	1.5	2.5	2	2.5
JPM	485	846	2.5	4.5	2	4.5
MS	307	569	1.5	3.0	2	3.0
STT	148	171	1.0	1.0	Both	1.0
WFC	171	336	1.0	2.0	2	2.0

Note: Estimates of Buckingham Research Group.

14.3   Risk-Weighted Assets Approach (RWA)

The Basel approach is in large part based on requiring capital in relationship to the riskiness of assets, the RWA approach. This is a highly
problematic enterprise given the difficulties of actually weighting
assets for risks. Basel I was built around the so-called standardized
approach where the regulators specified risk-weights, an inherently
impossible task. Attempts to set prices for goods and services, a much
easier task than pricing risk, have generally failed in the past. Basel I
required more capital for unsecured loans to private borrowers (100
percent RWA) than it did for any residential mortgages, including
subprime (50 percent), and assigned the same zero risk-weight to all
OECD sovereign bonds, which included Greece as well as the United
States. Underweighting of some risks while overrating of others distorted capital allocation.[27]

Recognizing that standardized risk-weights did not work, Basel II
gave large sophisticated banking institutions the right to use models,
with certain parameters, to estimate different risks, market, credit, and
operational risks. But this grants banks a large amount of discretion to
use models that underestimate risk, thereby artificially bolstering
reported capital ratios. Basel has already substituted more standardized calculations for models with respect to resecuritization exposures
including CDOs of ABS.[28] And the Basel Committee is currently reex-
amining risk-weighting models as part of the Basel III process and may
seek to use standardized methodology to set RWA floors—models
could only increase but not decrease risk estimates.[29] But this just brings
back the problems of the standardized approach. The general point
here is that we should not have a lot of faith in the ability of capital
requirements to limit risk, let alone avoid contagion.

14.4   Leverage Ratio Approach

In addition to RWA capital requirements, Basel III provides for a non–
risk-weighted tier I capital leverage ratio, provisionally set at 3 percent
of total assets and subject to adjustment during the phase-in.[30] The
United States currently employs two leverage ratio concepts. The "generally applicable" leverage ratio is the ratio of a firm's tier I capital to
its total consolidated balance sheet assets (but not off-balance sheet
items).[31] Under the current US regime, all BHCs and insured depository
institutions ("IDIs") must maintain a minimum generally applicable

leverage ratio of 4 percent.[32] Furthermore IDIs that are subject to the advanced approaches risk-based capital rules ("advanced approaches" IDIs) must comply with a "supplementary" leverage ratio requirement under which they must maintain a generally applicable leverage ratio of 5 percent to be considered "well-capitalized" for purposes of prompt corrective action and financial services holding company status. The "supplementary" leverage ratio is the ratio of tier I capital (the old Basel definition) to total leverage exposure, comprising total consolidated balance sheet assets plus many off-balance sheet exposures, including derivatives positions.[33] US regulators have proposed that this supplementary leverage ratio for the largest US BHCs and their IDIs be 5 percent and 6 percent, respectively.[34]

The case for the use of a leverage ratio to set capital requirements is bolstered by the deficiencies of the RWA approach. Andrew G. Haldane, Executive Director of Financial Stability at the Bank of England, has stated that in a financial environment filled with uncertainty, Basel III's complex risk-weighting system for capital adequacy may be less optimal than a simpler one. He finds that in the period leading up to the recent financial crisis, simple leverage ratios had greater power in predicting the failure of large global banks than the more complex risk-weighted measures of the Basel approach. Haldane determines that a simple market-based leverage ratio outperforms the more complex Basel III tier I capital ratio by a factor of 10 to 1 as an indicator of bank solvency. In addition Basel III's increased reliance on internal risk models has led in Haldane's judgment to overly complex measures with thousands, if not millions, of parameters.[35] Calibration of these parameters will likely require decades of data collection. In terms of capital regulation, and in particular the Basel approach, less may be more.

Though intended "as a backstop to the risk-based measures,"[36] a leverage requirement that does not rely on RWA seems to run counter to the basic premise of the Basel initiative from its start in 1988 that capital adequacy should not be judged without considering the riskiness of the assets.[37] A leverage ratio requires precisely the same amount of capital for high- and low-risk assets. Effectively, the risk-weight assigned to all assets under a leverage ratio is 100 percent, regardless of the actual riskiness of the asset. As a result, if the regulatory cost of capital for a bank is the same for high- and low-risk assets, this may give bank management an incentive to increase return on equity by investing in high-risk assets with higher returns. Such incentives are inconsistent with prudent risk management and sound banking practice. In theory, this could be avoided to some extent by employing both RWA and non–RWA-based requirements together. Another consequence of a binding leverage ratio is that when the Federal Reserve begins to reduce the size of its balance sheet then banks will be less able to buy and hold Treasuries and mortgage-backed securities to offset the decreased Fed role in these markets.[38]

14.5   Tighter Definitions of Capital

While Basel III increases minimum capital requirements through the direct measures described above, it also effectively increases the amount of capital required by restricting the range of instruments eligible for inclusion in the calculation of tier I capital.[39] In particular, Basel III calls for eliminating certain elements from qualifying common equity tier I capital ("CET1"), to be phased in gradually through 2018.[40] These eliminations include certain deferred tax assets, mortgage servicing assets, and significant investments in the common shares of unconsolidated financial institutions.[41]

14.6   Stress Tests

Finally, the Basel Committee addressed the stress-testing requirements established under Basel II through expansion of the internal capital adequacy assessment process ("ICAAP").[42] In general, stress tests are an analysis of a bank's capital adequacy under varying adverse economic scenarios. Stress tests augment the Basel capital requirements by requiring financial institutions to plan for highly adverse events. Basel requires banks to have a comprehensive stress-testing program that aims to address the possibility of severe shocks and changes in market conditions.[43] US regulators issued a final rule in November 2011 requiring all US-domiciled BHCs with consolidated assets of $50 billion or more to submit to an annual Comprehensive Capital Analysis and Review ("CCAR").[44] Each year, covered BHCs must develop and submit a three-year capital plan to the Federal Reserve. The Federal Reserve will then carry out a supervisory stress test based on a predetermined stress scenario that projects earnings, and losses. The Federal Reserve uses its own nondisclosed model to calculate losses. Based on the resulting determination of the adequacy of each firm's capital plan, the BHC may be required to forego capital distributions to shareholders in the form of dividends or share buybacks, or raise additional capital.[45] Some believe that US stress tests rather than the Basel RWA or leverage requirements are the binding constraint on the amount of capital banking organizations must hold, given the amount of capital that must make up for losses driven by the adverse scenarios.

Stress tests have their own methodological problems. First, the extreme adverse scenarios are very extreme. In the 2014 CCAR, projecting economic conditions over nine quarters, from Q4 2013 to Q4 2015, the scenario made the following assumptions (compared to what really happened in parentheses): real GDP decline of 4.75 percent (increased 2.4 percent), unemployment rate 11.5 percent (5.6 percent), deflation 1 percent (inflation 0.8 percent), equity prices fall 50 percent (11.4 percent increase, all time high), house prices fall 25 percent (4.6 percent gain).[46] Second, the Fed's model to analyze bank losses is a black box—we do not know what it is, so we cannot judge if it is any good. The Fed has argued that it if revealed its model, it would be gamed by the banks. Even if this is true, the fact remains that we have no way of judging the quality of the model.

In the context of contagion concerns, the stress test design really falls short. CCAR does not consider the possibility of runs by short-term creditors in the adverse scenarios.[47] The Office of Financial Research has pointed to two primary limitations of the current stress test designs: (1) a lack of fire-sale or run considerations and (2) a failure to capture potential feedback effects of external shocks, such as the potential reduction of credit availability to the firm resulting from its losses.[48] If capital requirements were actually stressed by runs, they would be sorely wanting, due to fire sales, and we would realize that capital requirements are a false palliative for anti-contagion weapons.

14.7   Calls for Even Higher Levels of Capital

The Basel III framework has been criticized by some for still not providing for enough capital.[49] In the United States, the Federal Reserve has already increased the capital requirement for US banks beyond the Basel requirement.[50] But these new capital requirements cannot prevent or provide an adequate buffer against contagion. During the crisis of 2008, most of the largest banks had a regulatory capital ratio that exceeds the new Basel III minimum ratio. Leading up to the financial crisis, in 2007, the average regulatory capital ratio for the top 20 US banks was 11.7 percent, which exceeded the then existing regulatory

Table 14.3
Large US bank capital ratios in 2007

Bank holding company	Tangible common equity to RWA	Tier I common equity to RWA
JPMorgan Chase	6.83	7.00
Bank of America	4.50	4.59
Citigroup	4.63	4.26
Wells Fargo	6.90	7.05
Bank of New York Mellon	5.52	15.24
Washington Mutual	5.51	5.37
Wachovia	4.95	4.69
State Street	7.46	6.50

minimums by 50 percent.[51] And as table 14.3 indicates, their ratio of tier I common equity to risk-weighted assets was higher than the new Basel III requirement of 4.5 percent and many had higher than the 7 percent requirement that includes the 2.5 percent buffer.[52]

By this time the major US investment banks had also implemented Basel II, pursuant to regulation by the SEC.[53] Yet, despite being effectively compliant under the Basel II framework before the financial crisis, these institutions still did not hold enough capital to survive the crisis without public support.

In fact the 2009 IMF Global Financial Stability Report found that risk-weighted capital adequacy ratios were unable to identify which institutions would require government assistance, even finding that capital ratios were higher on average for commercial banks needing intervention.[54] Furthermore bank default risk as measured by CDS spreads did not correlate meaningfully with regulatory capital ratios during the crisis, feeding "doubts ... in relation to the efficacy of the capital index tier I ratio as a safeguard against the risk of future default."[55] The fact that new minimum Basel III capital requirements, which were met by large banks during the crisis, did not capitalize US financial institutions sufficiently to avoid public support in the crisis, undercuts expectations for the framework's future performance.

A bill proposed in the US Senate in 2013 by Senators Sherrod Brown and David Vitter would substantially increase capital requirements for large banks and discard risk-weights in favor of an exclusive leverage requirement.[56] Under this proposal, regional banks would be required to hold 8 percent equity capital to total assets, while the largest banks would have a 15 percent requirement.[57] Regulators would be given the authority to increase these capital requirements further on a case-by-case basis as institutions grow larger.[58] However, even these increased levels of bank capital are not sufficient to have a meaningful effect in reducing the risk of contagion. The Brown–Vitter proposal also, incidentally, would prohibit the Federal Reserve and other banking regulators from providing discount window lending, short-term credit insurance, and other federal support programs to nonbank financial institutions.[59] Another bill passed by the House, the FORM Act, as previously discussed, would further restrict but not prohibit the Federal Reserve's ability to lend to nonbanks.[60] If either bill were implemented, it would dramatically *increase* the risk of contagion because short-term creditors would be much more inclined to run in the absence of any lender-of-last-resort support.[61]

One paper authored by economists at the Bank of England in 2011 called for bank equity capital requirements of between 16 percent and 20 percent of RWA.[62] A government-appointed commission of noted policy makers in Switzerland proposed heightened capital requirements for UBS AG and Credit Suisse as an additional prophylactic measure for the Swiss economy, under which both banks would be required to hold total capital of 19 percent and be subject to a 10 percent common equity minimum due to their designation as "too big to fail" (TBTF).[63] This "too-big-to-fail" legislation incorporating the so-called Swiss finish received final approval from both houses of the Swiss parliament in September 2011[64] and became effective on March 1, 2012, although implementation will be phased in through January 1, 2019.[65] Again, these higher capital requirements are still too low to have a meaningful impact on the probability of avoiding contagion.

14.8 Economic Impact of Capital Requirements

The Basel III requirements also come with high and uncertain costs to the real economy. One study estimates that Dodd–Frank and Basel III regulations would collectively lead to 20 percent fewer loans and result in 600,000 fewer home sales, ultimately costing one million housing starts and 3.9 million fewer jobs.[66] Although the precise economic impact on GDP is uncertain, several organizations have commissioned studies to make estimates. Studies have been published by the Macroeconomic Assessment Group ("MAG"), established by the Basel Committee, along with the FSB; the Institute of International Finance; the

IMF; the Organization for Economic Co-operation and Development; the Government Accountability Office ("GAO"); and a panel including staff from the FRBNY, Bank of Italy, BIS, ECB, European Commission, and IMF.[67] All of the studies predict that Basel III will have a negative impact on gross domestic product. Moreover the Institute of International Finance (IIF), an industry group, estimates that the various Basel III requirements (excluding the leverage ratio) will reduce the real GDP of the United States, the euro area, the United Kingdom, Switzerland, and Japan by about 3.2 percent, leading to 7.5 million fewer jobs being created by 2015.[68] In addition the FSB, in collaboration with the IMF and World Bank, has published a study that identified unintended consequences of regulatory reforms to emerging market and developing economies, particularly as it pertains to trade finance and restrained international capital flows.[69] Although mostly qualitative in nature, the analysis highlights the widespread economic impact of current regulatory reform measures.

But these studies fail to incorporate the dynamic impact that bank capital requirements will no doubt have in shifting risky activity, financed by short-term funding, to the nonbanking (i.e., "shadow banking") sector, which is subject to no or very low capital requirements. Thus the true economic cost of these new capital requirements, which could mean more risk to the economy from nonbank failures and contagion, is not taken into account.

14.9   Role of Markets in Setting Capital Levels

One solution to improving the determination of capital adequacy is to assign a larger role to the judgment to markets. The CCMR has conducted a study on capital regulation that examines a balanced approach to enhancing private market discipline, through better disclosure and requirements for capital instruments that cannot be bailed out, while strengthening the role of regulators.[70] A regulatory approach recognizing the dual roles of government and the private market in determining adequate capital might result in a stronger and safer financial system than can be achieved through public regulation alone. In general, the private market is much more effective and efficient at pricing risk than regulators, so policymakers should pursue a market-based approach that enhances the market discipline of banks, relying on the market to dictate optimal levels of capital. Market signals, such as debt yields or

CDS prices, may also better inform a regulator of capital deficiencies than strict adherence to government-imposed requirements.

The heaviest consideration weighing against reliance on capital requirements to control contagion, however, is that while capital *cushions* short-term creditors against having to absorb losses, perhaps deterring the impulse to run, it does not *foreclose* the risk of suffering impairment altogether. As long as a financial institution is reliant on short-term funds, in any significant amount, to support long-term investment, short-term creditors who supply those funds are exposed to potential losses incurred through fire sales. In a crisis, the rational option will be to run. When that happens, capital requirements can certainly lower public costs by ensuring that deeper reserves of private funding and capital are available to the distressed institution. What they cannot do is prevent the run in the first place, or stop it from becoming generalized to the financial system.

If the problems posed by contagion are solved through more effective means, then individual banks can be allowed to fail as a result of bank mismanagement without concerns that their failure will spread to other banks. Having effective anti-contagion weapons is just as important in dealing with the too-big-to fail problem as effective resolution procedures.

Capital will not stop contagion but it is still vitally important. A correlated negative shock causes the failure of many large financial institutions at the same time. This problem cannot be addressed by a lender of last resort because insolvent banks should not be eligible for such lending absent adequate collateral. Despite the limitations of capital requirements in addressing contagion, increased capital may provide a level of protection against correlation risk, since stronger banks can better withstand common external shocks, and ultimately limit the need for public injection of capital.

15 Liquidity Requirements

Liquidity is the second wing of regulatory reform, and one more aimed at preventing contagion than capital requirements. Minimum "private" liquidity requirements (as distinct from "public" liquidity supplied by the Fed) are supposed to assure banks' uninterrupted holding of a pool of high-quality liquid assets that can be sold (or pledged as collateral) to accommodate a sudden surge of withdrawals by depositors and other short-term debt holders during a serious crisis involving contagion.[1] In principle, maintaining sufficient high-quality assets should help financial institutions to withstand periodic instability created by the dependency on short-term funds. However, liquidity requirements are curiously in conflict with the Fed's monetary policy efforts, insofar that quantitative easing is intended to get financial institutions to hold riskier assets to raise interest rates, whereas liquidity rules require banks to hold assets with low rates of interest reflecting their liquidity.

Initially, liquidity requirements seem to represent a more promising regulatory approach to contagion than capital requirements, since contagion originates in and propagates through runs that are fundamentally liquidity driven. Four primary objections to over reliance on private liquidity requirements should be considered.

First, like capital requirements, the liquidity proposals discussed below (with the exception of redemption restrictions and liquidity requirements for money market funds discussed later in this part) apply only to depository institutions, for short banks. In modern financial panics, as in 2008, contagion spread beyond the traditional banking sector—a fundamental point that is made throughout this book.

Second, the stock of high-quality assets that banks can hold to meet private liquidity requirements is limited by nature. Basel's proposal, for instance, would require banks to retain sufficient liquid assets to match net cash outflows over 30 days.[2] However, it is quite possible that persistent disruption to short-term borrowing markets leading to sustained investor outflows stretching over a longer period could eventually overrun even the strongest portfolio of liquid assets, making it difficult to liquidate even "liquid" assets and forcing financial institutions into liquidating long-term assets to meet incremental redemptions. Short-term creditors of a financial institution subject to such liquidity requirements would thus still have an incentive to exit sooner, while that portfolio was still intact, rather than later, after waves of outflow have exhausted it.

Third, holding assets suited to meeting the purposes of liquidity requirements entails costs to financial institutions and to the economy, since every dollar of capital allocated to low-yielding, liquid, short-term securities is unavailable to finance longer term lending to borrowers. This theoretically lowers the amount of new credit that financial institutions can create and raises the overall cost of capital to the real economy. Further, when combined with the leverage requirement, banks will tend to hold only the minimum amount of liquidity required by regulation. Higher levels of safe assets, with low returns, will be limited by the capping effect of a leverage ratio.

Fourth, securing emergency liquidity to the financial system through limited private liquidity is less efficient than traditional use of central bank lender-of-last-resort authority to provide unlimited liquidity to solvent institutions in emergencies. Indeed private liquidity requirements may even undermine the efficacy of the lender-of-last-resort system if, by selling privately held high-quality liquid assets to meet liquidity needs (before going to the lender of last resort), banks deplete the store of collateral available for pledging to the government in exchange for central bank loans.

For these reasons, private liquidity requirements are both under-inclusive and over-inclusive: under-inclusive because they provide coverage that is limited in amount, do not apply to nonbank financial institutions, and will not always forestall runs by short-term creditors; over-inclusive because they may unnecessarily raise the cost of real economic activities that depend on the intermediation of financial institutions but do not create systemic risk. We now turn to the details of the new liquidity requirements.

15.1 Basel Liquidity Requirements

The Basel Committee has adopted a new liquidity standard for phase-in at the start of 2015, to be completed by 2019.[3] Basel's liquidity metric, known as the liquidity coverage ratio ("LCR"), requires banks to hold unencumbered high-quality assets sufficient to meet all outstanding 30-day-or-fewer liabilities.[4] Financial institutions that achieve compliant LCRs must hold a "stock of high-quality assets" equal to 100 percent or more of their net cash outflows over a 30-day period.[5] Maintaining a 100 percent LCR in principle is intended by Basel to enable an institution to use the sale of its own liquid assets to satisfy all potential net outflows during a full calendar month without impairing its capital by selling longer term assets at discounted prices, giving managers and regulators breathing room to devise a comprehensive response to a crisis or to wind down an institution, when necessary.[6]

Qualifying "high-quality assets" include liquid assets that can immediately be converted to cash equal to their carrying values.[7] Among other restricting criteria, qualifying assets must be unencumbered securities with low credit- and market-risk and performance that is not correlated to riskier asset classes. Further they must be exchange-listed, trade in active and liquid markets, and easily be susceptible of valuation.[8] Examples of high-quality assets satisfying Basel's multifactor standard are cash, central bank reserves, marketable securities with 0 percent Basel II risk-weightings, and domestic currency government debt.[9] Contractual committed liquidity facilities ("CLFs") provided by a central bank can also be included as high-quality liquid assets.[10] Originally the Basel Committee limited CLFs to jurisdictions that otherwise lacked sufficient liquid assets in the local currency, but it later expanded the permitted inclusion of CLFs more generally.[11] The Basel Committee has also released guidance for using market-based factors of liquidity that could cause regulators to drop certain assets from an otherwise "high-quality" classification (e.g., Greek debt).[12]

The effectiveness of the LCR at meeting demand for liquidity during a crisis depends on making an accurate regulatory judgment *ex ante* about the required quantity and quality of assets. This judgment involves significant guesswork about the severity of future crises and assumes that assets thought to be of high-quality today will remain so during a period of market dislocation. Likewise, to be effective, the LCR must accurately estimate the 30-day net cash outflow that would arise from a "combined idiosyncratic and market-wide shock."[13] Regulators have promulgated minimum 30-day runoff rates for various liability classes, but have provided little empirical evidence to support these predictions.[14] To some extent, these runoff rates are based on what happened in 2008, but the past is not always prologue.

Basel has also proposed a longer term metric called the net stable funding ratio ("NSFR") designed to secure institutions with enough liquidity support for one year, to be implemented by January 2018.[15] The components of "stable funding"[16] are capital, preferred stock, other liabilities with maturities of more than one year, plus "stable" deposits.[17] All components are discounted by weightings reflective of their relative stability.[18] One hundred percent NSFR-compliant institutions must maintain stable funding levels in excess of total assets (both on- and off-balance sheet), weighted according to liquidity and resilience in a period of stress.[19] In October 2014, the Basel Committee released its final NSFR standards.[20] The Basel Committee included three additional requirements under the final NSFR: interbank loans with residual maturities of under six months must be backed by at least 10 percent of their value in "stable funding"; the initial margin on any derivative contract must be backed by 85 percent "stable funding"; and the ability to offset derivative assets by derivative liabilities was reduced.[21] Under the NSFR, regulators are granted discretion in determining whether asset and liability items are sufficiently interdependent to be viewed as NSFR-neutral.[22]

Beyond LCR and NSFR, the Basel III proposal introduces other measurements oriented at facilitating supervisory monitoring of institution liquidity. Their focus is on maturity mismatching, wholesale funding dependency, and amount of available unencumbered assets. Finally, Basel endorses market-based liquidity monitoring using equity prices and CDS spreads.[23] Like the LCR, the NSFR requires regulators to make accurate forecasts about the stability of funding and the quality and liquidity of a bank's assets. It seems less justified than the NCR, since it is hard to imagine a year-long liquidity crisis for a bank.

15.2   US Implementation of Basel Liquidity Requirements

The US implementation of the Basel III LCR was proposed by regulators in November 2013, and was finalized in October 2014.[24] The US LCR applies to (1) large, internationally active banking organizations, (2) nonbank SIFIs regulated by the Federal Reserve that do not engage in substantial insurance activities, and (3) consolidated subsidiary depository institutions with total assets of greater than $10 billion.[25]

The US LCR requires all covered organizations to maintain a minimum LCR of 100 percent, calculated by dividing a bank's high-quality liquid assets by its total net cash outflow amount over a 30-day period.[26] It is substantially more severe than the Basel proposal. One of the most significant differences between the US LCR and the Basel III LCR lies in the assumed runoff rates for short-term creditors without a specific maturity date, including uninsured retail and wholesale depositors, the primary source of short-term funding for covered organizations.[27] The US LCR assumes that these short-term creditors would withdraw their funding immediately on day 1 (essentially, a single day stress scenario), whereas the Basel III LCR implicitly assumes that these funds are withdrawn at a constant rate through day 30.[28] The US LCR calculates the total net cash outflow amount based on the single day within a 30-day period with the highest amount of net cumulative outflows, while the Basel III LCR uses total cash outflows over a 30-day period.[29]

In order for an asset to qualify as a high-quality liquid asset under the Fed's rules, it must be liquid and readily marketable, a reliable source of funding in repurchase agreement or sales markets, and not an obligation of a financial company.[30] A standard stress scenario would assign specific outflow amounts to different categories of a bank's funding.[31] Importantly, during an idiosyncratic or systemic liquidity crisis, a covered organization would be permitted to convert its high-quality liquid assets into cash as necessary to meet withdrawals by short-term creditors, even if this required falling well below the minimum LCR.[32]

A Basel Committee Study assuming full implementation of the Basel III liquidity requirements as of December 31, 2013, found that for internationally active banks with over €3 billion in capital, the aggregate LCR shortfall at a minimum requirement of 100 percent is €353 billion, and is €158 billion at a minimum requirement of 60 percent.[33] The aggregate shortfall for the NSFR is €817 billion.[34] However, "the shortfalls in the LCR and the NSFR are not necessarily additive, as decreasing the shortfall in one standard may result in a similar decrease in the shortfall of the other standard, depending on the steps taken to decrease the shortfall."[35] The Basel III liquidity requirements, combined with a growing demand for safe collateral resulting from an increase in central clearing of derivatives,[36] will put upward pressure on the prices of liquid assets and cause further increases in funding costs. The liquidity requirements are likely to be expensive and may ultimately have more impact on bank lending activity than capital requirements.

Whatever the virtue of "private liquidity" it can never be a complete substitute for public liquidity through a strong LLR. Indeed it was the shortcoming of the private liquidity system of the clearinghouses in 1907 that led to the creation of the Fed as a public lender of last resort in 1913. Governor Tarullo has stated that while private liquidity can never be considered a complete substitute, it bolsters the stability of the financial system by giving the Fed a breathing room of 30 days to make a determination of whether to provide liquidity but this hero- ically assumes that private liquidity would not be exhausted much faster, if runoff rates exceed expectations.[37] Further any delay in lending to Bank X by the Fed will incentivize runs on other banks, which the Fed should seek to avoid. And, of course, there could be an immediate run on the shadow banking system that has no liquidity requirements. A recent Federal Reserve paper recognizes this problem by saying that only in the case of runs should the Fed act immediately. The paper thus acknowledges that private liquidity cannot be relied on in a run. Further, if the Fed were to wait 30 days to determine whether a run was taking place and discovered it was, the paper implicitly recognizes that this may be too late. Therefore the breathing space justification seems weak. Furthermore liquidity regulation may decrease lending between financial institutions, thus worsening a weak institution's options during a crisis. A recent study found that banks have reduced lending to financial institutions as a response to liquidity regulation, but not to nonfinancial institutions.[38] Critics of the LCR have also raised concerns that the rule locks up safe debt and increases more risky debt without any reduction of contagion risk.[39] William Dudley, President of the Federal Bank of New York, has suggested a willingness to address liquidity concerns through adjustments to regulation.[40]

The strongest argument for liquidity requirements is a political one, that bank liquidity requirements allow the Fed to say it will only rescue banks from contagion that have exhausted their own resources first. This is probably smart politics but bad policy insofar as the markets may believe it will in fact delay the Fed's response to a contagious run, thus causing the markets to run earlier and faster. Like the Dodd–Frank restrictions, it seems to put still another limit on the use of the Fed's power. In the end, private liquidity is not a substitute for public liquidity.[41]

16 Bank Resolution Procedures, Contingent Capital (CoCos), and Bail-Ins

If capital and liquidity are the wings to address contagion, better insolvency resolution procedures for banking organizations and other financial institutions are the prayer. Effective resolution procedures are primarily designed to address the TBTF problem by allowing banking organizations or other covered financial institutions to be resolved without public support. Those designing these procedures have recognized, however, that such resolutions must be conducted in a manner to avoid contagion. They seek to achieve this result by assuring all short-term creditors of subsidiaries that they will not lose any money, even if their institution goes into resolution, because resolution will only take place at the holding company or because all longer term creditors are subordinated to short-term creditors if resolution takes place within operating subsidiaries.

For contagion to be prevented by resolution, short-term creditors of an institution that may go into resolution must believe they have no risk of losing their money. If they do not believe this, then it is rational for them to run. Better safe than sorry. Moreover short-term creditors in other institutions, fearing resolution, will run as well. I believe that shortcomings in the design of the resolution procedures, as discussed below, will not provide such assurances. In any event, prudence dictates that we have strong measures in place if there is a run despite the resolution procedures. It is also important to realize that fear of initiating contagion, particularly if one has poor weapons to fight it, could deter use of resolution in the first place. And if that happens, the primary objective of better resolution procedures, avoiding TBTF, will not be achieved.

In this chapter we turn to the principal components of the new resolution system, CoCos and bail-ins.

16.1   Contingent Convertible Capital Instruments (CoCos)

The term "contingent capital" is the generic name given to a group of long-term hybrid debt instruments. The distinguishing characteristic of all contingent capital instruments is an embedded equity mandatory conversion provision, triggered automatically after the issuer's financial profile deteriorates below a defined threshold.[1] These instruments are thus designed to provide more capital when needed so as to avoid formal resolution. Contingent capital instruments incorporate long-term maturities that enhance the total loss-absorbing capital available to issuers, thus protecting all nonconvertible liabilities (including, indirectly, shorter term debt) against losses large enough to overwhelm common equity.[2] Like bail-in proposals, examined next, contingent capital instruments generally focus on the holding company level because generally only holding companies issue these instruments, not bank subsidiaries. Like bail-ins under the single point of entry (SPOE) approach, use of contingent capital at the holding company does not in and of itself recapitalize banking subsidiaries or other operating subsidiaries.

Since contingent capital is long-term debt,[3] it is arguably more economical to issue than equity given tax regimes permitting the deduction of interest on debt but not dividends on equity. Further, since contingent capital instruments convert automatically, they can absorb losses outside of a formal resolution process. In effect, they streamline loss absorption and internalization of costs beyond the common equity layer. For this reason, and owing to its substantive similarity to creditor bail-ins, contingent capital may be viewed as a form of resolution procedure rather than simply as an exotic variant of capital.

Analogous instruments predate the financial crisis in concept and practice. Reinsurance companies use contingent capital to manage risk from large, discrete loss exposures.[4] As one example, in 1997 LaSalle Re Holdings Ltd. issued $100 million of contingent capital structured as convertible preferred shares to cover "a major catastrophe or series of large catastrophes that cause[d] substantial losses" in the future.[5] The adoption of contingent capital by the banking industry is a more recent development that remains at a more conceptual stage.[6] Variations of contingent capital instruments customized for bank and nonbank financial institutions have, however, gained traction with some policy makers. Between 2009 and February 2015, $288 billion of CoCos were issued.[7] Significantly, $174 billion of these issuances occurred in 2014, demonstrating the growth of their popularity.[8] Chinese banks accounted for approximately one-third of these 2014 issuances, while European banks were responsible for slightly more than half of the amount.[9] As of April 2015, there have not yet been any United States issuances.[10]

US regulators and the Basel Committee have not permitted CoCos to satisfy capital requirements. Thus, in July 2011, the Basel Committee announced that the capital buffer for systemically important banks would be composed only of tier I common equity, rejecting the use of contingent capital to satisfy a SIFI surcharge.[11] Similarly the Federal Reserve's June 2013 final rules implementing Basel III in the United States require that the paid-in amount of any instrument be classified as equity under GAAP to qualify as tier I capital, which effectively prevents contingent convertible debt from qualifying prior to conversion.[12] Regulators have, however, acknowledged certain potential benefits of CoCos: FSOC determined that contingent convertible instruments can help financial institutions withstand losses at a cost cheaper than common equity[13] and Federal Reserve Board Governor Tarullo has stated that requirements for long-term convertible debt would "strengthen our domestic resolution mechanisms and be consistent with emerging international practice."[14]

With the so-called Swiss finish, Swiss policy makers have offered the most significant endorsement of contingent capital. Under the new Swiss regime, in addition to the Basel III tier I common ratio of 4.5 percent, the two systemically important Swiss banks are required to maintain an 8.5 percent capital conservation buffer, up to 3 percent of which may consist of contingent capital that converts to equity if tier I common falls below 7 percent of RWA ("high trigger CoCos").[15] The remaining 6 percent of RWA progressive surcharge may consist of contingent capital that converts when the tier I common ratio falls below 5 percent ("low trigger CoCos").[16]

Contingent capital is an attractive complement to common equity and nonconvertible long-term debt and offers several benefits. It minimizes the public externalities and market disruption of putting a SIFI through conservatorship or receivership.[17] Automating the restructuring motivates bondholders and equity holders to monitor risk-taking by issuers.[18] The current yield on contingent capital instruments serves as an objective leading indicator of the market's judgment of an issuer's financial strength. Contingent capital is cost-effective for issuers relative to permanent equity,[19] but more expensive than nonconvertible debt, supplying an *ex ante* source of market discipline.[20] The loss absorbency of contingent capital can shield short-term debt holders along with other creditors supplying credit not subject to conversion from impairment.[21] Finally, contingent capital has an established record of performance in the insurance industry. Nevertheless, two serious practical obstacles must be overcome before these potential benefits can be realized and before regulators will be willing to count these instruments as capital: (1) relative lack of investor demand and (2) design of an effective conversion trigger. In addition recent studies indicate that CoCo bonds may increase equity holders' risk taking.[22]

16.1.1 Demand for CoCos

Strong demand for contingent capital is essential to realizing the cost savings that these instruments offer relative to equity. Recent contingent convertible issuances show that investor demand is heavily dependent on the particular structure of the contingent capital instruments, while the structure itself generally hinges on the constraints imposed by regulators and ratings agencies.[23] Bert Bruggink, chief financial officer of Rabobank, reported ambivalence on the part of buyers about pricing the SCNs: "We met people who argued the pricing was completely wrong—overpriced—and others surprised we were even willing to pay a premium to our senior debt."[24] Similarly a disappointing UBS issuance in February 2012 shows that in some cases there is weak demand for the particular contingent convertible structures that banks are able to offer.[25]

Weak demand for contingent convertibles is partially explained by the fact that many current institutional investors participating in the market for nonconvertible subordinated debt instruments (classified as tier II debt under the existing Basel framework)[26] face statutory restrictions on owning common stock or convertible instruments.[27] Other investors might be reluctant to manage the tail-risk associated with conversion as a matter of investment policy.[28] Excluding these buyers from the marketplace could narrow the prospective investor base for contingent capital to pure fixed income funds and hedge funds with investment mandates that extend affirmatively to hybrid, convertible debt, and equity instruments.[29]

16.1.2 Conversion Triggers

One model, favored by the Basel Committee, assigns this decision to the discretion of the issuer's primary regulator. While the convertibility of the capital instruments is still subject to contract, the conditions triggering the convertibility are determined under the contract by regulators upon a finding that the issuer's financial condition is unsatisfactory, for example due to a negative stress-test result.[30] This flavor of a CoCo is really a bail-in, discussed below. A second model bases conversion on the adequacy of the issuer's capital ratios.[31] The Association for Financial Markets in Europe favors this model, and both the Lloyds and Rabaobank securities are patterned on it.[32] A third model employs market-based variables to determine when to convert,[33] such as an issuer's share price, credit spreads, or the CDS pricing on an issuer's long-term subordinated debt.[34] To ensure that a market-based trigger is activated only during a genuine market-wide downturn, some have suggested pairing any of these market measures of an issuer's individual riskiness with a secondary variable measuring overall market risk, for instance the level of an index of financial firms. Using an index-based component theoretically would help ensure that conversion of contingent capital instruments occurs only during a financial crisis, when all firms are faring poorly for systemic reasons, while restricting convertibility and leaving scope for resolutions through normal bankruptcy channels otherwise.

The market trigger model, unlike the regulatory- or some capital-based alternatives, is independent of regulatory discretion and observable in real time. Critics of a market trigger worry that it will expose conversion to arbitrary market volatility and possible manipulation by speculators[35] Risk of manipulation may be overstated, however. It is doubtful if even wide-scale manipulation by "speculators" or short-sellers could exercise enough influence on security prices to trigger a conversion event. This risk could easily be addressed, in any case, by adding an index-based conversion provision of the type described above, which would require a downturn in the performance of *all* of the financial institutions in the financial system before mandating conversion of any individual issuer's contingent capital.

Reliance on index-based triggering might, however, increase overall correlation risk among contingent capital issuers during a market-wide crisis. If a conversion event at one financial institution caused the securities prices of peer institutions to decline, for example, because investors become fearful of a more generalized crisis, this could inadvertently prompt conversion of contingent capital securities issued by other institutions. By linking the behavior of individual convertible instruments to the performance of financial institutions *other* than the issuer itself, an index trigger might introduce an additional source of correlation and connectedness, increasing systemic risk as a result.[36] Additionally both the index-based and the single-issuer market triggers, either separately or in conjunction, should incorporate a type of market variable that is impervious to the effects of market noise. If CDS prices, credit spreads, or share prices prove to be too easily distorted during a crisis, then use of a market trigger will have to be reevaluated. Indeed an FRBNY study has found that "trade frequency in single-name reference entities [is] relatively low."[37] This thin trading may suggest that CDS prices do not function as a high-quality proxy for the market's perception of a reference entity's likelihood of default and therefore might not provide a reliable conversion trigger.

Assuming these practical considerations may be resolved, contingent capital instruments may improve the existing framework for internalizing the costs of financial distress and might lessen the probability of failure by adding to the amount of capital on which financial institutions may draw. In this sense automatic resolution operating at the holding company level, may protect short-term creditors of banks and other operating subsidiaries, making contagious runs less likely. However, a conversion event might well intensify contagion as existing creditors and new potential investors might interpret the signal transmitted by the conversion of contingent capital into equity in one institution as a sign of fatal distress for their own institutions or for the financial system more generally.

Since contingent capital does not satisfy the systemic demand for liquidity created during a run, it can never serve as a useful tool for rescuing financial institutions affected by contagion. Proponents of contingent capital instruments who appreciate this limitation acknowledge the necessity of interim liquidity facilities, organized privately or in all likelihood by a public lender of last resort to steward issuers through a period of systemic crisis.[38]

16.2 Creditor Bail-ins by Regulators

Creditor bail-in transforms the basic loss absorbing functionality of contingent capital instruments into a more general and noncontractual method for restructuring a financial institution's liabilities without going through an extended resolution process. The bail-in procedure is generally patterned on a prepackaged restructuring that is intended to enable a struggling bank to recapitalize swiftly and free from the institutional value destruction or market disruption typical in a judicial or administrative reorganization.[39] We later discuss the use of bail-in techniques inside of resolution through the new Dodd–Frank Orderly Liquidation Authority but this section is addressed to bail-in outside of resolution. Nonetheless, many of the problems we identify with the use of bail-in outside of resolution are also present within resolution.

Bail-in refers to a set of related techniques that aim at forcing the creditors of a financial institution that is deemed by regulators to be in danger of failing to absorb the losses that it has incurred by swapping certain of their liability claims for new equity issued for the purpose of recapitalizing the financial institution's balance sheet. Bail-in uses debt-to-equity conversion to increase a troubled financial institution's total pool of available capital and to reduce its leverage in a period of stress.[40] Unlike contingent capital, bail-in is a stand-alone strategy for resolving distressed or failed institutions.[41] It is a systematic restructuring procedure, not a class of capital instruments, which is intended to automate the conversion and write-down of a designated portion of a financial institution's debt capital structure in response to a preceding regulatory determination or trigger event.[42] Conversion through a process of bail-in is not governed by contract and, as such, can embrace any or all parts of an institution's debt, including instruments that may not have been specified as convertible at the time of issuance. This is sharply different from contingent capital instruments, which are designated in advance to convert only under a defined set of contractual conditions.

Under most approaches envisioned by its sponsors, to institute a creditor bail-in regulators simply would require that designated liabilities (those that regulators have selected, whether or not they incorporate a preexisting contractual conversion feature) undergo a form of mandatory write-off or convert to equity.[43] One important consequence of this difference is that contingent capital is naturally limited in the amount of support it can provide to an ailing firm to the value of contingent capital instruments that are actually issued and outstanding. By contrast, creditor bail-in would potentially provide the same firm access to a much larger implied capital cushion, theoretically equal to the firm's entire financial indebtedness. This would enable bail-in to serve the role of a more comprehensive restructuring system during a crisis, rather than just supplying a novel form of supplementary capital.

16.2.1   Shortcomings of Bail-in outside Formal Resolution

One major shortcoming common to all forms of creditor bail-in is the legal uncertainty associated with implementing it. It would not appear that the FDIC or other US regulators currently possess bailout powers outside of a formal resolution procedure. It is true that the Federal Reserve can use the "source-of-strength" doctrine to force holding company parents to inject capital into their bank subsidiaries.[44] However, if that capital injection and any absorption of subsidiary losses put the holding company at risk of failure, then use of a formal resolution procedure to restructure the holding company (e.g., OLA) would be necessary.

Since the process of bail-in is designed to bypass ordinary bankruptcy channels (including chapters 7 and 11 of the Bankruptcy Code and the various forms of FDIC resolution) the automatic stay normally instituted against withdrawals by creditors in bankruptcy might not be available to prevent a mass exit,[45] though this shortcoming could be addressed in principle by extending the application of such a stay to cover debts subject to the bail-in. This seemingly would require new legislation. For example, §362 of the Bankruptcy Code automatically prohibits the creditors of an entity entering bankruptcy from enforcing financial claims against the debtor—apart from so-called qualified financial contracts (QFCs), such as repos and OTC derivatives, that they are entitled to terminate—a stay not available outside formal resolution.[46] Even if such a stay could be adapted to bail-in, however, it would not deter runs by anxious short-term creditors on institutions that had not yet become subject to bail-in.

Anticipatory runs by short-term creditors on institutions that have not yet, but could soon be, bailed-in thus present a major problem for the implementation of a bail-in regime, and this concern would be present whether we are dealing with bail-in in or outside of a formal resolution procedure. The main alternative—generally exempting short-term creditors from bail-in, for example by announcing an express carve-out of short-term debt or confining its reach to a financial institution's regulatory capital instruments only—could restrict its effectiveness in situations where severe losses overwhelm an institution's capital buffers. If the bail-in of non–short-term debt was insufficient to cover losses, short-term debt could still be at risk. Explicitly carving short-term debt out from the coverage of a bail-in regime might also promote a shift of institutional funding from unprotected longer term capital instruments into shorter maturity investments, increasing overall systemic dependency on short-term debt. This would increase the overall risk of contagion in the financial system rather than contain it.

16.2.2   Bailable Instruments and the Amount of Losses

Common to all forms of creditor bail-in, whether it occurs outside or within a formal bankruptcy procedure, is the question of which classes of debt instruments are eligible for impairment or conversion. Absent a special exemption from normal priority rules, applying debt-to-equity conversion across the entirety of a financial institution's capital structure will expose short-term unsecured debt holders to the risk of impairment, encouraging them to exit preemptively from an institution that is perceived to be in distress, considerably increasing the risk of a run. Shielding short-term debt holders (in particular, uninsured deposits including foreign deposits, nondeposit short-term debt, plus all the other systemically important liabilities that are likely to exit instead of accepting impairment) from the imposition of losses will, however, override ordinary rules of contractual priority controlling inter-creditor relationships outside of bankruptcy, altering the pricing of longer term bailable instruments that beforehand may have ranked equivalently with (or senior to) shorter term debt in order of recovery but now will in effect have been demoted.

At the least, the power of regulators conducting bail-in to unsettle existing inter-creditor contracts for the purpose of favoring systemically relevant debt is likely to raise the cost of unfavored bailable instruments proportionately. Further, short-term creditors that harbor doubt about whether exemptions will actually be given or the strength of the legal footing for a regulatory carve-out will rationally prefer to withdraw from a distressed institution rather than remain invested during a bail-in and, taking their chances in court. The FDIC's SPOE proposal, pursuant to OLA, discussed below, seeks to avoid these problems by limiting bail-in to the holding company, which is generally funded by only longer term debt. This in turn creates the necessity to downstream new capital from the restructured holding company to the banks and other operating subsidiaries, a matter we examine in our discussion of OLA.

The Basel Committee proposal on bail-ins limits bail-in conversion to noncommon tier I and tier II capital instruments only. Under this formulation, short-term debt presumably will be excluded from conversion, since it is not a capital instrument. This will reduce the danger of setting off a run or spreading contagion, since short-term debt would be protected. Limiting the selection of bailable instruments to tier I and tier II capital only, however, could restrict the total amount of capital potentially available to absorb losses, narrowing the usefulness of bail-ins to situations in which institutional losses are no greater than total existing capital. Short-term investors who suspect that their issuer's long-term debt and common equity are insufficient to facilitate the recapitalization will expect to be impaired too despite ex ante assurances of a carve-out, and may run anyway. This concern is even more acute in the case of an Institute of International Finance (IIF) proposal, which ordinarily reserves only subordinated debt, but not senior debt, for bail-in conversion, and thus increases the chance that a severely impaired firm will be unable to marshal the financial resources necessary to support a successful bail-in. Although the IIF proposal does permit bail-in of senior indebtedness in extraordinary circumstances, it would require a separate decision by regulators.[46] If short-term creditors had any doubt that this decision would be timely and forthcoming, they might panic and run.

Provided in table 16.1 is an illustrative bail-in based on Citigroup's consolidated balance sheet as of December 31, 2008. It depicts a bail-in at the holding company level.

As the table suggests, the firm possessed enough senior and subordinated long-term debt, about $1.9 billion, to support losses of 20 percent, or about $260 million, to its trading, investment, and loan portfolios through bail-in, without impairing guaranteed, short-term, and otherwise ineligible instruments. Losses greater than approximately 30 percent of the carrying value of these assets, however, would have exhausted the amount of long-term debt eligible for bail-in, requiring public support to fully restore the pre–bail-in leverage ratio without converting shorter term instruments. The issue of sufficient bailable instruments at the holding company level is a concern inside formal resolution like OLA, as well as outside formal resolution.

Under the IIF proposal, however, in which bail-in is confined (at least initially) to subordinated and junior subordinated debt instruments only, losses of 20 percent or more would exhaust bailable capital and subordinated debt, requiring public support or the conversion of senior indebtedness (via separate regulatory approval) to effectuate the bail-in. As of December 31, 2008, subordinated debt held at Citigroup's parent and subsidiaries levels totaled no more than $57.7 billion, or just 16 percent of Citi's cumulative long-term debt maturities recorded on

Table 16.1

Illustrative bail-in of Citigroup balance sheet as of December 31, 2008 (USD millions)

	12/31/2008	Realized impairment of:	
ASSETS	**Actual**	**20.0%**	**50.0%**
Cash, deposits, fed funds, and brokerage receivables[a]	$427,995	$427,995	$427,995
Trading account assets	380,043	304,034	190,022
Investments, available for sale and held to maturity	253,393	202,714	126,697
Loans, net of allowances	664,915	531,932	332,458
Other assets[b]	218,917	218,917	218,917
TOTAL ASSETS	$1,945,263	$1,685,593	$1,296,088
Total losses to be absorbed	-	($259,670)	($649,176)

LIABILTIES AND EQUITY		
Deposits	$774,185	
Repurchase agreements	205,293	Protected/ineligible
Brokerage payables	70,916	funding source that
Trading account liabilities	167,536	cannot be impaired
Short-term borrowings	126,691	through bail-in.
Other liabilities[c]	90,275	
Subtotal - Protected or ineligible liabilities	**1,434,896**	
Long-term debt	359,303	Available to absorb
Other secured debt	290	losses
Shareholders' equity	150,774	
TOTAL LIABILITIES AND EQUITY	$1,945,263		

	Actual	20.0%	50.0%
Tier I cap./Implied Tier I for constant ratio	$118,758	$102,905	$79,126
Tier I leverage ratio (Tier I capital/total assets)	6.10%	6.10%	6.10%
ILLUSTRATIVE LOSS ABSORPTION SCHEDULE			
Total losses to be absorbed		$259,670	$649,176
Less: Losses absorbed by Tier I capital		(118,758)	(118,758)
Residual losses to be absorbed by converting long-term debt		140,912	540,418
Add: Conversion of long-term debt to maintain Tier I leverage ratio		102,905	79,126
Total long-term debt required for bail-in		243,817	609,543
Actual long-term debt held on balance sheet		359,303	359,303
Implied bail-in funding surplus (deficit/required public support)		$115,486	($250,240)

Note: See Citigroup, Financial Information, Quarterly Financial Data Supplement, *supra* note 750.

a. Includes fed funds sold and securities borrowed/purchased under resale agreements.
b. Includes goodwill, intangible assets, mortgage servicing rights, and other.
c. Includes credit loss allowances for letters of credit.

balance sheet (the remaining $301.6 billion represented senior long-term instruments) (see table 16.2). A bail-in of Citigroup assuming even modest balance sheet losses would thus have overwhelmed the total amount of liability claims the IIF proposal would make available to regulators. The current solution to this problem for bail-ins within resolution is to impose minimum requirements of unsecured debt that would be available for potential bail-in, through TLAC, or total loss absorption capacity requirements, discussed below under OLA.[47]

Table 16.2
Illustrative bail-in of Citigroup under IIF proposal with subordinated debt only (USD millions)

Citigroup long-term debt maturities as of 12/31/2008:

Senior debt		
Senior notes - Parent	$138,005	Ineligible initially
Senior notes - Subsidiaries	105,629	for creditor bail-in
Senior notes - Other	57,994	under IIF proposal
Total senior debt	301,628	
Subordinated/junior subordinated debt		
Subordinated debt - Parent	54,276	
Subordinated debt - Subsidiairies	2,295	
Subordinated debt - Other	4	
Total subordinated debt	57,675	16.05%
Total long-term debt	$359,303	

LOSS ABSORPTION SCHEDULE ASSUMING LOSSES OF:	20.0%	50.0%
Total losses to be absorbed	$259,670	$649,176
Less: Losses absorbed by Tier I capital	(118,758)	(118,758)
Residual losses to be absorbed by converting long-term debt	140,912	530,418
Add: Conversion of long-term debt to maintain Tier I leverage ratio	102,905	79,126
Total long-term debt required for bail-in	243,817	609,543
Actual **subordinated** long-term debt held on balance sheet	57,675	57,675
Implied bail-in funding surplus (deficit/required public support)	($186,142)	($551,868)

16.2.3   Other Potential Obstacles to Bail-In

Regulators also face an array of practical obstacles similar to those confronted in the case of contingent capital. First, the impact on investor appetite of subjecting the debt of financial institutions to the risk of automatic conversion at the discretion of regulators is unknown, but it could be significant. The *Financial Times* reported the results of a customer survey by JPMorgan showing that one quarter of senior bondholders have indicated they would refuse to purchase instruments subject to bail-in risk.[48] This could raise average bank borrowing costs by 0.87 percent.[49] European banks' issuance of senior debt that can be subject to a bail-in is at its lowest in a decade as of mid-2013.[50] During September and October of 2014, European banks issued 14.5 billion euros of senior debt, down from 27 billion issued over that same period in 2013.[51]

Bail-in eligibility is also likely to impact the ratings and capital treatment of implicated instruments. In 2011, Moody's Investors Service cautioned that it would consider downgrades of junior bank debt subject to bail-in;[52] in February 2014, S&P issued a similar warning.[53] S&P followed through on its threat in August 2014, when the rating agency downgraded three Austrian banks, specifically citing new bail-in legislation that "indicates reduced predictability of extraordinary government support for systematically important banks, and for banks' hybrid capital instruments and grandfathered debt, than we previously envisaged."[54]

Second, the mechanics governing conversion must be designed and articulated.[55] If the "trigger" controlling when bail-in takes place is a pure function of regulatory discretion (rather than premising it on capital- or market-based variables), then at the very least regulators must define prospectively under what circumstances bail-in will occur (and which liabilities will be included or exempted from its sweep). This is the subject of considerable disagreement among advocates for the solution.[56] Many of the putative advantages of bail-in, for example, automating resolution, minimizing regulatory intervention, and promoting uniformity in reorganizational outcomes, all in a nondisruptive manner,[57] require investors to know ex ante which claims will bear these costs and under what circumstances, but many market participants echo doubts that certainty in this connection can be achieved.[58]

Third, bail-in may entail replacing the failed institution's old management with new management that commands the confidence of the market place following reorganization. This means that new managers may have to be found and installed before a bail-in can be completed, delaying the process. Completing a bail-in would furthermore involve a change of control that placed former debt holders into equity ownership of the failed institution. These debt holders may, however, be disqualified by regulators from the ownership of banking institutions under US law, for example, hedge funds or private equity firms.

The fourth major practical shortcoming of creditor bail-in is jurisdictional. To encompass a meaningful portion of the international financial system, a bail-in regime will need to be coordinated with insolvency laws and resolution procedures applicable in multiple national jurisdictions so that bail-ins can take place on a cross-border basis without violating or otherwise interfering with local laws.[59] This is crucial when large financial institutions with multinational operations are subjected to bail-ins during a crisis. These institutions—arguably the most complex in the financial system—are widely regarded as most in need of an efficient alternative to current resolution regimes. Cross-border resolution through bail-in is likely to be much more difficult outside of formal resolution—developing cross-border cooperation is primarily focused today on resolution within bankruptcy. Given the major obstacles to achieving coordinated bail-in policies in the near future, one could require new debt instruments issued by financial institutions to incorporate private contract terms authorizing conversion to equity upon a trigger signal from regulators of a specified country, as the Basel Committee and others such as Bates and Gleeson (2011) have suggested.[60] Under this alternative creditors would contract to apply the law of the bail-in jurisdiction in advance, so that conflicts of law and among local regulators would be minimized. In the variant of this approach outlined by Bates and Gleeson, a financial institution incorporated in a bail-in regime would be required by the law of that jurisdiction to contract ex ante with any creditors whose claims could potentially arise in a non–bail-in jurisdiction to submit to the effect of a bail-in if one were to occur.[61]

However appealing it may be in principle, "contracting" for cross-border bail-in presents daunting challenges in practice. Success depends, among other things, on *where* the long-term debt of large, complex financial institutions is issued and held, and at what level of the corporate structure. The paradigmatic case imagined by Bates and Gleeson contemplates one-company institutions where all subsidiaries are of a parent bank (though potentially with creditors in different jurisdictions) governed by bail-in rules applicable to all creditors. If all bailable debt were indeed issued at and held at the parent bank holding company level in a single jurisdiction, it might be relatively straightforward to require the institution to contract for uniform bail-in terms from all creditors. However, most large institutions hold debt at dozens or even hundreds of local subsidiaries in multiple jurisdictions (even if originally it was issued at the holding company level but then transferred downstream to those subsidiaries). Under these conditions, the contractual solution is unlikely to work. Lehman Brothers, for example, operated 433 subsidiaries in 20 different countries prior to its failure.[62] Many subsidiaries were subject to local regulation including capital. Local regulators responsible for managing the capital levels of local bank subsidiaries are unlikely to allow conversion of subsidiary-level debt for the purpose of restoring the consolidated capital ratio at the holding company-level in a different jurisdiction, or to uphold or even permit contract terms to require that such local debt be subject to the control of foreign regulators.

Even for regulators bailing-in a financial institution that is organizationally confined to a single jurisdiction, the challenge of coordinating the conversion of debt instruments outstanding across many different bank subsidiaries so that all of these subsidiaries, in addition to the parent holding company, are adequately (but not over-) capitalized after the bail-in, will be formidable. Contracting for bail-in of complex multinational financial institutions thus presents both a "vertical" problem (coordinating bail-in between the holding company and its bank subsidiaries) and a "horizontal" one (coordinating bail-in of debt in different jurisdictions). Furthermore relying on contract to streamline bail-in would transform it into a form of contingent capital, sacrificing its functionality as a substitute for formal resolution procedures by requiring that the major terms controlling conversion be stipulated in advance if it were to be acceptable in multiple jurisdictions.[63]

Bail-ins outside of resolution have significant problems, some of which can be addressed in a more formal resolution procedure. We now turn to the new Orderly Liquidation Authority, the new formal US framework for dealing with certain nonbank SIFIs including bank holding companies.

17 Dodd–Frank Orderly Liquidation for Nonbank SIFIs (Including Bank Holding Companies)

17.1 General Design of OLA and the SPOE Strategy

The orderly liquidation authority ("OLA") contained in Title II of the Dodd–Frank Act, created a new regime for receivership of nonbank financial companies whose failures "would have serious adverse effects on the financial stability in the United States."[1] As such, OLA is intended to offer regulators an alternative to bankruptcy proceedings. However, the FDIC has stated that bankruptcy remains the preferred resolution procedure despite the availability of OLA.[2] OLA applies to "financial companies," which includes BHCs, nonbank financial companies that have been designated as systemically important, and certain registered brokers and dealers.[3]

In order to be placed into receivership under OLA, the "covered" financial company must be designated as posing systemic risk in the event of failure, and it must be in default or in danger of default. The determination is made on the eve of bankruptcy by the Federal Reserve and FDIC with final approval by the Treasury Secretary upon consultation with the President. The decision to place a troubled financial institution under OLA is entirely separate and distinct from the determination of whether a nonbank financial institution is systemically important, with the associated consequence of Fed supervision. Use of OLA authority has been highly contentious, with some lawmakers asserting it will lead to more bailouts due to availability of Treasury funding described below. Whatever the merits of the contention, OLA designations will be politically charged. The upshot being that whatever the virtues of using OLA, its actual usage, even for important financial institutions, is far from assured. Short-term creditors, uncertain whether their institution will fall under OLA, and whether they will actually be protected if the institution was under OLA, will likely run well in advance of an OLA coverage determination being made. In this case OLA resolution would be too little too late to stem contagion.

Once the company is under OLA, the FDIC has broad authority to resolve the insolvent firm. The FDIC, in conjunction with the Bank of England, has stated its preference for a "single-point-of-entry" (SPOE) approach to resolving failed financial companies.[4] Under this approach the FDIC would be appointed as receiver to the top-tier parent of the failed holding company, in the case of banks, the BHC. Of course, FDIC would also have authority over the bank subsidiaries' resolution through its traditional bank resolution authority.[5] The first step would be the creation of a "bridge financial company," essentially a new financial service holding company, such as a bank holding company, where all the assets, primarily investments in subsidiaries, and a limited amount of the liabilities of the failed holding company would be transferred. The equity, subordinated debt, and senior unsecured debt of the failed holding company would be left behind as claims in a receivership, basically holding bad assets, to absorb the losses that triggered resolution. The receivership itself would hold the equity in the bridge financial company. Ultimately, upon valuing the bridge company equity, with consultation from accountants and investment bankers, the FDIC will issue new debt and equity securities of the bridge financial company, based on that valuation, to satisfy the claims of the receivership creditors.[6] The FDIC estimates that the valuation process and new issuance of securities will take six to nine months, during which time the bridge financial company will remain under FDIC control.[7]

The FDIC envisions that the swift creation of a well-capitalized bridge holding company will allow the bridge company to provide the necessary holding company support to its operating subsidiaries.[8] Furthermore, if either the parent or the subsidiaries are in need of temporary liquidity that the bridge holding company cannot obtain in the private market, the Dodd–Frank Act authorizes an orderly liquidation fund (OLF), funded by the Treasury, with proper approvals, to provide temporary funding to the bridge holding company, through the FDIC, secured by parent-level or subsidiary assets.[9]

In establishing a bridge financial company that is able to provide liquidity and necessary capital injections to operating subsidiaries, the SPOE approach aims to ensure that subsidiaries can continue operations without any restructuring. This is a clever solution to the potential problem of intervening at the operating subsidiary level where normal creditor priorities could require short-term unsecured creditors to absorb losses, thus triggering contagious runs. SPOE leaves all creditors of the operating subsidiaries, short- or long-term, unaffected by the restructuring. However, it bears noting that if the SPOE approach was able to successfully protect uninsured short-term creditors at the subsidiary level, then it could actually increase the overall riskiness of the consolidated banking organization. This is because uninsured bank creditors would now no longer have incentives to monitor and impose discipline on bank risk-taking. Indeed empirical studies have found that the discipline provided by uninsured bank creditors has reduced the cost of issuing long-term debt.[10] If the SPOE approach were to protect uninsured creditors from the risk of losses, then it would reduce these creditors' incentive to provide such discipline.

One important reason for the FDIC to be focused on use of SPOE at the holding company level is because its powers to protect the creditors of banks under the Federal Deposit Insurance Act, as amended by the Dodd–Frank Act, has been severely limited by the elimination of open bank assistance, which allowed the FDIC to provide loans, purchase assets, assume liabilities, and even provide cash contributions in order to prevent an insured bank from failing.[11]

For there to be a successful restructuring of the holding company under OLA, there must be enough long-term unsecured liabilities that can be bailed in or otherwise used together with any remaining equity to recapitalize the parent holding company on a consolidated basis at a sufficiently strong level (e.g., Basel III common equity tier I = 7 percent of RWA). A stable, adequately capitalized consolidated holding company is important to the continuing operation of the subsidiaries since customers and trading partners of the operating subsidiaries may pull their business if the consolidated holding company is still unstable, which could put the subsidiaries, and their creditors, at risk of failure. In addition the long-term unsecured liabilities used to recapitalize the parent holding company must be structurally or legally subordinate to short-term unsecured liabilities at the parent or operating subsidiary levels to reduce or eliminate the potential for contagion among short-term unsecured creditors throughout the financial system (albeit this cannot by itself stop contagion). The line between long-term and short-term unsecured liabilities could be drawn in a number of ways, for example liabilities with an original maturity of a year (some of which may be much less at the time of a run) or a remaining maturity of 30 days following the liquidity approach of the BIS. Unless long-term unsecured liabilities at the holding company level are legally subordinate to short-term liabilities at the holding company level, there must be no material amount of short-term liabilities at the holding company level in order to reduce or eliminate the risk of a run against the holding company.

Under OLA, the FDIC could use its authority to provide liquidity to the operating subsidiaries (e.g., banks or broker-dealers) by having the bridge financial company borrow from the Treasury's OLF. The bridge financial companies may last for only two years, or up to five years with extensions.[12] The FDIC may not use the OLF to capitalize the operating subsidiaries. However, the FDIC may lend the money to the holding company, which could downstream the proceeds to the operating subsidiaries in the form of capital, so the prohibition of FDIC itself recapitalizing the subsidiaries is somewhat meaningless. Any borrowing from OLF must be paid back with a reasonable rate of interest. If the assets of the company are insufficient to do so, then funding must be clawed back from creditors or assessed on other financial institutions. There are also limitations on how much can be borrowed. In the first 30 days, before the FDIC has had the opportunity to determine the real value of the company's assets, it can borrow only 10 percent of the assets reported on the company's last financial statement.[13] After that period, once the FDIC has established the "real" value, it may borrow up to 90 percent of the fair value of the assets. Provision of Treasury funding will be intensely political, as it will likely be attacked as another bailout.

17.2   Total Loss Absorption Capacity (TLAC) to Assure Holding Company Recapitalization

In an effort to ensure recapitalization, the FSB released in November 2014 a Consultative Document on the Adequacy of Loss-Absorbing Capacity of Global Systemically Important Banks (G-SIBs) in Resolution.[14] In the US context, given the SPOE approach, the FSB standards would apply to holding companies but for banks in other countries it could apply at the bank level. The Consultative Document defines international standards for minimum amounts of total loss-absorbing capital ("TLAC") to be issued by G-SIBs. Under the proposal the top-tier parent company of a US G-SIB will be required to issue eligible securities ("TLAC Instruments") in an amount at least equal to 16 to 20 percent of the consolidated group's RWA and at least 6 percent of its total assets.[15] This requirement excludes from TLAC Basel III discretionary countercyclical buffers, capital conservation buffers, and G-SIB surcharges.[16] Therefore a G-SIB with no countercyclical buffer, but with a standard 2.5 percent capital conservation buffer and a 2.5 percent G-SIB surcharge would effectively be required to hold 21 to 25 percent of RWA in TLAC Instruments.[17] The TLAC proposal does not explain why excluding buffers and surcharges is necessary. The FSB intends to select an actual value from the 16 to 20 percent range after conducting a Quantitative Impact Study ("QIS"). The QIS will evaluate consequences of the TLAC requirement, including bank funding costs and the historical record of bank losses and recapitalization needs. TLAC Instruments issued by one G-SIB cannot be held by another G-SIB.[18] On October 30, 2015, the Federal Reserve Board released its TLAC proposed rule, requiring domestic G-SIBs to hold minimum TLAC of 18 percent of risk-weighted assets and U.S. operations of foreign G-SIBs to hold 16 percent.[19]

TLAC Instruments must be unsecured,[20] and must have a minimum remaining maturity of at least one year.[21] In addition TLAC Instruments must be contractually or statutorily subordinated to a broad class of excluded liabilities, with limited exceptions.[22] Several important excluded liabilities are deposits, structured notes, callable debt, and any liability that is senior to vanilla unsecured debt under bankruptcy law.[23] Securities that qualify as Basel III regulatory capital are eligible TLAC Instruments.[24] However, the Proposal requires that at least 33 percent of the TLAC requirement must be satisfied with securities that do not qualify as regulatory capital.[25] For example, if a G-SIB issued sufficient equity to satisfy 100 percent of its TLAC requirement, it could only count 67 percent of this capital surplus toward its TLAC requirement. The justification for this requirement is not addressed in the proposal.

The Committee on Capital Markets Regulation has estimated that these TLAC requirements will lead to a "total gap to implementation for the eight US G-SIBs between $44.6 billion and $197 billion."[26] This is twice the average monthly issuance of *all* US corporate debt.[27] These estimates accord with other estimates. In particular, the Clearing House has estimated US G-SIB shortfalls between $104 and $195 billion,[28] while Standard & Poor's has estimated a shortfall of between $23.4 and $203.2 billion.[29] One concern with TLAC is that if it were ever used to actually recapitalize subsidiaries then the investors holding TLAC debt would experience large losses and as a result, demand for future TLAC debt could dry up.

17.3   Recapitalization of Operating Subsidiaries: Banks and Broker-Dealers

Quite apart from the recapitalization of the holding company, the bridge holding company must be able to downstream enough capital to absorb the losses in the operating subsidiaries. On the asset side of the holding company, the assets must be in a sufficient amount and eligible to be contributed to the operating subsidiaries. Eligible assets would include any assets held at the parent level that can be contributed to the subsidiaries, such as interests in solvent companies, cash, or portfolio securities, or a reduction or cancellation of loans (which are liabilities of the operating subs).

When considering the downstreaming of assets, the only eligibility restriction is that the subsidiary not be prohibited by regulation from owning the particular assets. For example, an insured bank subsidiary may not be able to own equity securities in a broker-dealer subsidiary that is engaged in activities that the bank is not permitted to engage in directly. In contrast, an insured bank subsidiary could accept the contribution of a receivable from a nonbank subsidiary without violating Section 23A of the Federal Reserve Act because the extension of credit would have been made by the parent, not the bank, and the acceptance of the contribution would not amount to a "purchase" of assets from an affiliate unless an express payment were made or liabilities assumed, which would not be the case here.[30]

An example of the bail-in of parent-level debt necessary to recapitalize the consolidated entity was illustrated previously in table 16.1, using Citigroup as an example. The point of that example is that bailable debt at the holding company level must be sufficient to cover the losses of the operating subsidiaries—because these losses directly impact their owner, the holding company.

As for the injection of capital into subsidiaries, consider the following example, illustrating the use of parent-to-sub loans for purposes of recapitalizing an operating subsidiary. For simplicity, assume that all assets have equal risk-weighting. Holdco is a bank holding company whose dominant holding is a large bank subsidiary, Bank Sub. In step 1, Bank Sub has tier I capital of $100 billion against RWA of $1.6 trillion, giving it an adequate tier I capital ratio of 6 percent. Holdco has tier I capital of $150 billion against consolidated RWA of $2.5 trillion, and is also adequately capitalized with a tier I capital ratio of 6 percent. In step 2, Bank Sub suffers a $75 billion loss, causing a reduction of its tier

I capital to $25 billion. Consequently Bank Sub is in need of a massive capital injection to avoid approaching insolvency and to re-establish an adequate capital ratio. Furthermore, as a result of this loss to Bank Sub, Holdco's tier I capital has also been reduced by $75 billion to $75 billion and Holdco is no longer adequately capitalized itself. Holdco needs to raise $75 billion in new capital to maintain an adequate capital ratio, which can be done through the bail-in of Holdco level debt. In step 3, a bail-in of $75 billion of Holdco level debt converts $75 billion of that debt into $75 billion of common equity, providing the necessary capital increase for Holdco. Holdco has increased its tier I capital back to $150 billion and is adequately capitalized. However, while the bail-in of Holdco level debt has re-established an adequate capital ratio for Holdco, Bank Sub has not yet received any new capital. Bank Sub continues to be inadequately capitalized with $25 billion of tier I capital and is in need of a $75 billion injection from Holdco. The question is: how does Holdco provide fresh capital to Bank Sub?

The main channel for injecting capital from Holdco to Bank Sub is through the cancellation of debt owed by Bank Sub to Holdco. Assume, as in figure 17.1, Holdco has a loan outstanding to bank sub in the amount of $100 billion. In step 4, Holdco can inject $75 billion of capital into Bank Sub by canceling $75 billion of the Debt-to-Holdco loans, which will increase Bank Sub's common equity by $75 billion. As a result Bank Sub's tier I capital is restored to $100 billion and it becomes adequately capitalized once again. Figure 17.2 illustrates this transmission mechanism.

At the same time, Holdco's capital remains at $150 billion after the cancellation of the loans. So long as the necessary capital injection is less than the amount of the Holdco-to-Bank Sub loan, this transmission channel will work for re-capitalizing a troubled subsidiary. However, if Bank Sub's initial loss were greater than $100 billion (the amount outstanding of Holdco-to-Sub loans), then a further transmission mechanism would be necessary, or losses would be imposed on the creditors of the bank subsidiary, including short-term uninsured creditors.

These holding company-to-subsidiary loans are common arrangements in US BHCs and could potentially serve as an adequate transmission channel for injecting capital into subsidiaries.

Table 17.1 shows a snapshot of the top 10 largest US BHCs and their respective largest bank subsidiaries as of March 31, 2012. These data provide insight into the potential for cancellation of holding company

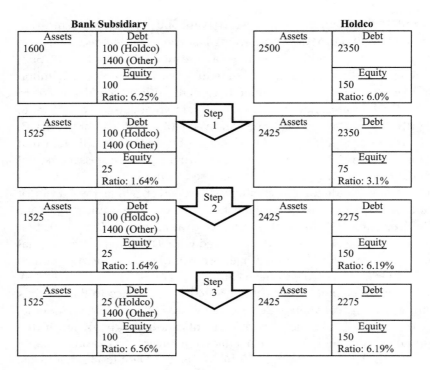

Figure 17.1
Recapitalization example

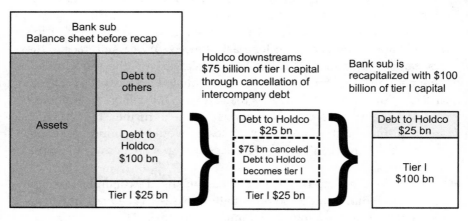

Figure 17.2
Capital downstream example

Table 17.1
Top 10 US bank holding company subsidiary data on loans to subs (USD millions)[a]

As of March 31, 2012	Tier I capital[b]	Tier I ratio[c]	BHC loans to bank subs (aggregate)[d]	BHC loans/ sub tier I capital (col. 3/col. 1)
JPMorgan Chase & Co. (BHC)				
JPMorgan Chase Bank, NA (Sub)	$100,846.0	9.58%	$40,809.00	40.47%
Bank of America Corporation				
Bank of America, National Association	$118,432.0	12.26%	$45,514.50	38.43%
Citigroup Inc.				
Citibank, National Association	$127,118.0	15.54%	$0.00	0.00%
Wells Fargo & Company				
Wells Fargo Bank, National Association	$93,339.0	10.13%	$20,874.00	22.36%
Goldman, Sachs Group Inc.				
Goldman Sachs Bank USA	$19,769.0	19.03%	$26.00	0.13%
MetLife, Inc.				
Metlife Bank, National Association	$1,310.7	21.29%	$1.70	0.13%
Morgan Stanley				
Morgan Stanley Bank, NA	$8,982.0	14.90%	$4,469.00[e]	49.76%
US Bancorp				
US Bank National Association	$26,071.3	9.89%	$6,291.82	24.13%
HSBC North America Holdings Inc.				
HSBC Bank USA, National Association	$16,119.6	13.54%	$5,000.00	31.02%
Bank of New York Mellon Corporation				
The Bank of New York Mellon	$12,872.0	14.75%	$4,511.00	35.05%

a. Top 10 by total consolidated assets; source: National Information Center as collected by the Federal Reserve System, www.ffiec.gov/nicpubweb/nicweb/Top50Form.aspx.

b. Includes perpetual preferred stock, noncontrolling interests in subsidiaries and trust preferred capital debt securities (i.e., not tier I common).

c. Source for BHCs: FDIC Bank Data & Statistics Call Reports; source: Parent Company: National Information Center/Federal Reserve, Company Filings.

d. Source: National Information Center/Federal Reserve, Company Filings; includes Loans, Advances, Notes and Bonds in both Bank Operating Subsidiaries as well as Subsidiary Bank Holding Companies.

e. Does not include $14.65 billion of loans to Subsidiary Bank Holding Companies, which includes nonbank subsidiaries.

loans to subsidiaries as the primary transmission channel for injecting capital. The final column shows holding company-to-subsidiary loans as a percentage of the bank subsidiary's tier I capital. While more specific loan detail is necessary for a complete analysis of intercompany loan cancellations as a viable transmission channel, this establishes an upper bound on the percentage of each bank subsidiary's tier I capital that could be injected through the cancellation of loans from the holding company to the bank subsidiary. For example, JPMorgan Chase & Co. (holding company) has its largest bank subsidiary, JPMorgan Chase Bank, NA (bank sub) holding $100.8 billion of tier I capital. JPMorgan Chase & Co. also has $40.8 billion of loans outstanding to its bank subsidiaries. If the entirety of those loans were to JPMorgan Chase Bank, NA,[31] JPMorgan Chase Bank, NA, could suffer up to a 40.47 percent loss of tier I capital that could be injected by the holding company through a cancellation of the $40.8 billion of loans. In its "Public Resolution Plan" submitted to the Federal Reserve as required by Dodd–Frank, JPMorgan does indeed indicate its intention to use the cancellation of intercompany loans as the primary mechanism for recapitalizing troubled bank subsidiaries under a Title II resolution.[32]

However, any substantial loss that severely impacts a bank subsidiary's balance sheet (i.e., losses that approach or result in insolvency) may not be sufficiently offset by a cancellation of the intercompany loans, since not every bank is like JPMorgan in this respect. In particular, half of the banks would be unable to support losses greater than 25 percent of tier I capital through cancellation of intercompany loans. In such cases of severe losses, the cancellation of intercompany loans is unlikely to be a sufficient means of injecting capital from the holding company into the bank subsidiary.

For this method of recapitalization to work, the regulators would have to require that important financial holding companies have sufficient debt to their operating subsidiaries (e.g., banks and broker-dealers), what some have called internal TLAC. This may be problematic for institutions whose operating subsidiaries do not need funding from the holding company do to their reliance on funding at the operating subsidiary level. This would be particularly true for retail banking organizations with a wide base of retail deposits. An intercompany loan requirement would require the holding companies to provide funding to banks that did not need or could not use it, imposing a substantial dead weight loss on such institutions.

17.4 Derivatives Contracts

Under the Bankruptcy Code derivatives counterparties facing a failing institution have a safe harbor that allows a nonfailing counterparty to terminate the derivative contract and take its collateral.[33] Normally, in bankruptcy all seizures of collateral are subject to an automatic stay that prevents such seizures. This safe harbor has the potential to impose further losses on the insolvent institution, and can accelerate its decline, as happened with Lehman. For example, Lehman owed one of its derivatives counterparties, JPMorgan, approximately $20 billion. Due to the derivatives safe harbor, JPMorgan was able both to freeze $17 billion of its Lehman collateral and to make a $5 billion collateral call days before Lehman's bankruptcy filing.[34] Although it may be difficult to quantify the value destruction that resulted from early termination, this accelerated imposition of losses undoubtedly contributed to overall losses to the estate that—according to Federal Reserve researchers— "could have been avoided in a more orderly process."[35]

OLA, however, like bank resolution conducted by the FDIC, institutes a one business day stay on the ability of counterparties to exercise their right to terminate, during which time the FDIC may find a third-party buyer to take the place of the nonfailing counterparty. In a bank holding company, derivative positions are either all held at the bank or operating subsidiary level, or held through SIVs that have higher credit ratings than the bank holding companies, rather than held at the holding company level. In the case of a large financial institution, finding such a buyer, especially in such a short period, is unrealistic given the difficulties in valuing a large and complicated derivatives book. It is more likely, that the stay would allow the authorities to restructure the holding company, and then to recapitalize its subsidiary banks, so that the banks were now solvent, such that their counterparties no longer had the right to terminate their contracts. There would be little to gain by transferring the banks' derivatives positions to the holding company which, unlike the banks, would not have access to discount window liquidity—as we have seen access for nonbanks (including holding companies) under Section 13(3) is much more problematic. Further, under the single point of entry policy, banks whose obligations would not be restructured, should have higher credit ratings than holding companies that can be restructured.

Although OLA imposes a stay on early termination rights, this restriction does not necessarily apply to swaps governed by foreign law or in a US non-OLA bankruptcy.[36] Under pressure from resolution authorities, in 2014, eighteen of the largest global dealer banks agreed to a stay of the longer of one business day or 48 hours (e.g., a weekend) on their derivatives termination rights in the event of a counterparty's bankruptcy.[37] Thus, if a counterparty enters bankruptcy, the largest dealer banks could not immediately terminate their open derivatives contracts with that counterparty or seize collateral from that counterparty. This could further facilitate leaving the derivatives book with the recapitalized banks. Global policy makers (particularly members of the FSB) are seeking to encourage additional derivatives counterparties to participate in this agreement, including through pursuing regulatory changes in their respective jurisdictions.[38] As of October 7, 2015, a total of 186 derivatives counterparties around the world had agreed to participate in this stay.[39]

17.5   International Coordination Problems

The use of the SPOE approach, as envisioned by the FDIC, requires cross-border cooperation of regulators to be successful. While SPOE resolution may be feasible when implemented within a single country, it becomes a much more difficult process across borders. In the case of OLA, the FDIC will need to give credible assurances to foreign authorities that subsidiaries operating within their borders will be given fair treatment regarding capital and liquidity injections.[40] In addition, the FDIC must ensure that the resolution strategy will preserve the critical functions operating in foreign jurisdictions.[41] Finally, equity holders and creditors must be given equitable treatment across borders.[42] Failure to credibly provide any of these assurances may induce a foreign jurisdiction to take independent action, thus disrupting a SPOE resolution.

In addition the United States may be concerned about the treatment of US subsidiaries of foreign banks when a foreign jurisdiction is in charge of the resolution of these entities—the failure of a foreign jurisdiction to adequately recapitalize US subsidiaries could give rise to losses for US creditors and could spark contagion in the United States. In the past the United States has ring-fenced the assets of foreign banks in the United States to provide the resources to protect US creditors.[43] To protect US creditors in foreign subsidiaries, the Federal Reserve has issued a final rule requiring foreign banking organizations to establish intermediate US holding companies in the United States with sufficient capital to cover losses of US subsidiaries.[44] This proposal has sparked foreign criticism and risks retaliation from other jurisdictions requiring their own intermediate holding companies for foreign banking organizations, such as the United States. This system of ring-fenced "trapped" capital is highly inefficient and significantly increases the capital needed by all multinational banking organizations.

The FSB has also envisioned a multiple-point-of-entry ("MPOE") approach in which various regulators intervene at different levels of a banking organization, namely some at holding company (or intermediate holding company) level and others at the operating sub (e.g., bank) level. This approach also requires cross-border cooperation to "avoid conflicts or inconsistencies that undermine the effectiveness of the separate resolution actions, a disorderly run on assets, and contagion across the firm."[45] Authorities must also agree to the scope of their respective resolution procedures to avoid a competition for assets of the firm, which would have a destabilizing effect. All of these international complications make the successful use of SPOE somewhat problematic.

~ ~ ~

The most important point about resolution, under the Bankruptcy Act, the FDIA or OLA, is that short-term creditors will be at risk, and thus contagion will not be abated; resolution helps with contagion but cannot by itself avoid it. Uninsured creditors have no priority under the Bankruptcy Act or FDIA, and recapitalization of the operating subsidiaries under OLA is far from certain. Institutions may never get to OLA, so their creditors will run fearing disposition under Bankruptcy; even if OLA were to apply, there is no guarantee that a method could be found to adequately recapitalize the operating subsidiaries, or that SPOE can be successfully deployed internationally. And these procedures have never been tested, let alone with the failure of a G-SIB or SIFI. We may pray that they will work but creditors who can run are not assured by prayers.

This is not to say resolution procedures are not important—they can preserve franchise value, minimize private and public losses, and permit large institutions to fail. And by minimizing the impact on short-term creditors they can help to avoid triggering or exacerbating contagion.

But even if resolution procedures were perfected their existence will not remove the need for a strong lender of last resort.[46] Runs can still occur at operating subsidiaries even with capital injections. Indeed, there is likely to be reputational contagion from the insolvent parent company to the solvent subsidiaries, leading to depositor flight from otherwise solvent subsidiaries.[47] Historical evidence supports this interpretation.[48] Short-term creditors would likely still redeem to be absolutely sure that they would not be hit with the costs of a creditor bail-in.[49] And creditors of institutions not in resolution but that could be will likely run—better safe than sorry. Effective resolution cannot by itself avoid contagion, and without weapons to fight contagion, placing a significant financial institution into resolution may itself ironically spark contagion.

18 Living Wills

Delay in resolution means more time for short-term creditors to run, and loss of franchise value. Following the financial crisis of 2007 to 2009, many believe these risks are acute for large, complex, or otherwise systemically important nonbank financial institutions as well as banks (including bank holding companies). Living wills[1] are intended to make resolution faster. But a faster procedure cannot assure short-term creditors of an unimpaired recovery of their investments, so they will not deter those creditors from withdrawing as soon as a struggling financial institution appears to be in danger of failing. Furthermore the very idea of planning the disposition of complicated corporate estates is dubious. In my view, living wills should focus on a key systemic risk posed by the failure of a few financial institutions—the potential loss of the provision of critical functions like clearing and settlement.

There is no doubt that resolution of large financial institutions pose great difficulty because of their complexity. Figures compiled by Kaufman (2010) show that Lehman Brothers Holdings incorporated nine banks, three insurance companies, 84 mutual and pension funds, 210 other financial subsidiaries, and 127 "nonfinancial" subsidiaries—in all, 433 subsidiaries in 20 countries—less than a year before its collapse. These numbers pale beside Citigroup, which encompassed 101 banks, 35 insurance companies, 706 mutual and pension funds, and over 1,500 other financial and nonfinancial subsidiaries at year end 2007. Statistics for other "large complex financial institutions" (LCFIs) such as Bank of America, JPMorgan Chase, and Deutsche Bank paint a similar portrait of geometric organizational complexity at the larger end of the financial services industry. Living wills are possibly one way to cope with these costs by requiring managers to maintain "inventor[ies of] ... all assets and liabilities," catalog derivatives counterparties, formulate a plan to maintain core operations and customer services during a workout, and take steps in advance to address complications related to the cross-border nature of contemporary banking. Living wills are in effect a way for managers and regulators to rehearse for resolution by choreographing the steps they would need to take when the time comes.

But it is far from clear that living wills will actually speed up resolution or what the systemic risk concern (as opposed to franchise value concern) is with not speedily disposing of thousands of relatively unimportant subsidiaries. Furthermore, if a living will is to serve as more than just an itemized list of assets and liabilities, it must make a complicated set of assumptions about the shape of the future financial crises in which it might be tested. Plans that are too specific will be ineffective in a wide range of possible alternative scenarios; those that are too broad in their design will require regulators to fill in most of the detail in the midst of a crisis, negating the public cost-savings that they promise in principle.

Living wills, it is hoped, may also encourage leaders of financial firms to simplify their organizational structures. Former FDIC chairman Sheila Bair stated "the FDIC and the Fed must be willing to insist on organizational changes that better align business lines and legal entities well before a crisis occurs." Bair contends that this structural simplification will allow management—as well as regulators—to better understand and monitor risks and interrelationships between business lines. Andrew Kuritzkes, who has argued in favor of a tax of $1 million per subsidiary on large financial institutions, sees additional benefits to structural simplification. Encouraging structural simplicity would combat large-firm externalities created by cross-border activity, legal complexity, and regulatory forum shopping.

Title 1, §165(d) of Dodd–Frank requires all SIFIs to develop advance resolution plans to be reviewed and approved by regulators. Specifically, the Act requires the Federal Reserve Board to require all supervised nonbank financial institutions and BHCs with greater than $50 billion in assets to make regular reports to the Federal Reserve, FSOC, and the FDIC on their advance planning for orderly resolution under the Bankruptcy Code. The FDIC and Federal Reserve approved a joint rule implementing the §165(d) requirements in September and October of 2011, respectively, and the rule became effective on November 30, 2011 (the "DFA Rule").[2] In January, 2012, the FDIC approved a complementary living will rule known as the Insured Depository Institution Rule (or "IDI Rule").[3] The IDI Rule requires insured depository institutions with $50 billion or more in assets to submit resolution plans to the FDIC under the Federal Deposit Insurance Act, with the FDIC as receiver.[4]

The Federal Reserve and the FDIC review plans submitted by covered institutions for credibility. Institutions that fail to submit living wills for review or that submit deficient plans may be subject to higher capital and liquidity requirements as well as more severe activity restrictions. Indeed Dodd–Frank empowers the Federal Reserve and the FDIC, in consultation with FSOC, to require institutions to divest "assets or operations" that would interfere with an orderly resolution. Under the DFA Rule, the Federal Reserve and the FDIC may direct an institution to divest assets and operations if it fails to submit an acceptable revised plan within two years of obtaining notice of the plan's deficiency.[5] The IDI Rule does not expressly provide for noncompliance sanctions.

Thomas Hoenig, Vice Chairman of the FDIC, has commented that the living will requirements are leading some firms to reduce their size.[6] Regarding the regulations' impact on organizational structure, he has remarked, "We're not going to break you up, but we want you to structure yourself so that your failure doesn't bring the economy down next time. If you can't get to that point with your current organization structure, then you should sell assets to get to that state."[7] However, the failure of an institution of any size can spark a contagious panic—the response to the failure of Lehman Brothers, which was less than half of the size of the largest banks, is a prominent example of this phenomenon. A "breakup" of big banks in any form is therefore unlikely to represent a meaningful check on the threat of contagion.

In August 2014, the Federal Reserve and the FDIC informed all eleven of the largest US banks of their failure to meet Dodd–Frank's living will standards.[8] The Federal Reserve and FDIC listed a number of reasons for the inadequacy of the living wills. First, the regulators indicated that the living wills did not put forth a credible bankruptcy plan; yet, the regulators were not clear what a living will must include in order to be deemed credible. Regulators further asserted that the banks did not articulate how different counterparties would respond in the event of a bank's downturn. However, it is essentially impossible to predict how counterparties would respond in the event of distress at a critically large banking institution. Finally, the regulators criticized the banks for failing to explain how cross-border jurisdictional issues would be resolved in the event of a bank's demise and for identifying the Federal Reserve as the lender of last resort in the context of living wills. However, it remains difficult for banks to determine how to resolve cross-border jurisdictional issues when US regulators have not yet come to a binding agreement with international counterparts. It is similarly difficult for banks to not acknowledge the key role the Federal Reserve would play in any large-scale banking crisis. In July 2015 the banks refiled their living wills, and they expect to receive feedback from the Federal Reserve and FDIC by the end of 2015.[9]

One very important issue that living wills should address is how critical functions performed by financial institutions, such as clearing of tri-party repos, custody or perhaps even asset valuation, can continue to be performed if a financial institution fails. This may require plans to isolate this activity from the rest of the institution or to transfer it seamlessly and quickly to another institution. If the function requires funding, plans should exist as to how that funding can be practically obtained from the private sector, and if need be the public sector. Without the assurance that critical functions can continue to be performed in the case of insolvency, financial institutions may be too critical to fail. Preservation of critical functions should be at the top of the priority list for living wills planning.

Living wills may help resolve complex banking institutions but they cannot stop short-term creditors from running on financial institutions that are in or might be in resolution—they are just another perhaps useful procedure to enable resolution.

Prime money market mutual funds are particularly susceptible to runs given the inherently short-term nature of their liabilities and the riskiness of their assets as compared with government funds. However, as discussed earlier, runs on such funds are unlikely to pose systemic risk concerns due to their role as funders of other financial institutions given the relatively low reliance large financial institutions have on funding from money market funds. But there is a legitimate concern, based on our experience in the crisis, that a run on money market funds could spark contagion in the rest of the financial system apart from any connectedness. Thus, it is a proper object of policy to minimize the possibility of prime money market fund runs. Accordingly, both FSOC and the SEC have addressed the issue with FSOC proposing recommendations to the SEC regarding money market mutual fund reform in 2012 and the SEC itself proposing rules in 2013.[1] The SEC issued its final rule on money market mutual funds in October 2014, with which funds will have two years to comply.[2]

As previously recounted, the Federal Reserve and the US Treasury instituted a number of programs during the financial crisis to stem the contagion in the MMF industry. The Federal Reserve extended indirect access to the discount window to money market funds through a $150 billion Asset-Backed Commercial Paper Money Market Mutual Fund Liquidity Facility ("AMLF"),[3] creating the $350 billion Commercial Paper Funding Facility ("CPFF")[4] and the Money Market Investor Funding Facility ("MMIFF").[5] The US Treasury provided an effective $3.2 trillion temporary guarantee of the liabilities of the money market funds through its Exchange Stabilization Fund.[6]

Despite the success of these programs, Dodd–Frank substantially curtailed the ability of the government to use similar tactics in the future to address contagion in the MMF industry. Future programs to inject Federal Reserve liquidity into the money market funds will require prior approval by the Secretary of the Treasury and must be programs that are applied on a broad basis only.[7] Furthermore Congress has explicitly prohibited the Treasury from using funds from the Economic Stabilization Fund to conduct a similar temporary guarantee program in the future. [8]

When evaluating the effectiveness of various MMF regulations, it is important to keep in mind that while regulations may be effective in combatting MMF contagion, the unintended consequence may be to push MMF activities into alternative, less-regulated sectors of the financial system. The MMF industry may be safer, but the financial system as whole would be no less vulnerable to contagion. Further any new proposals to address the contagion risks in the MMF industry should not simply be veiled attempts to eliminate money market funds by fundamentally compromising their business model. While many believe money market funds are the product of interest rate regulation under Regulation Q—and they may be right—this arbitrage has long ceased to exist. These funds serve an important function today as indicated by the fact that they have $2.7 trillion in assets.[9] Indeed they allow large depositors, including major firms, to hold funds with a stable asset value, that can be used to make payments, that provide a return (not the case with transaction accounts in banks) and most importantly are less risky than holding uninsured funds in banks—due to the fact that MMF assets are much more liquid and generally carry less risk than bank assets.

The SEC's approach to MMF reform incorporates three elements: (1) enhanced liquidity requirements, (2) a floating NAV requirement for certain classes of money market funds, and (3) the possibility of imposing liquidity fees and redemption gates on money market funds, which would limit rapid MMF creditor outflows in times of stress. It specifically rejected imposing a capital requirement on these funds. At the outset it should be clear that the concern with contagion should only be with prime money market funds and municipal funds, and not with government funds, which are all but immune from runs.

19.1   Enhanced Liquidity Requirements

In February 2010 the SEC amended rule 2a-7 to significantly increase the liquidity of money market funds. The SEC reduced the maximum permitted weighted average portfolio maturity of money market funds from 90 days to 60 days. Additionally money market funds have to invest at least 10 percent of their portfolios in "daily liquid assets" (cash, US government securities, and other securities that provide the holder the right to demand payment within one day) and 30 percent of their portfolio in weekly liquid assets (same as above, US government securities maturing in 60 days or less, and other securities maturing within five business days). The rule also prohibits money market funds from investing more than 5 percent of the fund's assets in illiquid securities. An illiquid security is any security that cannot be sold by the fund within seven days at approximately the value ascribed to it by the fund.[10] According to a recent study by James Angel, due to the 2010 amendments a MMF can withstand redemptions of 10 percent of its assets in a single day or 30 percent of its assets in a week without having to "sell a single asset into a fragile market."[11] The 2010 amendments also adopted rule 22(e)(3), which permits a MMF's Board of Directors to suspend redemptions when liquidating a fund. In a 2012 report the SEC argues that money market funds are more resilient under these new rules as funds are less likely to break the buck under the 2010 liquidity rules than under the previous rules.[12] However, the report also concludes that the Reserve Primary Fund would still have broken the buck under the new 2010 rules.[13]

19.2   The 2014 Reforms: Floating NAV, Redemption Fees, and Gates

The floating NAV reform under the SEC's 2014 rule will apply to prime institutional money market funds, as well as institutional municipal money market funds—often called tax-free money market funds, which invest in debt instruments issued by municipalities and state authorities[14]—that do not qualify for an exemption. A prime money market fund is any fund that invests more than 0.5 percent of its assets in private short-term debt. The final SEC rule exempts "retail" prime or municipal money market funds, as well as government funds, from the floating NAV reform, but applies the fees and gates reform to retail money market funds. A "retail" money fund is defined as a fund having "policies and procedures reasonably designed to limit all beneficial owners of the fund to *natural persons*."[15] Institutional prime money market funds were the only segment that suffered significant asset outflows during the 2008 financial crisis, with approximately $300 billion (or 14 percent of total assets) withdrawn during the week of

September 15, 2008.[16] While wholesale creditors that are better informed and more active in managing risk are more likely to run, retail investors might still run eventually as well—as noted before without the prompt adoption of Treasury guarantees, they might well have run in the crisis.

Government money market funds (regardless of whether investors are retail or institutional) are excluded from all of the reforms. To qualify as a government money market fund, a fund is required to invest at least 99.5 percent of its total assets in cash, government securities, and/or repurchase agreements that are collateralized exclusively by government securities or cash.[17] This threshold replaced a less stringent 80 percent threshold under rule 2a-7.[18] Again, the basis for the exemption is that runs on government funds did not happen in the crisis—there was indeed a run to such funds. And runs on such funds are highly unlikely in the future. We shall now look at these new rules in more depth.

19.3 Floating NAV

Under the SEC's final rule, institutional prime and municipal institutional money market funds are no longer eligible for two exemptions provided in rule 2a-7 that currently allow funds to maintain a stable NAV, namely to "sell and redeem [money market fund] shares at a stable share price without regard to small variations in the value of the securities that comprise its portfolio."[19] The first of these exemptions—amortized cost valuation—permits a fund to value its portfolio at cost, plus or minus adjustments for amortization of premium or accumulation of discount.[20] The second—"penny-rounding"—is a method of pricing fund shares that allows NAV to be rounded to the nearest one percent (or one penny for funds targeting a $1.00 share price).[21] Loss of these exemptions requires institutional money market funds to "sell and redeem shares based on the current market-based value of the securities in their underlying portfolios, rounded to the fourth decimal place (e.g., $1.0000),"[22] or in other words, adopt a "floating" NAV, with daily share prices generally tracking the mark-to-market value of portfolio assets.

It is highly questionable whether a floating NAV offers a solution to contagion—even if it provides more transparency of pricing to investors. A floating NAV does not reduce the underlying risk of MMF investments, including interest rate risk, credit risk and liquidity risk. MMF investors will continue to need ready access to their cash and have a low tolerance for risk. During stress events, these risk-averse investors are still able to pull back quickly and are incentivized to do so. For example, according to the ICI, "French floating NAV dynamic money funds ... lost about 40 percent of their assets over a three-month time span from July 2007 to September 2007."[23] It is true that under a fixed NAV, that overstates the true value of a fund, there is an incentive to withdraw early at par rather than to remain invested and suffer the actual losses. So if an investor can today withdraw for 100 when the true value is 98 he will do so. The floating NAV will mean the investor can only withdraw today for 98 but that will not stem withdrawals based on fears that the NAV will experience further declines (e.g., to 96). A floating NAV rule might address fairness among investors but early withdrawers from the funds will still get a better price since the fund will first liquidate its most liquid and best-priced assets to fund withdrawals—later withdrawals will be funded with the sales of less liquid and more poorly priced securities.[24] In any event, a floating NAV will not stem contagion.

19.4 Liquidity Fees and Redemption Gates

The SEC's rule also permits the board of a nongovernment money market fund to impose liquidity fees and redemption gates triggered by a fall in a fund's weekly liquid assets to below certain thresholds of the fund's total assets.[25] If a fund's weekly liquidity assets falls below 30 percent of its total assets, investor redemptions from the fund could be subject to a fixed "liquidity fee" of 2 percent, except where the fund's board of directors determines that imposition of such fee would not be in the best interests of the fund. And a fund's board, including a majority of independent directors, would be authorized temporarily to suspend redemptions from the fund, known as a "redemption gate." Any such gate must be lifted within 30 days, and no fund may institute a gate for more than 10 days in any 90-day period.[26] In addition, if such a fund's weekly liquidity assets fall below 10 percent of its total assets, the fund must impose a liquidity fee of one percent on all investor redemptions, unless the fund's board of directors determines the imposition of such a fee would not be in its best interest.[27] In the end all these decisions are left to boards and are not mandated.

The SEC's trigger may prove to render the liquidity fee and redemption gate moot. According to data assembled by Fidelity Investments,[28] money market funds currently hold liquidity in amounts far in excess of the requirements of either rule 2a-7 or the proposed 15 percent weekly liquid assets threshold. The Investment Company Institute (ICI) reports that, as of December 2013, prime money market funds held 23.30 percent of their portfolios in daily liquid assets and 36.29 percent in weekly liquid assets.[29] Consequently it is unlikely the liquidity fee and redemption gates would ever be triggered

In terms of the overall effectiveness of liquidity fees and redemptions, some claim that a fee or an outright redemption restriction would improve the liquidity position of money market funds by reducing MMF investors' incentives to flee, as they did when RPF broke the buck in September 2008. However, SEC Commissioner Kara Stein has emphasized that it is questionable whether the liquidity fee and redemption gate proposal would serve to check contagion, as the threat of such measures could conceivably accelerate redemptions as investors scramble to redeem their shares before the gates are lowered or a liquidation fee is assessed.[30] In unstable market environments, investors may choose to redeem *en masse* in order to avoid the impending redemption restrictions. Indeed, even the SEC acknowledges that "the fees and gates proposal ... would not fully eliminate the incentive to quickly redeem in times of stress, because redeeming shareholders would retain an economic advantage over shareholders that remain in a fund if they redeem when the costs of liquidity are high, but the fund has not yet imposed a fee or gate."[31] Furthermore BlackRock's client research revealed that, if a portion of balances is held back for 30 days and subordinated, MMF investors would redeem even sooner, "at the slightest sign of nervousness in the markets."[32] According to Black-Rock, the complexity of the redemption restriction model is a significant disadvantage in a crisis:

[W]e believe clients would not take the time to navigate the complex structure and would be more likely to redeem earlier—and in this model, 97% of balances are open for redemption. Rather than preventing runs, we believe this approach would act to accelerate a run.[33]

Prior to the adoption of federally insured deposits, withdrawal suspensions were commonly used to combat bank runs in the United States.[34] While these suspensions were a response to fleeing depositors, they were also a cause of depositor flight. If past experience suggests that a bank or a bank regulator will limit withdrawals or redemptions, rational market participants will almost certainly attempt to withdraw their funds prior to their suspension, accelerating the run. While redemption restrictions on bank deposits, in the form of historical bank holidays, were somewhat successful during the Great Depression, they were also accompanied by deposit insurance, which likely achieved more in terms of reassuring depositors. Such public insurance is, of course, not currently available for money market fund investors, as previously discussed. Finally, recent research suggests that money market fund managers may be reluctant to impose fees or restrictions on redemptions for fear that this could be the death knell for the future of such funds. A study of hedge funds that imposed discretionary liquidity restrictions (DLRs) on investors during the 2008 crisis found that the use of the restrictions impacted fund family reputations so that after the crisis funds from DLR families faced difficulty raising capital and were more likely to raise their fees.[35]

19.5 Capital Requirement

Although not adopted—or even proposed—by the SEC, a further reform that has been suggested by FSOC[36] and actually proposed for European funds by Michel Barnier, the EU's European Commissioner for Internal Market and Services,[38] is a requirement that money market funds hold a small capital buffer, such as the 3 percent of NAV proposed by Barnier, which would reduce the risk of a run on money market funds.[39] Research suggests that such a requirement could contribute to financial stability by increasing the ability of MMFs to absorb losses.[40] However, as former SEC Chairman Mary Schapiro suggested in Congressional testimony that "[t]he capital buffer would not necessarily be big enough to absorb losses from all credit events. Instead, the buffer would absorb the relatively small mark-to-market losses that occur in a fund's portfolio day to day, including when a fund is under stress."[41] In this manner the capital buffer would not prevent substantial losses that would come with a major credit event and/or fire sale of assets, which could more than overwhelm a small capital buffer. To the extent that MMF investors may run to avoid such large losses, the capital buffer would not seem to solve the problem of contagion.

19.6 Insurance

As previously noted, insurance for MMFs has also been proposed as a potential reform to prevent future contagion in the industry. In its October 2010 report on MMF reform, the President's Working Group on Financial Markets (PWG) noted that some form of insurance for MMF investors may be useful in "mitigating systemic risk posed by MMFs ...."[42] The report highlights the central role that the Treasury guarantee of MMFs played in stemming runs during the financial crisis and states that insurance would reduce the risk of future runs.[43] Possible insurance programs may be provided by the private sector, the public sector, or a hybrid of the two.[44] A more detailed discussion of MMF insurance is found in Part III, Chapter 11 B.

19.7 End of Public Institutional Prime MMFs?

In recent months there has been concern that there may be a significant reduction in the assets of institutional prime MMFs. Certain large asset managers have indicated that they will further reduce their offerings of institutional prime MMFs. Fidelity recently announced that the firm plans to stop offering prime MMFs and instead offer government money market funds.[45] Charles Schwab recently announced it will convert its institutional MMFs to retail funds and one of its prime funds to government.[46] Furthermore asset managers, including Blackrock and Federated, have indicated that they are considering offering private MMFs that have stable NAVs and no redemption restrictions, as an alternative to SEC publicly registered institutional prime MMFs.[47] Shifting from public to private funds does not eliminate such funds, in fact it makes them more risky since such funds would not even be subject to the 2010 SEC liquidity reforms. But a shift of these funds to government funds would eliminate the risk of runs in those funds; however, such risk would still exist for retail prime funds.

In my view, none of the existing reforms solves the problem of contagion. The options for doing so are: (1) prohibit prime funds, retail or institutional; (2) insure prime funds in some manner; or (3) provide strong lender of last resort to such funds.

20 Dependence of the Financial System on Short-Term Funding

Contagion depends critically on short-term funding, without such funding creditors cannot run. They can, however, refuse to lend more, and this was a major problem in the crisis—institutions that were dependent on short-term funding, like broker-dealers or corporate commercial paper issuers, could not get such funding. If one could design a financial system that was not critically dependent on short-term funding, the possibilities of contagion would be greatly diminished. In the extreme, if there were no private short-term funding, contagion would be impossible. This, of course, depends on one's definition of short-term funding—if short-term funding was defined as 30 days or less, and such funding was replaced by 31 day funding or even 60 day funding, there would still be a contagion concern, albeit it would take more time to unfold. This chapter and the next one explore how short-term funding could be sufficiently limited to control contagion to the point where the need for lender of last resort or guarantees was virtually eliminated, and concludes this is not feasible. It also explores the downside of the government replacing the private sector as supplier of short-term funding.

20.1 Quantifying Short-Term Funding

Financial institutions have increasingly relied on short-term instruments to meet their funding needs.[1] In quantifying an appropriate measure of this reliance on short-term funding, two measures are relevant: a gross amount and a net amount. We estimate both the gross amount, which is all "runnable debt" in the United States, and the net amount, in which we eliminate the double counting of liabilities that arise from financial intermediaries (namely, money market mutual funds and securities lenders). The gross amount is relevant since it is

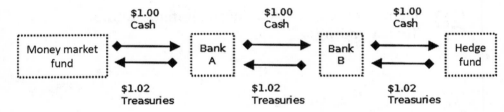

Figure 20.1
Intermediation chain in repo transaction

a measure of how vulnerable the financial system is to panicked runs as a result of short-term debt issuance, while the net amount is relevant to the chapter 21 discussion of how much debt the Treasury or the Fed would have to incur to crowd out private short-term debt with public short-term debt.

Consider the following example that illustrates the difference between the gross and net amounts. Suppose, as illustrated in figure 20.1, that a MMF wishes to lend $1.00 against $1.02 of collateral in a repo transaction, and that a hedge fund wishes to borrow $1.00 against $1.02 of collateral. If the two funds have institutional relationships with different banks (bank A and bank B), their single "net" trade could give rise to three "gross trades." If we are interested in crowding out, one would net the transactions, as the entire chain could be replaced by a single transaction with the Fed, so the net amount is the relevant measure. However, if we are interested in financial fragility, and where runs could start, we should consider each runnable step of the chain and the gross amount is the relevant measure.

20.1.1   Gross Funding
Summarized in table 20.1 are estimates of the $7.4 to $8.2 trillion in gross runnable short-term debt (with maturities of 30 days or less) at the end of 2014, based on the inclusion of repurchase agreements backed by US treasuries. A recent Federal Reserve note places the gross amount of runnable debt at a higher figure based on an inclusion of certain uninsured liabilities that may or may not be runnable. Either way, for contagion purposes, there is still a substantial amount of runnable debt.[2] As previously discussed in chapter 12, the size of the entire private uninsured short-term funding market is approximately $10.6 trillion, or 18.6 percent of the $57 trillion total US credit market, but this higher number is not restricted to 30 day or less maturities.[3]

Table 20.1
Level of runnable short-term debt

Type	USD billions
Runnable commercial paper	$787.9
Runnable repo	1,982.9 w/o treasury repo
	2,743.4 w/ treasury repo
Runnable deposits	2,537.0
Securities lending	720.6
Prime MMF shares	1,401.0
Total	$7,429.4 w/o treasury repo
	$8,189.9 w/ treasury repo

Our estimate of gross short-term funding includes five components: commercial paper, repurchase agreements, uninsured deposits, securities lending, and certain money market fund shares. We adjust these components to more narrowly identify debt of 30 days or less. First, we estimate the total amount of commercial paper with a maturity of thirty days or less to be $788 billion.[4] Second, we estimate the size of the market for repurchase agreements with maturities thirty days or less to be $1,983 billion to $2,743 billion. While the maturity structure of all repo is not available in public filings,[5] it is possible to roughly estimate this figure. Using money market fund repo holdings as proxy for the overall repo market, we estimate that 86 percent of *term* repo has a maturity of thirty days or less. Since the overall repo market (excluding repo purchased from the Fed through its reverse repo program ("RRP"), which is not runnable) is $3,190 billion, there is then roughly $2,743 billion of runnable repo.[6] However, that figure includes repo collaterized by treasuries. Exlcuding treasury-backed repos would drop the amount to $1,983 billion.[7] The inclusion of repos backed by treasuries depends on whether one thinks such repos are "runnable." Recent scholarship suggests that repo collateralized by treasuries is just as vulnerable to runs as other forms of repo, so we include both amounts.[8] Net repo lending from outside the financial sector tends to take place through tri-party repo. Copeland, Martin, and Walker (2014) provide evidence that Lehman Treasury tri-party repo experienced runs as severely as its other forms of tri-party repo. Third, runnable uninsured deposits are $2,537 billion.[9] Fourth, net securities lending liabilities amounts to $721 billion.[10] However, as noted by the New York Fed, most securities lending is conducted by asset managers, pension funds, or insurance companies that engage in the practice to increase yield, not to fund their operations.[11] As a result a run on securities lending will affect returns for these institutions, but not necessarily lead to solvency problems. Finally, we assume that only prime money market mutual funds are at risk of runs, which amount to $1,403 billion.[12] Therefore we estimate that the gross size of runnable private debt is around $7.4 to $8.2 trillion.[13]

20.1.2   Net Funding

We are also interested in estimating a measure of *net* runnable debt, since that is how much debt the Treasury or the Fed would have to incur to crowd out private short-term debt with public short-term debt. Since the *gross* amount double counts many liabilities, as illustrated above in the example of MMFs, the *net* figure should remove the double-counted liabilities. Therefore our estimate of the net amount of runnable debt does not include certain financial intermediaries in the calculation, namely money market mutual funds, and does not include certain financial intermediation transactions, namely securities lending, which are double counted in the gross figure. Further we consider only repo transactions with funding sourced from outside the banking sector since bank-to-bank repo transactions are simply a lengthening of the intermediation chain and are therefore double-counted in the *gross* amount (similar to MMFs). Therefore, to obtain the net amount we only include commercial paper, uninsured deposits, and net repurchase agreements funded outside the banking system (i.e., excluding intra-banking system repo).

As above, the total amount of commercial paper with a maturity of thirty days or less is estimated to be $788 billion and runnable uninsured deposits amount to $2,537 billion. For repos we are interested in the amount of short-term financing that originates from the nonbanking sector, thus excluding the repo transactions that occur entirely among banks. We estimate this amount by determining the quantity of repo assets held by major cash investors, namely money market funds, mutual funds, securities lenders' cash collateral reinvestment, GSEs, and the domestic nonfinancial sector. We then exclude the amounts of the holdings held in Fed RRPs, since those liabilities should not be considered "runnable." Our total estimate amounts to $1,172 billion.[14] However, some of the repo transactions in this figure have maturities greater than thirty days. Therefore, using our prior estimate that 86 percent of *term* repo has a maturity of 30 days or less, we calculate the runnable repo market to be $1,008 billion, including treasury-backed repo. Excluding treasury-backed repo reduces the amount to $729 billion.[15] In total, we estimate that the net size of runnable private debt is around $4.0 to $4.3 trillion.

20.1.3 Importance of Short-Term Funding

The scale of the gross runnable short-term funding market of $8.2 trillion is comparable to the total US government debt of $13 trillion.[16] However, it is nearly six times larger than the $1.4 trillion of US government debt issued with a maturity of less than one year.[17] It is also nearly twice the size of the Federal Reserve's $4.5 trillion balance sheet.[18]

Increased reliance on private short-term funding makes the financial system more susceptible to contagious panics, as illustrated by the run on money market mutual funds during the financial crisis. As noted in the 2014 International Monetary Fund's Global Financial Stability report, the growth in private short-term debt issuance (i.e., growth in the *supply* of short-term debt) may be driven by increased *demand* for money-like securities from large institutional cash pools.[19] These institutional cash pools include the cash balances of large nonfinancial corporations, large institutional investors and asset managers, and large sovereign wealth funds.[20] These cash pools have increased from $2 trillion in 1997 to approximately $6 trillion at the end of 2013.[21] These pools have large cash-management needs, and therefore represent a large and consistent source of demand for safe and liquid money-like claims.[22]

Consistent with this increased demand, recent research has found that the yield on safe short-term debt instruments is lower than would otherwise be expected by the added safety and liquidity of these instruments. They define and quantify this yield differential as the *"money premium."*[23] Indeed the money premium presumably reflects the fact that the recent increase in demand from these pools has not yet been met by a commensurate increase in supply of safe short-term debt instruments. The presence of a money premium therefore *incentivizes* private-sector firms to fund themselves by issuing short-term money-like claims to capture this premium. Issuers do not fully, if at all, internalize the increased risk of contagion created by this increased issuance.[24]

Although total short term funding has not decreased, as set forth in table 12.1 in the chapter 12 section on insuring short-term liabilities, US banks have generally become less reliant on wholesale short-term funding since the peak of the financial crisis. The composition of bank short-term funding in the United States has shifted increasingly from wholesale short-term funding to retail deposits. Wholesale short-term funding as a percentage of retail deposits has declined from roughly 140 percent in 2008 to 62 percent at the end of 2012.[25] While retail funding may not be as likely to disappear in a contagion situation, as reflected in the liquidity coverage ratio, it is still vulnerable to runs. And concern continues about the level of wholesale funding, however reduced. Further the shift of bank short-term funding to the nonbank sector, over which there is less control, arguably makes the situation not better but worse.

20.2   Caps on Short-Term Funding

Federal Reserve Governor Daniel Tarullo has noted the "considerable conceptual appeal" in proposals to actually cap short-term funding, although he also points out the problems with a cap and, therefore, has not endorsed this approach.[26] A short-term funding cap could be instituted through an aggregate industry cap, which would require a consideration of the appropriate threshold consideration what the cap should be, such as some specified percentage of GDP.[27] This approach would also require an analysis of the potential social cost from lost economies of scale and scope if financial institutions are forced to shrink to meet the cap.[28] Regulators must also consider the effects on the stability of the financial system if short-term funding were to switch to the less regulated shadow banking system.[29]

Another approach to limiting short-term funding, endorsed by the UK Independent Commission on Banking in its September 2011, the "Vickers report," would place a cap on the portion of a bank's balance sheet that may be funded with short-term liabilities. While the recently enacted UK Financial Services (Banking Reform) Act of 2013 does not include an explicit short-term funding cap, it does grant regulators authority to require banks to issue "debt instruments of a particular kind,"[30] leaving open the flexibility to limit short-term funding.

The focus on limiting wholesale short-term funding of financial institutions is supported by a number of recent academic studies which show that banks reliant on such funding are more likely to suffer distress.[31] The IMF has found that commercial and investment banks that required government assistance during the 2008 financial crisis held significantly higher ratios of short-term debt to total debt than did banks that did not require assistance.[32] Short-term wholesale funding has also been found to be the best predictor of a bank's contribution to systemic risk.[33]

A key question with regard to capping short-term funding is whether such funding could be limited sufficiently to appreciably reduce contagion risk. Limits on the use of short-term debt could be implemented in conjunction with an extended insurance regime for short-term liabilities, but there could be a practical inability to lower short-term debt to a level that would appreciably reduce the probability of contagion remains.

20.3 Indirect Limits on Short-Term Funding

Various academic studies have suggested indirect ways in which restrictions on short-term funding might be implemented. Many of these proposals are aimed at reforming the use of repurchase agreements and money market funds, which dominate the short-term financing markets, as asset backed commercial paper has largely disappeared as a funding instrument for financial institutions.[34]

One proposal is to reduce banks' reliance on short term funding by rolling back 2005 amendments to the Bankruptcy Code that added repurchase agreements on mortgage-related assets to the exemptions from the automatic stay, the normal bankruptcy rules preventing the seizure of collateral.[35] Prior to 2005, collateral in repurchase agreement transactions eligible for the automatic stay was limited to US government and agency securities, bank certificates of deposits, and bankers' acceptances. Rolling back this new exemption would arguably increase counterparty risks on these repurchase agreements thereby reducing the willingness of financial institutions to enter into them for short-term funding. Moreover, narrowing the safe harbors to only the most predictably liquid securities can help prevent these exemptions from exacerbating a liquidity crisis.[36] Although safe harbors are designed to insulate counterparties from default at the individual level, they can actually function to aggravate liquidity problems, as they facilitate "panic selling."[37]

Other proposals also focus on repurchase agreements, including calling for strict regulation of securities used as collateral in repurchase agreements, limiting such collateral to only the highest quality securities for banks.[38] One study has found that during the 2008 financial crisis, the contraction in repurchase agreements played a significant role for systemically important dealer banks. For example, nearly half of the repurchase agreements of Merrill Lynch, Goldman Sachs, and Citigroup with money market funds were backed by nonagency MBS/ABS and corporate debt, and almost all of this financing disappeared during the crisis.[39] The FSB has recommended that regulators consider mandatory haircuts on collateral for all repurchase agreements.[40]

Another future Fed action that could potentially affect the short-term funding market is the Fed's impending implementation of restrictive margin requirements for securities financing transactions.[41] While the Fed's main objective with the restrictions would likely be to address asset bubbles, higher margin requirements would directly reduce the amount of short-term funding that can be obtained with a given amount of collateral. The Office of Financial Research estimates this market to be $4.4 trillion.[42] However, the effect of higher margin requirements on short-term funding markets will be dampened because the new rules will likely exempt Treasurys and agency securities, which make up two-thirds of the market.[43] Regardless, as the increased restrictions limit the use of a portion of the securities financing market, the effect may be an overall increase in unsecured borrowing. Substituting unsecured borrowing for secured borrowing will consequently expose the financial system to greater risk, not less, which should be seriously considered as an unintended consequence in the wrong direction.

21 Government Crowding Out of Private Issuance of Short-Term Debt

Some have suggested that the government should increase the effective supply of public short-term debt in order to meet the demand by institutional cash managers for safe short-term debt. In the extreme case, if the government eliminated private issuance of short-term debt by issuing enough public short-term debt to satisfy this demand, then there could be no runs and no contagion. The same result could be achieved if the remaining short-term debt of the financial system was so small that runs would not be significant. These policies can be characterized as "crowding out" private short-term debt.

21.1 Crowding Out by the Treasury

As suggested by Greenwood, Hanson, and Stein (2015), and Carson et al. (2014), the Treasury could crowd out runnable private short-term debt by replacing a certain amount of long-term Treasury debt issuance with shorter term Treasury debt. Investors that would otherwise buy and hold private short-term debt would instead buy Treasuries. This approach, of course, raises the questions of whether the Treasury has the capacity to do so and what the consequences would be if it did.

At the end of 2014, the total US debt outstanding was over $13 trillion (excluding intra-governmental holdings),[1] $1.4 trillion of which was issued with a maturity of one year or less ("Treasury bills" or "T-bills").[2] T-bills are issued in various lengths: 4, 13, 26, or 52 weeks, and "cash management bills" can have maturities as short as a few days.[3] The weighted average maturity of T-bills was 90 days between 1995 and 2009. Evidence suggests that T-bills with shorter maturity provide the most significant short-term safety and thus substitutability with short-term private debt.[4] Thus, for purposes of crowding out private short-term debt, the US Treasury would have to shift its issuance to shorter maturities *within* T-bills.[5] A potential issue to consider is whether such a shift would have significant consequences for the dollar's status as a reserve currency. In February 2015, foreign holdings of US treasuries stood at roughly $4.1 trillion.[6] Of this, only around $350 billion (8.5 percent of total) was held in short-term Treasury bills.[7] If foreign governments have a preference for long-term debt, as appears to be the case, the shift to short-term issuance and corresponding decline in the supply of long-term Treasuries might weaken the dollar's status as a dominant reserve currency. However, recent history has also illustrated periods of higher relative preferences for short-term US treasuries with many periods substantially higher than the 8.5 percent listed above. The percentage has peaked at nearly 28 percent since 2000,[8] suggesting that a lowering of maturities may not significantly impact the dollar's status as a reserve currency.

In figure 20.1 of chapter 20 we estimated that there was roughly $4.3 trillion in net runnable short-term debt in the United States at the end of 2014. The net amount is more relevant for this analysis than the gross amount, since the crowding out of the net amount will also eliminate the financial intermediation of short-term liabilities that is included in the gross amount, as discussed in chapter 20. Therefore it is only necessary for the government to crowd out the net amount of short-term liabilities. Assuming that $1 of T-bills crowds out $1 of private short-term debt, then the Treasury would have to issue $4.3 trillion in short-term liabilities—in addition to the $1.4 trillion outstanding—to completely crowd out private issuance. As a result $5.7 trillion (or 44 percent) of the Treasury's $13 trillion total debt would have to be in T-bills in order to fully crowd out the $4.3 trillion private short-term debt market. Such a dramatic shift in the maturity structure of the Treasury's liabilities would have to be an incremental process. The Treasury could not simply issue $4.3 trillion in short-term Treasury debt in the immediate term. This would, of course, increase the total outstanding debt and violate debt-ceiling limits that only moderately exceed total current debt levels. However, if the US Treasury were to fund all future projected fiscal deficits and pay off all outstanding debt as it matures with T-bills, then we estimate that it would reach $5.7 trillion in outstanding T-bills in 2017.[9] Thus it is technically *possible* for this policy to fully crowd out private short-term debt issuance within a reasonably short time.

It is notable that even if the policy objective was a *partial* crowding out of private short-term debt issuance, then such a policy would still require a very large amount of increased T-bill issuance to meaningfully reduce contagion risk. As a counterfactual, if T-bill issuance were increased by $1 trillion, then this would only reduce the size of the private short-term debt market from $4.3 trillion to $3.3 trillion. A financial system with $3.3 trillion in private short-term debt is still quite vulnerable to contagion.

However, there are serious concerns with dramatically changing the maturity structure of US government debt that renders this approach impracticable. On the one hand, given a typically upward-sloping yield curve, lowering the maturity of debt issuance could reduce funding costs. On the other hand, switching government debt issuance to short-term maturities exposes the US government to the unpredictable fluctuations of future interest rates and forces the roll-over of substantial amounts of debt at one time.[10] This risk is highly problematic because it makes future budget planning, and thus future taxes, more unpredictable.[11] Additionally it may be important for the United States to lock in low long-term interest rates today, during a period of historically low interest rates. For example, while 30-year rates today are approximately 2.7 percent, historically, they have been much higher, averaging as high as 9 percent in 1990 and 6 percent in 2000.[12]

In a political climate of debt ceilings and government shutdowns, the risk of increased funding costs is even more problematic. Although the Treasury has very little risk of becoming insolvent, there is a small but nonnegligible probability that a failure to increase the debt ceiling could force a temporary "technical default," whereby the Treasury could not pay interest on all of its T-bills. During this time, it would be likely that the short-term creditors of the US Treasury would demand higher interest rates in order to bear this risk.[13]

21.2   Crowding Out by the Federal Reserve

The Federal Reserve could also "crowd out" private short-term debt, using its new tools of monetary policy—interest on excess reserves ("IOER") and reverse repurchase agreements ("RRPs"). It is important to understand how these tools are used to conduct monetary policy in order to assess whether efforts to crowd out private short-term funding with these tools could conflict with monetary policy. This section first presents a very general overview of how and why the Fed uses IOER and RRPs for monetary policy. It then describes how these tools could be used to crowd out private issuance of short-term debt, and concludes with an evaluation of this approach.

21.2.1 General Overview of Fed's Tools of Monetary Policy[14]

The federal funds rate ("FFR") is the rate at which banks lend reserves to one another overnight.[15] This rate is determined by the market, although the Fed uses its tools of monetary policy to guide market rates to the target FFR announced by the Federal Open Markets Committee.[16] The Fed establishes a baseline demand for reserves by setting reserve requirements, which are minimum amounts of reserves that depository institutions must hold against their deposits.[17] Historically the Fed would set a target FFR and guide market rates to the target by marginally adjusting the level of reserves in the banking system.[18] However, the total level of reserves and the overall size of the Fed's balance sheet grew dramatically after the financial crisis. Presently banks hold approximately $90 billion in required reserves and approximately $2.6 *trillion* in excess reserve balances with the Fed.[19] With the supply of reserves far exceeding banks' required reserves, modest adjustments to the total outstanding level of required reserves would clearly no longer result in a meaningful change in banks' ability or willingness to lend overnight at the FFR.[20] This is because banks are easily able to meet moderately higher minimum reserve requirements in an environment where $2.6 trillion in *excess* reserves exist.[21] As a result, while the Fed has historically used open market operations to set interest rates, recently rates are set by Fed guidance through announcements instead.[22]

It is important to note that the Fed *created* these excess reserves as part of their lending and buying programs during the financial crisis and quantitative easing programs after the crisis.[23] Indeed only the Fed can increase or decrease the total level of reserves in the banking system, as the total level of reserves "is not affected by banks' lending decisions."[24] While one bank may be able to marginally increase or decrease its level of reserves, this will necessarily be offset by an equal and offsetting increase or decrease in the reserves of another bank.[25]

21.2.2 Interest on Excess Reserves and Reverse Repo Program

Under current conditions the Fed must now use interest on excess reserves ("IOER") and its "trial" reverse repo program ("RRP") to set the effective floor of the FFR. IOER is simply an interest payment by the Fed on excess reserves. The Fed also pays interest on required reserves. An RRP is a short-term cash loan from an approved market participant (including nonbanks as well as banks), which is secured by collateral from the Federal Reserve's securities portfolio.[26] The Fed has implemented term RRPs of between one week and a month and overnight RRPs as part of their trial program. Current approved RRP counterparties include primary dealers, banks, MMFs, and GSEs.[27] The Fed has stated that the program is temporary and for monetary policy purposes.[28]

These programs guide market rates toward the target FFR by eliminating the incentive for banks and nonbanks to lend at rates lower than what the Fed is paying on IOER and RRPs, respectively. This is because the interest paid on reserves and RRPs are generally viewed as risk free; why loan to anyone else at a lower rate when you can get at least the same rate from the Fed risk free?[29] The IOER is currently set at 25 basis points.[30] However, the IOER cannot set the effective floor for the FFR by itself, since nonbank short-term lenders like MMFs and the GSEs cannot hold reserves and are therefore willing to lend at rates below the IOER. The Fed's RRP program sets the risk-free rate for these nonbank lenders. It is currently paying interest between 5 and 11 basis points.[31] While banks have an incentive to arbitrage away any difference between the IOER rate and the RRP rate (having access to both), they cannot entirely do so, given the deposit insurance premiums paid to the FDIC on deposits. The Fed is widely expected to raise the FFR this year and has stated that it will use both IOER and RRP to do so.

21.2.3 IOER and RRP Impact on Private Short-Term Debt Issuance

The impact that IOER and the RRP program, respectively, have on the private short-term debt market differs in important respects. With regard to IOER, simply increasing the interest paid on reserves does not directly "crowd out" private short-term debt issuance because it only affects banks and the banking system as a whole cannot meaningfully increase the total level of reserves held at the Fed. However, academics have found that the RRP program clearly has a "crowding out" effect on private short-term debt issuance.[32] Understanding why necessitates an explanation of how the RRP program affects the Fed's balance sheet. According to a recently released NY Fed study on the RRP program, "RRP take-up does **not** expand the size of the Federal Reserve's balance sheet ... [it] shifts the composition of the Federal Reserve's liabilities *from* [excess] reserves held by banks *to* RRPs that can be held by a wider range of institutions."[33] In other words, the amount of excess reserves *decreases*, as RRPs take up increases, and therefore the amount of total public (i.e., Fed) short-term liabilities stays neutral.

But if the total amount of public short-term liabilities does not increase, then why do RRPs "crowd out" private short-term debt issuance? According to the NY Fed, "the crowding out of private financing that results from greater use of RRPs largely represents a reduction in private lending by money market investors (with access to RRPs) to banks that are financing reserves."[34] Instead, these investors lend to the Fed.

This is best demonstrated with an example. For example, absent the RRP program, a money market fund would have been incentivized to enter into a repo with a bank or to buy commercial paper issued by a bank at a rate exceeding 0 percent. If the money market fund had previously deposited cash with the bank, then the switch to supplying funds to the Fed in the RRP would shrink the bank's deposits. The private short-term liability issued by the bank (the repo, commercial paper, or deposit) would have clearly counted toward the overall $8.1 trillion in private short-term debt, and such private short-term debt overall has been reduced.

21.2.4   Size of the RRP Program

The *size* of the RRP program (and therefore the extent to which it crowds out private short-term debt) depends on the interest rates offered by the Fed.[35] The Fed has found that whenever it offers rates that are slightly closer to prevailing short-term market repo rates—the RRP rate is generally lower than market repo rates—then it gets increased take up on its RRP program.[36]

This link between size of the RRP program and interest rates can also be clarified with an example. The current program, which is paying between 5 and 11 basis points, is not meeting its size caps. As of December 31, 2014, the Fed offered $600 billion in RRPs: $300 billion in overnight RRPs ("ON RRPs") and $300 billion in term RRPs and had total RRP take up of only $397 billion—$171 billion in ON RRPs and $226 billion in term RRPs.[37] Clearly, the Fed could increase uptake to the full $600 billion in RRPs by offering substantially higher rates (e.g., 1 percent). In this example money market investors that are lending at rates below 1 percent would be incentivized to enter into an RRP transaction with the Fed instead of lending to riskier private counterparties at a lower rate. However, raising the rate to 1 percent would of course be inconsistent with Fed's monetary policy goals, which currently require near zero interest rates. In a very low interest rate environment, it is difficult to use RRP to crowd out.

But the size of the RRP program is expected to grow if and when the Fed raises rates. According to the NY Fed, when the FOMC decides to raise the target FFR, the extent to which the RRP program "crowds out" private short-term debt will also increase.[38] Indeed, if the RRP program is to set the effective floor on the FFR, then the growth of the RRP program is likely. This is because in order to set the floor of the FFR, the RRP program must offer a sufficient supply of RRPs to meet the demand for RRPs at that interest rate.[39] Otherwise, money market investors will still be incentivized to lend in private markets at a rate below the interest rate paid by the RRP program. However, the extent to which the size of the RRP program will grow as the Fed raises rates is less clear (especially since the Fed has stated it is a temporary program). Certain market participants have estimated that the RRP program could grow to $1 trillion.[40] At the same time, while it is likely that the Fed must grow the RRP program to increase rates, there is a possibility that the Fed can announce rates rather than expand its balance sheet to set interest rates.[41] The Fed can also use both the RRP and the IOER to set interest rates wherever it wants.

21.2.5   Potential Conflicts between Monetary Policy and Increasing the RRP Program to "Crowd Out" Private Short-Term Debt

Banks currently hold $2.6 trillion in excess reserves with the Fed. Therefore the size of the RRP program could be increased to $2.6 trillion without the Fed having to create reserves by buying additional assets or lending. However, the relationship between the quantity of uptake on RRPs and the interest rate that must be offered on RRPs to achieve that uptake will determine whether RRPs can be used to crowd out private short-term debt issuance without conflicting with monetary policy goals.

Once again, an example is instructive. Suppose that the Fed wanted to set a floor interest rate of 1 percent in order to achieve its monetary policy objectives. Suppose further that the Fed, completely apart from its monetary policy objectives and in an effort to foster financial stability, also wanted to crowd out $500 billion of private issuance. If the take-up at 1 percent were less than $500 billion, the Fed would have to raise the RRP rate to achieve the desired level of crowding out. If only very minor adjustments to the rate paid on RRPs (0.01 percent) were necessary to achieve large increases in uptake (hundreds of billions), then the Fed would be able to substantially increase uptake without conflicting with monetary policy goals. However, if larger adjustments were necessary (0.25 percent or greater) to obtain a meaningful increase in uptake, then achieving an increase in size of the RRP program would clearly conflict with monetary policy goals. Note, however, that this may be less of a concern in practice because the financial markets will observe the RRP rates and adjust market rates accordingly.

The extent of uptake would depend in part on the spread between the Fed RRP rate and the rates paid in private repo markets. For example, if money market investors are collectively lending trillions at a rate only 0.01 percent above the Fed RRP rate, then it is likely that a very marginal increase in the Fed RRP rate could result in substantial uptake in the RRP program. However, if most money market investors are lending short term at rates substantially higher than the Fed RRP rate (suppose 0.5 percent), then the opposite may be true.

There is some evidence that there is a significant amount of lending taking place only marginally above the effective FFR, as the level of take-up on overnight RRPs with the Fed increases substantially with only very minor increases to the interest rate paid on RRPs relative to the "market repo rate."[42] The market repo rate is the interest rate paid on repo transactions between two private-sector firms. This suggests that, in the above example, only a very small increase in the RRP rate above 1 percent would be required to achieve the desired crowding out effect. In other words, if this holds true, then there is no significant conflict between monetary policy and crowding out.

However, if the Fed sought to crowd out more than $2.6 trillion in short-term debt, there could be a conflict with monetary policy because it would be increasing the total reserves in the system. For example, suppose that the Fed was seeking to reduce outstanding credit in the system ("tightening") by raising interest rates, while also crowding out private short-term debt by increasing RRP beyond $2.6 trillion. Reserves would have to be increased through asset purchases on the open market, which would increase the reserve balances of banks that sold assets. Holding all else equal, these asset purchases by the Federal Reserve would amount to a higher level of demand for debt instruments at a given interest rate. This higher level of demand would put downward pressure on interest rates, potentially interfering with the monetary policy objective of "tightening" credit conditions by raising interest rates.

21.2.6   Adverse Consequences of Partial and Full Crowding Out via RRP

If the Fed sought to avoid conflicts with monetary policy, by only using its RRP program to the extent of $2.6 trillion, the remaining $1.7 trillion in short-term debt (we assume total private short-term debt is $4.3 trillion) is still vulnerable to contagion. Thus, while the system would be less vulnerable to contagion ex ante, we will still need to be prepared to deal with it if it still occurs.

But even partially crowding out private-sector issuance raises a number of concerns. If public short-term debt issuance expands during a crisis, as opposed to before a crisis, it may create destabilizing effects for the residual private-sector issuance. Specifically, the expanding public issuance could exacerbate runs by allowing for "disruptive flight-to-quality flows during a period of financial stress and thus could undermine financial stability."[43] It is the rapid *change* of money market investors from private to public short-term funding that would be destabilizing,[44] since the sudden lack of funding sources may leave private institutions incapable of rolling over their debt.[45]

Further, if the Fed ultimately does succeed in crowding out enough private-sector issuance to appreciably lower contagion risks, the increase in liabilities from newly issued debt will require an increase in assets. In other words, the Fed will have to decide which securities to invest in on the left-hand side of its balance sheet as the liabilities increase on the right-hand side. Should it buy corporate commercial paper or corporate bonds? And if so, from which companies? There would also be the question of what counterparties the Fed would enter into RRPs with on the right-hand side of its balance sheet, raising fairness concerns and concerns about the appropriate role of government in a capitalist system.

In addition there would be the impact on financial institutions that must now replace the short-term debt absorbed by the Fed with longer term debt at higher cost. The impact to those entities no longer able to obtain short-term funding could be particularly damaging because certain valuable activities for the economy should in fact be funded with short-term liabilities. Broker-dealers fund very short-term assets with short-term liabilities, and this makes economic sense. We may make the system safer from contagion but at what cost?

Moreover, if the Fed did expand its balance sheet to appreciably crowd out private issuance,[46] the assets it adds would have to bear enough interest to finance payments on RRP. As a result the Fed may have to take on additional balance sheet risk. If the Fed invests in assets that lose value, or if they do not earn sufficient interest, Fed remittances to the Treasury would decrease and taxes or higher deficits would have to make up the difference.

An expanded balance sheet also raises questions about political economy. The average federal funds rate since 1954 is slightly above 5 percent. If the Fed paid this rate on $8.1 trillion of liabilities, this would amount to around $405 billion in interest payments annually. This is comparable to the Department of Defense's $496 billion budget in 2014.[47] Interest payments on this scale may be difficult to defend in the current political climate questioning the role of the Fed in general, and may therefore further jeopardize the Fed's independence.

My conclusion is that measures to limit short-term funding, particularly through the Fed, deserve further study. The costs of replacing this cheaper short-term funding with more expensive long-term funding, which may not be optimal for particular activities, such as broker-dealer activities, should also be examined. But for now, it would seem highly unlikely that short-term debt issued by the private sector could be sufficiently reduced to obviate the need for a strong lender of last resort and flexible guarantee system.

V Public Capital Injections into Insolvent Financial Institutions

This part focuses on public capital injections into banks, which for short we will call "bailouts," as distinct from liquidity support from the Federal Reserve or deposit or short-term liability insurance. While the central bank's role as lender of last resort is well established, bailouts are more controversial. As Bernardo, Talley, and Welch (2011) suggest, prior to 2007 most academic economists viewed government bailouts as "aberrations of developing countries, artifacts of political patronage, or idiosyncrasies of the banking industry."[1] Significant academic skepticism remains "about the wisdom of bailouts as a categorical matter."[2] However, as with TARP, bailouts are realistically the lesser of two evils, if economic collapse is the alternative.

While central bank liquidity and guarantees should be the first line of defense against contagion, one may still need to deal with the negative economic impact of the failure of large banks. Such multiple failures can arise due to correlation risk, the same negative external event, such as a sharp decline in housing prices. The first line of defense against insolvency is capital or increased TLAC to allow resolution, but even higher capital requirements or TLAC may be insufficient to protect the system against widespread, steep losses. While one can possibly envision resolving one or maybe even two of our largest financial institutions simultaneously in OLA, an entire insolvent system is another matter. Indeed, this is what Japan faced in the "lost decade."

Capital injections may become necessary when other measures, including central bank lending or government guarantees are no longer effective. If a large number of financial institutions are in trouble because significant losses have consumed their equity base, additional lending to the institutions may not help. To remain viable, the institutions may have to be recapitalized. As one commentator put it, no matter how much a central bank lends to entities with negative capital, "the capital is still negative."[3]

Bailouts through use of public funds are only necessary when efforts to raise private capital do not succeed. Private capital, however, may be insufficient and may therefore make public investments necessary. Due to asymmetric information, private investors may refuse to invest in troubled financial institutions; the government may be in a better position to overcome the information asymmetry.[4] In addition troubled financial institutions may not be able to attract new private equity because of the problem of "debt overhang." If a firm is heavily leveraged and is on the verge of bankruptcy, any increase in firm value due to an equity infusion largely goes to debt holders.[5] Government intervention thus becomes necessary to overcome the debt overhang problem.

In theory, troubled financial institutions could sell their illiquid and troubled assets to generate capital. Diamond and Rajan (2010) ask why new investors, such as vulture funds, did not step in to purchase those assets at a bargain price during the financial crisis.[6] They argue that the possibility of a future fire sale may explain banks' inability to dispose of toxic assets. Greenwood et al. contend that modest equity injections can dramatically reduce systemic risk if they are optimized to minimize the aggregate impact of fire sales.[7] Yet a recapitalization plan could be quickly rolled out and would have the added benefit of boosting lending activities.

Capital Purchase Program and Other TARP
Support Programs

We turn now to examining the Capital Purchase Program, the principal
form of capital injection used by the United States during the financial
crisis. As the earlier part of this book has discussed in detail, the collapse of Lehman Brothers triggered widespread turmoil in the global
financial market beyond the expectations of Chairman Bernanke and
Secretary Paulson.[8] Just two days after its bankruptcy, the Federal
Reserve had to extend an $85 billion emergency credit facility to AIG,
even though some might have considered a capital injection by Treasury to be the better response. The market was deeply confused by the
government's seemingly ad hoc bailout decisions. Who will be bailed
out? Who will be let go? Following Bear Stearns's rescue a few months
before, it was assumed that others would also be bailed out. When
Lehman sent the opposite message, the rescue of AIG just days later
was insufficient to stop contagion fueled by the continuing guessing
game. The government finally abandoned its ad hoc approach, which
had so far relied heavily on the Federal Reserve and the FDIC, and
decided to adopt a comprehensive and proactive plan with direct
involvement by the Treasury.

After the rescue of AIG on September 16,[9] it was highly uncertain
that a bailout plan could be quickly approved. Initially, members of
Congress were outraged by Secretary Paulson's original three-page
proposal—some called a "term sheet"—for granting Treasury broad
authority to purchase $700 billion of toxic assets.[10] Even after the pro-
posal was greatly elaborated, it was rejected by the House of Representatives on September 29, 2008, by a vote largely along party lines (with
Republicans opposing).[11] The S&P500 plummeted 8.5 percent after the
failure.[12] The Senate voted two days later to pass a revised bill and the
final bill passed the House on October 3 only after many members of

Congress reluctantly switched positions.[13] It was signed into law by President Bush on October 3.

22.1   Design of TARP

The resulting Emergency Economic Stabilization Act of 2008 (EESA) established the Troubled Asset Relief Program (TARP) to stabilize the US financial system.[14] The core of the recapitalization plan under TARP was the Capital Purchase Program (CPP), under which "healthy, viable" financial institutions would receive capital injections from Treasury.[15] The first nine recipients—the systematically important banks in the United States—had already agreed to the recapitalization plan when Secretary Paulson announced the plan on October 14, 2008.[16] Many of these banks were actively seeking to augment their capital bases or merge with a stronger bank at the early stage of the financial crisis. Shortly before the announcement of the Capital Purchase Program, both Goldman Sachs and Morgan Stanley were able to secure financing from sources such as Warren Buffet and foreign investors.[17]

The CPP was a program open to all qualified financial institutions approved by their respective banking regulators, whether large or small.[18] The government wanted the healthy as well as less healthy major banks—the first nine recipients—to take government assistance to avoid publicly identifying any banks as insolvent. However, it appears that analysts could independently distinguish the relative health of the banks.[19] As we will see, other countries did not follow this all banks approach. While it is clear that politics favored giving support to small as well as large banks, the failure of small banks (unless cumulatively significant) would not have endangered the system. The demand for CPP investments by smaller banks soared after the market considered receiving CPP funding as getting on the "survivor list" and those not receiving the investments as too unhealthy to be rescued.[20] Also adding to the demand was the opportunity the CPP presented for small banks to obtain a relatively cheap source of funding through the program. Between October 2008 and December 2009, Treasury invested a total of $205 billion in 707 banking institutions.[21] Although the initial investments in the nine financial institutions in October 2008 accounted for more than half of the total CPP investments[22] and ten of the largest firms received almost 70 percent of the funds under the CPP,[23] Treasury made numerous smaller investments in institutions of less than $100 million in assets.[24]

Participating financial institutions received capital injections under the same standard terms irrespective of their financial health.[25] Most investments were in the form of perpetual preferred shares, although those firms that could not issue preferred shares (e.g., S corporations) issued subordinated debt instead.[26] At the later stages of its investments in Citigroup, AIG, and other financial institutions, the US Treasury replaced its preferred stock with common stock.[27] But this replacement did not oust common entirely, it just diluted it.[28] Apart from the obvious benefit of savings on interest payments, one reason cited by the recipient banks for the conversion was the market's view that tangible common equity is an important measure of financial strength, even if preferred stock would also qualify for tier I capital.[29] Treasury agreed because it would be easier to sell the common than preferred when it later exited from its capital position.[30] In the end, only about 50 banks, mainly small community banks, issued subordinated debt instead of preferred shares.[31]

Preferred stock was also the primary investment tool used by the Reconstruction Finance Corporation during the Great Depression.[32] Many scholars have compared the current financial crisis with the Great Depression and pointed out that the Reconstruction Finance Corporation (RFC) became successful only after it switched from making loans to troubled banks to making preferred stock investments because the more RFC lent, the less likely that unsecured creditors could recoup their investments.[33] As a result studies have found that the more banks borrowed from the RFC during the Great Depression, the more likely they were to fail.[34] Bailout therefore plays a role that may not be fulfilled by other forms of public assistance.

Preferred stock has several advantages over other instruments. First, it can be structured to qualify for the firm's tier I capital, while retaining debt-like characteristics of deductible interest payments that could be relevant to investors who might later buy the stock from the government. Since cumulative perpetual preferred stock does not qualify as tier I capital under the US Basel IIII rules,[35] this capital treatment will require the preferred stock to be noncumulative perpetual with no dividend rate step-ups. On the other hand, interest payments, if made on preferred stock, put a burden on the financial institution that common stock does not. A second advantage of preferred stock is it allows the government, as preferred stockholder, to rank between debt holders and common stockholders in terms of priority. It is therefore possible to dilute or eliminate common stockholders' interests while protecting the value of the company's other debt securities. Third, preferred stock does not put the government in the limelight as the outright owner of an institution, even though it may exert considerable influence on management through contractual arrangements granting the holder voting power and/or veto power on strategic issues, as well as the power to appoint directors and remove the board.[36]

One of the drawbacks of preferred stock is that it preserves the claim of common shareholders, thus giving them an upside in the case of recovery. Given the complete paybacks of most financial firms that received TARP assistance, and all the large ones including AIG, the preservation of this upside is significant. Arguably, for moral hazard purposes, it would be better to dispossess equity entirely in any capital injection program, or at the very least heavily dilute it.

Below is a summary of the key investment terms under the CPP. According to the Congressional Oversight Panel, the documentation for CPP investments was "quite similar to, and appears to be based on," the documentation for Warren Buffet's earlier investment in Goldman Sachs.[37]

As of December 31, 2014, 673 of the 707 financial institutions that received capital under the CPP had exited the program.[38] 254 of the firms that had exited as of that date did so via repurchase of their preferred shares or subordinated debentures and 185 institutions had their investments sold at auction.[39] In addition 137 community banks refinanced their CPP investments into Treasury investments under the Small Business Lending Fund and 28 banks converted their CPP investments into investments under the Community Development Capital Initiative under TARP.[40] Thirty-two of these exits occurred via bankruptcy or receivership.[41]

The US government made it clear that it was only reluctantly helping troubled banks when the TARP bailout legislation was passed. Chairman Bernanke said: "Government assistance should be provided with the greatest reluctance and only when the stability of the financial system, and thus the health of the broader economy, is at risk. In those cases when financial stability is threatened, however, intervention to protect the public interest may well be justified."[42] The sentiment was echoed by then-Secretary Paulson: "We regret having to take these actions. Today's actions are not what we ever wanted to do—but today's actions are what we must do to restore confidence to our financial system."[43]

More important, bailouts are now regarded as politically taboo under the anti-bailout consensus in Washington, and concern with capital injections, even more so than with lender of last resort or guarantees, is at the heart of the bailout concern. While those powers were severely restricted, the capital injection program was abolished altogether.

22.2 Expiration and Wind-Down of TARP

Authority to make and fund commitments to purchase assets under the TARP programs, including the CPP, could only take place for a limited period of time, as prescribed by the 2008 Emergency Economic Stabilization Act ("EESA") that created TARP. Pursuant to Section 120 of the EESA, TARP authority was initially set to terminate on December 31, 2009, but the Treasury Department had authority under that section to extend the TARP commitment period to October 3, 2010.[44] In December 2009, the Treasury Department did so.[45] In July 2010, the Dodd–Frank Wall Street Reform and Consumer Protection Act separately decreased TARP purchase authority from $700 billion to $475 billion.[46] Dodd–Frank also expressly prohibited TARP authority under the EESA from being used to incur any obligation for a program or initiative that was not initiated before June 25, 2010.[47]

Accordingly, no new funds can now be committed to a TARP program and no new TARP programs can be established. Furthermore Section 106(d) of the EESA requires that when recipients of funds that were disbursed by TARP programs pay back their funds that such funds be deposited with the US Treasury, so that they cannot be used to further fund any future disbursements.[48] In other words, TARP funds cannot be reused once then have been disbursed to a private borrower and paid back to the US Treasury. Dodd–Frank made this point crystal clear, by amending the EESA's text to remove any potential ambiguities in the language about the funds' reuse.[49] However, the Treasury has the statutory authority under Section 106(e) of the EESA to continue to disburse the funds that were already allocated for each TARP program before October 3, 2010, but have not yet been actually disbursed to private borrowers.[50]

TARP programs for banks have essentially been wound-down, as there are no funds allocated to banks generally that have not been used. The only reason that the programs are not completely wound down is that certain small banks that received $625 million funds from these

Table 22.1
Standardized investment terms under the Capital Purchase Program

Size	• 1–3% of RWA (increased to 5% for small banks) but no more than $25 billion.
Preferred securities issued	• Senior perpetual nonconvertible preferred shares at $1,000 per share.
Dividend rights	• Quarterly cumulative compounding dividends for institutions that are not subsidiaries of BHCs. (Note this requirement does not apply to most of the large recipients, as CPP investment is required to occur at the highest holding level.) Noncumulative dividends for those that are subsidiaries of BHCs in order to qualify as tier I capital.
	• 5% per annum for the first five years, 9% thereafter.
Voting rights	• Limited customary voting rights for preferred stock.[a]
	• If dividends are not paid for six quarters, holders of preferred shares have the right to elect two directors to board.
Redemption of preferred shares	• Preferred shares cannot be redeemed within the first three years unless a qualified equity offering occurs. (This requirement was later changed by the American Recovery and Reinvestment Act of 2009 [ARRA],[b] which permits redemption in full subject to consultation with appropriate banking regulators.)
Warrants issued	• In addition to nonconvertible preferred shares, for a *public company*, Treasury receives warrants to purchase common stock in an amount equal to 15% of Treasury's preferred stock investment at exercise price. Exercise price equals average market price of the common stock in the 20-day period prior to the acceptance of the application by Treasury. For a *private company*, Treasury receives warrants to purchase a separate series of preferred stock (with a dividend rate of 9%) in an amount up to 5% of its original preferred stock investment. Treasury will exercise these warrants immediately.[c]
	• Warrants valid for 10 years.
	• The investee has the right to reduce the number of shares underlying the warrants by half if it raises 100% of the issue price of the preferred stock in qualified offerings before the end of 2009.
Repurchase of warrants	• The issuer has right to repurchase any equity securities (including warrants) held by Treasury at fair market value once the preferred shares are redeemed or transferred.
	• If the issuer does not repurchase the warrants, Treasury may sell them by auction.

Table 22.1 (continued)

Covenants	• Dividends on common stock must be capped at the last quarterly level in the first three years. For private companies, dividend payments could increase only 3% each year thereafter and no dividend permitted after 10 years.[d]
	• Executive compensation practices to comply with EESA requirements, as subsequently amended by AARA and interpreted by Treasury regulations. These restrictions include (1) prohibition on bonus payments during TARP assistance to the five senior executive officers and the next 20 most highly compensated employees except in the form of limited long-term restricted stock, (2) prohibition on severance payments to the five senior executive officers and the next five most highly compensated employees during TARP assistance, (3) adoption of governance standards that eliminate unnecessary risk-taking incentives and prohibit plans encouraging earnings' manipulation,[e] and (4) clawback of improperly determined payments to the five senior executive officers and the next 20 most highly compensated employees.
	• There is no covenant as to the use of proceeds, the adoption of a restructuring plan or other restriction on business activities.

Note: This summary is based on the acquisition agreement for Treasury's investment in JPMorgan Chase investment, which is available at http://www.treasury.gov/initiatives/financial-stability/programs/investment-programs/cpp/Documents_Contracts_Agreements/JPMorgan_Chase_Agreement_Dated_26_October_2008.pdf, and information in July SIGTARP Report, *supra* note 1592, at 76.

a. By design, the Treasury will not explicitly exercise day-to-day control of the CPP recipients. Such control is indirectly achieved through measures such as a contractual requirement on management compensation and Treasury's implicit threat to take over the bank by converting its holdings into common stock.

b. American Recovery and Reinvestment Act of 2009, Pub. L. No. 111–5, 123 Stat. 115.

c. The difference in treatment of public and private companies largely stems from the fact that Treasury will hold privately issued securities with no readily available market prices. Treasury may also, as a result, hold the securities for a longer period of time.

d. American Recovery and Reinvestment Act of 2009, *supra* note 1607, at 516–20.

e. Id.

programs have yet to repay these funds. As noted above, these funds must be paid straight to the US Treasury, thus once they are repaid these TARP programs will cease to exist.[51] Since minimal commitments remain in the TARP programs, and no new commitments to these programs can be made, there is no standing TARP authority to capitalize future troubled banks. The below table details the status of these programs, ordered from largest to smallest based on the initial investment. The "Initial Investment" column refers to the total amount Treasury invested in the particular TARP program. The "Lifetime income (cost)" column refers to the overall income or expenses incurred for the program, from inception to expiration. The source for this table is the Government Accountability Office's ("GAO") January 2015 TARP update.

We have already discussed the CPP. The Automotive Industry Financing Program ("AIFP") refers to Treasury's investments in automakers Chrysler and GM and other auto financing companies; such investments were justified as needed to stabilize the automotive industry, although no convincing case was made that the failure or restructuring of that industry would be a source of systemic risk[52] After the first stage of TARP that involved the CPP, the second stage of TARP assistance included the Systemically Significant Failing Institutions ("SSFI") program, created to provide support to AIG and subsequently renamed the American International Group, Inc. (AIG) Investment Program.[53] According to the Congressional Budget Office (CBO),[54] "AIG has fully exited the TARP; the company repaid its line of credit, and the Treasury recouped $34 billion from the sale of its shares of AIG common stock at an average price of about $31— bringing the total amount repaid or recovered to $54 billion out of the $68 billion originally disbursed. The final net subsidy cost to the Treasury for [sic]the assistance that was provided to AIG through the TARP was $15 billion."[55] However, because the Treasury (with the Federal Reserve) also supported AIG through non-TARP assistance in exchange for common shares of AIG, the Treasury will actually wind up with a net profit of $5 billion on its overall AIG assistance.[56] The Federal Reserve profited $17.7 billion on its overall AIG assistance.[57]

Additionally the Targeted Investment Program ("TIP") refers to Treasury's case-by-case investments in critical financial institutions; only Citigroup and Bank of America participated in this program, each receiving $20 billion in exchange for preferred stock and warrants.[58]

Table 22.2

Remaining financial-crisis TARP commitments as of Jan. 2015, reproduced per GAO update (apart from housing programs)

	Program start date	Program status	Initial investment (USD billions)	Lifetime income (cost) (USD billions)
Capital Purchase Program (CPP)	October 2008	$625 million outstanding. No set exit date.	204.9	16.1
Automotive Industry Financing Program (AIFP)	December 2008	Treasury retains a 13% ownership share of Ally Financial. No set exit date for Ally Financial. Treasury has exited other portions of the AIFP program.	79.7	(12.2)
American International Group, Inc. (AIG) Investment Program	November 2008	Exited December 2012.	67.8	(15.2)
Targeted Investment Program (TIP)	December 2008	Exited January 2011.	40.0	4.0
Public–Private Investment Program (PPIP)	September 2009	No funds outstanding, only the completion of wind-down activities remains before exit. Treasury expects exit by December 31, 2014.	18.6	2.7
Community Development Capital Initiative (CDCI)	February 2010	$465 million outstanding, No set exit date. Treasury has limited control over when participants choose to exit the program.	0.57	(0.11)
Small Business Administration Securities Purchase Program	March 2010	Exited January 2012.	0.37	0.004
Term Asset-backed Securities Loan Facility (TALF)	March 2009	No loans outstanding, only the completion of wind-down activities remains before exit.	0.1	0.6
Asset Guarantee Program	January 2009	Exited January 2011.	0.0	4.0
Capital Assistance Program	February 2009	This program was never utilized.	0.0	0.0

Note: US Government Accountability Office, *Troubled Asset Relief Program* 1, 10 (Jan. 2015), *available at* http://www.gao.gov/assets/670/667833.pdf.

The Public–Private Investment Program ("PPIP") refers to Treasury's purchase of residential and commercial mortgage-backed securities in coordination with private firms.[59] The Community Development Capital Initiative ("CDCI") refers to Treasury's investment in Community Development Financial Institutions through which Treasury received preferred stock and subordinated debentures.[60] The Small Business Administration Securities Purchase Program refers to Treasury's investments in the secondary markets for government-guaranteed small business loans under the 7(a) SBA loan program.[61] The Term Asset-backed Securities Loan Facility ("TALF") refers to Treasury's further investments in the securitization market, enabling credit access throughout the crisis period.[62] The Asset Guarantee Program refers to a program that provided federal government guarantees for financial institution assets; only Citigroup participated in this program, while Bank of America also considered it.[63] Through this program, Citigroup received loss protection on $301 billion of assets.[64] Finally, the Capital Assistance Program was created to provide capital to financial institutions that were unable to meet stress test requirements under the Supervisory Capital Assessment Program; this program was ultimately not funded or initiated.[65]

Ultimately the ten TARP programs described above invested a total of $412 billion, with only $12.4 billion outstanding as of 2014.[66] As of October 9, 2015, TARP has recovered 98.7 percent of funds invested.[67] However, the remaining $625 million in CPP assets, $465 million in CDCI assets, and 13 percent share in Ally Financial acquired through the AIFP program will likely turn these modest losses into a net profit. It is worth noting that, aside from the relatively minor loss from the CDCI illustrated above, TARP losses are not attributable to the bank investment programs; instead, the AIFP and AIG Investment Program are responsible for the most significant losses. The outcome of TARP is broadly consistent with the experience of Fannie Mae and Freddie Mac, which received $187 billion in government aid during the crisis and ultimately returned $192 billion by 2014.[68]

While TARP has now expired, consideration should be given to provide a standing program for capital injections with significant design improvements from TARP. The program could be on the shelf ready to be used by regulators, subject to appropriate findings and high-level approvals, if events required this. The reality is that currently few would support rational planning for the future, since political opponents would accuse the planners of being pro-bailout.

22.3   TARP Housing Programs Have Not Been Wound Down

In contrast to the programs described above, TARP housing programs have not been wound down because these programs received funding commitments from TARP before October 2010 and have yet to disburse this all of that funding. But with the rest of TARP, no new commitments can be made after October 2010.

TARP instituted three relevant housing programs: the Making Home Affordable ("MHA") program, the Hardest Hit Fund, and the Federal Housing Authority ("FHA") Short Refinance program.[69] The MHA program primarily assists borrowers with reducing monthly payments on first-lien mortgages and coordinating efficient short sales.[70] The Hardest Hit Fund is focused on those states with the highest unemployment rates; the program specifically seeks to help individuals in those states make mortgage payments and reduce their overall principal.[71] Finally, the FHA Short Refinance program enables individuals to refinance when their mortgages exceed the value of their homes.[72]

The GAO reports that, as of September 2014, 13.7 billion, or 36 percent, of the 38.5 billion in TARP housing program funding has been disbursed.[73] Accordingly, each of the housing programs authorized under TARP remain ongoing, as the housing programs still have access to the funds allocated before the October 2010 cutoff applicable to all TARP programs. As described above, these funds were never disbursed to private borrowers, so that is why these programs still have unused funding. The Treasury has extended the time period to disburse these already allocated funds under the MHA program until December 2016, although officials have indicated that an earlier wind-down may occur depending upon "market conditions, program volume, and other factors."[74] Similarly states have until December 31, 2017, to commit funds for the TARP Hardest Hit fund; states are also allowed to continue to spend Hardest Hit funds after 2017 deadline.[75] Finally, FHA's short refinance program was expected to end on December 31, 2014, but was extended by two years until December 31, 2016.[76] These disbursements are, of course, limited to the total funding provided to these programs before the October 2010 cutoff. Further extensions to disburse funds from these TARP housing programs beyond 2016/2017 is also feasible, as the EESA does not set explicit deadlines for when TARP programs can disburse unused funds.[77] The TARP housing programs are subject to the same statutory scheme as the other TARP programs, but the Treasury makes clear that "the funds committed for TARP's housing programs were never intended to be recovered,"[78] so long as the housing programs continue to operate within the basic parameters and budgets set forth in 2009 and 2010 under TARP. Such ongoing activity ensures that the GAO and other organizations will continue to monitor the TARP wind-down in subsequent years.

A separate question remains. Could Congress "activate" TARP by passing legislation that repeals any prohibition in the EESA and Dodd–Frank on the use of TARP funds? While lending authority has expired, the shell of the program remains. While this is technically possible, it is, of course, politically impracticable in the current climate. One theoretical advantage to such an approach is that the "old" TARP authorities could be quickly activated under similar terms as existed in 2008, instead of drafting language at the last minute like last time. However, this would not be the optimal solution, since it would be preferable to detail a new more detailed TARP that builds on lessons learned from the use of the old TARP.

The EESA TARP authorities are broad and undetailed. Section 101(a) authorizes the Secretary of the Treasury to establish TARP "to purchase, and to make and fund commitments to purchase, troubled assets from any financial institution, on such terms and conditions as are determined by the Secretary, and in accordance with this Act and the policies and procedures developed and published by the Secretary."[79]

While the TARP bailout fund to deal with the 2008 banking crisis has expired, it bears mentioning that there is still a standing fund to deal partially with bank failures in the form of the deposit insurance fund. As of June 2014 this fund stood at $51.1 billion,[80] and is financed on an ongoing basis by premiums paid by the banks at a rate of between 2.5 basis points and 45 basis points, depending on a bank's risk category.[81] This fund is basically designed to pay off depositors or assist in acquisitions or restructurings, but it can no longer be used for capital injections as part of open bank assistance. Section 1106(b) of Dodd–Frank effectively eliminated the systemic risk exception to the FDIC's least-cost resolution obligation under the Federal Deposit Insurance Act, thereby foreclosing this possibility. The DIF is not relevant to an OLA resolution, since it is only available when a bank is in receivership, and as designed by the FDIC under SPOE, OLA is intended to restructure only holding companies, not operating subsidiaries such as banks. In any event, $51.1 billion is far short of what would be needed, in a 2008 repeat.

23 Criticisms of Bailouts Generally

We now turn to five general criticisms of government bailout efforts: (1) taxpayers can suffer losses, (2) bailouts may not work or may be prolonged, (3) bailouts create moral hazard, (4) government decisions over bailout may be political and ad hoc, and (5) bailouts may fail to boost lending activities.

23.1 Taxpayer Loss

Historically bailouts have had varying impact on taxpayers. The Reconstruction Finance Corporation ("RFC") during the Great Depression had a cumulative profit of $160 million on its capital of $500 million.[1] However, the bailout of Continental Illinois National Bank eventually cost the FDIC $1.1 billion[2] and taxpayers paid for "$123.8 billion, or 81 percent of the total costs" of the savings and loans crisis.[3] As discussed above, TARP's bank bailout programs will not result in any tax dollar loss; indeed they will be profitable. However, were they profitable enough in light of the risk Treasury took?

Even though bailouts may, in the end, not be costly for taxpayers, one does not know this in advance of the expenditure. At the time TARP was authorized by the Congress, the estimated cost to taxpayers was much higher.[4] However, if the objective is to avoid taxpayer losses, one can provide that financial institutions or their investors—or some subset of them—bear any eventual losses through ex post assessments. Section 134 of the Emergency Economic Stabilization Act of 2008, which authorized TARP, provides that the President shall submit a legislative proposal that recoups from the financial industry an amount equal to the shortfall of TARP to ensure that the bailout does not add to the deficit or national debt.[5] Pursuant to this Section 134, President Obama in 2013 proposed the "Financial Crisis Responsibility Fee," which would be imposed on certain financial institutions with $50 billion or more in consolidated assets.[6] The President included this fee in his budget proposal for fiscal year 2014, aiming to collect roughly $59 billion in such fees over a ten-year period.[7] However, the President's proposal has never been acted on, and as stated there have been no losses from the CPP program.

At the request of G20 leaders, the IMF in June 2010 proposed two general alternatives to shift the burdens associated with government interventions to the financial sector: (1) a financial stability contribution levied upon financial institutions based on certain attributes such as size and riskiness, or (2) a financial activities tax based on bank profits.[8] These proposals were not limited to financing government past losses from interventions, as more fully developed below.

The plan to impose a global tax was subsequently shelved but various European countries have considered similar national legislation.[9] In September 2011 the European Commission also proposed a Europe-wide financial transaction tax (FTT).[10] In May 2012 the European Parliament passed the FTT[11] and in January 2013 approved a plan to allow 11 European Union countries to pursue a FTT.[12] Nevertheless, this European FTT has encountered multiple delays and is expected to be implemented no earlier than 2017.[13]

The imposition of such a "Tobin tax" would supposedly curb what some see as useless financial activities. The proceeds from the FTT, which has received support from French and German leaders but staunch opposition from the United Kingdom,[14] would be used to compensate European governments for rescue costs during the financial crisis, but also, more generally, to "contribute to the public finances" during the ongoing European fiscal crisis.[15] The FTT has also been justified as a form of compensation for an implicit state guarantee, a roughly-fashioned (but explicit) premium for an implicit bailout guarantee.[16] However, the FTT is poorly designed for this purpose, since it taxes all financial transactions indiscriminately, rather than charging those firms that are most likely to be bailed out, based either on their size or the riskiness of their activities.[17]

There are several concerns with the ex post tax assessment approach to pay for bailouts. First, it is hard to determine how such ex post assessments should be apportioned, such as to banks and nonbanks.[18] The challenges are essentially the same as those for an insurance regime funded through ex post assessments, as previously discussed in chapter 12. Second, failing global coordination, banks may be subject to double or even triple taxation.[19] Third, there is some concern that such taxes could turn out to be politically unenforceable when the financial crisis is over, but taxpayers should blame politicians and not banks for that outcome.[20] Finally, there is the fear that the government could use the opportunity to overtax the banks, as the EU financial transactions tax proposal arguably demonstrates, to achieve other objectives.

23.2 Bailouts May Not Work or Be Prolonged

Before the 2008 financial crisis, the most successful bailout in mature economies was probably the Swedish bank bailout in the early 1990s. The collapse of the property market left several Swedish banks with large quantities of soured real estate loans. The government announced a blanket guarantee of bank debt and took over the major banks. Sweden eventually incurred minimum cost after selling its bank interests several years later.[21] However, bailout does not always work. It may carry the risk that one bailout will evolve into multiple efforts to prop up insolvent banks for an extended period of time without any real hope of recovery.

The Japanese "lost decade" is a prominent example of a prolonged bailout. Until very recently large and small Japanese banks have been saddled with bad loans since the collapse of its stock and real property markets in 1990.[22] Through the 1990s the government purchased non-performing loans (NPL) from banks and tried other rescue measures. However, it continued to delay in recognizing the full scale of the NPL problem by endorsing questionable accounting practices due to the high social cost that would follow from corporate bankruptcies and the political consequences of admitting large losses.[23] In 1998, when the level of NPL became extremely high, the government purchased 1.8 trillion yen ($16 billion) in subordinated debt and preferred shares in 21 major banks that were undercapitalized. The bailout failed to stabilize the market and the government nationalized two major banks, the Long-Term Credit Bank of Japan and Nippon Credit Bank, followed by another injection of 7.5 trillion yen ($71 billion) in 15 banks the next year.[24] Bailouts continued thereafter, including the injection of 1.96 trillion yen (around $19 billion) in Resona in 2003. The government also consolidated the biggest banks during this period to create some of the largest banks in the world.

The Japanese financial system finally began to stabilize after its economy started to recover and the government began to address the

NPL problem seriously around 2003.[25] By 2006 banks appeared to be able to repay public funds within a few years. The largest ones have already done so,[26] but regional banks continue to struggle.[27] Some nationalized banks were sold to nonbanking and foreign owners.[28]

The Japanese experience demonstrates that fundamental problems with banking systems may only be prolonged, but not resolved, through bailouts. Bailouts may be the beginning and not the end of financial recovery. Bailing out banks without dealing with the NPL problem was throwing good money after bad. The Congressional Oversight Panel in early 2009 agreed that CPP and other bank investment programs would work based on the key assumption that the financial crisis was in large part the product of temporary liquidity constraints resulting from non-functioning markets for troubled assets.[29] In other words, bailouts should only be used to curb risk contagion and stabilize the market so that the government could have breathing time to implement *other* cleanup efforts such as proactive write-downs, reform of banking practices and gradual sales of assets.

23.3   Creation of Moral Hazard and Too-Big-to-Fail Competitive Advantage

The fear of moral hazard is the strongest argument against government bailouts. Both individual firms and the market may have perverse incentives if they know the government will come to the rescue. The consequence of this moral hazard is that firms will take on more risk than would otherwise be optimal because risk taking becomes a one-sided bet.[30] Investors, especially debt investors, may have less incentive to monitor the performance of the firm. As the firm becomes too big to fail, meaning presumptively entitled to a bailout, it may also enjoy an unfair competitive advantage over other firms because its cost of financing could be cheaper.[31] These concerns are similar to the ones regarding insurance or guarantees.

Summers identifies an excessive fear of moral hazard among a group he calls "moral hazard fundamentalists," and suggests these fundamentalists are misguided in three respects as they analogize the moral hazard of bailout to the moral hazards raised by insurance: first, individual actors in the financial world may underestimate the role of contagion and the benefits that their own insurance will have on other actors; thus they will tend to underinsure (suggesting the free market may not be an adequate way to address the risks they pose). Second, institutions may fail simply because of a loss of confidence, rather than because of increased risk taking. In these cases, the possibility of bailout can help to avoid panic and contagion. However, confidence (of short-term creditors) is better addressed through the lender of last resort. Finally, unlike insurance, bailout can actually leave taxpayers better off, for example, when a government program like TARP is potentially profitable. For all these reasons, policy should not be developed simply on the basis of "avoiding moral hazard," but rather must take into account contagion, potential liquidity runs and the benefits of quelling panic, and the potential costs and benefits of a bailout to taxpayers.[32]

In my view, however, bailouts (public capital injections) are not the answer to contagion; this can be avoided by a strong lender of last resort and guarantees. Nor are bailouts necessary to avoid single large bank failures (this may be different in countries where one or two banks dominate an economy), assuming there are effective resolution proce-dures and the preservation of critical functions. Bailouts like TARP should be reserved in the United States for correlation related systemic risk when multiple large banks are rendered insolvent by a common external event. There is no denying that bailouts increase moral hazard and put taxpayers at risk, so they should only be used when there is no feasible alternative. Even when necessary bailouts should be designed to minimize moral hazard.

Government bailouts should wipe out existing common sharehold-ers, thus helping reduce moral hazard; at the very least the common should be heavily and permanently diluted through the creation of new common. Government bailouts could also be combined with some hit on longer term creditors (e.g., through bail-ins), as discussed in chapter 16. These longer term creditors should therefore have incentive to monitor risk.[33] Indeed, since bond losses are tightly linked to ratings, and rating agencies are usually not certain that a given financial institu-tion will be bailed out, they may downgrade poorly capitalized banks, a threat also reducing incentives of managers to take undue risk. Rating agencies obviously consider implicit government backing in its rating decisions. In 2011 S&P downgraded Bank of America, Citigroup, Goldman Sachs, Morgan Stanley, JPMorgan, and Wells Fargo.[34] In Sep-tember 2011, Moody's also downgraded Citigroup, Bank of America and Wells Fargo. Both rating agencies that believed the government to be less likely to assist these banks going forward than during the finan-cial crisis when contagion risk was high.[35] Moody's also considered the enactment of Dodd–Frank Act as showing the government's intent to impose losses on bondholders in future crises.[36] In 2012, citing the "clear intent of government around the world to reduce support for creditors," Moody's downgraded five of the six largest US banks: JPMorgan, Bank of America, Citigroup, Goldman Sachs, and Morgan Stanley.[37] More recently, in November 2013, Moody's further downgraded JPMorgan, Goldman Sachs, Morgan Stanley, and Bank of New York Mellon.[38] A managing director at the rating agency explained that "rather than relying on public funds to bail out one of these institutions, we expect that bank holding company creditors will be bailed-in and thereby shoulder much of the burden to help recapitalize a failing bank."[39]

Bernardo, Talley, and Welch, using a model that focuses exclusively on moral hazard, show that bailouts can be welfare-enhancing if (1) they are only used sparingly, where social externalities are large and subsidies are small; (2) the government eliminates incumbent owners, board, and managers to improve a priori incentives; and (3) the bailout is funded through redistributive taxes on healthy firms rather than forcing recipients to repay in the future, as the government has already fully expropriated existing owners and managers.[40] With regard to the problem that bank managers may take excessive risks in exchange for large bonuses and then leave before the ship sinks, even a no-bailout rule could not correct the problem and the solution may lie elsewhere, such as compensation reforms and clawback requirements. Goodhart and Avgouleas argue that a bail-in may "be much superior to [a] bailout in the case of idiosyncratic failure."[41] However, "bail-in regimes will not eradicate the need for injection of public funds where there is a threat of systemic collapse."[42]

23.4 Bailout Decisions May Be Political and Ad Hoc

Some have claimed that the use of TARP funds was determined based on political rather than actual systemic risk grounds.[43] One prominent example was the bailout of GMAC, which showed that the presence of systemic risk was not a condition for granting public assistance because GMAC's rescue had little or nothing to do with mitigating the financial crisis.[44] Some claim that some companies are simply "too connected to fail" due to their executives' extensive connections with the key decision makers within the federal government.[45] Further the assistance given to small banks under TARP had little to do with concern with systemic risk.

Public confidence in the bailout effort can be seriously damaged if it is perceived by the public that the government did not follow any clearly articulated goals and principles in making important decisions.[46] This was particularly the case in the pre-TARP period. Bailouts often seemed to be ad hoc responses to an impending crisis—"when a major financial institution got into trouble, the Treasury Department and the Federal Reserve would engineer a bailout over the weekend and announce that everything was fine on Monday."[47] This is another reason why it may be better to have a standing program rather than responding ad hoc.

23.5 Bailouts May Fail to Boost Lending Activities

Bailout efforts often serve the twin purposes of stabilizing the financial system and alleviating the adverse impacts on the real economy caused by the collapse of the lending market. Obviously there is some inherent tension between the two purposes—if the financial system fails largely due to the failure of businesses in the real economy, as in the case of Japan, extending credit to these failed businesses would simply generate new bad debt. However, if the real economy could have maintained its good shape under normal lending conditions and the crisis is caused by a failure within the financial system itself, as many consider to be the case in the recent crisis, a government bailout of the financial system should increase business lending, grow the real economy, boost the financial performance of the banks and in turn facilitate the government's exit from its investments.

Although general lending conditions have significantly improved since the peak of the financial crisis in 2008, many blamed TARP for failing to revive the real economy. To start, critics of TARP often point to the flaw in CPP's design. When the UK government made equity investments in RBS and Lloyds, there were explicit contractual requirements that they maintain their level of lending at pre-crisis levels.[48] On the contrary, no similar requirement was imposed by US Treasury for CPP participants. To be fair, the FDIC has instructed the banks it regulates to monitor the use of TARP funds as well as the use of money raised with FDIC debt guarantees.[49] In addition an interagency statement urges all banking organizations to make loans to creditworthy borrowers.[50]

Treasury was also faulted for failing to implement proper measures to monitor the actual use of TARP funds, prompting the Congressional

Oversight Panel to repeatedly ask Treasury where the money went.[51] Treasury's response was that money was fungible so it was impossible to correlate the TARP funds with specific uses of funds.[52] As pointed out by the Panel, Treasury's claims were challenged by a survey of the Special Inspector General for the Troubled Asset Relief Program (SIGTARP) demonstrating that banks could provide meaningful information on their use of TARP funds without much difficulty.[53] The Panel also pointed out that some banks voluntarily disclosed information on the use of their TARP funds in public filings.[54] But all said, it is likely the low level of lending was dictated by low demand, not just low supply, due to the general economic stagnation brought on by the financial crisis.

I would conclude that despite the criticisms, which may be largely justified, under dire circumstances, like those that existed in October 2008, bailouts may be the only tenable solution. Simultaneous bail-ins of several large financial institutions, assuming such bail-ins would work perfectly, could still leave the financial system so weak that it could not finance the recovery of the real economy. In any event, the bailout option should exist if needed. A standing TARP's design should benefit from a diagnosis of how the old TARP was found wanting and could be improved. We turn to that issue in the next chapter.

24 Specific Criticisms of TARP

There have been several criticisms of TARP laying the basis for possible improvements that could be made if such a program were adopted in the future. The major criticisms are (1) too favorable terms for recipients, (2) too much or too little interference in recipient operations, and (3) lack of enforcement of the terms of support.

24.1 Too Favorable Terms for CPP Participants

All CPP recipients received government funds on the same terms, and the terms have been criticized for being too favorable. As the Congressional Oversight Panel's February 2009 report pointed out, the valuation firm hired by the Panel, Duff & Phelps, found that of the $184 billion in TARP funds that it analyzed, the securities that Treasury received in exchange had a market value of only $122 billion, or 66 percent of its face value.[1] Similar results were found by another study by the Congressional Budget Office.[2] There was also a short-lived criticism from the Panel that in some early exits the Treasury did not receive adequate compensation for the warrants that it received for its investments.[3] The Panel, however, acknowledged in a later report that the prices for subsequent sales or redemptions were very close to its own estimate.[4] SIGTARP also found separately that the government received a fair price for most of the warrants.[5]

The Treasury designed the terms for the CPP to be favorable for the banks to increase their capital base, to rescue the financial system, not to make money. Excessively demanding terms might have undermined the banks' ability to participate in the program, thereby making it difficult to achieve the objective of stabilizing the financial sector.

The Treasury also did not want to signal which banks were worse off by differentiation of its terms—this was an extension of its policy requiring the nine initial recipients to take funds whether or not they were needed.[6] This made it very difficult, for example, to eliminate all equity claimants or to impose some losses on longer term creditors. Further the Treasury acquired the ability in these deals to change the terms in the future, an option not valued in the Panel's analysis.[7] Other countries, as we will see, did not design broad programs and had different terms for different recipients, but this raised the ad hoc favoritism problem. Another criticism, as previously discussed, was not ousting or heavily diluting the common shareholders. Further, in a future TARP, some additional losses could be placed on creditors in combination with new capital injections. Bailouts could act in tandem with bail-ins.

24.2   Interference with Firm Operations

As most of the largest banks exited CPP within a year of its implementation, discussions about potential excessive government interference in the day-to-day management of rescued firms concentrated on a few institutions such as Citigroup and AIG, in which the government held its position for a longer period—Treasury sold its final Citigroup and AIG shares in December 2010[8] and December, 2012,[9] respectively. According to the Treasury, it developed several core principles to guide its oversight including (1) acting as a reluctant shareholder, (2) not interfering in day-to-day management decisions, (3) ensuring a strong board of directors, and (4) exercising voting rights only in core areas.[10] On the one hand, many still criticized the government's involvement as excessive, especially the engagement of a "pay czar" to set compensation standards for key employees.[11] On the other hand, some criticized the Treasury for not interfering enough, particularly in not firing key management, as did the Japanese in their rescues during the lost decade.[12]

Some analysts have suggested that Treasury could have resolved the dilemma of acting both as a regulator and a controlling shareholder in its implementation of TARP by creating a separate corporation holding its TARP investments.[13] The corporation would hire professional managers to manage the investments. The predominant strategy should be investment management, not politics.[14] The corporation would report its holdings based on appropriate accounting standards.[15] Commentators pointed to the example of RFC, which was an agency independent from the Treasury.[16] Another example would be the UK Financial

Investments Limited, which was the separate vehicle holding and managing UK government's investments in Northern Rock, RBS, and other firms receiving government funds.[17] The UK Treasury, however, had the final say on key issues and only left routine decisions to the management of the holding company.[18]

24.3   Lack of Enforcement of the CPP's Contractual Terms

Another criticism of the CPP is that certain terms governing banks' participation in the program have been ineffective. Although, as discussed above, the vast majority of CPP recipient institutions have exited the program, those that remain illustrate this problem. As of December 31, 2014, 76 percent of the remaining outstanding CPP investments were attributable to just 10 of the 34 institutions that had not yet exited the program ($359.7 million of the $470.3 million remaining).[19] A majority of the remaining CPP institutions are smaller banks that were on the FDIC's "problem bank list" as of December 31, 2014.[20] As of that date, 26 of the 34 remaining CPP participants were not current on their dividend (or interest) payments to Treasury—25 of these banks were overdue by at least six payments.[21] Under the terms of CPP investments summarized above, if a participant misses six quarterly dividend (or interest) payments, Treasury has the right to appoint up to two additional members to the bank's board. Although 25 of the 34 remaining participants had missed six or more dividend payments as of December 31, 2014, none of these institutions have board members appointed by the Treasury.[22] It is worth nothing that delinquencies were not entirely concentrated among the stragglers to exit the program—the aggregate amount of missed dividend (or interest) payments among all CPP banks as of that date was $520.9 million, for which 175 banks were responsible over time.[23]

24.4   Comparisons with Foreign Bailout Efforts in the 2008 Crisis

It is instructive to see how foreign bailouts compare with TARP. Legislative bodies in many countries aside from the United States introduced recapitalization measures during 2008 and 2009 (this is before the eurozone crisis).[24] As seen in table 24.1, the US CPP is the largest program in absolute amounts ($205 billion in commitments versus $107 billion for second-ranked Germany); but as a percentage of GDP, the US program was more modest. The Netherlands had the largest exposure with 4.3 percent of GDP committed, while the United States with 1.8 percent committed ranked at the bottom, also below Ireland (3.8 percent), the United Kingdom (3.5 percent), Germany (3.2 percent), and France (2.0 percent). In terms of participation, the US CPP has the largest number of beneficiaries with 707 recipients compared to 18 recipients of the European programs combined. The sheer size of the US CPP is due to the program's openness to any US financial institution, whether systemically important or not.[25] However, participation as a percentage of total assets in the banking system is highest in France (92.6 percent), followed by the United States (75.8 percent), Ireland (74.2 percent), the Netherlands (65.9 percent), the United Kingdom (34.1 percent), and Germany (18.5 percent). The option for large banks to opt out of the programs in the United Kingdom (Barclays PLC) and Germany (Deutsche Bank) explains the large contrast in participation rates.[26]

Analysis of the nonprice conditions set forth in the various recapitalization programs shows the US CPP with a relatively small set of such conditions (i.e., no restructuring requirements, few limits on executive compensation, and no binding lending requirements).[27] By contrast, the United Kingdom prohibited bonuses for 2008 and required restoration of mortgage lending to small and medium enterprises to 2007 levels, while France prohibited stock options and stock grants to senior executives and required a 3 to 4 percent annual increase in overall lending levels.[28]

Table 24.1
International CPP comparison

Program	Amount committed		Outlay ($ bn)[a]	Recipients		Instrument	Dividend/ interest rate	Covenants and restrictions				
	Total ($ bn)	% GDP (2008)[b]		#	% asset[c]			Exec comp	Ordinary dividend ban[d]	Board of Directors appointment	Required lending	Required Restructuring
US (TARP)												
CPP[e]	$250	1.8	$204.9 (16.42)	707 (352)	75.8	NCP, warrants	Initial: 5% / 5 yrs: 9%	✓		✓[f]		
TIP[g]	—	—	$40 (0)	2 (0)	—	NCP, Warrants	8%	✓	✓			
AIG[h]	$70	0.05	$48 (35.85)	1 (1)	—	NCP, Warrants	10%	✓	✓	✓		
UK (GRS)	$86.5	3.5	$113.84 (113.84)	2 (2)	34.1	NCP, Common	Initial: 12% / 5 yrs: LIBOR +7%	✓	✓	✓	✓	✓
Germany (SoFFin)	$107	3.2	$40.28 ($27.5)	4 (4)	18.5	Silent Participation	Average 9–10% + dividend-linked rate[j]	✓		✓	✓	✓
France (SSPE)	$55	2	$28.53 (0)	6[i] (0)	92.6	NCP, or TSS securities	Initial: average 8% / 5 yrs: CDS-linked rate[k]	✓		✓	✓	
Ireland	$9.63	3.8	$14.71 (2)	3 (3)	74.2	NCP, Warrants	8%	✓	✓	✓	✓	✓
Netherlands	$27.5	4.3	$18.9 (5.16)	3 (2)	65.9	Convertible securities	Dividend-linked[l] w/floor of 8.5%	✓	✓	✓	✓	✓

Table 24.1 (continued)

Japan								
1998 Financial Functions Stabilization Act	$157.3	2.6	$21.97 (2.3)	21 (2)	—		Mostly subordinated debt	Varied, average Libor+1.15% 9SD) for first 5 years.
1999 Early Strengthening Act	$302.5	5	$104.12 (8.42)	32 (5)	—	Varied^m	✓	✓	Varied, average 1% (CP) or Libor+1% (SD) before step-up date.

Note: US Government Accountability Office, Troubled Asset Relief Program 1, 5 (Jan. 2015), available at http://www.gao.gov/assets/670/667833.pdf.

a. Converted using October 2008 exchange rate. Japanese programs were converted using the March 1998 and March 1999 exchange rates, respectively.

b. The percentages for the Japanese programs were converted using the 1998 and 1999 GDP, respectively.

c. Percent of total banking assets in program, calculated using data from approximately 12/31/2008.

d. Includes "effective" ban on dividends. For example, the TIP limited dividends to $0.01, and the SSFI prevented AIG from increasing its dividends from $0 for five years.

e. This chart summarizes the CPP terms for public institutions. Terms for public, private, S-corporation, and mutual banks were slightly different.

f. Only effective after nonpayment of dividends for six quarterly periods (whether or no consecutive).

g. TIP is the Targeted Investment Program and it refers to the Treasury's case-by-case investments in Citigroup and Bank of America.

h. The AIG Investment Program was formerly called the Systematically Significant Failing Institutions Program (SSFI).

i. For each €4.4 million in dividends (€5.9 million in the second Commerzbank tranche), interest rates increase by 0.01 percent.

j. Dexia, not included in the six because its recapitalization arose in different isolated event, was also recapitalized using SPPE funding in coordination with Belgium and Luxembourg.

k. For TSS: EURIBOR +250 bps +5 x CDS (senior 5 years). For preferred shares, the higher of: (1) TSS interest rate increased by 24 bps every year or (2) rate equal to 105 percent of the dividends per ordinary share in 2009, 110 percent in 2010, 115 percent for 2011–2017, and 125 percent for 2018 and after.

l. 110 percent of the dividends per ordinary share in 2009, 120 percent in 2010, and 125 percent in 2011 and after.

m. Includes convertible preferred shared, nonconvertible preferred share, and subordinated debt. Loan amount, coupon rate, and step-up date varied across

25 Standing Bailout Programs

25.1 Standing Bailout Programs in the European Union and Japan

In the European Union, as a result of the eurozone crisis, and in Japan as a result of the lost decade, standing support programs have been created that can be used to bail out failing banks, and in the case of Japan nonbanks as well, in the future. Other countries such as China effectively guarantee the solvency of banks without setting up a program. The point being that the United States is rather unique in its apparent resolve, however unrealistic it may be, to foreswear any use of bailouts in the future.

25.1.1 Eurozone

Bank stability in the eurozone is of particular importance since bank failures can create sovereign debt crises. Weak banks, especially those that are large compared to national GDP, can spread panic to sovereign debt markets if a solvent sovereign needs to borrow heavily to recapitalize its banks, as was the case of Ireland during the global financial crisis. The problem can also be the reverse. Government debt defaults may lead to bank failures when banks holding sovereign debt need to write it down. In February 2010 German and French banks alone had over $900 billion of exposure to Greece, Portugal, Ireland, and Spain.[1]

The Single Resolution Mechanism and Single Resolution Fund The eurozone (EZ) crisis led to fundamental changes in the regulation of banking in the EZ. In June 2012, the European Council agreed to create a banking union that would allow for centralized *supervision* by the ECB (transferring it from national authorities) of large banks through the Single Supervisory Mechanism ("SSM") and centralized *resolution* of euro area banks through the Single Resolution Mechanism ("SRM").

The SRM also applies to financial holding companies, investment firms, and other financial institutions that are subject to consolidated supervision by the ECB.[2]

These actions parallel the US restructuring of bank supervision by centralizing supervision of $50 billion banks, plus nonbank SIFIs in the Federal Reserve System, and creating new resolution authority for systemically important banking organizations under the OLA, as previously discussed. However, unlike the United States, which prevents the government making injections of capital into banks under OLA or FDIC procedures, the EU's SRM does have this capability.

In connection with SRM, the EZ countries have created a Single Resolution Fund (SRF) to recapitalize failed banks and to provide liquidity financed by bank levies—this is entirely separate from deposit guarantee funds. The SRF will be built up to €55 billion within the next eight years, or 1 percent of total deposits for banks covered by the SRF.[3] The SRF is financed ex ante by bank levies raised at the national level and will be kept at the national level for a ten-year transition period.[4] First losses of at least 8 percent of liabilities must be covered by bail-ins.[5] While the United States rescinded the ability of the FDIC to use its guarantee fund for open bank assistance,[6] and designed OLA to impose all losses on private creditors (only liquidity is available through OLF) through the TLAC mechanism, the EZ handles failed banks by a combination of bailout and bail-in, and the bail-out component is pre-funded.[7]

The European Stability Mechanism   In addition to the SRF, the European Union also created a new permanent bailout mechanism in 2010, the European Stability Mechanism ("ESM"), primarily intended to bailout sovereigns. But sovereigns can use loans from the ESM to inject capital into banks. And to a limited extent the ESM can inject capital directly into EZ banks.

The ESM raises funds in capital markets to finance loans to euro area member states. ESM bonds are backed by guarantees provided on a pro-rata basis by each member state. The ESM's current lending capacity is €500 billion.[8] The funds are backed by €80 billion paid-in capital contributed by EZ members in five installments and the ESM has an additional call on the member states for €622 billion—to cover potential losses.[9] ESM funding is conditional on reform and austerity measures taken by borrowing states.

There is also authority for ESM to make direct loans to banks, and its funds can also be used to backstop the SRM. The size of this program, the direct bank recapitalization instrument, is capped at €60 billion.[10] To be eligible for ESM recapitalization, the bank or its holding company must have exhausted all other sources of funding, private creditors must have been bailed-in, and the bank must have been designated by the ESM Board of Governors as systemically important or likely to pose a serious threat to the financial stability of the euro area.[11] The ESM Board of Governors makes such a determination.[12] However, there are no publicly available guidelines on the criteria, or how/when such a determination would be made. Although not explicitly required, the ESM has stated that it will only recapitalize institutions "whose viability can be secured through a capital injection and restructuring plan."[13] Direct bank recapitalization is only available after creditors have been bailed-in and the Single Resolution Fund has made a contribution to the bank.[14] The recently adopted minimum requirement for own funds and eligible liabilities ("MREL") consultation outlines minimum levels of debt that will be available for bail-in.[15]

The major point about the EU approach is that it uses pre-funded bailouts of banks as a major way of dealing with insolvent or inadequately capitalized banks. The procedures for using these funds in resolution are being developed in detail, so that a full and transparent system will be on the shelf. Thus the European Union not only has a strong lender of last resort, it also is ready to inject capital into failing banks if warranted.

25.1.2 Japan

The Japanese government also has standing authority to use public funds to recapitalize solvent banks and solvent financial institutions. The Japanese government further has the authority to nationalize insolvent banks and to provide limited assistance to insolvent financial companies. The government is also permitted to nationalize an insolvent financial institution following a systemic risk determination.

Capital Injections for Banks Chapter VII-1 ("Measures against a Financial Crisis") of the Deposit Insurance Act ("DIA"), provides the Deposit Insurance Company of Japan ("DICJ") with the authority to inject capital into solvent banks, provided that the Prime Minster determines that failing to do so would create a serious risk to financial stability.[16] The government is also permitted to temporarily nationalize an insolvent bank following a similar systemic risk determination.[17] Of course, nationalization would also lay the predicate for a capital injection.

Chapter VII-1 was adopted in 2000, after a wave of large bank failures during the Asian financial crisis illustrated the need for extraordinary intervention during crisis periods. The DIA generally seeks to resolve troubled banks through either an insurance payoff approach in which the bank is liquidated and insurance proceeds are paid to protected depositors; through a purchase and assumption transaction; or through the establishment of a bridge bank in anticipation of finding a buyer for a purchase and assumption transaction.[18] In the second and third cases, the DICJ is authorized to provide financial support up to the equivalent amount that would be paid in an insurance payoff approach through, for example, loan guarantees to the bridge bank.[19]

The systemic risk exception of Chapter VII-1 grants the DICJ authority, when the Prime Minister, in consultation with the Council for Financial Crises, determines that exercising exceptional authorities is necessary to "maintain ... an orderly credit system,"[20] to provide support in excess of the amount that would be paid in an insurance payoff approach.[21] If the bank is solvent, the DICJ is specifically authorized to use public funds to recapitalize the bank or underwrite its stock issuance.[22] Chapter VII-1 does not include any express limitations on the maximum amount of capital that can be injected into a solvent bank. It also does not specify the source of public funds for recapitalization, although it will presumably draw on the deposit insurance fund if necessary. In this sense, the exceptional measures permitted under the systemic risk exception may be partially pre-funded. But prefunding is much more limited than in the EU.

Public capital injections are unavailable to *nonbanks* under Chapter VII-1. This generally includes a trouble bank's nonbank affiliates. However, the DICJ is permitted to temporarily inject capital into a holding company of a bank, provided that the holding company uses the proceeds to recapitalize the bank subsidiary.[23] Chapter VII-1 authorities were used in 2003, when the DICJ acquired approximately 70 percent of voting shares in Resona Bank for roughly $20 billion.[24]

If a bank is *insolvent* and the Prime Minister, in consultation with the Council for Financial Crisis, has made a systemic risk determination, the troubled bank can be temporarily nationalized.[25] The most important characteristic of nationalization is that existing shareholders are completely wiped out, an approach whose possible virtues we have previously discussed. For example, in 2003 Ashikaga Bank was temporarily nationalized to avoid financial crisis. The DICJ used approximately $4 billion from the deposit insurance fund to lend to the failed institution, and to purchase some of its assets.[26] Public funds were repaid when Ashikaga was purchased by a consortium in 2008.[27]

Capital Injections for Solvent Financial Institutions   Whereas Chapter VII-1 only applies to banks, Chapter VII-2 of the DIA grants the DICJ a broad array of special authorities over financial companies. Under limited circumstances these authorities include an ability to use public funds to recapitalize a distressed firm or to guarantee its debt. Financial companies covered by Chapter VII-2 are defined as banks, bank holding companies, subsidiaries of banks and holding companies, insurance companies and their subsidiaries, securities firms, and the parent companies and subsidiaries of certain large securities firms.[28] So banks can be dealt with under either Chapter VII-I or II.

Once Chapter VII-2 is triggered with respect to a specific financial company, the troubled financial company "must submit to oversight by the DICJ."[29] If the firm is solvent, then the DICJ can provide it with liquidity or guarantee its debt.[30] Subject to additional approval by the Prime Minister, the DICJ is also authorized to use public funds to recapitalize the solvent firm or underwrite a share issuance.[31] A firm is solvent if it is able "to satisfy its obligations in full with its assets," it is not "likely to face a situation where it is unable to satisfy its obligations in full with its assets," it has not "suspended payment of obligations," and it is not "likely to suspend payment of obligations."[32] This is a more restrictive standard than the one applicable to Chapter VII-1 recapitalization. Costs of a recapitalization will be recouped by ex post assessments on all financial institutions.[33] The assessment can be waived if payment would trigger financial instability.[34] Chapter VII-2 does not have an explicit cap on the maximum amount of capital injections, and does not create a pre-funded facility designed for recapitalization.

If Chapter VII-2 is triggered with respect to an insolvent financial company, the DICJ has certain limited authorities to provide the company with financial assistance. For example, the DICJ can transfer "systemically important transactions," namely transactions whose failure would disrupt the financial system, to a bridge bank.[35] In addition the DICJ can lend to the institution to avoid financial instability.[36]

These authorities do not include nationalization or debt guarantees, as under Chapter VII-1.

25.2 Virtues of Standing Bailout Authority

Advance bailout authority and capability is the third method, along with lender of last resort and guarantees, to deal with a financial crisis. In the United States, while we greatly limited the lender of last resort and guarantee weapons, we did not abandon them altogether as we did with TARP, putting the new OLA resolution procedure, without the possibility of public support, in its place.

This is not sound public policy for designing a stable financial system. Suppose that all of our 8 G-SIBs were insolvent at the same time as a result of an operational failure due to a cyberattack or another form of terrorism? Do we really think the answer would be to put them all in OLA? How about just one, JPMorgan? In my view, a responsible Secretary of the Treasury or the President would not want to do so in either case, whatever the moral hazard implications. And in extreme circumstances, would it not be better for the entire country, the taxpayers, to pay for a failure, with a high prospect of repayment, rather than impose the loss on creditors, which could include major institutions like pension funds and insurance companies (and ultimately the policy holders of such companies)?

So, if we don't put our heads in the sand, we would design and fund such a capability in advance rather than have our Secretary of Treasury run into Congress at the last minute with a term sheet in hand. At the very least we would design the program in advance (even without funding) to make changes to the approach we used in TARP based on our experience with TARP. Key design issues for consideration would be: First, does it make sense to require all big banks to take assistance for fear of identifying the ones that are insolvent—who was really fooled by this? Second, should we really be giving assistance to every bank, or just systemically important ones? Third, could we combine capital assistance with some degree of private loss, as the EU has the ability to do, even where we would not want to impose total loss? Fourth, how would we value the shares received in return for capital—would we want to assure a market rate of return for Treasury, or not? Fifth, should we close out common shareholders entirely by nationalizing banks, as can be done in Japan, and presumably Europe? Sixth, could we impose more conditions on recipients, including wholesale replacement of top management? Seventh, should we be able to recapitalize banks and other financial institutions before they become insolvent, and if so how? Do we really want to think through these issues in the grip of panic, and where Congress is terrified by voting for an actual bailout under the gun? Some argue that having a plan, and particularly funding it in advance, will just encourage moral hazard. In my view, this concern can be met by deciding in advance what the criteria for its use would be—an extreme circumstance where no other alternative, including most importantly bail-in, is more attractive. And the keys to turn the program on could be very tough. Not only requiring the same actions that are needed to put an institution into OLA, votes by supermajority of the Fed and FDIC, and approval of the Secretary of the Treasury after consultation with the President. It could even include, if necessary, a joint resolution of Congress. That procedure would be far better than what we now have. Who is fooling whom? The market will believe that bailouts will be used in extreme circumstances even if the program is not on the shelf, so it is better to have a good one there than none at all.

And the advance funding would not necessarily involve government appropriations. As is the case with the EZ SRF, the funding could come from assessments on the financial sector, or as in the case of the EZ ESM, come from some government capital leveraged through borrowing authority with a government guaranty.

26 Conclusion

This book's central concern is the fundamental stability of our financial system upon which the viability of our economy, and ultimately our polity, rests. This stability depends on the ability of the government, and especially our central bank, the Federal Reserve, to deal with panic runs—contagion—as it did during the financial crisis of 2008. The failure to do so in the future could put our country's survival at risk. It could lead not only to a depression but could result in revolt—challenges to our political system itself. Our world power would be dealt a severe blow. The reserve status of our currency could well come to an end. A world crisis set off by a US depression would be a threat to our national security. Bad monetary policy might destroy a country in years, but bad lender of last resort policy can destroy a country in weeks.

In the aftermath of the crisis, those that saved our country during the crisis—the Fed, FDIC, and Treasury—were demonized as bailing out Wall Street. As a result the powers of the government to deal with contagion in the future have been severely constrained. This is not a popular subject to complain about—anyone, whether in industry or in government, seeking to restore and even improve our powers to deal with contagion will again be attacked as bailing out Wall Street. But given the stakes, this is no excuse for silence.

In the 2008 financial crisis we witnessed a severe plunge in real estate prices that led to significant losses for financial institutions exposed to residential mortgages and commercial real estate. This book demonstrates that it was "contagion," not "connectedness," that was the most potentially destructive feature of that crisis and that contagion remains the most virulent and important part of systemic risk still facing the financial system today. Connectedness is the possibility that the failure of one institution would bankrupt other institutions directly overexposed to them, resulting in a chain reaction of failures. Contagion is an indiscriminate run on financial institutions that can render them insolvent due to fire sales of assets necessary to fund withdrawals.

The book shows that connectedness was not the problem in the crisis. No significant Lehman counterparties were rendered insolvent by Lehman's failure, with the exception of the Reserve Primary Fund where investors only lost a few pennies on a dollar. And no significant counterparties would have been rendered insolvent by AIG's failure. This is because sophisticated financial institutions routinely manage counterparty risk by limiting their capital exposure, demanding adequate collateral, or hedging. Yet Dodd–Frank is largely premised on the idea that connectedness was the major problem in the crisis. This is reflected in Dodd–Frank's requirements for central clearing of over-the-counter derivatives (swaps), net exposure limits for banks, and the designation of banks and other financial institutions as systemically important financial institutions (SIFIs) and therefore subject to heightened supervision by the Federal Reserve.

However desirable these Dodd–Frank policies may be, the real problem in the crisis was the contagion that smoldered before Lehman's failure and broke out in a full blaze afterward. The losses from contagion and the impact on our economy and country would have been much worse but for heroic efforts by the Federal Reserve to expand its role as lender of last resort, by the FDIC to expand the amount of its insurance, by the Treasury to temporarily guarantee the money market funds, and by the government under TARP to make capital injections in some major banks that were insolvent, or on the brink of insolvency. But the powers of the Fed, FDIC, and Treasury were barely adequate to the task. While the lesson of the crisis should have been that Congress must strengthen their powers, its actual response was to weaken them.

The Federal Reserve was created in 1913 to stem such panics, which were rife in the nineteenth century and culminated in the panic of 1907, through acting as the lender of last resort. As the book describes, the United States came late to the party in creating a central bank. This was largely because of the bad political odor left by our early experiment from 1791 to 1832 with the First and Second National Banks. These were both full-scale federal banks (private in form but government controlled) with broad powers to lend commercially, not just to other banks. But these two National Banks could and did come to the aid of illiquid state banks by modulating use of their ownership of state bank notes to demand specie redemptions from the state banks. The National Banks came to an end in 1832 when newly reelected President Jackson, who had campaigned against these banks as too powerful and too federal, refused to back reauthorization. This bad odor is still with us. The current attack against the Fed's power as lender of last resort is often premised on the idea that the federal government should not make any loans to the private sector, whether those loans are made to commercial establishments, banks or other financial institutions.

As a result of the anti-bailout sentiment following the 2008 crisis, the Fed's power as lender of last resort was significantly restricted by the Dodd–Frank Act, particularly as a lender of last resort to nonbanks under Section 13(3) of the Federal Reserve Act. Having a strong lender of last resort for nonbanks is increasingly important, as nonbanks have issued approximately 60 percent of the estimated $7.4 to $8.2 trillion in runnable short-term liabilities in the financial system.

The Fed can now only lend to nonbanks under a broad program, only with the approval of the Secretary of the Treasury, only if the nonbanks are solvent, and only with heightened collateral requirements. The Fed must also make prompt disclosure of any loans to nonbanks to leaders in the Congress. Discount window loans to banks can also no longer be used to fund nonbank affiliates of banks like broker-dealers. Moreover the Fed knows that any future use of its powers a lender of last resort will be controversial, further threatening its independence and powers. This may inhibit its willingness to act in the future, even within the scope of its newly restricted legal powers.

It is eye opening that the Fed ranks last in its lender of last resort powers to nonbanks as compared to its peer central banks, the Bank of England (BoE), the European Central Bank (ECB), and the Bank of Japan (BOJ). None of these institutions differentiate their lending powers between banks and nonbanks or are prohibited from lending to single nonbanks. None have as demanding disclosure policies as the Fed. The ECB has what amounts to constitutional independence, and while the BoE and BOJ require Treasury approval or request for emergency lending, both operate in parliamentary democracies where the government also controls the Parliament. The biggest threat to Fed independence is the Congress (which can create and destroy the Fed), and which the Administration (even if of the same party) cannot control.

The Fed's main partner in fighting contagion during the 2008 crisis was the FDIC, which was created in 1933 during the Depression. The fundamental idea behind its creation, which remains valid today, was that depositors in banks would not run if their deposits were insured. During the 2008 crisis the FDIC expanded the amount of insurance—granting unlimited insurance to transaction accounts and higher limits for other accounts. The FDIC also guaranteed the issuance of senior debt. In addition the Treasury stepped forward to temporarily guarantee the money market funds, where the contagion blaze first broke out. These FDIC powers were taken away by Dodd–Frank, and, in the case of the Treasury, by the earlier TARP legislation.

Some argue that the old powers to fight contagion are no longer necessary because we have put in place new ex ante regulations to prevent future contagion—namely enhanced capital requirements, new liquidity requirements, and new resolution procedures, what I have termed the two wings and prayer approach. Capital and liquidity requirements, the wings, are ex ante policies designed to prevent contagion, not to deal with it if it does occur. It would be foolhardy to believe we can completely avoid contagion by adopting such policies. Capital requirements only apply to banks and a few specific nonbanks (e.g., the three nonbank SIFIs, for which the requirements have not yet been determined), and could never be at a high enough level to assure short-term creditors that capital would not be seriously eroded by the fire sale of assets in a crisis. In addition the very methodology for designing capital requirements, whether through Basel requirements or stress tests geared to risk, is under serious attack.

New liquidity rules also only apply to banks, whereas short-term liabilities are increasingly held outside the banking system. Liquidity requirements seek to assure that banks have liquid assets to cover withdrawals in a run. But they are based on dubious assumptions about the withdrawal rates of different kinds of bank funding, and ultimately cannot avoid the need of a central bank to act as a lender of last resort when "private" liquidity fails. At best liquidity requirements can buy some breathing room for the central bank to determine what to do, but the fact of the matter is that it must act very quickly.

New resolution authority under the Orderly Liquidation Authority ("OLA") in Dodd–Frank is the prayer. First, its use is not assured. It only comes into play if a financial institution on the brink of insolvency is determined to be a threat to the financial stability of the United States. Second, while procedures are being designed with the objective of making sure no short-term creditors of banks and other subsidiaries of financial holding companies, like broker-dealers, would lose money in an OLA procedure (as opposed to equity and longer term debt), these procedures may not prove effective or credible enough to stop runs on still solvent institutions. Short-term creditors may flee these institutions because they believe it is better to be safe than sorry.

Money market fund reforms, which include a floating NAV for prime institutional and municipal funds, and the powers of fund boards to impose liquidity fees or stop redemptions, are also inadequate to address contagion in that industry. Indeed the prospect of liquidity fees and redemption fees will only accelerate runs. Runs on money market funds can only be stopped the way they were in the crisis, by guarantees and a lender of last resort.

Some have proposed yet another ex ante policy to stop contagion, directing the short-term funding of the financial system away from the private sector into the public sector, because holders of public short-term debt would not run. The problem with this solution is whether it could be adopted on a sufficient scale, both within and outside the banking system, to eliminate the risk of contagion. This seems unlikely given the $7.4 to $8.2 trillion total size of runnable short-term debt, here defined as 30 days or less. Redirection of this amount of short-term funding to the Federal Reserve, through setting adequate rates to attract these funds, could conflict with monetary policy objectives. On the left-hand side of the Fed's balance sheet it would raise credit allocation concerns—in what assets would the Fed invest its massively expanded balance sheet, and on the right-hand side it would raise fairness issues—from what private investors would the Fed accept funds. This approach would therefore inject the Fed into even a greater role in controlling our economy, a prospect unacceptable to many. Although this approach deserves further consideration, it is for now just a dream to go along with two wings and a prayer. Ex ante policies alone, including heightened macroprudential regulation, will be insufficient to manage the next crisis. Strengthening ex ante policies is no reason to weaken ex post protections.

Strengthening the contagion fighting powers described throughout this book would enable the government to credibly allow a large financial institution to fail. This is because such a failure would not spark contagion, as the market could rest assured that the government had the necessary authorities in place to protect the remaining solvent financial institutions. Thus strengthening the contagion fighting powers would actually reduce moral hazard, since the government would no longer have to "bail out" a large insolvent financial institution out of fear that contagion could spread to solvent financial institutions. Nonetheless, a strong lender of last resort should operate under a well-defined framework—such specification of actions that might be taken in a contagious panic could well forestall the panic in the first place and there is a need for the Fed to be transparent and accountable without weakening its ability to deal with crisis.

The last part of the book is focused on TARP, which is properly described as a bail out. In the end the government invested about $250 billion in capital in troubled financial institutions (out of a $700 billion authorization), starting with the nine largest banks and the refinancing of the Fed's position in AIG. The taxpayer actually made money from this venture, as banks have more than repaid their investments.

Authority to make new investments in banks, post-2010, no longer exists. However, in a severe future financial crisis, involving the insolvency of a large number of financial institutions, bailouts and the invention of a new TARP would again be necessary. Without such an intervention the financial system would stop working and the real economy would plunge into a depression. We are fooling ourselves to believe that such a widespread insolvency will never occur. Of course, this could involve financial institutions of any size, so long as the insolvency is sufficiently widespread that the financial system seizes up. Resolution procedures can deal with restructuring insolvent institutions but cannot assure that they will remain solvent or be strong or big enough to continue to finance the economy. Both the Eurozone and Japan have standing TARP-like authority, and Congress should enact such an authority, whether or not it is pre-funded. We have learned many lessons from how TARP operated and we should put a better-designed TARP on the shelf, only to be used in dire future circumstances and with the highest levels of approvals, perhaps even a resolution of Congress.

There is one strong argument that restoring the government's contagion fighting powers is unnecessary—that is, if we are looking over the precipice, as we were in 2008, then the Secretary of the Treasury, Federal Reserve and the Congress will do the right thing. While this is possible, as the Federal Reserve could use its Section 13(3) authorities, with the agreement of the Treasury, to lend to a wide range of financial institutions, we take a big risk that by the time the precipice is cleared, it will already be too late. Can the Federal Reserve convince the

Secretary of Treasury that there is a precipice before a run has started and perhaps gotten out of control? The Secretary and the Fed will have to contend with restrictions that they cannot get around, like the express prohibition of lending to an insolvent institution, heightened collateral requirements and prompt disclosure to Congress. We do not want a system where we have to approach a precipice—we want a clear and strong deployment of weapons long in advance. This was not even possible under the old Section 13(3). And remember there is nothing that the Secretary and the Fed chair can do alone to deploy guarantees or a new TARP. Both require congressional action, and those voting yes on these measures will be putting their political future in jeopardy just as many democrats did when they voted for TARP in 2008.

One of the most challenging aspects of writing this book is knowing that those in and out of the government privately agree with many of my conclusions, particularly the need for Congress to strengthen the lender of last resort and establish a stronger guarantee system, but will not speak out for fear of being accused of trying to bail out Wall Street. However, this issue involves the very preservation of our country, with its economy, way of life, and role in the world. Our leaders need to speak out on this issue, even recognizing that there may be serious adverse consequences to their own careers or institutions. We need profiles in courage not fear.

Appendix

A.1 Asset Interconnectedness Literature Review

Much of the recent literature on asset connectedness provides theoretical support for the conjecture of Haldane (2009) that a densely connected financial system is "robust yet fragile" so that "[w]ithin a certain range [of negative shocks], connections serve as a shock-absorber [and] [c]onnectivity engenders robustness, [but outside that range] the system [flips to] the wrong side of the knife-edge" and distress spreads.[1] So asset connectedness may actually be a way to absorb shocks rather than a cause for meltdown. For example, Acemoglu, Ozdaglar, and Tahbaz-Salehi (2015)[2] study a banking network connected by a cross-holding of unsecured debt contracts. This model includes a "small shock" regime and a "large shock" regime. In the small shock regime, "a more diversified pattern of interbank liabilities implies that the burden of any potential losses [from a borrowing bank] is shared among more banks, creating a more robust financial network."[3] However, in the large shock regime, "dense interconnections act as a channel through which shocks to a subset of the financial institutions transmit to the entire system creating a vehicle for instability and systemic risk."[4] The dividing line between the large and small shock regimes is a negative shock equal to the "total excess liquidity available to the financial network as a whole."[5] Specifically, the dividing line is an idiosyncratic shock equal to all cash held by banks that is not required to meet external liabilities.[6] Like other models of asset connectedness, this dividing line is too high to offer a plausible explanation of the 2008–2009 financial crisis, or prospective future crises.

Other recent literature has added some insight to the relationship between asset connectedness and contagion. For example, Elliot, Golub, and Jackson (2014)[7] analyze a model of connectedness that looks at the effects of integration (i.e., a measure of a firm's asset exposure to other firms) and the effects of diversification (i.e., the number of firms that a given firm is exposed to). Under this model, an initial shock can be amplified when one bank loses value discontinuously after its value falls below a certain critical threshold. Elliot, Golub, and Jackson offer a variety of explanations for the sharp drop in value. For example, a bank might be downgraded, pushing up its cost of capital. More generally, "many of these discontinuities stem from … illiquidity which then leads to an inefficient use of assets."[8] In other words, a small initial shock can be amplified by a sudden withdrawal of liquidity (runs on the bank) that destroys value and magnifies an otherwise minor event into a systemic crisis. They find that an economy is most susceptible to the chain reaction of failures (cascading failures) in the middle region—a system that include firms that are both partially integrated and partially diversified.[9] While asset connectedness plays an important role in shaping the propagation and magnitude of the crisis, the root cause of collapse is value destruction related to illiquidity and contagion. Although they focus on chain reaction failures, which were not observed during the crisis, it may be the case that their results could apply to "cascading losses" that fall short of actual insolvency. For example, suppose Bank A owns the debt of Bank B. If Bank B suffers a shock, which is amplified by illiquidity costs, Bank A will also experience a discontinuous drop in asset prices, as the value of its Bank B debt holdings also dropped discontinuously. Importantly, the mechanism driving the cascade is amplification of the initial shock by run behavior.

Simulation studies are a partial substitute for empirical studies of bank failure, which are often impractical owing to the infrequency of financial crises and the tendency of governments to intervene when they do occur. Upper (2011) reviews a large body of literature that uses "counterfactual simulations to estimate the danger of [cascading failures] owing to exposures in the interbank loan market."[10] He finds that the vast majority of this literature "focus[es] on the unanticipated failure of individual banks," but observes that historical banking crises were not caused by "the domino effects of idiosyncratic failures."[11] Upper observes that one important shortcoming of these models is the assumption that "banks sit tight as problems at their counterparties mount," until an unanticipated default triggers a cascade of failures.[14] However, in reality, counterparties "react by cutting credit lines, [by] not rolling over maturing debt, [and] by novating derivatives contracts."[12] These simulation studies cannot account for the events witnessed in the 2008–2009 financial crisis.

A.2 Liability Interconnectedness Literature Review

This literature can be broadly categorized into two groups. The first group uses network theory to evaluate how an illiquidity shock to one firm propagates to others. The second group identifies liability connectedness through reliance on a "common liquidity pool."

A.2.1 Liability Connectedness through the Lens of Network Theory

One body of literature uses the tools of network theory to examine how a funding shock to one firm spreads to other firms through the interbank lending market. These papers attempt to characterize how the structure of linkages between individual institutions affects the likelihood and severity of a systemwide funding dry up. According to this literature, the complexity of direct and indirect linkages between institutions within a financial network is a critical component of a network's resilience. Many studies have analyzed how direct funding linkages, while introducing the possibility of systemic failure, can also prevent such failure where banks engaging in cross-holdings of deposits effectively insure each individual bank against an idiosyncratic liquidity shock. For example, if Bank A and Bank B each hold one another's deposits, a liquidity shock to Bank A can be met simply by liquidating its holdings in Bank B.[13] Such a network works well when there is sufficient aggregate liquidity in the system to meet demand, but in the case where demand exceeds supply even a small, localized liquidity shock to one bank can spread rapidly through the entire financial network through direct interbank lending arrangements. When an initial shock causes a bank to fail, this failure reduces the overall pool of common liquidity available for the remaining solvent banks in the network. A negative feedback cycle can afflict the system whereby insolvency reduces liquidity, which then causes further insolvency, and so on. The end result can be complete systemic collapse. To a degree, the numerous interconnections between banks within a network serve as a "shock absorber," diffusing the shock throughout the vastness of the financial system, much as does asset connectedness as discussed above. The network provides mutual insurance to each institution, and negative shocks dissipate with no systemic consequences. However, the range of absorbable shocks is bounded by a "tipping point." Beyond this point, interconnections no longer dampen the shock to the system but rather serve to amplify and propagate the damage; this is the same analysis as discussed above for asset connectedness. "The system acts not as a mutual insurance device but as a mutual incendiary device."[14] While the precise threshold of absorbable shocks can be difficult to specify, the existence of such "tipping points" in a connected network can be shown.[15]

The concentration of institutions within a financial network also plays an important role in the propagation of a shock through the system. A more concentrated ("fat-tailed") network is one with a small number of highly connected key players, where connectedness refers to both the number of interbank relationships and the total value of those relationships.[16] A concentrated network is more robust to random shocks than less concentrated networks, provided the shocks are within a given range.[17] However, for shocks outside that range, "higher concentration in the network makes the system more susceptible to a systemic liquidity crisis."[18] Furthermore, since concentrated networks are vulnerable to shocks targeting the key players, when the initial shock hits the most connected interbank lender, the likelihood of systemic failure increases.[19] However, it may require an exceptionally large liquidity shock to destabilize the system. For example, in Gai, Haldane, and Kapadia (2011) instability is triggered by a sudden doubling of repo haircuts.[20] The only plausible explanation for such a tremendous liquidity shock is run-like behavior (i.e., contagion), so connectedness absent contagion would not be a serious problem.

Over the decade preceding the 2008 financial crisis, US financial networks increased in complexity, concentration, connectedness, and homogeneity. From a network theory perspective, such a combination leads to fragility.[21] Securitization and derivatives have lengthened the network chains, while also multiplying the number of links between institutions. Over the past two decades, nodes in the financial network have increased fourteen-fold and "links have become fatter and more frequent, increasing roughly 6-fold."[22] As firms diversified and engaged in risk management strategies with common characteristics, the diversification of individual firms created less diversity in the aggregate system. The network became more homogeneous. Finally, the international finance network has increasingly displayed the characteristics of a fat-tailed network, comprising a relatively small number of highly connected financial institutions.[23]

These features have resulted in a "robust-yet-fragile" system, well equipped to absorb adverse shocks within a given range but vulnerable to failure in the case of shocks outside that range. In addition to the relative magnitude of the shock, the location of a shock in the network (i.e., hitting a so-called super-spreader) can have catastrophic consequences for systemic stability.[24] The basic fragility of the US financial network is best illustrated by the fact that, while the system demonstrated resilience to "fairly large shocks prior to 2007 (e.g., 9/11, the Dotcom crash and the collapse of Amaranth to name a few),"[25] the past fifteen years were in fact a "lengthy period of seeming robustness (the Golden Decade from 1997 to 2007) ... punctuated by an acute period of financial fragility."[26]

Importantly, in most theoretical network models of liability connectedness, the destabilizing mechanism is not a cessation of lending due to default of a lender. Instead, the financial system is disrupted by contagious waves of liquidity hoarding. The structure of the network determines how an initial shock is transmitted throughout the system, but the fundamental destabilizing force is an abrupt onset of liquidity hoarding behavior, often without regard the credit quality of a bank's counterparties. Hence liability connectedness itself is less problematic than contagious run-like behavior.

A.2.2 Liability Connectedness through Reliance on a Common Pool of Liquidity

A second body of literature examines how banks are exposed to funding shocks through reliance on a common pool of liquidity. Empirical studies have documented that market liquidity (the ease with which an asset is traded) co-varies with market prices and volatility,[27] and that an asset's sensitivity to market liquidity is priced (e.g., the less liquid, the lower price).[28] The value of liquidity provides some explanation for the "flight to quality" or "liquidity hoarding" that takes place during crises. Archarya and Pedersen (2005) set forth an equilibrium model that explains these phenomena. Brunnermeier and Pedersen (2009) propose a model that further explains these phenomena and includes a feedback mechanism that illustrates how this need for liquidity can create financial fragility. In their framework, an "asset's market liquidity is linked with investors' "funding liquidity (i.e., the ease with which a firm or more generally an investor can obtain funding)." When market liquidity decreases, and the value of assets decrease as a result, margin requirements will increase. But, if funding liquidity also decreases, it will be difficult to obtain such margin. Thus a small shock to market liquidity can produce outsize effects on market prices through "margin spirals" and "loss spirals." In a loss spiral, firms are forced by a drop in market prices to liquidate assets, which further impairs market liquidity and also asset prices. As a result firms are faced with ever more increased demands for collateral. In a margin spiral, increased demands for collateral prompt firms to sell into an illiquid market, feeding back into the loss spiral. This mechanism creates multiple equilibria in which "a small change in fundamentals can lead to a large jump in illiquidity" and a corresponding decline in asset prices. These spirals may be transmitted between markets and institutions. According to Kodres and Pritsker (2002), "the correlated liquidity shock channel posits that when some market participants need to liquidate some of their assets to obtain cash, perhaps due to a call for collateral, they chose to liquidate assets in a number of markets, effectively transmitting the shock." This illustrates how contagion can spread throughout the financial sector via fire sales, even absent direct balance sheet links between institutions. A similar point is made in Liu (2015), that "indirect interconnectedness" can occur though fire sales and mark-to-market accounting practices.[29] However, these are really consequences of contagion and not the chain reaction of failures that is the key feature of interconnectedness. While Liu (2015) also posits that correlation of CDS spreads is evidence of interconnectedness, that is more indicative of correlation, discussed below.

A.3 Measures of Systemic Risk

Adrian and Brunnermeier's (2010) CoVaR estimates the value at risk of a given financial institution conditional on financial distress occurring at other financial institutions in the industry.[30] A financial insititution's systemic risk measure is therefore defined as the difference between the firm's CoVaR when in a distressed state and the firm's CoVaR when in a stable state. Adrian and Brunnermeier attempt to use firm characteristics such as size, leverage, and maturity mismatch to construct forward-looking measures of CoVar and therefore predict systemic risk (systemic risk as defined by the authors). In effect, the CoVar analysis is really predicting changes in correlation without providing any direct measure of connectedness or contagion. The measure therefore leaves a wide hole in systemic risk predictions since it does not predict systemic risk that results from contagion or connectedness.

While the CoVaR measure may be a useful tool in monitoring correlation, its failure to address the most significant driver of systemic risk—contagion—is a major limitation.

Acharya et al.'s (2011) systemic expected shortfall (SES) estimates a given financial institution's expected loss conditional on substantial losses to the rest of the financial industry.[31] In particular, the SES measure focuses on the likelihood of losses large enough to result in a firm's undercapitalization, namely failure. The higher a firm's SES, the more it contributes to systemic risk under this analysis. Further Acharya et al. propose a "systemic risk tax" on financial institutions based on their SES. However, similar to the issues with the CoVaR measure, the SES measure is merely a conditional loss-probability-based measure, in that it primarily captures correlation among financial institutions without providing any quantifiable measure of connectedness or contagion. While there is value in the SES measure for purposes of correlation, the risk of contagion is absent in the analysis.

Finally, Billio et al. (2012) attempt to complement the conditional loss-probability-based CoVaR and SES systemic risk measures by providing a measure of connectedness for financial instituions.[32] They use a principal component analysis to estimate the return correlations among financial institutions, finding that the monthly returns of hedge funds, banks, broker-dealers, and insurance companies have become more correlated over the past ten years. While Billio et al. declare that their return correlation measurements are "metrics [gauging] the degree of connectedness of the financial system," the analysis does not in fact directly measure connectedness, but merely makes an inference that connectedness must be present to explain the return correlations. As I have explained above, connectedness, contagion, and correlation are distinct factors in systemic risk that should not be conflated. The presence of one factor does not imply the other. Therefore Billio et al. (2012) have provided evidence of correlation, but they fail to measure connectedness or contagion.

A.4   Correlation Literature Review

The potential for widespread correlated losses is intimately related to the degree of herding behavior exhibited by banks and other investors. If bank portfolios are homogeneous across individual firms, for example, if all banks lend to the same type of borrower, they can become vulnerable to a correlated shock. Scharfstein and Stein (1990)[33] study mechanisms that can lead to this herding behavior in investment decisions. They suggest that individual managers may have an incentive to follow herd behavior, even despite "substantive private information" suggesting that the path is ill-advised. They believe there is safety in just being part of a herd. In addition to maximizing value for their current employer, managers have an incentive to preserve their reputations. As a result managers may make suboptimal investments because "an unprofitable decision is not as bad for reputation when others make the same mistake." This reasoning is equally applicable to asset managers who, during times of market distress, "rush to the exit" and collectively shun many asset classes. Archarya and Yorulmazer (2008) construct a model in which rational profit-maximizing banks have an incentive to herd into similar positions, because contrarian banks that do not follow the herd may face higher borrowing costs, and therefore lower profits.

Reinhart and Rogoff (2009) document 800 years of systemic crises and identify real estate price bubbles as a major contributor to systemic risk.[34] Allen and Carletti (2009) "argue that the main cause of the crisis was that there was a bubble in real estate in the U.S."[35] In addition to the papers that identify correlated shocks as the proximate cause of crisis, another body of literature identifies correlated losses as the trigger of an amplification mechanism. For example, Elsinger Lehar and Summer (2006)[36] study the effects of a correlated shock on a banking network connected through asset connectedness. They find that studying the effects of a single idiosyncratic shock "underestimates the impact of bank defaults on the rest of the system by a considerable margin."[37] However, losses in the housing market amounted to roughly $100–200 billion. This correlated shock alone is insufficient to explain the $8 trillion loss of equity market capitalization witnessed during the crisis. As previously argued, indiscriminate waves of run-like behavior depressed asset prices far below their fundamental values. Although correlation played an important role in this process, contagion is what transformed an otherwise minor shock into a major systemic crisis.

Notes

Introduction

1. See S&P/Case-Shiller U.S. National Home Price Index, S&P Dow Jones Indices, http://us.spindices.com/indices/real-estate/sp-case-shiller-us-national-home-price -index(lastupdatedSep.29,2015).

2. See id.

3. Real Capital Analytics, Moody's/RCA CPPI, available at: https://www.rcanalytics .com/Public/rca_cppi.aspx

4. On September 25, 2008, the bank subsidiary of Washington Mutual was placed into FDIC receivership. Its parent company, Washington Mutual Inc. filed for Chapter 11 bankruptcy. See Status of Washington Mutual Bank Receivership, *Federal Deposit Insurance Corporation*, available at https://www.fdic.gov/bank/individual/failed/wamu _settlement.html.

5. Peter Dattels and Laura Kodres, Further action needed to reinforce signs of market recovery: IMF, *IMF* (Apr. 21, 2009), available at http://www.imf.org/external/pubs/ft/ survey/so/2009/RES042109C.htm.

6. GDP growth (annual %), data, World Bank, available at http://data.worldbank.org/ indicator/NY.GDP.MKTP.KD.ZG?page=1.

7. Timothy F. Geithner, *Stress Test: Reflections on Financial Crises* 515 (New York: Crown, 2014).

8. Henry M. Paulson, Jr., *On the Brink: Inside the Race to Stop the Collapse of the Global Financial System* 1, xxviii (2013).

9. Warren Buffet, Financial Crisis Inquiry Commission Interview, available at http:// fcic.law.stanford.edu/interviews/view/19.

Chapter 1

1. Tobias Adrian and Hyun Song Shin, Liquidity and financial contagion, *Fin. Stability Rev.*, special issue on liquidity, 1 (Feb. 2008).

2. Christian Upper, Simulation methods to assess the danger of contagion in interbank markets, 7 (3) *J. Fin. Stability* 111, 112 (2011) (indicating an absence of such events, while noting that this scenario almost unfolded when Herstatt failed in 1974).

Chapter 2

1. See, for example, Milton Friedman and Anna Schwartz, *A Monetary History of the United States 1867–1960*, 1, 299–419 (1963) (discussing the role of contagion in US banking crises of the early 1930s); Milton Friedman and Anna Schwartz, *The Great Contraction 1929–1933*, 1 (1965); Alan Greenspan, Chairman, Board. of Governors of the Federal Reserve System, Remarks at the 8th Frankfurt International Banking Evening (May 7, 1996), available at https://fraser.stlouisfed.org/historicaldocs/852/download/28572/Greenspan_19960507.pdf (warning of the consequences to the contemporary financial system of a contagious "chain reaction" of institutional failures in a period of financial crisis).

2. See George Kaufman, Bank contagion: Theory and evidence (Fed. Res. Bank of Chicago, Working Paper 92–13, June 1992), available at https://www.chicagofed.org/digital_assets/publications/working_papers/1992/WP-92-12.pdf. "Panic," a popular and historical term that is substantially synonymous with contagion, will be used interchangeably throughout this book.

3. See Ted Temzelides, Are bank runs contagious?, *Federal Reserve Bank of Philadelphia Business Review* 3 (Nov./Dec.1997), available at https://www.philadelphiafed.org/research-and-data/publications/business-review/1997/november-december/brnd97tt.pdf.

4. Id. at 4–6.

5. Jean-Claude Trichet, President, European Central Bank, Text of the Clare Distinguished Lecture in Economics and Public Policy (Dec. 10, 2009), available at http://www.ecb.europa.eu/press/key/date/2009/html/sp091210_1.en.html (analyzing the linkage between systemic risk and contagion).

6. George Kaufman, Bank contagion: Theory and evidence 1, 3 (Fed. Res. Bank of Chicago, Working Paper 92–13, June 1992), available at https://www.chicagofed.org/digital_assets/publications/working_papers/1992/WP-92-12.pdf.

7. Mark Carlson and David Wheelock, The lender of last resort: Lessons from the Fed's first 100 years (Fed. Res. Bank of St. Louis, Working Paper 2012–056B, 2013), available at https://research.stlouisfed.org/wp/2012/2012-056.pdf.

8. See Adam Zaretsky, Learning the lessons of history: The Federal Reserve and the payments system, *Regional Economist* (July 1996), available at https://www.stlouisfed.org/publications/re/articles/?id=1805; Jeffrey Lacker, President Federal Reserve Bank of Richmond, Speech at Christopher Newport University, A look back at the history of the Federal Reserve (Aug. 29, 2013), available at https://www.richmondfed.org/press_room/speeches/president_jeff_lacker/2013/lacker_speech_20130829.cfm.

9. Stephen Williamson, Bank failures, financial restrictions, and aggregate fluctuations: Canada and the United States, 1870–1913, *Fed. Res. Bank of Minneapolis Quart. Rev.* 1 (Summer 1989), available at https://www.minneapolisfed.org/publications_papers/pub_display.cfm?id=218.

10. Richard Scott Carnell, Jonathan R. Macey, and Geoffrey P. Miller, *The Law of Banking and Financial Institutions*, 1, 11 (Austin: Wolters Kluwer Law & Business, 4th ed. 2008).

11. Id. at 11.

12. Williamson, *supra* note 9, at 3 (finding that banks subject to a unit banking restriction are less diversified, "more sensitive to idiosyncratic shocks, and … experience runs and fail with higher probability").

13. Id. at 3–6, 13–19.

14. Id. at 24.

15. Id. at 5; see also Friedman and Schwartz, *The Great Contraction*, *supra* note 1, at 352–53 (discussing absence of runs on Canadian banks during the Depression and its impact on the money supply).

16. Williamson, *supra* note 9, at 20; see also Ted Temzelides, *supra* note 3, at 8

(discussing Williamson's findings).

17. Charles Calomiris and Joseph Mason, Contagion and bank failures during the Great Depression: The June 1932 Chicago banking panic, 87(5) *Am. Econ. Rev.* 863, 881 (1997), available at http://www.jstor.org/stable/2951329?seq=1#page_scan_tab_contents (finding "failures during the [Chicago] panic reflected relative weakness of failing banks in the face of a common asset value shock rather than contagion").

18. Id. at 865. In total there were forty-nine bank failures in Illinois in June 1932. Id.

19. Id. at 881.

20. Id.

21. Id. at 864.

22. Id. at 864, 868–69 (noting that "at least one solvent bank" was saved from failing through the assistance of the Chicago clearing house banks).

23. See Martin Wolf, *Fixing Global Finance*, 1 (Johns Hopkins University Press 2008).

24. Nicolas Dumontaux and Adrian Pop, Contagion effects in the aftermath of Lehman's collapse: Measuring the collateral damage, 14 (Working Paper, Dec. 2009), available at http://congres.afse.fr/docs/2010/836939dp2010_lehman.pdf.

25. Id. at 15.

26. Id. at 15–16 (calling the "market reaction to Lehman's failure … selective and well-informed, rather than random and indiscriminate").

27. William Sterling, Looking back at Lehman: An empirical analysis of the financial shock and the effectiveness of countermeasures, 57(2) *Musashi Univ. J.* 53 (2009).

28. Id.

29. Jian Yang and Yinggang Zhou, Credit risk spillovers among financial institutions around the global credit crisis: Firm-level evidence, 59(10) *Managem. Sci.* 2343 (2013).

30. Id.

31. See JPMorgan Chase, *Letter to Shareholders: Annual Report*, 28 (2009), available at http://files.shareholder.com/downloads/ONE/1017247059x0x362440/1ce6e503-25c6-4b7b-8c2e-8cb1df167411/2009AR_Letter_to_shareholders.pdf.

32. Sam Jones, The run on Morgan Stanley, FTAlphaville (Sep. 18, 2008), available at http://ftalphaville.ft.com/2008/09/18/16082/the-run-on-morgan-stanley/ (reporting that JPMorgan "[was] thought" to have received $40 billion in prime brokerage inflows in the two days following the bankruptcy of Lehman Brothers).

33. JPMorgan Chase, *Letter to Shareholders, supra* note 31.

34. See Rick Rothacker and Kerry Hall, Wachovia faced a "silent" bank run, *Charlotte Observer* (Oct. 2, 2008).

35. See E. Scott Reckard, Deposit run at WaMu forced their hand, regulators say, *Los Angeles Times* (Sep. 25, 2008).

36. William Dudley, President and Chief Executive Officer of the Federal Reserve Bank of New York, Remarks at the Center for Economic Policy Studies (CEPS) Symposium, Princeton, NJ, More lessons from the crisis (Nov. 13, 2009), available at http://www.newyorkfed.org/newsevents/speeches/2009/dud091113.html.

37. Hal S. Scott, How to improve five important areas of financial regulation, *Kaufman Task Force on Law, Innovation, and Growth*, 113, 117–18, available at http://www.kauffman.org/~/media/kauffman_org/research%20reports%20and%20covers/2011/02/rulesforgrowth.pdf.

38. For a summary, see Hal S. Scott and Anna Gelpern, *International Finance, Transactions, Policy, and Regulation*, University Casebook Series 1, 44–84 (20th ed. 2014).

39. For a summary of systemic risk measures, see Christopher Bierth, Felix Irresberger, and Gregor Weiss, Systemic risk of insurers around the globe, *J. Bank. Fin.* 55 (2015) 232–45.

40. Douglas Diamond and Philip Dybvig, Bank runs, deposit insurance, and liquidity, 24 *Fed. Res. Bank of Minneapolis Q. Rev.* 14 (2000), available at http://minneapolisfed.org/research/QR/QR2412.pdf; Gary Gorton, Banking panics and business cycles, 40 *Oxford Econ. Papers* 751 (1988).

41. See Hal S. Scott and Anna Gelpern, *International Finance, Transactions, Policy, and Regulation*, University Casebook Series 1, 26 (Eagan, MN: Foundation Press, 20th ed. 2014).

42. See Sushil Bikhchandani, David Hirshleifer and Ivo Welch, A theory of fads, fashion, custom, and cultural change as informational cascades, 100(5) *J. Polit. Econ.* 992, 1012–13 (1992).

43. Id. (comparing the initiation of a bank run to "a cascade in which small depositors fear for the solvency of a bank and act by observing the withdrawal behavior of other depositors"); see also Charles Kindleberger, *Manias, Panics, and Crashes: A History of Financial Crises* 1, 38, 145 (5th ed., Wiley, Hoboken, NJ, 2005).

44. See, for example, Morgan Ricks, Shadow banking and financial regulation, 3, 13 (Columbia Law and Econ., Working Paper 370, Aug. 30, 2010) (extending the economic explanation for run behavior to the so-called shadow banking system).

45. Douglas Diamond and Philip Dybvig, Bank runs, deposit insurance, and liquidity, 24 *Fed. Res. Bank of Minneapolis Q. Rev.* 14, 15 (2000), available at https://minneapolisfed.org/research/QR/QR2412.pdf.

46. Douglas Diamond and Philip Dybvig, Bank runs, deposit insurance, and liquidity, 91(3) *J. Polit. Econ.* 401, 410 (1983).

47. See Scott, *supra* note 37, at 114.

48. Diamond and Dybvig, *supra* note 45.

49. Markus Brunnermeier, Deciphering the liquidity and credit crunch 2007–2008, 23 *J. Econ. Persp.* 77, 79 (Winter 2009).

50. Diamond and Dybvig, *supra* note 46, at 403; see also Gerald Corrigan, Are banks special? Federal Reserve Bank of Minneapolis (January 1982), available at https://www .minneapolisfed.org/publications/annual-reports/ar/annual-report-1982-complete-text (noting that "[o]nly banks issue transaction accounts; that is, they incur liabilities payable on demand at par and are readily transferable by the owner to third parties").

51. Carnell et al., *supra* note 10, at 310 (characterizing uninsured depositors as "fac[ing] a collective action problem of the sort game theorists call the *prisoner's dilemma*"); see also Ricks, *supra* note 44, at 3, 13.

52. See, for example, Hal S. Scott, The reduction of systemic risk in the United States financial system, 33(2) *Harvard J. Law Pub. Pol.* 671, 674–75 (2010) (describing the prototypical depositor-initiated contagious run and linking it to the broader problem of systemic risk in the financial system); Andrei Shleifer and Robert Vishny, Fire sales in finance and macroeconomics, 25(1) *J. Econ. Persp.* 29 (2011); Ted Temzelides, *supra* note 3, at 5.

53. Shleifer and Vishny, *supra* note 52, at 37 (discussing the impact of margin requirements and collateral liquidations on fire sales).

54. Friedman and Schwartz, *A Monetary History, supra* note 1, at 355 (reporting that "impairment in the market value of assets held by banks, particularly in their bond portfolios, was the most important source of impairment of capital leading to bank suspensions, rather than the default of specific loans or of specific bond issues [of the early 1930s]").

55. Paul Masson, Contagion: Monsoonal effects, spillovers, and jumps between multiple equillibria, 1 (IMF Working Paper 98/142, Sep. 1998).

56. Ali Hortacsu, Gregor Matvos, Chaehee Shin, Chad Syverson, and Sriram Venkataraman, Is an automaker's road to bankruptcy paved with customer beliefs?, 101(3) *Am. Econ. Rev.* (May 1, 2011), available at http://papers.ssrn.com/sol3/papers. cfm?abstract_id=2158358.

57. Id. at 1.

58. Gary Gorton and Andrew Metrick, Securitized banking and the run on repo, 104(3) *Journal of Financial Economics* 425 (2012).

59. Id.

60. Gary Gorton and Guillermo Ordoñez, Collateral crises, 104(2) *Am. Econ. Rev.* 343 (2014).

61. Tobias Adrian and Hyun Shin, Paper prepared for the Federal Reserve Bank of Kansas City Symposium at Jackson Hole, Aug. 21–23, 2008, Financial intermediaries, financial stability and monetary policy, 1 (Aug. 5, 2008), available at http://www .iepecdg.com.br/uploads/seminario/Shin.08.06.08.pdf.

62. Tobias Adrian and Markus K. Brunnermeier, CoVaR (Working Paper, 2010); Viral Acharya, Lasse H. Pedersen, Thomas Philippon, and Matthew Richardson, Measuring

systemic risk (Working Paper 2010); Monica Billio, Andrew W. Lo, Mila Getmansky, and Loriana Pelizzon, Econometric measures of connectedness and systemic risk in the finance and insurance sectors, 104(3) *J. Fin. Econ.* 535 (2012).

Chapter 3

1. Monica Billio, Andrew W. Lo, Mila Getmansky, and Loriana Pelizzon, Econometric Measures of Connectedness and Systemic Risk in the Finance and Insurance Sectors, *J. Fin. Econ.* 104 (2012).

2. Markus Brunnermeier, Deciphering the liquidity and credit crunch 2007–2008, 23(1) *J. Econ. Persp.* 77 (2009).

3. See Andrew Haldane, Speech at the London Business School, 2–5 (April 4, 2014), available at http://www.bankofengland.co.uk/publications/Documents/speeches/2014/speech723.pdf.

4. Financial Stability Board, *Assessment Methodologies for Identifying Non-bank Non-insurer Global Systemically Important Financial Institutions* 1 (2015), available at http://www.financialstabilityboard.org/2015/03/assessment-methodologies-for-identifying-non-bank-non-insurer-global-systemically-important-financial-institutions/.

5. Id.

6. Mark Carlson, A brief history of the 1987 stock market crash with a discussion of the Federal Reserve response 10 (2007), available at http://www.federalreserve.gov/Pubs/feds/2007/200713/200713pap.pdf.

7. Id. at 17.

8. Id.

Chapter 4

1. See Deal Journal, From general store to titan: A brief history of Lehman, *Wall St. J.* (Sep. 15, 2008), available at http://blogs.wsj.com/deals/2008/09/15/from-general-store-to-titan-a-brief-history-of-lehman/.

2. Voluntary Petition, *In re* Lehman Bros. Holdings Inc., No. 08-13555 (Bankr. SDNY Sep. 15, 2008).

3. Sam Mamudi, Lehman folds with record $613 billion debt, *MarketWatch* (September 15, 2008), available at http://www.marketwatch.com/story/lehman-folds-with-record-613-billion-debt?siteid=rss.

4. Voluntary petition at exhibit A, *In re* Lehman Bros. Holdings Inc., No. 08-13555 (Bankr. SDNY Sep. 15, 2008).

5. Debtors' disclosure statement for joint Chapter 11 plan of Lehman Brothers Holdings Inc. and its affiliated debtors pursuant to section 1125 of the Bankruptcy Code at exhibit 2A, *In re* Lehman Bros. Holdings Inc. et al., No. 08-13555 (Bankr. SDNY Apr. 14, 2010).

6. Twenty-four LBHI affiliates subsequently filed for Chapter 11 in the United States. Two of these cases were dismissed, and the rest are being jointly administered with LBHI's. See *Case Information, General Information* (LBH), available at http://dm.epiq11.com/LBH/Project (2013).

7. See Report of Anton Valukas, Examiner 631, *In re* Lehman Bros. Holdings Inc. et al., No. 08-13555 (Bankr. SDNY March 11, 2010); see also William Dudley, Transcript of the Federal Open Market Committee Meeting (March 18, 2008) ("In my view, an old-fashioned bank run is what really led to Bear Stearn's demise.").

8. Report of Anton Valukas, Examiner 631, *In re* Lehman Bros. Holdings Inc. et al., No. 08-13555, at 1643 (Bankr. SDNY Mar. 11, 2010).

9. Id. at 634.

10. Id. at 1464.

11. See, for example, Hearing before the Financial Crisis Inquiry Commission 1 (Sep. 1, 2010) (statement of Richard S. Fuld, Jr.), available at http://fcic-static.law.stanford.edu/cdn_media/fcic-testimony/2010-0901-Fuld.pdf (lamenting that "Lehman's demise was caused by uncontrollable market forces and the incorrect market perception and accompanying rumors that Lehman did not have sufficient capital to support its investments").

12. Report of Anton Valukas, Examiner 631, *In re* Lehman Bros. Holdings Inc. et al., No. 08-13555, at 214–215 (Bankr. SDNY March 11, 2010) (noting that there was enough evidence to suggest the firm had overvalued some of its Principal Transaction Group real estate assets and its Archstone Bridge equity investment).

13. Sheila Bair, Road to safer banks runs through Basel, *Financial Times* (August 23, 2010), available at http://www.ft.com/cms/s/0/a1dfbd02-aee8-11df-8e45-00144fe-abdc0.html#axzz1uqOCR300; see Thomas Russo and Aaron Katzel, The 2008 financial crisis and its aftermath: Addressing the next debt challenge 12 (Group of Thirty, Occasional Paper No. 82, 2011) (arguing that the 2008 financial crisis was fundamentally "caused by excessive leverage at each level of the economy").

14. Financial Crisis Inquiry Commission, *The Financial Crisis Inquiry Report*, at xix (2011), available at http://www.gpo.gov/fdsys/pkg/GPO-FCIC/pdf/GPO-FCIC.pdf.

15. Report of Anton Valukas, Examiner 631, *In re* Lehman Bros. Holdings Inc. et al., No. 08-13555, at 43 (Bankr. SDNY March 11, 2010).

16. Id. at 62.

17. Id. at 4, n.13.

18. Id. at 45.

19. Id. at 224.

20. Id. at 45.

21. Id. at 616, 642–43.

22. Id. at 645.

23. Id. at 647–48.

24. See id. at 642.

25. Linda Sandler and Bob Ivry, Lehman borrowed $18 billion from previously secret Fed program, (July 7, 2011), available at http://www.bloomberg.com/news/articles/2011-07-06lehman-borrowed-18-billion-from-undisclosed-fed-program-during-08-crisis

26. See id. at 667–68.

27. See id. at 678–81.

28. See id. at 690–91.

29. See id. at 693–95.

30. Id. at 697.

31. Id. at 699–700.

32. See Order Under 11 USC §§105(a), 363, and 365 and Federal Rules of Bankruptcy Procedure 2002, 6004 and 6006 Authorizing and Approving (A) the Sale of Purchased Assets Free and Clear of Liens and Other Interests and (B) Assumption and Assignment of Executory Contracts and Unexpired Leases, *In re* Lehman Bros. Holdings Inc. et al., No. 08-13555 (Bankr. SDNY Sep. 20, 2008). In the transaction, Barclays also purchased, *inter alia*, Lehman's global headquarters and two data centers. See Asset Purchase Agreement among Lehman Brothers Holdings Inc., Lehman Brothers Inc., LB 745 LLC and Barclays Capital Inc. §1.1, at 2, 6–8, Schedule 2 (Sep. 16, 2008).

33. Report of Anton Valukas, Examiner 631, *In re* Lehman Bros. Holdings Inc. et al., No. 08-13555, at 706–07, 709 (Bankr. SDNY Mar. 11, 2010).

34. Id. at 707.

35. See id. at 706.

36. James Stewart and Peter Eavis, Revisiting the Lehman Brothers bailout that never was (Sep. 29, 2014), available at http://www.nytimes.com/2014/09/30/business/revisiting-the-lehman-brothers-bailout-that-never-was.html?_r=0.

37. Id.

38. Report of Anton Valukas, Examiner 631, *In re* Lehman Bros. Holdings Inc. et al., No. 08-13555, at 1550 (Bankr. SDNY Mar. 11, 2010).

39. See PricewaterhouseCoopers, *Lehman Brothers International (Europe) (in Administration): Joint Administrators' Progress Report for the Period 15 September 2008 to 14 March 2009*, at 9 (Apr. 14, 2009).

40. Id. at 4–5, 8.

41. Order Commencing Liquidation, *In re* Lehman Bros. Inc., No. 08-01420 (SIPA) (SDNY Sep. 19, 2008).

42. *Trustee's Preliminary Investigation Report and Recommendations* 2–3, Exhibit C-6, *In re* Lehman Bros. Inc., No. 08-01420 (SIPA) (SDNY Sep. 19, 2008).

43. See Report of Anton Valukas, Examiner 631, *In re* Lehman Bros. Holdings Inc. et al., No. 08-13555 (Bankr. SDNY Mar. 11, 2010).

44. See Joseph Checkler, Lehman creditor plan heads for vote, *Wall St. J.* (Aug. 31, 2011), available at http://www.wsj.com/articles/SB10001424053111904332804576540641768081466.

45. *In re* Owens Corning, 419 F.3d 195, 202 (3d Cir. 2005).

46. Eastgroup Props. v. S. Motel Ass'n, Ltd., 935 F.2d 245, 248 (11th Cir. 1991).

47. See, for example, Report of Anton Valukas, Examiner 631, *In re* Lehman Bros. Holdings Inc. et al., No. 08-13555 (Bankr. SDNY Mar. 11, 2010).

48. The plan was originally filed on March 15, 2010. Joint Chapter 11 Plan of Lehman Brothers Holdings Inc. and Its Affiliated Debtors, *In re* Lehman Bros. Holdings Inc. et al., No. 08-13555 (Bankr. SDNY Mar. 15, 2010). It was slightly revised and re-filed on April 14 in conjunction with a disclosure statement. Notice of Filing of Revised Chapter 11 Plan, *In re* Lehman Bros. Holdings Inc. et al., No. 08-13555 (Bankr. SDNY Apr. 14, 2010); see also Disclosure Statement for Initial Plan, *In re* Lehman Bros. Holdings Inc. et al., No. 08-13555 (Bankr. SDNY Apr. 14, 2010).

49. See Debtors' Disclosure Statement for First Amended Joint Chapter 11 Plan of Lehman Brothers Holdings Inc. and Its Affiliated Debtors Pursuant to Section 1125 of the Bankruptcy Code, *In re* Lehman Bros. Holdings Inc. et al., No. 08-13555 3–50 (Bankr. SDNY Jan. 25, 2011).

50. *Compare* Joint Substantively Consolidating Chapter 11 Plan for Lehman Brothers Holdings Inc. and Certain of Its Affiliated Debtors Other Than Merit, LLC, LB Somerset LLC and LB Preferred Somerset LLC Proposed by the Ad Hoc Group of Lehman Brothers Creditors, *In re* Lehman Bros. Holdings Inc. et al., No. 08-13555 (Bankr. SDNY Dec. 15, 2010); Disclosure Statement for the Joint Substantively Consolidating Chapter 11 Plan for Lehman Brothers Holdings Inc. and Certain of Its Affiliated Debtors Other Than Merit, LLC, LB Somerset LLC and LB Preferred Somerset LLC Proposed by the Ad Hoc Group of Lehman Brothers Creditors, *In re* Lehman Bros. Holdings Inc. et al., No. 08-13555 (Bankr. SDNY Dec. 15, 2010); *with* Joint Chapter 11 Plan for Lehman Brothers Holdings Inc. and Its Affiliated Debtors Other Than Merit, LLC, LB Somerset LLC and LB Preferred LLC Proposed by Non-Consolidation Plan Proponents, *In re* Lehman Bros. Holdings Inc. et al., No. 08-13555 (Bankr. SDNY Apr. 25, 2011).

51. See First Amended Joint Chapter 11 Plan of Lehman Brothers Holdings Inc. and Its Affiliated Debtors, *In re* Lehman Bros. Holdings Inc. et al., No. 08-13555 (Bankr. SDNY Jan. 25, 2011); Amended Joint Substantively Consolidating Chapter 11 Plan for Lehman Brothers Holdings Inc. and Certain of Its Affiliated Debtors Other Than Merit, LLC, LB Somerset LLC and LB Preferred Somerset LLC, Proposed by the Ad Hoc Group of Lehman Brothers Creditors, *In re* Lehman Bros. Holdings Inc. et al., No. 08-13555 (Bankr. SDNY Apr. 27, 2011).

52. See Modified Third Amended Joint Chapter 11 Plan of Lehman Brothers Holdings Inc. and Its Affiliated Debtors, *In re* Lehman Bros. Holdings Inc. et al., No. 08-13555 (Bankr. SDNY Nov. 29, 2011). In this book, the disclosure statement for the Third Amended Plan will be used to explicate elements of the Modified Third Amended Plan.

53. Order Confirming Modified Third Amended Joint Chapter 11 Plan of Lehman Brothers Holdings Inc. and Its Affiliated Debtors, *In re* Lehman Bros. Holdings Inc. et al., No. 08-13555 (Bankr. SDNY Dec. 6, 2011).

54. Notice of Effective Date and Distribution Date in Connection with the Modified Third Amended Joint Chapter 11 Plan of Lehman Brothers Holdings Inc. and Its Affiliated Debtors, *In re* Lehman Bros. Holdings Inc. et al., No. 08-13555 (Bankr. SDNY Mar. 6, 2012).

55. See Notice Regarding Initial Distributions Pursuant to the Modified Third Amended Joint Chapter 11 Plan of Lehman Brothers Holdings Inc. and Its Affiliated Debtors at Exhibit B, *In re* Lehman Bros. Holdings Inc. et al., No. 08-13555 (Bankr. SDNY Apr. 11, 2012).

56. See Debtors' Disclosure Statement for Third Amended Joint Chapter 11 Plan of Lehman Brothers Holdings Inc. and Its Affiliated Debtors Pursuant to Section 1125 of the Bankruptcy Code, *In re* Lehman Bros. Holdings Inc. et al., No. 08 13555 Annex A-2 (Bankr. SDNY Aug. 31, 2011).

57. Josh Fineman and Christopher Scinta, Credit Suisse Group selling $1 billion Lehman claim, *Bloomberg* (Sep. 24, 2009), available at http://www.bloomberg.com/apps/news?pid=newsarchive&sid=a08KzEnlvIrk.

58. See Disclosure Statement for Initial Plan, *In re* Lehman Bros. Holdings Inc. et al., No. 08-13555, Exhibit 5 (Bankr. SDNY Apr. 14, 2010).

59. See id.

60. Michael J. Fleming and Asani Sarkar, The failure and resolution of Lehman Brothers, 20(2) *Fed. Res. Bank of New York Econ. Pol. Rev.* 175 (2014), available at http://www.ny.frb.org/research/epr/2014/1412flem.html.

61. Id.

62. Joseph Checkler, Lehman trustee begins third payout to brokerage creditors, *Wall St. J.* (Sep. 9, 2015), available at http://www.wsj.com/articles/lehman-trustee-begins-third-payout-to-brokerage-creditors-1441805748.

63. See Interconnectedness, fragility and the financial crisis: Hearing before the Financial Crisis Inquiry Commission 4–5 (Feb. 26–27, 2010) (statement of Randall Kroszner).

64. Jean Helwege and Gaiyan Zhang, Financial firm bankruptcy and contagion (Working Paper, July 31, 2012).

65. See Mark Roe and Stephen Adams, Restructuring failed financial firms in bankruptcy: Selling Lehman's derivatives portfolio, 32 *Yale J. Regul.* (forthcoming, summer 2015); see generally Mark J. Roe, The derivatives market's payment priorities as financial crisis accelerator, 63(3) *Stan. L. Rev.* 539 (2011).

66. Id.

67. Alvarez & Marsal, *Lehman Brothers Holdings Inc.: The State of the Estate* 23 (Sep. 22, 2010). Note that these figures from the estate's September 2010 update do not precisely match the "Filed amount per Epiq" in the disclosure statement for the Initial Plan.

68. See Disclosure Statement for Initial Plan, *In re* Lehman Bros. Holdings Inc. et al., No. 08-13555, Annex A-2 (Bankr. SDNY Apr. 14, 2010).

69. Fleming and Sarkar, *supra* note 60, at 177.

70. See Disclosure statement for initial plan, *In re* Lehman Bros. Holdings Inc. et al., No. 08-13555, Annex A-4 (Bankr. SDNY Apr. 14, 2010).

71. Id. at Annex A-3.

72. First Amended Joint Chapter 11 Plan of Lehman Brothers Holdings Inc. and Its Affiliated Debtors, *In re* Lehman Bros. Holdings Inc. et al., No. 08-13555 (Bankr. SDNY Jan. 25, 2011).

73. See Debtors' Disclosure Statement for First Amended Joint Chapter 11 Plan of Lehman Brothers Holdings Inc. and Its Affiliated Debtors Pursuant to Section 1125 of the Bankruptcy Code at 3–50, In re Lehman Bros. Holdings Inc. et al., No. 08-13555, Exhibit 6-2-6-6 (Bankr. SDNY Jan. 25, 2011).

74. The estate's characterization of claims has been subject to dispute. While one might argue that the estate's estimates therefore understate economic exposure, these estimates are still the most reliable basis for analysis. Slightly higher estimates would not materially change the thrust of this work's findings.

75. Debtors' Disclosure Statement for Third Amended Joint Chapter 11 Plan of Lehman Brothers Holdings Inc. and Its Affiliated Debtors Pursuant to Section 1125 of the Bankruptcy Code, In re Lehman Bros. Holdings Inc. et al., No. 08-13555, Annex A-2 (Bankr. SDNY Aug. 31, 2011). Secured claims allowed under the Modified Third Amended Plan are omitted from all claims analysis because the estate does not include them in its estimate of claim amounts (it adds them as a plan adjustment), these claims are small in magnitude ($3.4 billion), and they are projected to receive 100 percent recovery. See id. at Exhibit 5, Annex A-2.

76. Id.

77. Debtors' Disclosure Statement for First Amended Joint Chapter 11 Plan of Lehman Brothers Holdings Inc. and Its Affiliated Debtors Pursuant to Section 1125 of the Bankruptcy Code at 3–50, In re Lehman Bros. Holdings Inc. et al., No. 08-13555, Exhibit 9–8 to 9–9 (Bankr. SDNY Jan. 25, 2011).

78. Debtors' Disclosure Statement for Third Amended Joint Chapter 11 Plan of Lehman Brothers Holdings Inc. and Its Affiliated Debtors Pursuant to Section 1125 of the Bankruptcy Code, In re Lehman Bros. Holdings Inc. et al., No. 08 13555, Annex A-2 (Bankr. SDNY Aug. 31, 2011).

79. Standard & Poor's, *Broader Lessons from Lehman Brothers' Bankruptcy*, RatingsDirect 3 (Sep. 17, 2008).

80. Disclosure Statement for Initial Plan, In re Lehman Bros. Holdings Inc. et al.,

No. 08-13555, Annex A-3, Exhibit 4–1 (Bankr. SDNY Apr. 14, 2010).

81. Takahiko Hyuga et al., *Japan Banks, Insurers Have $2.4 Billion Lehman Risk*, Bloomberg (Sep. 17, 2008), available at http://www.bloomberg.com/apps/news?pid=newsarchive &sid=a3mSQ9tXT.5w&refer=japan.

82. Id.

83. Id.

84. Disclosure Statement for Initial Plan, In re Lehman Bros. Holdings Inc. et al., No. 08-13555, Annex A-2 (Bankr. SDNY Apr. 14, 2010).

85. Disclosure Statement for Third Amended Joint Chapter 11 Plan of Lehman Brothers Holdings Inc. and Its Affiliated Debtors Pursuant to Section 1125 of the Bankruptcy Code, In re Lehman Bros. Holdings Inc. et al., No. 08-13555, Annex A-2 (Bankr. SDNY Aug. 31, 2011).

86. See id. at Exhibit 19–9.

87. Id. at Exhibit 11-1.

88. See id. at 49.

89. Id. at 52.

90. See id. at Exhibit 6–3.

91. Id. at Exhibit 6–3.

92. See id. Exhibit 6–4.

93. See id.

94. See id.

95. See Seth Brumby and Nicoletta Kotsianas, Lehman Brothers special financing's derivatives claims secondary market grows after proof-of-claims revision, *Debtwire* (Jul. 8, 2009); Josh Fineman and Christopher Scinta, Credit Suisse Group selling $1 billion Lehman claim, *Bloomberg* (Sep. 24, 2009), available at http://www.bloomberg.com/apps/news?pid=newsarchive&sid=a08KzEnlvIrk.

96. See Brumby and Kotsianas, *supra* note 94.

97. SecondMarket, *Claims Trading: Year in Review, 2010*, at 6 (2011); SecondMarket, *2011 Year-in-Review Bankruptcy Claims Trading Report* (2012).

98. See Disclosure Statement for Third Amended Joint Chapter 11 Plan of Lehman Brothers Holdings Inc. and Its Affiliated Debtors Pursuant to Section 1125 of the Bankruptcy Code, In re Lehman Bros. Holdings Inc. et al., No. 08-13555, Exhibit 5 (Bankr. SDNY Aug. 31, 2011).

99. See, for example, Hearing before the H. Comm. on Fin. Servs., 111th Cong. 1 (Apr. 20, 2010) (statement of Henry M. Paulson, Jr.), available at http://archives.financialservices.house.gov/media/file/hearings/111/paulson_testimony__-_4.20.10.pdf (noting that "[t]he possibility of a Lehman failure especially concerned [him] because [of] … how deeply interconnected the firm was with various other parts of our financial system [through] … [a]mong other things, [its] derivatives contracts"). See also Gary Gensler, Clearinghouses are the answer, *Wall Street Journal* (Apr. 21, 2010), http://online.wsj.com/article/NA_WSJ_PUB:SB10001424052748704671904575194463642611160.html (arguing that "interconnectedness is a direct result of the unregulated over-the-counter derivatives market where financial institutions are contractually obligated to each other through trillions of dollars of derivatives contracts").

100. See Report of Anton Valukas, Examiner 631, *In re* Lehman Bros. Holdings Inc. et al., No. 08-13555, at 1841, 1843, 1845 (Bankr. SDNY Mar. 11, 2010).

101. Id. at 1845.

102. Id. at 1846. The firms—Barclays, Goldman Sachs, Morgan Stanley, JPMorgan, Citadel, and DRW Trading—were selected on the basis of their capital and risk management expertise as well as market concentration considerations. Id.

103. Id. at 1854–55.

104. Id. at 1851.

105. Id. at 1853.

106. Id. at 1852, 1854.

107. Id. at 1855.

108. See, for example, Jean Helwege, Samuel Maurer, Asani Sarkar, and Yuan Wang, *Credit Default Swap Auctions* 1 (Fed. Res. Bank of New York, Staff Rep. No. 372, May 2009) (remarking that "market participants feared that sellers of CDS contracts would face

large losses based on the gross notional value of Lehman's CDS contracts, even though the net value of the positions was substantially smaller").

109. Projections regarding the total notional of CDS written on Lehman span from a low of $72 billion to the "widely cited industry estimate of $400 billion." See Robert Pickel, Insight: The CDS sector is not the central villain, *Financial Times* (Oct. 29, 2008), available at http://www.ft.com/intl/cms/s/0/9e609634-a5d4-11dd-9d26-000077b07658. html#axzz3nuBRvxVo (referring to the $400 billion estimate); René M. Stulz, Credit default swaps and the credit crisis, 24 *J. Econ. Persp.* 73, 80 (Winter 2010) (noting the range).

110. Lehman had about $136 billion in senior unsecured debt outstanding around the time of its filing. See Debtors' Disclosure Statement for First Amended Joint Chapter 11 Plan of Lehman Brothers Holdings Inc. and Its Affiliated Debtors Pursuant to Section 1125 of the Bankruptcy Code, *In re* Lehman Bros. Holdings Inc. et al., No. 08-13555, Exhibit 9–8 to 9–9 (Bankr. SDNY Jan. 25, 2011). But under the ISDA protocol for the Lehman CDS auction, only about $72 billion notional of this debt could actually be used by a CDS buyer to physically settle its contract. See ISDA CDS Market Place, *CDS FAQ* (2015), http://www.isdacdsmarketplace.com/about_cds_market/cds_faq.

111. See Shannon Harrington and Neil Unmack, Lehman credit-swap auction sets payout of 91.38 cents, *Bloomberg* (Oct. 10, 2008), available at http://www.bloomberg.com/apps/news?pid=newsarchive&sid=aLkOZnNcDmSQ&refer=home; Helwege et al., *supra* note 107, at 19 tbl. 2.

112. Fannie Mae and Freddie Mac, which also triggered an event of default and thus a CDS auction, actually accounted for a much larger amount of CDS notional than did Lehman. Although estimates of Fannie and Freddie CDS were on the order of $1.4 trillion, the CDS payout in these cases was much smaller than in the case of Lehman because the settlement values of Fannie and Freddie CDS were in the nineties (implying a payout of less than ten cents for every dollar of CDS notional). See Gerson Lehrman Group Research, *Lehman CDS Settlement—The Dog That Didn't Bark* (2008).

113. See Geoffrey Rogow, The looming Lehman CDS unwind, *MarketBeat* (Oct. 9, 2008), available at http://blogs.wsj.com/marketbeat/2008/10/09/the-looming-lehman-cds -unwind/.

114. Matthew Goodburn, Markets fret over "day of reckoning" on crucial Lehman CDS auction, *Citywire* (Oct. 10, 2008), available at http://citywire.co.uk/money/markets-fret -over-day-of-reckoning-on-crucial-lehman-cds-auction/a317207.

115. Press Release, Depository Trust & Clearing Corp., DTCC Trade Information Warehouse completes credit event processing for Lehman Brothers (Oct. 22, 2008), available at http://www.dtcc.com/news/press/releases/2008/dtcc_processes_lehman_cds.php.

116. See Stulz, *supra* note 108, at 80.

117. *See* Anne Duquerroy, Mathieu Gex, and Nicolas Gauthier, Banque de France, Credit default swaps and financial stability: Risks and regulatory issues, 13 *Fin. Stability Rev.* 75, 79 tbl. 2 (Sep. 2009).

118. Press Release, Depository Trust & Clearing Corp., *DTCC Successfully Completes Greek CDS Restructuring Credit Event Processing* (Mar. 27, 2012).

119. Katy Burne, Nearly $3 billion changed hands under Greek CDS settlement-DTCC, *Dow Jones Newswires* (Mar. 27, 2012).

120. See Helwege et al., *supra* note 108, at 10.

121. See *BIS Q. Rev.*, Statistical annex A121, tbl.19 (Jun. 2010).

122. The BIS calls this market value measure "gross market value" because derivatives are, by definition, zero sum such that their net market value would be zero. It arrives at the measure by summing the positive market value of all reporting parties' contracts and, in absolute terms, the negative market value of reporting parties' contracts with nonreporting parties. *BIS Q. Rev.*, Statistical annex A112 (Jun. 2010).

123. BIS, *OTC Derivatives Market Activity in the First Half of 2009*, at 9, available at http://www.bis.org/publ/otc_hy0911.pdf.

124. Id.

125. ISDA, *OTC Derivatives Market Analysis*, at 5 (Jun. 30, 2011), available at http://www2.isda.org/attachment/Mzg2Mg==/OTC%20Derivatives%20June%202011%20Market%20Analysis%20FINAL.pdf.

126. See Helwege et al., *supra* note 108, 13, 19 tbl 2.

127. See id. at 19 tbl.2.

128. See Shannon Harrington and Neil Unmack, Lehman credit-swap auction sets payout of 91.38 cents, *Bloomberg* (Oct. 10, 2008).

129. See, for example, id.

130. *Derivatives Market Trades on Sunday to Cut Lehman Risk*, Reuters (Sep. 14, 2008), available at http://www.reuters.com/article/2008/09/15/us-lehman-specialsession -idUSN1444498020080915.

131. Report of Anton Valukas, Examiner 631, *In re* Lehman Bros. Holdings Inc. et al., No. 08-13555, at 572 (Bankr. SDNY Mar. 11, 2010).

132. This approximation is based on a time-weighted linear interpolation of BIS's reported June 2008 gross market value of $20.4 trillion and its reported December 2008 gross market value of $33.9 trillion. *BIS Q. Rev.*, at 285 (Jun. 2009).

133. Sheri Markose, Simone Giansante, Mateusz Gatkowski, and Ali Rais Shaghagi, Too interconnected to fail, at 5 (Ctr. for Computational Fin. and Econ. Agents, ECB Workshop Paper, Oct. 2009). The market value of Lehman's CDS holdings in isolation is unclear, but as of May 31, 2008, the combined net market value of its interest rate, currency, and credit derivatives portfolios was approximately $16 billion. Report of Anton Valukas, Examiner 631, *In re* Lehman Bros. Holdings Inc. et al., No. 08-13555, at 572 (Bankr. SDNY Mar. 11, 2010).

134. See *BIS Q. Rev.*, A121 tbl.19 (Jun. 2010).

135. See Alvarez & Marsal, *supra* note 66, at 20. As of June 2009, LBSF accounted for approximately 75 percent of Lehman's derivatives trades, 80 percent of its receivables (i.e., the amount owed Lehman for its derivatives), and 75 percent of its payables (the amount Lehman owed). See id. at 21.

136. As the overall number of outstanding trades is not a commonly reported statistic, it is difficult to precisely estimate the percentage of OTC trades that Lehman accounted for. Still, there is reason to believe that the percentage was nonnegligible. The DTCC, for example, reported that it held 2.3 million CDS contracts in its Trade Information

Warehouse as of April 2010. Press Release, Depository Trust & Clearing Corp., *supra* note 117. Adjusting for the roughly 50 percent decline in total CDS notional between June 2008 and December 2009 and assuming both that CDS accounted for about 8 percent of Lehman's trades (based on the percentage of overall derivatives notional that came from CDS in June 2008 as reported by the BIS) and that they did not make up a disproportionate share of Lehman's holdings, one could reasonably conclude that Lehman held about 2 percent of all outstanding derivatives contracts. See *BIS Q. Rev.*, A121 tbl.19 (Jun. 2010).

137. In using the term "in-the-money" to denote a contract for which a party is owed money (i.e., a contract that is an asset to the party and a liability in an equal amount to its counterparty), this book is equating "in-the-money" with "positive net present value" (NPV). In market practice, however, the terms are not the same, and the more relevant measure in assessing exposure is in fact positive NPV, which refers to the total value of a derivatives contract, encompassing both intrinsic value ("moneyness") and time value. Significantly, a derivative can be "out-of-the-money" as the term is used in market practice (meaning it has no intrinsic value) but can still have positive NPV (because it has time value). So, while "positive NPV" is therefore the technically correct term, for convenience this book uses "in-the-money" to denote the same concept.

138. See 11 USC §§101, 741, 761 (2006).

139. See 11 USC §§362(b)(17), (27), 560 (2006).

140. See id. §546(g), (j).

141. See, for example, Patrick Bolton and Martin Oehmke, Should derivatives be privileged in bankruptcy, *J. Fin.* (forthcoming, 2015). (concluding that "[w]hile derivatives are value-enhancing risk management tools, seniority for derivatives can lead to inefficiencies"). See also Mark Roe, The derivatives market's payment priorities, *supra* note 64 (arguing that derivatives priorities undermine market discipline).

142. *See* OCC, *OCC's Quarterly Report on Bank Trading and Derivatives Activities First Quarter 2012* tbl.2 (Mar. 31, 2012); *see also* OCC, *OCC's Quarterly Report on Bank Trading and Derivatives Activities Second Quarter 2011* tbl.2 (Jun. 30, 2011) (also suggesting concentration of nearly 96 percent as of the end of the second quarter of 2011).

143. Id.

144. See Bob Ivry et al., Missing Lehman lesson of shakeout means too big banks may fail, *Bloomberg* (Sep. 8, 2009), available at http://www.bloomberg.com/apps/news?pid=newsarchive&sid=aX8D5utKFuGA.

145. The Initial Plan suggested that about $74 billion in third-party derivatives claims were brought against LBHI on account of its guarantees of affiliates, and approximately the same amount of claims was brought against the affiliates directly. See Disclosure statement for Initial Plan, *In re* Lehman Bros. Holdings Inc. et al., No. 08-13555, Annex A-2, A-3 (Bankr. SDNY Apr. 14, 2010).

146. See, for example, Disclosure statement for First Amended Joint Chapter 11 Plan of Lehman Brothers Holdings Inc. and Its Affiliated Debtors Pursuant to Section 1125 of the Bankruptcy Code, *In re* Lehman Bros. Holdings Inc. et al., No. 08-13555, Exhibit 6–5 (Bankr. SDNY Jan. 25, 2011); Debtors' disclosure statement for Third Amended Joint Chapter 11 Plan of Lehman Brothers Holdings Inc. and Its Affiliated Debtors Pursuant to Section 1125 of the Bankruptcy Code, *In re* Lehman Bros. Holdings Inc. et al., No. 08-13555, Exhibit 6–6 (Bankr. SDNY Aug. 31, 2011).

147. See Alvarez & Marsal, *supra* note 66, at 16 (noting that, before the 50 percent adjustment in the Amended Plan described below, Big Banks accounted for 48 percent of about $45 billion in then-extant claims).

148. See Disclosure statement for Initial Plan, *In re* Lehman Bros. Holdings Inc. et al., No. 08-13555, Annex A-2 (Bankr. SDNY Apr. 14, 2010).

149. ISDA, 1992 Master Agreement (Multi-Currency–Cross Border) §5(a)(vii); ISDA, 2002 Master Agreement §5(a)(vii).

150. Agreements may provide for "automatic early termination," in which case the nondefaulting party has to terminate upon an event of default. ISDA, 1992 Master Agreement (Multi-Currency–Cross Border) §6(a); ISDA, 2002 Master Agreement §6(a). Notably, the Bankruptcy Code generally disregards such *ipso facto* clauses. See 11 USC §365(e)(1) (2006). However, the Code's "safe harbor" provisions exempt swap agreements and other important derivatives from both this rule and the automatic stay. See, for example, Id. §§362(b). Thus early termination under an ISDA Master Agreement is normally considered valid, and parties may seize any collateral posted pursuant to the agreement. See id. §362(a) (prohibiting, *inter alia*, "any act to … enforce any lien against property of the estate").

151. See Alvarez & Marsal, *supra* note 66, at 19–20 (reporting that as of January 2, 2009, 888,000 of 906,000 trades had been terminated); see also Notice of debtors' motion for an order pursuant to Sections 105 and 365 of the Bankruptcy Code to Establish Procedures for the Settlement or Assumption and Assignment of Prepetition Derivative Contracts at 4, *In re* Lehman Bros. Holdings Inc. et al., No. 08-13555 (Bankr. SDNY Nov. 13, 2008) (indicating that as of November 13, 2008, approximately 733,000 contracts had been terminated).

152. See Disclosure statement for Initial Plan, *In re* Lehman Bros. Holdings Inc. et al., No. 08-13555, at 275 (Bankr. SDNY Apr. 14, 2010).

153. See Notice of deadlines for filing proofs of Claim 4–5, *In re* Lehman Brothers Holdings Inc. et al., No. 08-13555 (Bankr. SDNY Jul. 8, 2009).

154. Lehman Brothers Derivative Questionnaire §4(c).

155. Id. §4(f).

156. Id. §4(e).

157. The 1992 Master Agreement permits parties to choose between either the "market quotation" method or the "loss" method. See ISDA, 1992 Master Agreement, §6(e)(i)(1)-(2). The "market quotation" method entitles the nondefaulting party to a settlement amount reflecting (1) net unpaid amounts owed to the party and (2) market quotations from at least three reference market-makers for replacement transactions. See id. §§6(e)(i)(1), 12. The latter method entitles the nondefaulting party to "an amount that party reasonably determines in good faith to be its total losses" from the terminated transactions. See id. §§6(e)(i)(2), 12. The 2002 Master Agreement employs the "closeout amount" approach, which, like the market quotation method, entitles the nondefaulting party to any unpaid amounts as well as a "closeout" amount representing the costs "that are or would be realized under then prevailing circumstances in replacing [or] providing … the economic equivalent of" the terminated trades." See ISDA, 2002 Master Agreement, §6(e)(i). Id. §14. Like the loss method, the closeout amount approach allows the determining party to "use [any] commercially reasonable procedures in order to produce a commercially reasonable result." Id. at §14.

158. Disclosure Statement for Initial Plan, *In re* Lehman Bros. Holdings Inc. et al., No. 08-13555, at 62 (Bankr. SDNY Apr. 14, 2010).

159. See, for example, Proof of Claim, Goldman Sachs Bank USA, Claim No. 28103, at 4, *In re* Lehman Brothers Holdings Inc. et al., No. 08-13555 (Bankr. SDNY Sep. 22, 2009) (noting that "instances of exact replacement trades were few").

160. A nondefaulting party might have considerable leeway in arriving at estimates for replacement costs, particularly under the closeout amount and loss approaches, provided that these figures are "commercially reasonable." See ISDA, 2002 Master Agreement 1, 22–23 (2002); ISDA, 1992 Master Agreement 15 (1992). And even under the market quotation approach, which ostensibly takes third-party quotations into account, a nondefaulting party must resort to the less restrictive loss method when quotations either cannot be determined or are not commercially reasonable. See ISDA, ISDA 1992 Master Agreement, at 15–16 (1992). Following Lehman's default, bid-offer spreads and illiquidity increased considerably, and nondefaulting parties may not have been able to obtain the requisite three quotations for certain contracts or the quotations that they received may not have been reasonable. Disclosure statement for Third Amended Joint Chapter 11 Plan of Lehman Brothers Holdings Inc. and Its Affiliated Debtors Pursuant to Section 1125 of the Bankruptcy Code, In re Lehman Bros. Holdings Inc. et al., No. 08-13555, Exhibit 6–6(ii) (Bankr. SDNY Aug. 31, 2011).

162. Derivatives Claims Settlement Framework, *In re* Lehman Brothers Holdings Inc. et al., No. 08-13555, at 4 (Bankr. SDNY May 27, 2011).

163. See id. at 9–11, 13. The thirteen big banks include Bank of America, Barclays, BNP Paribas, Citigroup, Credit Suisse, Deutsche Bank, Goldman Sachs, JPMorgan, Merrill Lynch, Morgan Stanley, the Royal Bank of Scotland, Société Générale, and UBS. Id. at appendix 3.3.

164. See id. at 12.

165. OCC, *OCC's Quarterly Report on Bank Trading and Derivatives Activities Third Quarter 2008*, at 12, available at http://www.occ.gov/topics/capital-markets/financial-markets/trading/derivatives/dq308.pdf.

166. JPMorgan Chase & Co., Form 10-K (2008), available at http://investor.shareholder.com/JPMorganChase/secfiling.cfm?filingID=950123-09-3840.

167. Bank of America, Form 10-K (2008), available at http://services.corporate-ir.net/SEC/Document.Service?id=P3VybD1hSFIwY0RvdkwyRndhUzUwWlc1cmQyb-DZZWEprTG1OdmJTOWtiM2R1Ykc5aFpDNXdhSEEvWVdOMGFXOXVQVkJFUmlac GNHRm5aVDAyTVRjeU1UWTJKbk4xWW5OcFpEMDFFOdz09JnR5cGU9MiZmbj-1CYW5rb2ZBbWVyaWNhQ29ycG9yYXRpb25fMTBLXzIwMDkwMjI3LnBkZg==.

168. Citigroup Inc., Form 10-K (2008), available at http://www.citigroup.com/citi/fin/data/ar08c_en.pdf.

169. HSBC, Form 10-K (2008), available at http://www.sec.gov/Archives/edgar/data/83246/000095012309003735/c49379e10vk.htm.

170. See Report of Anton Valukas, Examiner 631, *In re* Lehman Bros. Holdings Inc. et al., No. 08-13555, at 572 (Bankr. SDNY Mar. 11, 2010).

171. See, for example, Debtors' Disclosure Statement for First Amended Joint Chapter 11 Plan of Lehman Brothers Holdings Inc. and Its Affiliated Debtors Pursuant to Section 1125 of the Bankruptcy Code at 3–50, In *re* Lehman Bros. Holdings Inc. et al., No.

08-13555, at 53 (Bankr. SDNY Jan. 25, 2011) (noting that "the Debtors often are unable to agree with counterparties on the amount due to the Debtors in connection with the Debtors' 'in the money' Derivative Contracts and in collecting such amounts").

172. Katy Burne, Lehman seeking to collect $3.2 billion on derivatives through 2015, *Wall St. J.* (Jul. 24, 2013).

173. Joseph Checkler, Filing shows Lehman still had billions in assets at end of 2013, *Wall St. J.* (Apr. 3, 2014).

174. See Report of Anton Valukas, Examiner 631, *In re* Lehman Bros. Holdings Inc. et al., No. 08-13555, at 574 (Bankr. SDNY Mar. 11, 2010).

175. Id. at 575.

176. Henny Sender, Lehman creditors in fight to recover collateral, *Financial Times* (Jun. 21, 2009), available at http://www.ft.com/intl/cms/s/0/909ba63c-5e99-11de-91ad -00144feabdc0.html#axzz3nuBRvxVo (noting that JPMorgan was Lehman's largest counterparty); Report of Anton Valukas, Examiner 631, *In re* Lehman Bros. Holdings Inc. et al., No. 08-13555, at 573 (Bankr. SDNY Mar. 11, 2010) (reporting that Lehman's largest counterparties by deal count as of May 2008 were, in order of their size, Deutsche Bank, JPMorgan, and UBS).

177. See Proof of Claim, JPMorgan Chase & Co., Claim No. 27189, at 9–10, 12, *In re* Lehman Bros. Holdings Inc. et al., No. 08-13555 (Bankr. SDNY Sep. 22, 2009).

178. See Report of Anton Valukas, Examiner 631, *In re* Lehman Bros. Holdings Inc. et al., No. 08-13555, at 1068 (Bankr. SDNY Mar. 11, 2010).

179. See id. at 1119.

180. See id. at 1115–16 (explaining the August agreements), 1152–54 (outlining the September agreements).

181. See ISDA, Margin Survey 2007, at 4, available at http://www.isda.org/c_and_a/ pdf/ISDA-Margin-Survey-2007.pdf; *see also* Kimberly Summe, Misconceptions about Lehman Brothers' bankruptcy and the role derivatives played, 64 *Stan. L. Rev.* 16, 20 (2011) (arguing that insufficient collateralization of derivatives was, contrary to popular belief, not a problem for Lehman counterparties).

182. See IMF, *Global Financial Stability Report* 9 (Apr. 2010) (suggesting that central clearing of Lehman's credit derivatives might have reduced the fallout from its failure); Managing the Lehman Brothers' default, *LCH.Clearnet*, available at http://www.lch-clearnet.com:8080/swaps/swapclear_for_clearing_members/managing_the_lehman_ brothers_default.asp(2015) (noting that $9 trillion notional of Lehman's interest rate swaps were successfully cleared by LCH.Clearnet); *see also* Darrell Duffie, Ada Li and Theo Lubke, Policy perspectives on OTC derivatives market infrastructure 11–12 (MFI Working Paper Series, No. 2010–002, Jan. 2010) (suggesting that by the end of 2009, about 35 percent of all interest rate derivatives were centrally cleared).

183. CCP12, Central counterparty default management and the collapse of Lehman Brothers (Apr. 2009).

184. Managing the Lehman Brothers' default, *supra* note 182.

185. Bank of England, *Financial Stability Report* 20 (Oct. 2008).

186. *See* Viral Acharya and Alberto Bisin, Counterparty risk externality: Centralized versus over-the-counter markets 37 (Jun. 2010), available at http://econ.as.nyu.edu/docs/IO/17314/Acharya_20100910.pdf.

187. Darrell Duffie et al., *supra* note 182, at 11.

188. Darrell Duffie, The failure mechanics of dealer banks, 24(1) *J. Econ. Persp.* 51, 67 (Winter 2010).

189. See id.

190. Writedowns & credit losses vs. capital raised, *Chart View 10/01/07–3/31/10*, Bloomberg (2015).

191. *See* OCC, *OCC's Quarterly Report on Bank Trading and Derivatives Activities First Quarter 2009* tbl.2 (Mar. 31, 2009). Goldman Sachs and Morgan Stanley did not appear in the OCC's holding company data for the fourth quarter of 2008 because their filings as holding companies had not been made publicly available in time for the report. However, given the considerable gap between them and the sixth largest holding company in the report for the first quarter of 2009, it can be assumed that they were among the top five derivatives holders in the fourth quarter of 2008.

192. *See* Board of Governors of the Federal Reserve System, *The Supervisory Capital Assessment Program: Overview of Results* 9 (May 7, 2009).

193. Id.

194. Merrill Lynch, through Merrill Lynch International and Merrill Lynch Capital Services Inc., filed claims for a combined $2.523 billion. Goldman Sachs, through Goldman Sachs Bank USA and Goldman Sachs International, filed claims for a combined $2.519 billion. See Proof of Claim, Merrill Lynch Int'l, Claim No. 20149, *In re* Lehman Bros. Holdings Inc. et al., No. 08-13555 (Bankr. SDNY Sep. 21, 2009); Proof of Claim, Merrill Lynch Capital Servs. Inc., Claim No. 20148, *In re* Lehman Bros. Holdings Inc. et al., No. 08-13555 (Bankr. SDNY Sep. 21, 2009); Proof of Claim, Goldman Sachs Int'l, Claim No. 28105, at 5, *In re* Lehman Bros. Holdings Inc. et al., No. 08-13555 (Bankr. SDNY Sep. 22, 2009).

195. See Robert McDonald and Anna Paulson, AIG in hindsight, 29(2) *J. Econ. Persp.* 81, 88 (Spring 2015).

196. Cong. Oversight Panel, *June Oversight Report: The AIG Rescue, Its Impact on Markets, and the Government's Exit Strategy* 131 (Jun. 10, 2010).

197. See McDonald and Paulson, *supra* note 195.

198. Id. at 19.

199. Id. at 20.

200. Financial Crisis Inquiry Commission, *supra* note 14, at 350.

201. 12 USC §343 (2006) (providing that "[i]n unusual and exigent circumstances, the Board of Governors of the Federal Reserve System ... may authorize any Federal reserve bank ... to discount for any participant in any program or facility with broad-based eligibility, notes, drafts, and bills of exchange when such notes, drafts, and bills of exchange are indorsed or otherwise secured to the satisfaction of the Federal Reserve bank").

202. As codified in 12 USC §221 et seq.

203. See Press Release, Board of Governors of the Federal Reserve System (Sep. 16, 2008), *available at* http://www.federalreserve.gov/newsevents/press/other/20080916a.htm.

204. See Press Release, Board of Governors of the Federal Reserve System (Oct. 8, 2008), http://www.federalreserve.gov/newsevents/press/other/20081008a.htm.

205. See Press Release, Board of Governors of the Federal Reserve System (Nov. 10, 2008), http://www.federalreserve.gov/newsevents/press/other/20081110a.htm.

206. Peter Wallison, The error at the heart of the Dodd–Frank Act, *American Enterprise Institute Financial Services Outlook* 6 (Sep. 7, 2011) (going on to emphasize that AIG's activities should not be grounds for regulating CDS as such a response would be "like regulating all lending because one lender made imprudent loans").

207. See American International Group, Form 10-K, at 121 (2007); Financial Crisis Inquiry Commission, *supra* note 14, at 139–40.

208. See American International Group, Form 10-K, at 130–31 (2008).

209. Id. at 122.

210. See id. at 130–31.

211. See, for example, id. at 139 (breaking down AIG's multi-sector CDO portfolio by underlying collateral, credit rating, and vintage).

212. American International Group, Form 10-K, at 122 (2007).

213. See American International Group, Form 10-K, at 146 (2008).

214. See id. at 4.

215. See Financial Crisis Inquiry Commission, *supra* note 14, at 344.

216. See id. at 376; Cong. Oversight Panel, *June Oversight Report, supra* note 196, at 145–47.

217. Dodd–Frank Act §165(e).

218. Goldman Sachs, Form 10-Q, at 90 (May 30, 2008).

219. Of course, this does not take into account the effect of other losses that Goldman Sachs might have suffered on account of AIG's default (e.g., from securities lending arrangements).

220. See American International Group, Form 10-K, at 122 (2007); American International Group, Form 10-K, at 133 (2008).

221. See Cong. Oversight Panel, *June Oversight Report, supra* note 196, at 92 n.428; David Henry, Matthew Goldstein and Carol Matlack, How AIG's credit loophole squeezed Europe's banks, *Bloomberg* (Oct. 15, 2008).

222. See, for example, American International Group, Form 10-K, at 130 (2008); Roddy Boyd, *Fatal Risk: A Cautionary Tale of AIG's Corporate Suicide* 90 (Hoboken, NJ: Wiley 2011) (noting that "[t]o this day … [the regulatory capital portfolio] appears to have performed quite well").

223. See David Henry et al., *supra* note 219.

224. See Cong. Oversight Panel, *June Oversight Report*, *supra* note 196, at 220 (noting that "there is no market for the regulatory capital hedges").

225. See Financial Crisis Inquiry Commission, *supra* note 14, at 348.

226. See, for example, Cong. Oversight Panel, *June Oversight Report*, *supra* note 196, at 92.

227. See id. at 92–93.

228. See PricewaterhouseCoopers, *supra* note 39, at 1 (Apr. 14, 2009).

229. See Lindsay Fortado, Lehman hedge fund clients to Get $3.3 billion payout, *Bloomberg* (Oct. 21, 2009), available at http://www.bloomberg.com/apps/news?pid=newsarchive&sid=axgsS0Sa0nZI.

230. PricewaterhouseCoopers's estimate that LBIE held $32 billion in Trust Assets as of September 15, 2008, coupled with the estimate that LBIE had rehypothecated about $22 billion in client funds, suggests that the failed entity held around $54 billion in total client assets. See PricewaterhouseCoopers, Lehman Brothers International (Europe) (in administration)—Claim resolution agreement receives overwhelming support (Dec. 29, 2009), available at http://www.businesswire.com/news/home/20091229005334/en/Lehman-Brothers-International-Europe-administration-Claim-Resolution#.VhV0orRViko. For other estimates, see James Mackintosh, Lehman collapse puts prime broker model in question, *Financial Times* (Sep. 24, 2008), http://www.ft.com/intl/cms/s/0/442f0b24-8a71-11dd-a76a-0000779fd18c.html#axzz3nuBRvxVo(suggesting that LBIE held $40 billion); Ianthe Dugan and Cassell Bryan-Low, In a suicide, crisis and life cross, *Wall Street Journal* (Nov. 15, 2008) (suggesting that it held $65 billion).

231. See James Mackintosh, Lehman collapse puts prime broker model in question, *Financial Times* (Sep. 24, 2008).

232. See Manmohan Singh and James Aitken, The (sizable) role of rehypothecation in the shadow banking system 4 (IMF Working Paper No. 10/172, Jul. 2010).

233. See id.

234. See PricewaterhouseCoopers, *FAQs for Trust Property 19/3/09*, http://www.pwc.co.uk/eng/issues/lehman_faqs_trust_property_client_assets.html (2015).

235. See id.

236. See Witness Statement of Steven Anthony Pearson, In the Matter of Lehman Bros. Int'l (Eur.) (in administration) and In the Matter of the Insolvency Act 1986, at 28 (The Court of High Justice Oct. 7, 2008) (Claim No. 7942); DealBook, Wachtell Lipton's lessons from Lehman, *NY Times* (Nov. 12, 2008).

237. Tom Cahill, Lehman hedge-fund clients left cold as assets frozen, *Bloomberg* (Oct. 1, 2008).

238. See Ianthe Dugan and Cassell Bryan-Low, In a suicide, crisis and life cross, *Wall Street Journal* (Nov. 15, 2008); Proof of Claim, Olivant Investments Switzerland, Claim No. 22636, *In re* Lehman Brothers Holdings Inc. et al., No. 08-13555, at 6 (Bankr. SDNY Sep. 21, 2009).

239. Jeff Nash, Broker biz up for grabs after bear buyout, *Crain's New York Business* (Apr. 7, 2008).

240. See Merrill Lynch Global Mkts. & Investment Banking, *The Multi-Prime Broker Environment: Overcoming the Challenges and Reaping the Benefits* 2 (Mar. 2007).

241. Id. at 1.

242. See Cassell Bryan-Low, U.K. ruling spells out Lehman asset protections, *Wall St. J.* (Dec. 15, 2009); Lindsay Fortado, CRC wins Appeals Court ruling it can access Lehman client-money accounts, *Bloomberg* (Aug. 2, 2010).

243. *Lehman Brothers Int'l* (Europe) (in Administration) *v. CRC Credit Fund Ltd. and Others,* [2009] EWHC (Ch) 3228 (Eng.).

244. *Lehman Brothers Int'l* (Europe) (in Administration) *v. CRC Credit Fund Ltd. and Others,* [2010] EWCA (Civ) 917 (Eng.).

245. See Fortado, *supra* note 240.

246. Martin Arnold, Lehman's UK unit administrators foresee £5bn surplus, *Financial Times* (Mar 5, 2014).

247. See Securities Litigation & Consulting Group, *Structured Products in the Aftermath of Lehman Brothers* 2 (2009).

248. See id. at 2–3.

249. See id. at 15, 18.

250. Id. at 15.

251. Disclosure statement for Initial Plan, *In re* Lehman Bros. Holdings Inc. et al., No. 08-13555 Annex A-3 (Bankr. SDNY Apr. 14, 2010); see *Lehman Programs Securities* (Jul. 17, 2009), *available at* http://www.svsp-verband.ch/download/faq/20090724_program _securities_list_de.pdf.

252. See Disclosure statement for First Amended Joint Chapter 11 Plan of Lehman Brothers Holdings Inc. and Its Affiliated Debtors Pursuant to Section 1125 of the Bankruptcy Code, *In re* Lehman Bros. Holdings Inc. et al., No. 08-13555, Exhibit 9-9 (Bankr. SDNY Jan. 25, 2011).

253. See *infra* text accompanying note 259.

254. See Financial institutions offering to repurchase Lehman Notes in some countries while fighting investors in others, *LehmanNotes.com* (Nov. 16, 2010).

255. See, for example, Securities Litigation & Consulting Group, *Structured Products in the Aftermath of Lehman Brothers* 1, 2 (2009).

256. Id. at 3–4.

257. See Disclosure statement for Initial Plan, *In re* Lehman Bros. Holdings Inc. et al., No. 08-13555, at 37 (Bankr. SDNY Apr. 14, 2010).

258. Id.

259. Id. at annex A-3.

260. See Disclosure statement for First Amended Joint Chapter 11 Plan of Lehman Brothers Holdings Inc. and Its Affiliated Debtors Pursuant to Section 1125 of the Bankruptcy Code, *In re* Lehman Bros. Holdings Inc. et al., No. 08-13555, Exhibit 11-1 (Bankr. SDNY Jan. 25, 2011).

261. Freshfields Bruckhaus Deringer, An overview of the Lehman Brothers minibonds saga 1 (Dec. 16, 2008), available at http://www.freshfields.com/uploadedFiles/Site Wide/Knowledge/An%20overview%20of%20the%20Lehman%20Brothers%20mini bonds%20saga.pdf.

262. See Valerie Chew, Nat'l Library Bd. Singapore, Lehman Brothers minibond saga, *Singapore Infopedia* (Mar. 19, 2010), available at http://infopedia.nl.sg/articles/ SIP_1654_2010-03-19.html; Freshfields Bruckhaus Deringer, An overview of the Lehman Brothers minibonds saga 1 (Dec. 16, 2008), available at http://www.freshfields.com/ uploadedFiles/SiteWide/Knowledge/An%20overview%20of%20the%20Lehman%20 Brothers%20minibonds%20saga.pdf.

263. See Mark Pittman and Bob Ivry, London suicide connects Lehman lesson missed by Hong Kong woman, *Bloomberg* (Sep. 9, 2009).

264. The good inside the bad, *The Economist* (Mar. 31, 2011).

265. Naohiko Baba, Robert N. McCauley, and Srichander Ramaswamy, U.S. dollar money market funds and non-U.S. banks, *BIS Q. Rev.* 65, 68 (Mar. 2009).

266. See Written Testimony before the H. Comm. on Fin. Servs., 111th Cong. (statement of Timothy Geithner, Secretary, US Dep't of the Treasury) (Apr. 20, 2010), http://www .treasury.gov/press-center/press-releases/Pages/tg645.aspx.

267. Naohiko Baba et al., *supra* note 263, at 68.

268. Id. at 71–72.

269. A prime money market fund typically "hold[s] a variety of taxable short-term obligations issued by corporations and banks, as well as repurchase agreements and asset-backed commercial paper." Money Market Fund Reform; Amendments to Form PF, 78 Fed. Reg. 36,836 (File Number S7–03–13, RIN 3235 AK 61) (proposed Jun. 19, 2013).

270. Investment Company Institute, *Report of the Money Market Working Group* 59 (Mar. 17, 2009), available at http://www.ici.org/pdf/ppr_09_mmwg.pdf.

271. Id.

272. Naohiko Baba et al., *supra* note 263, at 72.

273. Investment Company Act of 1940, 15 USC §80a-22(e) (2012).

274. In the Matter of The Reserve Fund, Investment Company Act Release No. 28386 (Sep. 22, 2008) (order).

275. See Press Release, The Primary Fund: A Statement Regarding Calculations of Potential Distributions on a Pro Rata Basis, *The Reserve* (Aug. 25, 2009), available at http:// www.primary-yieldplus-inliquidation.com/pdf/Press_Release_StmtReCalc_082509 .pdf.

276. See Press Release, The Primary Fund, Additional Information Regarding the Reserve Primary Fund, *The Reserve* (May 27, 2010), available at http://www.primary-yieldplus -inliquidation.com/pdf/AdditionalInformation_PrimaryFund_052710.pdf.

277. See Press Release, The Primary Fund, Reserve Primary Fund to Distribute $215 Million, *The Reserve* (Jul. 15, 2010), available at http://www.primary-yieldplus-inliqui dation.com/pdf/PrimaryDistribution_71510.pdf.

278. See, e.g., DTCC, *Understanding Interconnectedness Risks*, Oct. 2015, *available at*: http://www.dtcc.com/~/media/Files/Downloads/WhitePapers/Interconnectedness WP-101815.pdf?la=en.

279. Direct credit exposures of UK banks to other financial institutions has decreased since 2008. See Zijun Liu and Stephanie Quiet, Banking Sector Interconnectedness: what is it, how can we measure it and why does it matter?,55(2) *Bank of England, Q. Bull.* 133 (2015 Q2), available at http://www.bankofengland.co.uk/publications/Documents/quarterlybulletin/2015/q2.pdf.

280. Tobias Adrian and Hyun Song Shin, Liquidity and Financial Contagion, *Fin. Stability Rev.*—Special issue on liquidity (Feb. 2008).

281. Id.

Chapter 5

1. See, for example, Franklin Allen and Douglas Gale, Financial contagion, 108(1) *Journal of Political Economy* 1, 4 (2000); Xavier Freixas, Bruno Parigi, and Jean-Charles Rochet, Systemic risk, interbank relations, and liquidity provision by the central bank, 32(3) *J. Money, Credit, Bank.* 611 (Aug. 2000).

2. See, for example, Douglas Diamond and Raghuram Rajan, Liquidity shortages and banking crises, 60(2) *J. Fin.* 615 (Apr. 2005).

3. Lehman Brothers Holdings Inc., Form 10-Q, at 23 (May 31, 2008).

4. Using the $1,739bn total 2008 market figure from Richard Anderson and Charles Gascon, The commercial paper market, the Fed, and the 2007–2009 financial crisis, *Federal Reserve Bank of St. Louis Review* 589, 594 (Nov./Dec. 2009), available at https://research.stlouisfed.org/publications/review/09/11/Anderson.pdf.

5. Id.

6. Id.

7. The $10m estimate is from Gary Gorton and Andrew Metrick (Yale ICF Working Paper No. 09–14, 12, Nov. 2010). However, the total size of the repo market can only be estimated and is not known with specificity. See Adam Copeland, Isaac Davis, Eric LeSueur, and Antoine Martin, Mapping and sizing the U.S. repo market (Jun. 25, 2012), available at http://libertystreeteconomics.newyorkfed.org/2012/06/mapping-and-sizing-the-us-repo-market.html.

8. David Scharfstein, Perspectives on Money Market Mutual Fund Reforms,Testimony before the S. Comm. on Banking, Hous. & Urban Affairs (Jun. 21, 2012), available at http://www.banking.senate.gov/public/index.cfm?FuseAction=Files.View &FileStore_id=ca1f8420-b2de-46dd-aee1-9a22d47b198c.

9. Id. at 2.

10. Id. at 2.

11. Marco Cipriani, Antoine Martin, and Bruno M. Parigi, Money market funds intermediation, bank instability, and contagion, *Fed. Res. Bank of New York*, Staff Report No. 599 (Feb. 2013).

12. Sean Collins and Chris Plantier, Do U.S. Banks Rely Heavily on Money Market Funds? No., *Inv. Co. Inst.* (Nov. 14, 2012).

13. Prime MMF funding, Top 50 holding companies, Fed. Fin. Inst. Examination Council, Crane Data (Jun. 30, 2013), available at http://www.cranedata.com.

14. Naohiko Baba, Robert N. McCauley, and Srichander Ramaswamy, U.S. dollar money market funds and non-U.S. banks, *BIS Q. Rev.* 65 (Mar. 2009).

15. Sean Collins and Chris Plantier, Money market funds continued to reduce eurozone holdings in November (Dec. 16, 2011), available at http://www.ici.org/viewpoints/view_11_mmfs_holdings_update.

16. Adam Copeland, Antoine Martin, and Michael Walker, Repo runs: Evidence from the tri-party repo market, *Federal Reserve Bank of New York*, Staff Report No. 506, at 9 (Jul. 2011; revised Aug. 2014), available at http://www.newyorkfed.org/research/staff_reports/sr506.html (noting that "[b]efore Lehman declared bankruptcy, almost $2.5 trillion worth of collateral was posted in the tri-party repo market each day"). See also Eric Rosengren, Short-term wholesale funding risks, *Federal Reserve Bank of Boston* (Nov. 2014), available at http://www.bostonfed.org/news/speeches/rosengren/2014/110514/110514text.pdf.

17. Tri-Party Repo Statistical Data, *Federal Reserve Bank of New York* (Oct. 2013), available at http://www.newyorkfed.org/banking/tpr_infr_reform_data.html.

18. Copeland et al., *supra* note 16, at 9.

19. Goldman Sachs, Form 10-K, at 167, 209 (2014). JPMorgan Chase & Co., Form 10-K, at 32, 128 (2014). Citigroup, Form 10-K, at 27, 204 (2014). Bank of America, Form 10-K 27, 224 (2014). Morgan Stanley, Form 10-K, at 58, 310 (2014).

20. Task Force on Tri-Party Repo Infrastructure, *Federal Reserve Bank of New York*, at 3 (May 17, 2010), available at http://www.newyorkfed.org/prc/files/report_100517.pdf.

21. Id.

22. See, for example, William C. Dudley, Fixing wholesale funding to build a more stable financial system, Remarks at New York Bankers Association's 2013 Annual Meeting & Economic Forum (Feb. 1, 2013), available at http://www.newyorkfed.org/newsevents/speeches/2013/dud130201.html; see also Bruce Tuckman, Systemic risk and the tri-party repo clearing banks, Center for Financial Stability Policy Paper (2010).

23. Press Release, Tri-Party Repo Infrastructure Reform, *Federal Reserve Bank of New York* (2015), available at http://www.newyorkfed.org/banking/tpr_infr_reform.html.

24. See, for example, Progress report, Task Force on Tri-Party Repo Infrastructure, *Federal Reserve Bank of New York* (Jul. 6, 2011), available at http://www.newyorkfed.org/tripartyrepo/pdf/tpr_progress_report_110706.pdf; Press release, Tri-Party Repo Infrastructure Reform Task Force issues progress report on direction of reform, *Federal Reserve Bank of New York* (Jul. 6, 2011), available at http://www.newyorkfed.org/tripartyrepo/pdf/PR_110706.pdf; Final report, Task Force on Tri-Party Repo Infrastructure, *Federal Reserve Bank of New York* (Feb. 15, 2012), available at http://www.newyorkfed.org/tripartyrepo/pdf/report_120215.pdf; website, Tri-Party Repo Infrastructure Reform Task Force, *NewYorkFed.org* (2015), available at http://www.newyorkfed.org/tripartyrepo/.

25. See White Paper, Tri-Party Repo Infrastructure Reform, *Federal Reserve Bank of New York* (May 17, 2010), available at http://www.newyorkfed.org/banking/nyfrb_triparty_whitepaper.pdf.

26. See Press Release, Recent developments in tri-party repo reform, *NewYorkFed.org* (Dec. 20, 2012), available at http://www.newyorkfed.org/newsevents/statements/2012/1220_2012.html (noting that JPMC has stopped the daily unwind of non-maturing repo trades, and BNYM has implemented changes to eliminate intraday credit that BNYM provides to dealers against privately issued securities that settle through the Depository Trust Company). See also Press Release, J.P. Morgan achieves major milestone in tri-party repo market reforms (Nov. 19, 2012).

27. Update on Tri-Party Repo Infrastructure Reform, *Federal Reserve Bank of New York* (Jun. 24, 2015), available at http://www.newyorkfed.org/newsevents/statements/2015/0624_2015.html

28. Final Report, Task Force on Tri-Party Repo Infrastructure, *Federal Reserve Bank of New York*, at 3 (Feb. 15, 2012), available at http://www.newyorkfed.org/tripartyrepo/pdf/report_120215.pdf.

29. Id. at 4.

30. See Statement, Recent developments in tri-party repo reform, *Federal Reserve Bank of New York* (Dec. 20, 2012), available at http://www.newyorkfed.org/newsevents/statements/2012/1220_2012.html. For example, the Federal Reserve reiterated to the clearing banks that final settlement of tri-party repo transactions should be completed sufficiently in advance of the Fedwire® Funds close in order to provide enough time for successive funds transfers. Id.

Chapter 6

1. Dodd–Frank Act §929-Z.

2. Dodd–Frank Title VII.

3. Dodd–Frank Act §165(e).

4. Dodd–Frank Act §113.

5. Darrell Duffie, The failure mechanics of dealer banks, 24(1) *Journal of Economic Perspectives* 51, 67 (Winter 2010); see Darrell Duffie, Ada Li, and Theo Lubke, Policy perspectives on OTC derivatives market infrastructure 11 (MFI Working Paper Series, No. 2010-002, Jan. 2010).

6. See Darrell Duffie et al., *supra* note 5, at 11; see also Darrell Duffie and Haoxiang Zhu, *Does a Central Clearing Counterparty Reduce Counterparty Risk?*, at 2 (Mar. 6, 2010), available at http://www.stanford.edu/~duffie/DuffieZhu.pdf (noting that "[c]learing also reduces the degree to which the solvency problems of a market participant are suddenly compounded by a flight of its OTC derivative counterparties").

7. Duffie and Zhu, *supra* note 6, at 2.

8. See id.

9. See Dodd–Frank Act §§723(a), 763(a).

10. Id.

11. See id.

12. Neal Wolin, Deputy Secretary, US Dep't of the Treasury, Remarks at the ISDA 25th Annual Meeting (Apr. 22, 2010), available at http://www.treasury.gov/press-center/press-releases/Pages/tg656.aspx.

13. See Darrell Duffie et al., *supra* note 5, at 8; Manmohan Singh, Making OTC derivatives safe—A fresh look, at 10–11 (IMF, Working Paper 11/66, Mar. 2011), http://www.imf.org/external/pubs/ft/wp/2011/wp1166.pdf.

14. Ben Bernanke, Chairman, Board of Governors of the Federal Reserve System, Remarks at the 2011 Financial Markets Conference: Clearinghouses, Financial Stability, and Financial Reform, at 2 (Apr. 4, 2011), available at http://www.federalreserve.gov/newsevents/speech/bernanke20110404a.pdf.

15. Duffie and Zhu, *supra* note 6, at 3.

16. See Singh, *supra* note 13, at 5.

17. See Dominic Hobson, Collateral makes the world go around ..., *Fin. News* (Sep. 3, 2012).

18. Id.

19. Dodd–Frank Act §165.

20. Dodd–Frank Act §164.

21. Dodd–Frank Act §165(e).

22. Enhanced Prudential Standards and Early Remediation Requirements for Covered Companies, 77 Fed. Reg. 594 (proposed Jan. 5, 2012).

23. Id. (to be codified at 12 CFR §252.93(b)).

24. See Letter from Goldman Sachs Group, Inc. to the Federal Reserve regarding 77 Fed. Reg. 594 (Apr. 30, 2013); Letter from JPMorgan Chase & Co. to the Federal Reserve regarding 77 Fed. Reg. 594 (Apr. 30, 2013); Letter from The Clearing House Association LLC to the Federal Reserve regarding 77 Fed. Reg. 594 (Apr. 30, 2013).

25. Letter from Comm. on Capital Mkts. Reg. to the Federal Reserve regarding Enhanced Prudential Standards and Early Remediation Requirements for Covered Companies, 77 Fed. Reg. 594 (Apr. 30, 2012).

26. Id.

27. Dodd–Frank Act §113(a)(2)(G).

28. Dodd–Frank Act §113(a)(2)(C).

29. Authority to Require Supervision and Regulation of Certain Nonbank Financial Companies, Final Rule RIN 4030-AA00, at 14–15, available at http://www.treasury.gov/initiatives/fsoc/documents/nonbank%20designations%20-%20final%20rule%20and%20guidance.pdf.

30. Letter from Comm. on Capital Mkts. Reg. to the Federal Reserve, at 2, available at http://capmktsreg.org/app/uploads/2015/04/04_01_15_G-SIB_capital_surcharge_letter.pdf.

31. Id.

Chapter 7

1. See George Kaufman, Bank contagion: Theory and evidence (Fed. Res. Bank of Chicago, June Working Paper Series, WP-92–13, Jun. 1992), available at http://www .chicagofed.org/digital_assets/publications/working_papers/1992/WP-92-12.pdf.

2. See Ted Temzelides, Are bank runs contagious? *Fed. Res. Bank of Philadelphia Bus. Rev.* 3, 3–14 (Nov./Dec. 1997), available at http://www.philadelphiafed.org/research-and -data/publications/business-review/1997/november-december/brnd97tt.pdf.

3. Id. at 4–6.

4. Jean-Claude Trichet, Pres., Eur. Cent. Bank, Text of the Clare Distinguished Lecture in Economics and Public Policy (Dec. 10, 2009), available at http://www.ecb.int/press/ key/date/2009/html/sp091210_1.en.html (analyzing the linkage between systemic risk and contagion).

5. Morgan Ricks, Shadow banking and financial regulation, 1, 3, Columbia Law and Economics, Working Paper No. 370 (Aug. 30, 2010).

6. For discussion of the increasing complexity in the contemporary financial system and its role in the financial crisis of 2007–2009, see, for example, Hal S. Scott and Anna Gelpern, *International Finance, Transactions, Policy, and Regulation,* University Casebook Series 1, 778–873 (20th ed. 2014).

7. Gary Gorton, Slapped in the face by the invisible hand: Banking and the panic of 2007, 1, 43 (Yale and NBER, May 2009), available at http://www.frbatlanta.org/news/ CONFEREN/09fmc/gorton.pdf (concluding that "[r]eforms to the current system must address the reality of [the] shadow banking system as a banking system").

8. The term "shadow banking system" is attributed to Paul A. McCulley, managing director at PIMCO. It has since been widely adopted by the financial press. Paul McCulley, *Teton Reflections,* PIMCO (Sep. 2007); see also Zoltan Pozsar, Tobias Adrian, Adam Ashcraft, and Hayley Boesky, Shadow banking 11–14 (Fed. Res. Bank of New York, Staff Report No. 458, Jul. 2010), available at http://www.newyorkfed.org/research/staff _reports/sr458.pdf.

9. Gary Gorton and Andrew Metrick, Securitized lending and the run on the repo, 104 *J. Fin. Econ.* 425 (2012).

10. Hal S. Scott, How to improve five important areas of financial regulation, Kaufman Task Force on Law, Innovation, and Growth 113, 117, available at http://www.kauffman. org/~/media/kauffman_org/research%20reports%20and%20covers/2011/02/rulesfor-growth.pdf. The FSB has defined "shadow banking" as "credit intermediation involving entities and activities outside the regular banking system." FSB, Global Shadow Banking Monitoring Report 2012 (Nov. 18, 2012). The FSB has recognized a distinction between "entity-focused" shadow banking, which involves nonbank entities, and "activity-based" shadow banking, in which banks may also participate. Id.

11. See also Zoltan Pozsar , Shadow banking, 1, 11–14 (Fed. Res. Bank of New York, Staff Report No. 458, Feb. 2012), available at http://www.ny.frb.org/research/staff_reports/ sr458.pdf.

12. Hyun Song Shin, *Macroprudential Policies beyond Basel III,* 1, 8 (2010).

13. Zoltan Pozsar et al., Shadow banking 1, 10–11 (Fed. Res. Bank of New York, Staff Report No. 458, Feb. 2012), available at http://www.ny.frb.org/research/staff_reports/sr458.pdf.

14. Id. at 12.

15. Id. at 12.

16. Id. at 12.

17. Id. at 13; see also Hal S. Scott and Anna Gelpern, *International Finance, Transactions, Policy, and Regulation*, University Casebook Series 1, 789–92 (20th ed. 2014) (describing the steps in the process of creating a CDO).

18. Zoltan Pozsar et al., Shadow banking, 1, 13 (Fed. Res. Bank of New York, Staff Report No. 458, Feb. 2012), available at http://www.ny.frb.org/research/staff_reports/sr458.pdf.

19. Id. at 13.

20. Id. at 14.

21. Richard Anderson and Charles Gascon, The commercial paper market, the Fed, and the 2007–2009 financial crisis, *Fed. Res. Bank of St. Louis Rev.* 589, 590 (Nov./Dec. 2009), available at http://research.stlouisfed.org/publications/review/09/11/Anderson.pdf.

22. Russ Wermers, Money fund runs, 1 (Sep. 2010) (noting that "[i]n the eyes of some investors, money market funds have become a substitute for bank deposits"); see also Morgan Ricks, Shadow banking and financial regulation, 3, 4 (Columbia Law and Econ., Working Paper No. 370, Aug. 30, 2010) (noting that "the short-term financing sources on which [the system of money market funds and other credit intermediaries] relies are the functional equivalent of bank deposits"); see also Gary Gorton, Slapped in the face by the invisible hand: Banking and the panic of 2007, 1, 30 (Yale and NBER, May 2009) (arguing that "[r]epo is essentially depository banking, built around informationally-insentive debt").

23. Morgan Ricks, Shadow banking and financial regulation, 3, 6, 9–11 (Columbia Law and Econ., Working Paper No. 370, Aug. 30, 2010); see, for example, Brooke Masters and Jeremy Grant, Finance: Shadow boxes, *Fin. Times* (Feb. 2, 2011) (defining and describing "shadow banking" and noting that "[s]ome non-banks … engage in what is known as 'maturity transformation' … [s]ometimes … within a single institution but … also … in long chains that encompass everything from mortgage brokers and packagers of loans into securities, to the money market funds and special-purpose vehicles that hold them").

24. Morgan Ricks, Shadow banking and financial regulation, 3, 11 (Columbia Law and Economics, Working Paper No. 370, Aug. 30, 2010).

25. Zoltan Pozsar et al., Shadow banking, 1, 5 (Fed. Res. Bank of New York, Staff Report No. 458, Feb. 2012), available at http://www.ny.frb.org/research/staff_reports/sr458.pdf.

26. Naohiko Baba, Robert N. McCauley, and Srichander Ramaswamy, U.S. dollar money market funds and non-U.S. banks, *BIS Q. Rev.* 65, 68 (Mar. 2009).

27. Fed. Deposit Ins. Corp., 2008 Annual Report 12, 53 (Jun. 2009), available at

http://www.fdic.gov/about/strategic/report/2008annualreport/index_pdf.html.

28. Ben Bernanke, Remarks at the Fed. Res. Bank of Kansas City's Annual Economic Symposium, Jackson Hole, WY (Aug. 21, 2009).

29. Inv. Co. Inst., Report of the Money Market Working Group 59 (Mar. 17, 2009).

30. Id. at 59.

31. Naohiko Baba et al., U.S. dollar money market funds and non-U.S. banks, *BIS Q. Rev.* 65, 72 (Mar. 2009).

32. See id.

33. Eleanor Laise, "Breaking the buck" was close for many money funds, *Wall St. J.* (Aug. 10, 2010).

34. Hugh Hoikwang Kim, Contagious runs in money market funds and the impact of a government guarantee (Pension Research Council, Wharton School of the University of Pennsylvania, Working Paper 2013-31, Sep. 19, 2012).

35. Naohiko Baba et al., U.S. dollar money market funds and non-U.S. banks, *BIS Q. Rev.* 65, 72 (Mar. 2009).

36. David Serchuk, Another run on money market funds? *Forbes* (Sep. 25, 2009).

37. Id.

38. Naohiko Baba, et al., U.S. dollar money market funds and non-U.S. banks, *BIS Q. Rev.* 65, 70–72 (Mar. 2009).

39. Federal Reserve Release, *Volume Statistics for Commercial Paper Issuance* (2015), http://www.federalreserve.gov/releases/CP/volumestats.htm; Bryan Keogh and Christopher Condon, Commercial paper falls most ever as ConEd sells bonds, *Bloomberg* (Jul. 16, 2009).

40. Marcin Kacperczyk and Philipp Schnabl, When safety proved risky: Commercial paper during the financial crisis of 2007–2009, 24 *J. Econ. Persp.* 29, 41 (Winter 2010), available at https://www.aeaweb.org/articles.php?doi=10.1257/jep.24.1.29; Chris Reese, US asset-backed commercial paper shrinks markedly, Reuters (Sep. 18, 2008).

41. Marcin Kacperczyk and Philipp Schnabl, When safety proved risky: Commercial paper during the financial crisis of 2007–2009, 24 *J. Econ. Persp.* 29, 40 (Winter 2010), available at https://www.aeaweb.org/articles.php?doi=10.1257/jep.24.1.29. For example, when Lehman filed for bankruptcy, the spread between overnight ABCP and the federal funds rate ballooned to over 300 basis points, up dramatically from already steep spreads of 25 to 30 basis points over the previous weeks.

42. Id. at 30; Press Release, US Dep't of the Treasury, Treasury announces temporary guarantee program for money market funds (Sep. 29, 2008).

43. Marcin Kacperczyk and Philipp Schnabl, When safety proved risky: Commercial paper During the Financial Crisis of 2007–2009, 24 *J. Econ. Persp.* 29, 46 (Winter 2010), available at https://www.aeaweb.org/articles.php?doi=10.1257/jep.24.1.29.

44. Financial Crisis Inquiry Comission, *The Financial Crisis Inquiry Report* ix, 394 (2011), available at http://www.gpo.gov/fdsys/pkg/GPO-FCIC/pdf/GPO-FCIC.pdf.

45. Id. at 355. For discussion of the wider impact of the financial crisis of 2007–2009 on the real (nonfinancial) economy, see id. at 389–410; Thomas Russo and Aaron Katzel, The 2008 financial crisis and its aftermath: Addressing the next debt challenge, 7, 61–62 (Working Draft, Oct. 25, 2010).

46. Gavin Finch and Kim-Mai Cutler, Libor jumps as banks seek cash to shore up finances, *Bloomberg* (Sep. 24, 2008).

47. Id.

48. LIBOR-OIS Spread [Functions: LOIS], Bloomberg Terminal, Bloomberg LP (2015). The LIBOR-OIS spread measures the difference between the London Interbank Offered Rate (LIBOR) and the overnight indexed swap (OIS) rate. The 3-month LIBOR is the rate at which banks borrow unsecured funds from other banks in the London wholesale money market for a 3-month period. An OIS allows a bank to exchange a fixed rate of interest on a notional amount for a reference floating rate (typically the federal funds rate) on that notional amount. The OIS rate is generally viewed as a measure of investor expectations of the effective federal funds rate, whereas LIBOR reflects credit risk and expectations of future overnight rates. The LIBOR-OIS spread can therefore be viewed as the premium banks are willing to pay to avoid the need to roll over the funds on a daily basis at changing overnight rates. Rajdeep Sengupta and Yu Man Tam, The LIBOR-OIS spread as a summary indicator, Fed. Res. Bank of St. Louis (2008), available at http://research.stlouisfed.org/publications/es/08/ES0825.pdf. See also Financial Crisis Inquiry Comission, *The Financial Crisis Inquiry Report* ix, 355 (2011), available at http://www.gpo.gov/fdsys/pkg/GPO-FCIC/pdf/GPO-FCIC.pdf.

49. *See* Markus Brunnermeier, Deciphering the liquidity and credit crunch 2007–2008, 23 *J. Econ. Persp.* 77, 85 (Winter 2009) (noting the utility of the TED spread as a measure of liquidity in the financial system).

50. Bloomberg.com Ted Spread Index, *Bloomberg* (depicting historical data).

51. Gavin Finch and Kim-Mai Cutler, Libor jumps as banks seek cash to shore up finances, *Bloomberg* (Sep. 24, 2008).

52. Financial Crisis Inquiry Comission, *The Financial Crisis Inquiry Report* ix, 355 (2011), available at http://www.gpo.gov/fdsys/pkg/GPO-FCIC/pdf/GPO-FCIC.pdf.

53. See figures 2.3 and 2.4.

54. Rick Rothacker and Kerry Hall, Wachovia faced a "silent" bank run, *Charlotte Observer* (Oct. 2, 2008); Markus Brunnermeier, Deciphering the liquidity and credit crunch 2007–2008, 23 *J. Econ. Persp.* 77, 90 (Winter 2009) (noting silent run on Washington Mutual prior to its being placed in receivership and sold to JPMorgan Chase).

55. News Release, Wells Fargo & Company, Wells Fargo and Wachovia merger completed (Jan. 1, 2009); News Release, Wells Fargo & Company, Wells Fargo's merger with Wachovia to proceed as whole company transaction with all of Wachovia's banking operations (Oct. 9, 2008).

56. Press Release, Fed. Deposit Ins. Corp., JPMorgan Chase acquires banking operations of Washington Mutual (Sep. 25, 2008), available at http://www.fdic.gov/news/news/press/2008/pr08085.html.

57. *See* Gary Gorton and Andrew Metrick, Securitized lending and the run on the repo, 104 *J. Fin. Econ.* 425 (2012) (finding that increases in repo spreads and repo haircuts during the financial crisis of 2007–2009 were correlated with uncertainty concerning counterparty risk and collateral values, respectively).

58. Id.

59. Id. The authors' data set focuses on interdealer repo markets and excludes the tri-party repo market.

60. Financial Crisis Inquiry Comission, *The Financial Crisis Inquiry Report* ix, 355 (2011), available at http://www.gpo.gov/fdsys/pkg/GPO-FCIC/pdf/GPO-FCIC.pdf. (noting effect of hedge fund withdrawals of assets held by Merrill Lynch prior to the closing of its merger with Bank of America and flows to "large commercial banks with … more diverse sources of liquidity"); Allan Sloan, A year after Lehman, Wall Street acting like Wall Street again, *Wash. Post* (Sep. 8, 2009).

61. The run on Morgan Stanley, FT.com/Alphaville (Sep. 18, 2008); Saijel Kishan and Katherine Burton, Morgan Stanley loses hedge-fund clients on stock drop, *Bloomberg* (Sep. 18, 2008).

62. Financial Crisis Inquiry Comission, *The Financial Crisis Inquiry Report* ix, 361 (2011), available at http://www.gpo.gov/fdsys/pkg/GPO-FCIC/pdf/GPO-FCIC.pdf.

63. Id. at 361 n.34.

64. Manmohan Singh and James Aitken, Counterparty risk, impact on collateral flows, and role for central counterparties, 1, 7–8 (IMF, Working Paper No. 09/173, Aug. 2009), http://www.imf.org/external/pubs/ft/wp/2009/wp09173.pdf.

65. Id.

66. Christine Harper, Morgan Stanley said to weigh deal with Wachovia as shares sink, *Bloomberg* (Sep. 17, 2008); Tiernan Ray, Goldman shares off 33% for week as CDS fears spread, *Barron's* (Sep. 17, 2008), available at http://blogs.barrons.com/stockstowatchto-day/2008/09/17/goldman-shares-33-off-this-week-as-cds-fears-spread/.

67. Financial Crisis Inquiry Comission, *The Financial Crisis Inquiry Report* ix, 361 (2011), *available at* http://www.gpo.gov/fdsys/pkg/GPO-FCIC/pdf/GPO-FCIC.pdf. This increase in CDS spreads affected both dealers and end clients. See Or Shachar, Exposing the exposed: Intermediation capacity in the credit default swap market (Stern School of Business, New York University, Working Paper, Mar. 2012). Shachar examined sample CDS contracts among the top dealers from 2007 to mid-2009, and found that after Lehman's bankruptcy, dealers found it more difficult to offset their positions, so the interdealer market was "congested" and dealers' ability to provide liquidity to their clients also decreased.

68. Christine Harper, Morgan Stanley, Goldman plummet after AIG takeover, *Bloomberg* (Sep. 17, 2008).

69. Id.

70. See Press Release, Bd. of Governors of Fed. Res. Sys. (Sep. 21, 2008).

71. *See* Press Release, Fed. Deposit Ins. Corp., FDIC announces plan to free up bank liquidity (Oct. 14, 2008).

72. Press Release, Bd. of Governors of Fed. Res. Sys. (Dec. 12, 2007).

73. Press Release, Bd. of Governors of Fed. Res. Sys. (March 7, 2008).

74. Bd. of Governors of Fed. Res. Sys., Term securities lending facility (2015), available at http://www.federalreserve.gov/monetarypolicy/tslf.htm; see also Press Release, Bd. of Governors of Fed. Res. Sys. (Mar. 11, 2008).

75. Press Release, Bd. of Governors of Fed. Res. Sys. (Mar. 16, 2008); Fed. Res. Bank of New York, Primary dealer credit facility: Frequently asked questions, available at http:// www.newyorkfed.org/markets/pdcf_faq.html (2015); Fed. Res. Bank of New York, Primary dealer credit facility: Program terms and conditions, available at http://www. newyorkfed.org/markets/pdcf_terms.html (2015).

76. Report Pursuant to Section 129 of the Emergency Economic Stabilization Act of 2008: Secured credit facility authorized for American International Group, Inc. on September 16, 2008, available at http://www.federalreserve.gov/monetarypolicy/files/ 129aigseccreditfacility.pdf.

77. Henry Paulson, On the brink, *Business Plus* 1, 229 (2011).

78. Bd. of Governors of Fed. Res. Sys., Asset-backed commercial paper money market mutual fund liquidity facility (2015), available at http://www.federalreserve.gov/mon etarypolicy/abcpmmmf.htm.

79. Press Release, US Dep't of the Treasury, Treasury announces temporary guarantee program for money market funds (Sep. 29, 2008).

80. Joint Press Release, Bd. of Governors of the Fed. Reserve Sys. & US Dep't of the Treasury, U.S. Treasury and Federal Reserve Board announce participation in AIG restructuring plan (Mar. 2, 2009), available at http://www.federalreserve.gov/newsev ents/press/other/20090302a.htm; Press Release, Bd. of Governors of the Fed. Reserve Sys. (Nov. 10, 2008).

81. Id.

82. Press Release, Fed. Deposit Ins. Corp., FDIC announces plan to free up bank liquidity (Oct. 14, 2008); see also Fed. Deposit Ins. Corp., Temporary Liquidity Guarantee Program, available at http://www.fdic.gov/regulations/resources/tlgp/index.html (2015).

83. Press Release, Fed. Deposit Ins. Corp., Emergency Economic Stabilization Act of 2008 temporarily increases basic FDIC insurance coverage from $100,000 to $250,000 per depositor (Oct. 7, 2008), available at http://www.fdic.gov/news/news/press/2008/ pr08093.html.

84. Bd. of Governors of the Fed. Reserve System, Commercial Paper Funding Facility (2015), available at http://www.federalreserve.gov/monetarypolicy/cpff.htm.

85. Press Release, Bd. of Governors of the Fed. Reserve Sys. (Nov. 25, 2008).

86. Colleen Baker, The Federal Reserve's use of international swap lines, 55 *Ariz. L. Rev.* 603 (2013).

87. Id.

88. Id.

89. Kathryn Judge, Three discount windows, 99 *Cornell Law Rev.* 795, 825 (2014).

90. Federal Housing Finance Agency Office of Inspector General, Recent trends in Federal Home Loan Bank advances to JPMorgan Chase and other large banks, 1 (Apr. 16, 2014), *available at* http://fhfaoig.gov/Content/Files/EVL-2014-006_1.pdf.

91. Adam Ashcraft et al., The Federal Home Loan Bank System: The lender of next-to-last resort, 42.4 *J. Money, Credit Bank.* 551 (2010).

92. Id.

93. See 12 USC §1430(a)(3) for a complete list of eligible collateral.

94. See Adam Ashcraft Morton L. Bech, and W. Scott Frame, The Federal Home Loan Bank System: The lender of next-to-last resort, 42.4 *J. Money, Credit Bank.* 551 (2010).

95. Id. at 552–54.

96. See Adam Ashcraft et al., The Federal Home Loan Bank System: The Lender of Next-to-Last Resort, 42.4 *J. Money, Credit Bank.*551 (2010); *see also* Kathryn Judge, Three discount windows, 99 *Cornell L. Rev.* 795 (2014).

97. See Adam Ashcraft et al., The Federal Home Loan Bank System: The lender of next-to-last resort, 42.4 *J. Money, Credit Bank.* 551 (2010).

98. Kathryn Judge, Three discount windows, 99 *Cornell Law Rev.* 795, 814–15 (2014).

99. Adam Ashcraft et al., The Federal Home Loan Bank System: The lender of next-to-last resort, 42.4 *J. Money, Credit Bank.* 551, 579 (2010).

Chapter 8

1. Speech by Mario Draghi, president of the European Central Bank (ECB), at the Global Investment Conference in London (Jul. 26, 2012), available at http://www.ecb.europa.eu/press/key/date/2012/html/sp120726.en.html.

2. Walter Bagehot, *Lombard Street: A Description of the Money Market*, E. Johnstone, Hartley Withers, eds. (Henry S. King, London, 1873).

3. Sir Francis Baring, *Observations on the Establishment of the Bank of England and on the Paper Circulation of the Country* 1, 22 (1797).

4. Walter Bagehot, *Lombard Street: A Description of the Money Market* 1 (1873).

5. See id. at 64.

6. Paul Tucker, The repertoire of official sector interventions in the financial system: Last resort lending, market-making, and capital, Speech at the Bank of Japan 2009 International Conference 1, 5 (May 28, 2009).

7. Walter Bagehot, *Lombard Street: A Description of the Money Market* 1, 25 (1873).

8. *See* Thomas Humphrey, Lender of last resort: The concept in history, *Fed. Res. Bank of Richmond Econ. Rev.* 8, 12–16 (Mar./Apr. 1989).

9. Michael Bordo, The lender of last resort: Alternative views and historical experience, *Fed. Res. Bank of Richmond Econ. Rev.* 18, 24 (Jan./Feb. 1990).

10. Id. at 27.

11. Marvin Goodfriend and Robert King, The incredible Volcker disinflation. 36 *J. Mon. Econ.* 1 (2007).

12. Id.

13. John Holdsworth, *The First and Second Banks of the United States* 1, 126 (Government Printing Office, Washington, DC, 1902).

14. Id. at 109.

15. Davis Dewey, *The Second United States Bank*, Washington, DC: National Monetary Commission 1, 154 (1911).

16. Id. at 156.

17. See id. at 163.

18. David Cowen, The First Bank of the United States and the securities market crash of 1792, 60 *J. Econ. Hist.* 1041, 1042 (2000).

19. Id.

20. Louis Johnston and Samuel Williamson, What was the U.S. GDP then? Measuring worth (2015), available at http://www.measuringworth.com/usgdp/.

21. Richard Timberlake Jr., *Monetary Policy in the United States: An Intellectual and Institutional History*, University of Chicago Press 1, 6 (1993).

22. John Holdsworth, *The First and Second Banks of the United States* 1 (1902).

23. John Holdsworth, *The First and Second Banks of the United States* 1, 132 (1902); see also Ralph Catterall, *The Second Bank of the United States*, University of Chicago Press 1, 23 (1902).

24. Ralph Catterall, *The Second Bank of the United States*, University of Chicago Press 1, 431 (1902).

25. *Id.*.

26. Fred Gotthiel, *Principles of Macroeconomics*, South-Western College Pub 1, 278 (7th Ed. 2013).

27. Ralph Catterall, *The Second Bank of the United States*, University of Chicago Press 1, 431 (1902).

28. Richard Timberlake Jr., *Monetary Policy in the United States: An Intellectual and Institutional History*, University of Chicago Press 1, 19 (1993).

29. *Id.*.

30. Edward Green, Economic perspective on the political history of the Second Bank of the United States, *Fed. Res. Bank of Chicago* 59, 63 (2003).

31. Id.

32. Richard Timberlake Jr., *Monetary Policy in the United States: An Intellectual and Institutional History*, University of Chicago Press 1, 38 (1993).

33. Id. at 10.

34. Id. at 38.

35. Id.

36. Richard Painter, Ethics and corruption in business and government: Lessons from the South Sea Bubble and Bank of the United States, University of Chicago Fulton Lectures 1, 17 (2006).

37. Richard Timberlake Jr., *Monetary Policy in the United States: An Intellectual and Institutional History*, University of Chicago Press 1 (1993).

38. Id.

39. James Wettereau, New light on the First Bank of the United States, 61.3 *Penn. Mag. Hist. Bio.* 263, 270 (1937).

40. Id. at 282.

41. Id.

42. See US Congress, House Committee to Investigate the Bank of the United States 279 (1832).

43. H. Wayne Morgan, The origins and establishment of the First Bank of the United States, 30 *Bus. Hist. Rev.* 472, 474 (1956).

44. Greg Gilner, Global macro trading: Profiting in a new world economy, *Bloomberg* 1, 9 (2014).

45. John Holdsworth, *The First and Second Banks of the United States* 1, 197 (1902).

46. Philadelphia Federal Reserve, The First Bank of the United States: A chapter in the history of central banking 1 (Jun. 2009), available at http://philadelphiafed.org/publications/economic-education/first-bank.pdf.

47. Fritz Redlich, *The Molding of American Banking: Men and Ideas, in Two Parts*, Johnson Reprint Corporation 1, 10 (New York, 1968).

48. Raymond Walters Jr., The origins of the Second Bank of the United States, 53 *J. Polit. Econ.* 115, 122 (1945).

49. Id.

50. Id. at 128.

51. Id. at 129.

52. US Congress, 22d. Cong., 1st sess., Reports of Committees, House Report No. 460 341 (1832).

53. Ralph Catterall, *The Second Bank of the United States*, University of Chicago Press 1, 451 (1902).

54. Id.

55. Philadelphia Federal Reserve Bank, The Second Bank of the United States: A chapter in the history of central banking 1, 8 (Dec. 2010), available at https://www.philadelphiafed.org/publications/economic-education/second-bank.pdf.

56. Ralph Catterall, *The Second Bank of the United States*, University of Chicago Press 1, 84 (1902).

57. Richard Timberlake Jr., *Monetary Policy in the United States: An Intellectual and Institutional History*, University of Chicago Press 1, 25 (1993).

58. Philadelphia Federal Reserve Bank, The Second Bank of the United States: A chapter in the history of central banking 1, 8 (Dec. 2010), available at https://www.philadelphiafed.org/publications/economic-education/second-bank.pdf.

59. Ralph Catterall, *The Second Bank of the United States*, University of Chicago Press 1, 70 (1902).

60. Philadelphia Federal Reserve Bank, The Second Bank of the United States: A chapter in the history of central banking 1 (Dec. 2010), available at https://www.philadelphiafed .org/publications/economic-education/second-bank.pdf.

61. Jay Shambaugh, An experiment with multiple currencies: The American monetary system from 1838 to 60 (2005) (manuscript on file with Dartmouth College) 1, 12, available at http://www.dartmouth.edu/~jshambau/Papers/AntebellumExchRtsJCS-5-2005 .pdf.

62. Id.

63. Davis Dewey, *The Second United States Bank*, Washington, DC, National Monetary Commission 1, 193 (1911).

64. Id.

65. Jane Knoddell, Profit and duty in the Second Bank of the United States Exchange Operations, 10 *Fin. Hist. Rev.* 5 (2003).

66. Bray Hammond, Jackson, Biddle, and the Bank of the United States, 7 *J. Econ. Hist.* 1, 3 (1947).

67. Id.

68. Richard Timberlake Jr., *Monetary Policy in the United States: An Intellectual and Institutional History*, University of Chicago Press 1, 38–39 (1993).

69. Id.

70. Letter from William H. Crawford to William Jones (Jun. 30, 1818).

71. Ralph Catterall, *The Second Bank of the United States*, University of Chicago Press 1, 148 (1902).

72. Id. at 150.

73. J. Laurence Broz, The origins of central banking: Solutions to the free-rider problem, 52.2 *Int'l Organ.* 231, 258 (Spring 1998).

74. Id.

75. Ralph Catterall, *The Second Bank of the United States*, University of Chicago Press 1, 249 (1902).

76. Id. at 250.

77. Id.

78. See, for example, *Osborne v. Bank of the United States*, 22 US 738 (1824); *McCulloch v. Maryland*, 17 US 316 (1819).

79. Bray Hammond, Jackson, Biddle, and the Bank of the United States, 7 *J. Econ. Hist.* 1, 5 (1947).

80. Id.

81. Timberlake, *supra* note 596 at 39.

82. Curzio Giannini, "Enemy of none but a common friend of all"? An international perspective on the lender-of-last-resort function, 214 *Essays Int'l Fin.* 24 (1999).

83. Richard Timberlake Jr., *Monetary Policy in the United States: An Intellectual and Institutional History*, University of Chicago Press 1, 39 (1993).

84. Id.

85. Miller Center, University of Virginia, Domestic affairs: Rotation in office and the spoils system, *American President: A Reference Resource*, available at: http://millercenter. org/president/jackson/essays/biography/4

86. Id.

87. Davis Dewey, *The Second United States Bank*, Washington, DC, National Monetary Commission 1, 299 (1911).

88. Id. at 299, 305.

89. H. W. Brands, *Andrew Jackson: His Life and Times*, Anchor 1, 486 (Oct. 10, 2006).

90. Asaf Bernstein, Eric Hughson, and Marc D. Weidenmier, Central banking and funding liquidity 1, available at http://www.usc.edu/schools/business/FBE/semi nars/papers/M_WEIDERMEYER_v9-16-2010.pdf.

91. Id. at 23.

92. Fabian Valencia and Luc Laevan, Systemic banking crises database, *IMF Econ. Rev.* 61(2), 225–270 (2013). Charles Calomiris and Luc Laeven, Political foundations of the lender of last resort: A global historical narrative (Dec. 19, 2014).

93. *See* Gary Gorton and Andrew Metrick, The Federal Reserve and financial regulation: The first hundred years 1, 8 (NBER Working Paper No. 19292, 2013).

94. Id. at 23.

95. Id. at 23.

96. See Panic of 1907, Fed. Res. Bank of Boston (1990), available at http://www.boston fed.org/about/pubs/panicof1.pdf.

97. Id. at 11. ("Senator Nelson Aldrich of Rhode Island summed up the general feeling. 'Something has got to be done,' he declared; 'We may not always have Pierpont Morgan with us to meet a banking crisis.'").

98. Id.

99. See Mark Carlson and David Wheelock, The lender of last resort: Lessons from the Fed's first 100 years (Fed. Reserve Bank of St. Louis, Working Paper 2012–056B, 2013), available at http://research.stlouisfed.org/wp/2012/2012-056.pdf.

100. *Id.* at 3.

101. Id. at 11.

102. Id. at 7.

103. Id. at 7.

104. Howard Hackley, Lending functions of Federal Reserve banks: A history 1, 124 (1973), available at https://fraser.stlouisfed.org/docs/publications/books/lendfunct _hackley1973o.pdf.

105. Id. at 101.

106. As originally enacted, the provision would have expired in March 1933. However, the Emergency Banking Act of 1933 lengthened its duration and authorized the Federal Reserve to make equivalent loans to nonmember banks. According to one Senator instrumental in extending the authority to nonmember banks, the expanded powers sought "to place the State banks nearer on a parity with member banks." While the expanded authority to lend to non-member banks expired in 1934, the Banking Act of August 1935 extended its other provisions indefinitely and permitted lending during ordinary periods. Howard Hackley, Lending functions of Federal Reserve banks: A history 1, 124–125 (1973), available at https://fraser.stlouisfed.org/docs/publications/books/lendfunct _hackley1973o.pdf; Mark Carlson and David Wheelock, The lender of last resort: Lessons from the Fed's first 100 years 1 (Fed. Res. Bank of St. Louis, Working Paper 2012–056B, 2013), available at http://research.stlouisfed.org/wp/2012/2012-056.pdf.

107. Kenneth J. Robinson, Depository Institutions Deregulation and Monetary Control Act of 1980, Federal Reserve Bank of Dallas (March 1980), *available at*: http://www .federalreservehistory.org/Events/DetailView/43.

108. See Bd. of Governors of the Fed Res. Sys., *The Federal Reserve Discount Window* (2015); *see also* 12 USC 347b(a); *see also* Bd. of Governors of the Fed Res. Sys., *Advances to Individual Member Banks* (2015) .

109. 12 USC 347b(a).

110. Id.

111. Section 10B requires that loans are "secured to the satisfaction of [the] Federal Reserve Bank. 12 USC 347b(a). For a summary of Federal Reserve lending programs and collateral accepted, see, for example, Fed. Res. Bank of New York, Forms of Federal Reserve lending (2015), available at http://www.newyorkfed.org/markets/Forms_of _Fed_Lending.pdf.

112. Federal Reserve Act Section 10A. 12 USC §347a.

113. 12 USC §347a.

114. *See* Martin Hellwig, Financial Stability and Monetary Policy, MPI Collective Goods Preprint, No. 2015/10, 12-13 (August 2015), available at: http://ssrn.com/abstract =2639532.

115. Sourced from Bloomberg.

116. Howard Hackley, Lending functions of Federal Reserve banks: A history 1, 128 (1973), available at https://fraser.stlouisfed.org/docs/publications/books/lendfunct_ hackley1973o.pdf; Mark Carlson and David Wheelock, The lender of last resort: Lessons from the Fed's first 100 years 1, 11–12 (Fed. Res. Bank of St. Louis, Working Paper 2012–056B, 2013), available at http://research.stlouisfed.org/wp/2012/2012-056.pdf.

117. Howard Hackley, Lending functions of Federal Reserve banks: A history 1, 128 (1973), available at https://fraser.stlouisfed.org/docs/publications/books/lendfunct _hackley1973o.pdf; Mark Carlson and David Wheelock, The lender of last resort: Lessons from the Fed's first 100 years 1, 11 (Fed. Res. Bank of St. Louis, Working Paper 2012–056B, 2013), available at http://research.stlouisfed.org/wp/2012/2012-056.pdf.

118. Alexander Mehra, Legal authority in unusual and exigent circumstances: The Federal Reserve and the financial crisis, 13 *U. Pa. J. Bus. L.* 221, 233 (2010–2011).

119. Initially the 13(3) required that the lending be "indorsed *and* secured to the satisfaction of the Federal Reserve bank" (emphasis added). However, the Banking Act of 1935 amended the language to require that the lending be "indorsed *or* secured to the satisfaction of the Federal Reserve bank" (emphasis added). Banking Act of 1935, available at http://www.federalreservehistory.org/Media/Material/Event/26-284.

120. Howard Hackley, Lending functions of Federal Reserve banks: A history 1, 128 (1973), available at https://fraser.stlouisfed.org/docs/publications/books/lendfunct _hackley1973o.pdf.

121. Alexander Mehra, Legal authority in unusual and exigent circumstances: The Federal Reserve and the financial crisis, 13 *U. Pa. J. Bus. L.* 221, 233 (2010–2011).

122. Hackley, *supra* note 653 at 128.

123. Id. at 128.

124. FDIC Act of 1991 §473, available at https://fraser.stlouisfed.org/docs/historical/congressional/pl102_242.pdf.

125. Mehra, *supra* note 655 at 232.

126. Binyamin Appelbaum and Neil Irwin, Congress's afterthought, Wall Street's trillion dollars, *Washington Post* (May 30, 2009).

127. Federal Reserve Act §13(3)(A).

128. Id.

129. Federal Reserve Act §13(3)(A).

130. Press Release, Bd. of Governors of the Fed. Res. Sys. (Mar. 16, 2008), Press Release, Bd. of Governors of the Fed. Res. Sys. (Sept. 16, 2008).

131. 12 USC §355 (2012).

Chapter 9

1. Press Release, US Department of the Treasury (Jul. 18, 2012).

2. The institutions designated are The Clearing House Payments Company, LLC, CLS Bank International, Chicago Mercantile Exchange, The Depository Trust Company, Fixed Income Clearing Corporation, ICE Clear Credit LLC, National Securities Clearing Corporation, and The Options Clearing Corporation.

3. Colleen Baker, The Federal Reserve as last resort, 46 (1) *University of Michigan Journal of Law Reform* (Dec. 19, 2012), available at: http://ssrn.com/abstract=2191784 (contending that broker-dealers may be designated as financial market utiltiies, and thus that Title VIII can function as a backdoor lender of last resort to broker-dealers).

4. Dodd–Frank Act §1101(a)(2), (6) (requiring lending facilities to be structured with "broad-based eligibility" with "the purpose of providing liquidity to the financial *system*, and not to aid a failing financial *company*" and stating that a "program or facility that is structured to remove assets from the balance sheet of a *single and specific company* … shall not be considered a program or facility with broad-based eligibility") (emphasis added).

5. Timothy Geithner, *Stress Test: Reflections on Financial Crises*, vol. 1 (Crown Publishers, New York, 2014), 515.

6. See Report Prepared by the Republican Staff of the House Committee on Financial Services, *Failing to End "Too Big to Fail": An Assessment of the Dodd–Frank Act Four Years Later* 1 (Jul. 2014).

7. Starr International Company, Inc. v. United States, 121 Fed. Cl. 428 (2015).

8. Extensions of Credit by Federal Reserve Banks, 79 Fed. Reg. 615 (proposed Dec. 23, 2014).

9. Id.

10. Letter from Jeb Hensarling, Chairman of the House Financial Services Committee, to Ben Bernanke (Jan. 13, 2014).

11. Letter from Elizabeth Warren, member of the Senate Committee on Banking, Housing, and Urban Affairs to Janet Yallen (Aug. 18, 2014).

12. Extensions of Credit by Federal Reserve Banks, 80 Fed. Reg. 246 (effective Dec. 23, 2015).

13. Id.

14. Dodd–Frank Act §1101(a)(6) ("(B) … (iv) The Board may not establish any program or facility under this paragraph without the prior approval of the Secretary of the Treasury").

15. Allan Meltzer, *A History of the Federal Reserve*, vol. 1 (University of Chicago Press, 2003).

16. Id. at 85.

17. Id.

18. William Silbre, *Volcker: The Triumph of Persistence*, vol. 1 (Bloomsbury Press, 2013), 170.

19. Id. at 95.

20. See id. at 92, 128–29.

21. Id. at 128–29.

22. Id. at 132.

23. Id. at 576.

24. Gary Richardson Alejandro Komai, and Michael Gou, Banking Act of 1935, Federal Reserve History, available at http://www.federalreservehistory.org/Events/Detail View/26.

25. Mark Carlson and David Wheelock, The lender of last resort: Lessons from the Fed's first 100 years 1, 12 (Fed. Res. Bank of St. Louis, Working Paper 2012–056B, 2013), available at http://research.stlouisfed.org/wp/2012/2012-056.pdf.

26. Howard Preston, The Banking Act of 1935, 43.6 *J. Polit. Econ.* 743, 753 (1935).

27. Gary Richardson Alejandro Komai, and Michael Gou, Banking Act of 1935, Federal Reserve History, available at http://www.federalreservehistory.org/Events/Detail View/26.

28. Frederick Bradford, The Banking Act of 1935, 25.4 *Am. Econ. Rev.* 661, 665; see also Howard Preston, The Banking Act of 1935, 43.6 *J. Polit. Econ.* 743, 756 (1935).

29. Gary Richardson Alejandro Komai, and Michael Gou, Banking Act of 1935, Federal Reserve History, available at http://www.federalreservehistory.org/Events/Detail-View/26; Frederick Bradford, The Banking Act of 1935, 25.4 *Am. Econ. Rev.* 661, 665; Howard Preston, The Banking Act of 1935, 43.6 *J. Polit. Econ.* 743, 755 (1935).

30. Id.

31. Marriner Stoddard Eccles, *Beckoning Frontiers: Public and Personal Recollections* 1, 382 (Knopf, New York, 1951).

32. Allan Meltzer, *A History of the Federal Reserve*, vol. 1 (University of Chicago Press, 2003), 711–12.

33. Id. at 712.

34. US Dept. of the Treasury, *Financial Regulatory Reform: A New Foundation* 1, 16 (Jun. 17, 2009), available at http://www.treasury.gov/initiatives/wsr/Documents/FinalReport_web.pdf. ("We will propose legislation to amend Section 13(3) … to require the prior written approval of the Secretary of the Treasury.)

35. Financial Services Oversight Council Act of 2009 (Jul. 22, 2009), available at http://www.llsdc.org/assets/DoddFrankdocs/dodd-frank-act_admn-reg-reform-bill.pdf.

36. Consumer Protection and Regulatory Enhancement Act (Jul. 23, 2009), available at http://www.gpo.gov/fdsys/pkg/BILLS-111hr3310ih/pdf/BILLS-111hr3310ih.pdf.

37. HR 3996, 111th Cong. (2009).

38. HR 4173, 111th Cong. (2009).

39. Id.

40. Section 1701(c)(1) included FSOC certification of a liquidity event and Section 1701(c)(6) included a congressional veto. Text available at https://www.congress.gov/bill/111th-congress/house-bill/4173/text/eh#toc-H857A300094C24DA9B74429C21B9C5D32.

41. Section 1701(c)(1) included FSOC certification of a liquidity event and Section 1701(c)(6) included a congressional vet. Text available at https://www.congress.gov/bill/111th-congress/house-bill/4173/text/rfs#toc-H336DEE05F3944DD6A6665676C74A2C52.

42. Title XI, Sections 1151–1159 include the provisions affecting the Federal Reserve. Section 1151 was the major provision affecting Section 13 of the Federal Reserve Act, and it did not include the FSOC certification of Congressional veto. Text available at https://www.congress.gov/bill/111th-congress/house-bill/4173/text/eas.

43. Timothy Geithner (telephone discussion with Hal Scott on Aug. 1, 2014).

44. Hal S. Scott (testimony before the Committee on Financial Services, US House of Representatives) (Jan. 26, 2011) (urging that the Treasury Secretary "may be reluctant to approve needed lending facilities for fear of political consequences").

45. Jeffrey Gordon and Christopher Muller, Confronting Financial Crisis: Dodd–Frank's Dangers and the Case for a Systemic Emergency Insurance Fund, 28 *Yale J. Reg.* 151 (2011).

46. Ben Bernanke, Liquidity and the lender of last resort, Closing keynote address, Brookings Institution 1, 178 (Apr. 30, 2014), http://www.brookings.edu/~/media/events/2014/04/30%20liquidity%20lender%20of%20last%20resort/20140430_liquidity_transcript.pdf.

47. Ben Bernanke, *The Courage to Act: A Memoir of a Crisis and Its Aftermath* (Norton New York, 2015), 464.

48. Federal Reserve Act §13(3), 12 USC §343 (2012).

49. Federal Reserve Act §13(3), §3(B)(ii).

50. 12 CFR Chapter II.A Part 201.

51. Bd. of Governors of the Fed. Res. Sys., Discount window lending (2015), available at http://www.federalreserve.gov/newsevents/reform_discount_window.htm.

52. 12 CFR §201.4(a).

53. Bd. of Governors of the Fed. Res. Sys., The Federal Reserve discount window (2015), available at https://www.frbdiscountwindow.org/Home/Pages/General-Information/The-Discount-Window.

54. Id.

55. Id.

56. §142 of the FDICIA amended §10B of the Federal Reserve Act to set time periods beyond which the Federal Reserve may not lend to undercapitalized and critically undercapitalized banks without incurring liability to the FDIC.

57. 12 CFR §201.4(b).

58. Id.

59. 12 CFR §201.5(b). However, "[i]n unusual circumstances, when prior consultation with the Board is not possible, a Federal Reserve Bank should consult with the Board as soon as possible."

60. Letter from Jeb Hensarling, Chairman of the House Financial Services Committee, to Ben Bernanke (Jan 13, 2014); letter from Elizabeth Warren, member of the Senate Committee on Banking, Housing, and Urban Affairs to Janet Yallen (Aug. 18, 2014).

61. Extensions of Credit by Federal Reserve Banks, 80 Fed. Reg. 243 78959, 78960 (published Dec. 18, 2015).

62. Maurice Obstfeld, Lenders of last resort in a globalized world, Keynote address prepared for the 2009 International Conference, Institute for Monetary and Economic Studies 1, 6 (May 27–28, 2009).

63. James Stewart and Peter Eavis, Revisiting the Lehman Brothers bailout that never was (Sep. 29, 2014), available at http://www.nytimes.com/2014/09/30/business/revisiting-the-lehman-brothers-bailout-that-never-was.html?_r=0.

64. See Marc Farag, Bank capital and liquidity, Bank of England 1 (2013), available at http://www.bankofengland.co.uk/publications/Documents/quarterlybulletin/2013/qb130302.pdf; see also James Stewart, Solvency, Lost in the fog at the Fed, *NY Times* (Nov. 7, 2014).

65. Paul Tucker, The lender of last resort and modern central banking: Principles and reconstruction, 79 *BIS Papers* 10, 22.

66. Paul Tucker, The repertoire of official sector interventions in the financial system—Last resort lending, market-making, and capital, Remarks at the Bank of Japan 2009 International Conference (May 27–28 2009).

67. Eric Rosengren, Short-term wholesale funding risks, *Boston Fed. Res.* 1, 7 (Nov. 5, 2014), available at http://www.bostonfed.org/news/speeches/rosengren/2014/110514 /110514text.pdf.

68. See Financial Stability Oversight Council, *2013 Annual Report* I (2013).

69. Id. at 139.

70. §1101(a)(6)(B)(i).

71. *See* §1101(a)(6)(B)(i).

72. Paul Tucker, The repertoire of official sector interventions in the financial system— Last resort lending, market-making, and capital, Remarks at the Bank of Japan 2009 International Conference (May 27–28 2009).

73. Kenneth Kuttner, The Federal Reserve as Lender of Last Resort during the Panic of 2008 1 (Working Paper, Jan. 13, 2008), available at http://capmktsreg.org/education -research/the-federal-reserve-as-lender-of-last-resort-during-the-panic-of-2008/.

74. Press Release, Bd. of Governors of the Fed. Res. Sys. (Mar. 20, 2015).

75. Gross collections were around $3.06 trillion in 2014. IRS, gross collections, by type of tax and state, fiscal year 2014 (2015), available at http://www.irs.gov/file_source/ pub/irs-soi/14db05co.xls.

76. Section 1101 of Dodd–Frank amended Section 13 of the Federal Reserve Act to require detailed disclosure of 13(3) lending to the Senate Committee on Banking, Housing, and Urban Affairs. Section 1103 requires this report to be published on the Federal Reserve website. ("The Board shall place on its home Internet website ... relevant information including ... the reports to the Committee on Banking, Housing, and Urban Affairs of the Senate required under section 13(3) relating to emergency lending authority").

77. Dodd–Frank Act §1103(b).

78. Id. at §1101(a)(6).

79. See Renee Haltom, Stigma and the discount window, Fed. Res. Region Focus First Quarter 1, 6 (2011), available at http://www.richmondfed.org/publications/research/ region_focus/2011/q1/pdf/federal_reserve.pdf.

80. See Sriya Anbil, Managing stigma during a financial crisis (Sep. 3, 2015), available at http://ssrn.com/abstract=2655747.

Chapter 10

1. This chapter is based on my article, The Federal Reserve: The weakest lender of last resort among its peers, *International Finance* 18 (3): 321–42 (2015).

2. Bank of England, *Bank of England Legislation* (2015), available at http://www .bankofengland.co.uk/about/Pages/legislation/default.aspx. Subsequent legislation includes the Bank Charter Act 1844, the Bank of England Act 1946, the Charter of the Bank of England 1998, the Bank of England Act ("1998 Act"), the Banking Act of 2009, and the Financial Services Act 2012.

3. Speech, Mark Carney, Governor of the Bank of England, One Mission. One Bank. Promoting the good of the people of the United Kingdom 1, 3 (Mar. 18, 2014), available at http://www.bankofengland.co.uk/publications/Documents/speeches/2014/speech715 .pdf.

4. Bank of England, *Bank of England Legislation* (2015), available at http://www.bankofengland.co.uk/about/Pages/legislation/default.aspx.

5. Speech, Mark Carney, Governor of the Bank of England, *One Mission. One Bank. Promoting the good of the people of the United Kingdom* 1, 3 (Mar. 18, 2014), available at http://www.bankofengland.co.uk/publications/Documents/speeches/2014/speech715.pdf.

6. Id.; see also Bank of England, Bank of England: Monetary Policy Framework, available at http://www.bankofengland.co.uk/monetarypolicy/Pages/framework/framework.aspx. The 1998 Act provides that the government may give instruction to the Bank in extreme circumstances if the national interest demands it.

7. Id.

8. Ian Plenderleith, Review of the Bank of England's Provision of Emergency Liquidity Assistance in 2008–09 1, 22, available at http://www.bankofengland.co.uk/publications/Documents/news/2012/cr1plenderleith.pdf.

9. Bank of England, *One Mission* (2015), available at http://www.bankofengland.co.uk/about/Pages/onemission/default.aspx.

10. Id.

11. Speech, Minouche Shafik, Deputy Governor of the Bank of England, *Fixing the Global Financial Safety Net: Lessons from Central Banking* (Sept. 22, 2015).

12. Bank of England, Bank of England Sterling Monetary Framework, available at http://www.bankofengland.co.uk/markets/pages/money/default.aspx; Bill Winters, Review of the Bank of England's Framework for Providing Liquidity to the Banking System 1, 5 (Oct. 2012), available at http://www.bankofengland.co.uk/publications/Documents/news/2012/cr2winters.pdf

13. Id.

14. Id. at 18 (quoting "The Development of the Bank of England's Market Operations").

15. Id. at 5–6.

16. Bank of England, The Bank of England's Sterling Monetary Framework 1 (Nov. 2014), available at http://www.bankofengland.co.uk/markets/Documents/money/publications/redbook.pdf.

17. Id. at 6.

18. Id. at 6, 13; Bank of England, Contingent Term Repo Facility (2015), available at http://www.bankofengland.co.uk/markets/Pages/money/ctrf/default.aspx.

19. *See* Bank of England, The Bank of England's Sterling Monetary Framework 1, 7 (Nov. 2014), available at http://www.bankofengland.co.uk/markets/Documents/money/publications/redbook.pdf.; Bank of England, SMF Application Form—for applicants wishing to become participants in the Bank of England's Sterling Monetary Framework facilities 1 (Nov. 2014), available at.

http://www.bankofengland.co.uk/markets/Documents/money/documentation/smfapplicationform.pdf.

20. See Bank of England, Banks and Building Societies Lists (2015), available at http://www.bankofengland.co.uk/pra/Pages/authorisations/banksbuildingsocietieslist.aspx.

21. Bank of England, Terms and Conditions for Participation in the Bank of England's Operations under the Sterling Monetary Framework 1 (Nov. 5, 2014), available at http://www.bankofengland.co.uk/markets/Documents/money/documentation/smfterms.pdf.

22. Bank of England, Widening access to the Sterling Monetary Framework (2014), available at http://www.bankofengland.co.uk/publications/Pages/news/2014/144.aspx. Tobias Adrian, Christopher R. Burke, and James J. McAndrews, The Federal Reserve's Primary Dealer Credit Facility, *Fed. Res. Bank of New York Curr. Issues Econ. Fin.* 15, 4 (Aug. 2009), available at http://newyorkfed.org/research/current_issues/ci15-4.pdf

23. See, for example, Bank of England, The Bank of England's Sterling Monetary Framework: SMF operating procedures 2.1 (Nov. 2014), available at http://www.bankofengland.co.uk/markets/Documents/money/documentation/smfopprocs.pdf; Bank of England, The Bank of England's Sterling Monetary Framework 1, 7 (Nov. 2014), available at http://www.bankofengland.co.uk/markets/Documents/money/publications/redbook.pdf.

24. Id. at 13.

25. See Bank of England, The Bank of England's Sterling Monetary Framework: SMF operating procedures 2.1 (Nov. 2014).

26. Speech, Mark Carney, remarks given at the Lord Mayor's Banquet for Bankers and Merchants of the City of London 1, 10 (Jun. 12, 2014), available at http://www.bankofengland.co.uk/publications/Documents/speeches/2014/speech736.pdf.

27. Bank of England, The Bank of England's Sterling Monetary Framework 1, 6 (Nov. 2014), available at http://www.bankofengland.co.uk/markets/Documents/money/publications/redbook.pdf.

28. Id. at 6–7.

29. Speech, Mark Carney, Remarks at the 125th Anniversary of the Financial Times. Full text of Mark Carney's speech (Oct. 25, 2013) available at http://www.ft.com/intl/cms/s/0/17a07314-3d44-11e3-b754-00144feab7de.html#axzz3TNhX5iz2.

30. Bank of England, The Bank of England's Sterling Monetary Framework 1, 7, 12 (Nov. 2014), available at http://www.bankofengland.co.uk/markets/Documents/money/publications/redbook.pdf.

31. Id. at 7, 12.

32. Id. at 7, 12.

33. Bank of England, The Bank of England's Sterling Monetary Framework 1, 7–8 (Nov. 2014), available at http://www.bankofengland.co.uk/markets/Documents/money/publications/redbook.pdf; see also Bank of England, Sterling Monetary Framework: Summary of haircuts for securities eligible for the Bank's lending operations (Nov. 2014), available at http://www.bankofengland.co.uk/markets/Documents/money/publications/summary_haircuts.pdf.

34. See Bank of England, Sterling Monetary Framework: Eligible collateral 2015), available at http://www.bankofengland.co.uk/markets/Pages/money/eligiblecollateral.aspx; Bank of England, Sterling Monetary Framework: Summary of haircuts for securities eligible for the Bank's lending operations (Nov. 2014), available at http://www.bankofengland.co.uk/markets/Documents/money/publications/summary_haircuts

.pdf; Bank of England, Bank of England Discount Window Facility—Indicative pricing spreadsheet (2015), available at www.bankofengland.co.uk/markets/Documents/dwf spreadsheet.xlsx.

35. Tim Wallace, Bank of England plans to accept equities as collateral from banks, Telegraph (July 13, 2015), *available at*: http://www.telegraph.co.uk/finance/bank-of -england/11736422/Bank-of-England-to-accept-equities-as-collateral-from-banks.html.

36. Bank of England, The Bank of England's Sterling Monetary Framework 1, 12 (Nov. 2014), available at http://www.bankofengland.co.uk/markets/Documents/money/publications/redbook.pdf;

37. Id.

38. Bank of England, The Bank of England's Sterling Monetary Framework: SMF operating procedures 6.23–6.25 (Nov. 2014), available at http://www.bankofengland.co.uk/markets/Documents/money/documentation/smfopprocs.pdf.

39. Bank of England, DWF Transaction Notice (Oct. 13, 2014), available at http://www.bankofengland.co.uk/markets/Documents/money/discount/dwftrannotice.pdf.

40. Paul Fisher, Liquidity support from the Bank of England: The Discount Window Facility, Speech at National Asset-Liability Management Global Conference, London, Mar. 29, 2012, available at http://www.bankofengland.co.uk/publications/Documents/speeches/2012/speech561.pdf

41. Id.

42. Id. This determination is made at the discretion of the Bank. See also Bank of England, The Bank of England's Sterling Monetary Framework: SMF operating procedures 6.8 (Nov. 2014), available at http://www.bankofengland.co.uk/markets/Documents/money/documentation/smfopprocs.pdf.

43. Bank of England, The Bank of England's Sterling Monetary Framework: SMF operating procedures 6.9–6.12 (Nov. 2014), available at http://www.bankofengland.co.uk/markets/Documents/money/documentation/smfopprocs.pdf

44. The Bank of England's Sterling Monetary Framework 1, 13 (Nov. 2014), available at http://www.bankofengland.co.uk/markets/Documents/money/publications/redbook.pdf; Bank of England, The Bank of England's Sterling Monetary Framework: SMF operating procedures 6.14 (Nov. 2014), available at http://www.bankofengland.co.uk/markets/Documents/money/documentation/smfopprocs.pdf.

45. Bank of England, The Bank of England's Sterling Monetary Framework: SMF operating procedures 6.14 (Nov. 2014), available at http://www.bankofengland.co.uk/markets/Documents/money/documentation/smfopprocs.pdf.

46. The Bank of England's Sterling Monetary Framework 1, 12 (Nov. 2014), available at http://www.bankofengland.co.uk/markets/Documents/money/publications/redbook.pdf.

47. See, for example, Thomas M. Humphrey, The lender of last resort: The concept in history at 8, *Fed. Res. Bank of Richmond Econ. Rev.*, Mar./Apr. 1989.

48. Speech, Mark Carney, Remarks at the 125th Anniversary of the *Financial Times*, Full text of Mark Carney's speech (Oct. 25, 2013), available at http://www.ft.com/intl/cms/s/0/17a07314-3d44-11e3-b754-00144feab7de.html#axzz3TNhX5iz2.

49. The Bank of England's Sterling Monetary Framework 1, 13 (Nov. 2014), available at http://www.bankofengland.co.uk/markets/Documents/money/publications/redbook.pdf.

50. Id.

51. Ian Plenderleith, Review of the Bank of England's Provision of Emergency Liquidity Assistance in 2008–09 1, 91, available at http://www.bankofengland.co.uk/publications/Documents/news/2012/cr1plenderleith.pdf; see also Bank of England, Bank of England Market Notice, Indexed long-term repo operations and Contingent Term Repo Facility 1, (Jan. 16, 2014), available at http://www.bankofengland.co.uk/markets/Documents/marketnotice140116.pdf. The Contingent Term Repo Facility was formerly called the Extended Collateral Term Repo (ECTR) Facility.

52. The Bank of England's Sterling Monetary Framework 1, 13 (Nov. 2014), available at http://www.bankofengland.co.uk/markets/Documents/money/publications/redbook.pdf.

53. Id. at 11, 13.

54. Id. at 13.

55. Bank of England, The Bank of England's Sterling Monetary Framework: SMF operating procedures 5.23–5.25 (Nov. 2014), available at http://www.bankofengland.co.uk/markets/Documents/money/documentation/smfopprocs.pdf.

56. The Bank of England's Sterling Monetary Framework 1, 13 (Nov. 2014), available at http://www.bankofengland.co.uk/markets/Documents/money/publications/redbook.pdf.

57. Bank of England, Contingent Term Repo Facility—Results (2015), available at http://www.bankofengland.co.uk/markets/Pages/money/ctrf/results.aspx.

58. Financial Services Act of 2012, 2012 c. 21, Part 4, available at http://www.legislation.gov.uk/ukpga/2012/21/part/4/enacted; HM Treasury, Bank of England, and Prudential Regulation Authority, Memorandum of understanding on financial crisis management §1 (2012), available at http://www.bankofengland.co.uk/about/Pages/mous/default.aspx.

59. See, generally, Review of the Bank of England's provision of emergency liquidity assistance in 2008–09, Report by Ian Plenderleith (Oct. 2012), at 51 available at http://www.bankofengland.co.uk/publications/Documents/news/2012/cr1plenderleith.pdf. "The purpose of this review is to learn lessons to inform the way the Bank conducts ELA operations for individual financial institutions. Such support operations will, in due course, be conducted under the new Crisis Management Memorandum of Understanding, which was published in January 2012. The review will build on the lessons learned in relation to the ELA provided to Northern Rock in 2007, as set out in the Treasury Committee's report "The Run on the Rock."" Bank of England News Release: Court of the Bank of England commissions a set of reviews to learn lessons (May 21, 2012), available at: http://www.bankofengland.co.uk/publications/Pages/news/2012/049.aspx

60. Bank of England, The Bank Return (2015), available at http://www.bankofengland.co.uk/publications/Pages/bankreturn/default.aspx.

61. Bank of England, Changes to the Bank's weekly reporting regime 1 (Jun. 30, 2014), available at http://www.bankofengland.co.uk/publications/Documents/quarterlybulletin/2014/qb300614.pdf.

62. Id.

63. Id.; Banking Act of 2009 §245, available at http://www.legislation.gov.uk/ukpga/2009/1/pdfs/ukpga_20090001_en.pdf.

64. Bank of England, *Weekly Report* (2015), available at http://www.bankofengland.co.uk/publications/Pages/weeklyreport/default.aspx.

65. Bank of England, Changes to the Bank's weekly reporting regime 1, 2 (Jun. 30, 2014), available at http://www.bankofengland.co.uk/publications/Documents/quarterlybulletin/2014/qb300614.pdf.

66. Id.

67. HM Treasury, Bank of England, and Prudential Regulation Authority, Memorandum of understanding on financial crisis management §5 (2012), available at http://www.bankofengland.co.uk/about/Pages/mous/default.aspx.

68. Id. at §12.

69. Ian Plenderleith, Review of the Bank of England's provision of emergency liquidity assistance in 2008–09 1, 91, available at http://www.bankofengland.co.uk/publications/Documents/news/2012/cr1plenderleith.pdf.

70. Id. at 10, 57, 81.

71. See, generally, Kenneth N. Kuttner, The Federal Reserve as lender of last resort during the Panic of 2008 (Dec. 30, 2008).

72. See id.

73. HM Treasury, Bank of England, and Prudential Regulation Authority, Memorandum of understanding on Ffinancial crisis management §25 (2012), available at http://www.bankofengland.co.uk/about/Pages/mous/default.aspx.

74. Id.

75. Financial Services Act of 2012, 2012 c. 21, Part 4 §58, 62, available at http://www.legislation.gov.uk/ukpga/2012/21/part/4/enacted; HM Treasury, Bank of England, and Prudential Regulation Authority, Memorandum of understanding on financial crisis management §4 (2012), available at http://www.bankofengland.co.uk/about/Pages/mous/default.aspx.

76. HM Treasury, Bank of England, and Prudential Regulation Authority, Memorandum of understanding on financial crisis management §26 (2012), available at http://www.bankofengland.co.uk/about/Pages/mous/default.aspx.

77. Id.

78. Id. at §26, 30.

79. Id. at §32.

80. Id.

81. Id.

82. See Hanspeter Scheller, The European Central Bank, History, role and functions 1, 28–29 (2004), available at https://www.ecb.europa.eu/pub/pdf/other/ecbhistoryrolefunctions2004en.pdf.

83. European Union, European Central Bank (2015), available at http://europa.eu/about-eu/institutions-bodies/ecb/index_en.htm; European Union, Protocol on the Statute of the European System of Central Banks and of the European Central Bank, Article 2, available at https://www.ecb.europa.eu/ecb/legal/pdf/en_statute_2.pdf.

84. Id.

85. The ECB makes its mind up: The launch of euro-style QE, *The Economist* (Jan. 22, 2015), available at http://www.economist.com/blogs/freeexchange/2015/01/ecb-makes-its-mind-up; European Union, Protocol on the Statute of the European System of Central Banks and of the European Central Bank, Article 1, available at https://www.ecb.europa.eu/ecb/legal/pdf/en_statute_2.pdf.

86. European Central Bank, *Tasks* (2015), available at https://www.ecb.europa.eu/ecb/tasks/html/index.en.html.

87. Id.

88. European Central Bank, Annual Report 1999 (Mar. 2000) 1, 98, available at https://www.ecb.europa.eu/pub/pdf/annrep/ar1999en.pdf.

89. European Union, Protocol on the Statute of the European System of Central Banks and of the European Central Bank, Article 14.4, available at https://www.ecb.europa.eu/ecb/legal/pdf/en_statute_2.pdf; see also Rosa Lastra, International financial and monetary law 1, 337 (2015); Jeremie Cohen-Setton, ECB liquidity and the return of National Central Banks (Apr. 8, 2011), available at http://www.bruegel.org/nc/blog/detail/article/569-ecb-liquidity-and-the-return-of-national-central-banks/.

90. European Central Bank, ELA procedures (the procedures underlying the Governing Council's role pursuant to Article 14.4 of the Statute of the European System of Central Banks and of the European Central Bank with regard to the provision of ELA to individual credit institutions), available at http://www.ecb.europa.eu/pub/pdf/other/201402_elaprocedures.en.pdf

91. European Central Bank, Emergency liquidity assistance (ELA) and monetary policy (2015), available at https://www.ecb.europa.eu/mopo/ela/html/index.en.html; The Economist explains what emergency liquidity assistance means, *The Economist* (Feb. 8, 2015), available at http://www.economist.com/blogs/economist-explains/2015/02/economist-explains-5; European Central Bank, Introduction, The eurosystem's instruments (2015), available at https://www.ecb.europa.eu/mopo/implement/intro/html/index.en.html.

92. See European Central Bank, Collateral (2015), available at https://www.ecb.europa.eu/mopo/assets/html/index.en.html.

93. European Central Bank, Guideline of the European Central Bank of 20 September 2011 on monetary policy instruments and procedures of the eurosystem, Section 1.5, *Official J. European Union* (2011), available at https://www.ecb.europa.eu/ecb/legal/pdf/l_33120111214en000100951.pdf; European Central Bank, Guideline (EU) 2015/XX* of the European Central Bank of 19 December 2014 on the implementation of the eurosystem monetary policy framework (recast) (ECB/2014/60) 1(20), Article 2(72) (2014), available at https://www.ecb.europa.eu/ecb/legal/pdf/en_ecb_2014_60_f_sign.pdf.

94. Id.

95. Id. at Part 1, Article 2(59) and (70); see also Press Release, ECB announces a new Guideline on the implementation of monetary policy (Feb. 20, 2015), available at http://www.ecb.europa.eu/press/pr/date/2015/html/pr150220.en.html.

96. European Central Bank, Guideline (EU) 2015/XX* Article 55(a) (2015), available at https://www.ecb.europa.eu/ecb/legal/pdf/en_ecb_2015_11_signed__f.pdf.

97. Austrian Federal Ministry of Finance, Basel III changes in the regulatory framework (2015), available at https://english.bmf.gv.at/financial-sector/basel-III.html.

98. See Silvia Merler, *Preserving the Greek Financial Sector: Options for Recap and Assistance*, Bruegel (Jul. 12, 2015), http://bruegel.org/2015/07/preserving-the-greek-financial-sec tor-options-for-recap-and-assistance/; Raoul Ruparel, *ECB Asks: Are Greek Banks Insolvent?* Forbes (Feb. 20, 2015), http://www.forbes.com/sites/raoulruparel/2015/02/20/are-greek-banks-insolvent/.

99. See European Commission, *CRD IV/CRR – Frequently Asked Questions* (Mar. 21, 2013), http://europa.eu/rapid/press-release_MEMO-13-272_en.htm; Merler, *supra* note 1.

100. The Economist explains what emergency liquidity assistance means, *The Economist* (Feb. 8, 2015), available at http://www.economist.com/blogs/economist-explains/2015/02/economist-explains-5.

101. European Central Bank, The EU arrangements for financial crisis management, *ECB Monthly Bulletin* 1, 80 (Feb. 2007), available at https://www.ecb.europa.eu/pub/pdf/mobu/mb200702en.pdf.

102. European Central Bank, *The Financial Risk Management of the Eurosystem's Monetary Policy Operations* 1, 35 (Jul. 2015), https://www.ecb.europa.eu/pub/pdf/other/finan cial_risk_management_of_eurosystem_monetary_policy_operations_201507.en.pdf

103. European Central Bank, The EU arrangements for financial crisis management, *ECB Monthly Bulletin* 1, 81 (Feb. 2007), available at https://www.ecb.europa.eu/pub/pdf/mobu/mb200702en.pdf.

104. Jeff Black, ELA Funds to euro-area banks probably jumped, ECB data show, *Bloomberg* (May 29, 2012); see also ELA Procedures, see *supra* note 820.

105. European Central Bank, Emergency liquidity assistance (ELA) and monetary policy 1 (2015), available at https://www.ecb.europa.eu/pub/pdf/other/elaprocedures .en.pdf.

106. Claire Jones, Q&A: The ECB's warning shot to Greece, *Financial Times* (Feb. 5, 2015), available at http://www.ft.com/intl/cms/s/2/197a2706-ac93-11e4-beeb-00144feab7de. html#axzz3UYsL1nOk. As Tyler Durden (played by Brad Pitt) explains in the 1999 film, "The first rule of Fight Club is: you do not talk about Fight Club. The second rule of Fight Club is: *you do not talk about Fight Club."*

107. European Central Bank, Emergency liquidity assistance (ELA) and monetary policy (2015), available at https://www.ecb.europa.eu/mopo/ela/html/index.en.html.

108. Dara Doyle and Jeff Black, Frozen Europe means ECB must resort to ELA for banks, *Bloomberg* (May 24, 2012).

109. Id.; see Paul Carrel and Eva Kuehnen, ECB extends Cyprus emergency funding until Monday, *Reuters* (Mar. 21, 2013).

110. See, for example, Charles Goodhart and Dirk Schoenmaker, The ECB as lender of last resort? (Oct. 23, 2014), available at http://www.voxeu.org/article/ecb-lender-last -resort.

111. Id.; see, for example, Christos Ziotis and Jeff Black, ECB gives smallest aid increase yet for Greek banks as talks due, *Bloomberg* (May 20, 2015), available at http://www .bloomberg.com/news/articles/2015-05-20/ecb-said-to-raise-greek-bank-emergency -cash-by-200-million-euros. See also George Georgiopoulos, ed. Crispian Balmer, ECB ups emergency funding cap for Greek banks by 600 million euros, *Reuters*, (Mar. 12, 2015), available at http://uk.reuters.com/article/2015/03/12/uk-greece-banks-ecb -idUKKBN0M81GK20150312.

112. See Rosa Lastra, *International Financial and Monetary Law* 151, 378 (Oxford, UK: Oxford University Press, 2015).

113. European Central Bank, Emergency liquidity assistance (ELA) and monetary policy 1 (2015), available at https://www.ecb.europa.eu/pub/pdf/other/elaprocedures.en.pdf (the procedures underlying the Governing Council's role pursuant to Article 14.4 of the Statute of the European System of Central Banks and of the European Central Bank with regard to the provision of ELA to individual credit institutions).

114. See, for example, George Georgiopoulos, ECB ups emergency funding cap for Greek banks by 600 million euros, *Reuters* (Mar. 12, 2015).

115. European Union, Protocol on the Statute of the European System of Central Banks and of the European Central Bank, Article 14.4, available at https://www.ecb.europa .eu/ecb/legal/pdf/en_statute_2.pdf.

116. European Central Bank, Emergency liquidity assistance (ELA) and monetary policy 1, 2 (2015), available at https://www.ecb.europa.eu/pub/pdf/other/elaprocedures .en.pdf.

117. Id.

118. Letter from Mr. Mario Draghi to Mr. Andreas Pitsillides, (Jan. 28, 2014), available at https://www.ecb.europa.eu/pub/pdf/other/20140128_pitsillides.en.pdf.

119. See, for example, European Commission, *Banking Union* (2015), available at http:// ec.europa.eu/finance/general-policy/banking-union/index_en.htm.

120. Rosa Lastra, *Int.l Fin. Monet. Law* 1, 157 (2015).

121. Rosa Lastra, *Int.l Fin. Monet. Law* 1, 157, 380 (2015); Press Release, European Commission, State aid: Commission approves UK rescue aid package for Northern Rock (Dec. 5, 2007).

122. Practical Law, Northern Rock: European Commission weighs in (Apr. 28, 2008), available at http://us.practicallaw.com/9-381-4487?q=&qp=&qo=&qe=#a977796.

123. Id.

124. European Commission, Communication from the Commission on the application, from 1 August 2013, of state aid rules to support measures in favor of banks in the context of the financial crisis 2013/C 216/01 1 (2013), available at http://eur-lex.europa.eu/ legal-content/EN/TXT/HTML/?uri=CELEX:52013XC0730(01)&qid=1443291537319&fr om=EN.

125. Id.

126. Dietrich Domanski and Vladyslav Sushko, Rethinking the lender of last resort: workshop summary, 79 *BIS Papers* 1, 3, available at http://www.bis.org/publ/bppdf/bispap79a_rh.pdf.

127. Id.

128. Treaty on the Functioning of the European Union, Article 123, available at http://eur-lex.europa.eu/legal-content/en/ALL/?uri=CELEX:12012E/TXT.

129. Akina Miyamoto, Consideration of central banks' authorities as lender of last resort (LLM Long Paper, Harvard Law School, on file with author, 2014).

130. European Union, Protocol on the Statute of the European System of Central Banks and of the European Central Bank, Article 18, available at https://www.ecb.europa.eu/ecb/legal/pdf/en_statute_2.pdf.

131. Id.

132. *See* Rosa Lastra, *Int.l Fin. Monet. Law* 1, 377 (2015).

133. European Union, Protocol on the Statute of the European System of Central Banks and of the European Central Bank, Article 18, available at https://www.ecb.europa.eu/ecb/legal/pdf/en_statute_2.pdf.

134. European Central Bank, ECB: Open market operations (2015), available at https://www.ecb.europa.eu/mopo/implement/omo/html/index.en.html.

135. Paul De Grauwe, London School of Economics and Political Science Blog (Mar. 9, 2012), available at http://blogs.lse.ac.uk/europpblog/2012/03/09/ecb-lender-last-resor/; David Enrich and Charles Forelle, ECB Gives banks big dollop of cash, *Wall St. J.* (Mar. 1, 2012).

136. David Enrich and Charles Forelle, ECB gives banks big dollop of cash, *Wall St. J.* (Mar. 1, 2012); Press Release, European Central Bank, ECB announces measures to support bank lending and money market activity (Dec. 8, 2011).

137. European Central Bank, The ECB's response to the financial crisis 59, 63, 66.

138. See Peter Praet, Member of the Executive Board of the ECB, The crisis response in the euro area, Speech at Pioneer Investments' Colloquia Series (Apr. 17, 2013), available at http://www.ecb.europa.eu/press/key/date/2013/html/sp130417.en.html; Press Release, European Central Bank, Press Release, Annual accounts of the ECB for 2013 (Feb. 20, 2014), available at http://www.ecb.europa.eu/press/pr/date/2014/html/pr140220.en.html.

139. *See* Rosa Lastra, *Int.l Fin. Monet. Law* 1, 380 (2015).

140. Id. at 159.

141. Mario Draghi, President of the ECB, Introductory statement to the press conference (with Q&A) (Sep. 6, 2012), available at http://www.ecb.europa.eu/press/pressconf/2012/html/is120906.en.html.

142. European Central Bank, Verbatim of the remarks made by Mario Draghi, Speech by Mario Draghi, President of the European Central Bank at the Global Investment Conference (Jul. 26, 2012), available at http://www.ecb.europa.eu/press/key/date/2012/html/sp120726.en.html.

143. See, for example, Guntramm Wolff, The ECB's OMT Programme and German constitutional concerns 1, 27 (2013), available at http://www.brookings.edu/~/media/Research/Files/Reports/2013/08/g20%20central%20banks%20monetary%20policy/TT20%20european%20union_wolff.pdf; David Keohane, ECJ: OMT OK (ish), *Financial Times* (Jan. 14, 2015).

144. Akina Miyamoto, Consideration of central banks' authorities as lender of last resort 1, 11 (LLM Long Paper, Harvard Law School, on file with author, 2014).

145. Id. at 12–13.

146. Id. at 13.

147. Id. at 14, 19.

148. Id. at 20–21.

149. Id. at 21, quoting Bank of Japan, "independence" and "transparency" of the Bank of Japan—outline of the new Bank of Japan Act," available at http://www.boj.or.jp/about/outline/expdokuritsu.htm/ (Japan); See also Bank of Japan, History (2015), available at https://www.boj.or.jp/en/about/outline/history/index.htm/.

150. Akina Miyamoto, Consideration of central banks' authorities as lender of last resort 1, 23 (2014).

151. *Current Developments in Monetary and Financial Law,* vol. 6, International Monetary Fund 1, 181 (Feb. 2013); see also Akina Miyamoto 9/9/14 correspondence.

152. Bank of Japan Act, Japanese law translation (transl. date: Apr. 1, 2009), Chapter IV, Article 33, available at http://www.japaneselawtranslation.go.jp/law/detail/?vm=04&id=92&re=02.

153. Bank of Japan, Bank of Japan Guidelines on Eligible Collateral (2015), available at https://www.boj.or.jp/en/mopo/measures/term_cond/yoryo18.htm/#hyou1.

154. Akina Miyamoto, Consideration of central banks' authorities as lender of last resort 1, 23 (2014); Bank of Japan, *Outline of Financial System Stability* (2015), available at http://www.boj.or.jp/en/finsys/outline/index.htm/.

155. See Bank of Japan, Principal terms and conditions for funds-supplying operations against pooled collateral (2013), available at http://www.boj.or.jp/en/mopo/measures/term_cond/yoryo33.htm/; Bank of Japan, Establishment of temporary rules for funds-supplying operations against pooled collateral (Oct. 5, 2010), available at http://www.boj.or.jp/en/announcements/release_2010/un1010a.pdf; Bank of Japan, Principal terms and conditions for temporary lending facility (2014), available at http://www.boj.or.jp/en/mopo/measures/term_cond/yoryo20.htm/; Bank of Japan, On monetary policy decisions (Dec. 19, 2008), available at http://www.boj.or.jp/en/announcements/release_2008/k081219.pdf.

156. See Bank of Japan, Monetary base and the Bank of Japan's transactions (2015), available at http://www.boj.or.jp/en/statistics/boj/other/mbt/index.htm/.

157. Id.

158. Bank of Japan Act, Japanese law translation (transl. date: Apr. 1, 2009), Article 38, available at http://www.japaneselawtranslation.go.jp/law/detail/?vm=04&id=92&re=02.

159. Akina Miyamoto, Consideration of central banks' authorities as lender of last resort 1, 25 (2014).

160. Id. at 28.

161. See, for example, Transcript of the Finance Committee of the Lower House (May 7, 1997), available at http://kokkai.ndl.go.jp/SENTAKU/syugiin/140/0140/main.html (available in Japanese).

162. Bank of Japan Act, Japanese law translation (transl. date: Apr. 1, 2009), Article 38, available at http://www.japaneselawtranslation.go.jp/law/detail/?vm=04&id=92&re =02.

163. Hiroshi Nakaso, Challenging the Bagehot rules and revisiting the Secular Stagnation thesis, Luncheon keynote address (Oct. 25, 2014), available at http://www.law .harvard.edu/programs/about/pifs/symposia/japan/2014-japan/speech---nakaso.pdf; GAO, *Bank Regulatory Structure Japan* Chapter 4:2 (Dec. 1996), available at http://www .gpo.gov/fdsys/pkg/GAOREPORTS-GGD-97-5/html/GAOREPORTS-GGD-97-5.htm; Akina Miyamoto, *Consideration of Central Banks' Authorities as Lender of Last Resort* 1, 25 (2014).

164. Bank of Japan, *The Bank of Japan's Business for Ensuring Financial System Stability* 1, 156, available at http://www.boj.or.jp/en/about/outline/data/foboj08.pdf.

165. Id.

166. Id.

167. Id.; Hiroshi Nakaso, Challenging the Bagehot rules and revisiting the Secular Stagnation thesis, Luncheon keynote address (Oct. 25, 2014), available at http://www.law .harvard.edu/programs/about/pifs/symposia/japan/2014-japan/speech---nakaso.pdf.

168. Bank of Japan, *The Bank of Japan's Business for Ensuring Financial System Stability* 1, 157, available at http://www.boj.or.jp/en/about/outline/data/foboj08.pdf.

169. Bank of Japan, *On Financial Stability* (May 28, 1999), available at https://www.boj. or.jp/en/announcements/release_1999/fss9905a.htm/.

170. Akina Miyamoto, *Consideration of Central Banks' Authorities as Lender of Last Resort* 1, 25, 28 (2014); See, for example, November 29, 2003 Press Release re: Ashikaga Bank, available at http://www.boj.or.jp/announcements/release_2003/giji03122.htm/ (in Japanese).

171. Id. at 28.

172. Id.

173. Bank of Japan, *Functions and Operations of the Bank of Japan* 1, 157 (2nd ed. 2011), available at http://www.boj.or.jp/en/about/outline/data/fobojall.pdf.

174. *Id*; Akina Miyamoto, *Consideration of Central Banks' Authorities as Lender of Last Resort* 1, 27 (2014).

175. Id.

176. Id.

177. Bank of Japan Act, Japanese law translation (transl. date: Apr. 1, 2009), Article 37, available at http://www.japaneselawtranslation.go.jp/law/detail/?vm=04&id=92&re =02; Akina Miyamoto, Consideration of central banks' authorities as lender of last resort 1, 24 (2014).

178. Id.

179. Akina Miyamoto, Consideration of central banks' authorities as lender of last resort 1, 27 (2014).

180. Bank of Japan Act, Japanese law translation (transl. date: Apr. 1, 2009), Article 37(2), available at http://www.japaneselawtranslation.go.jp/law/detail/?vm=04&id=92&re =02.

181. Bank of Japan, On financial stability (May 28, 1999), available at https://www.boj. or.jp/en/announcements/release_1999/fss9905a.htm/.

182. Akina Miyamoto, Consideration of central banks' authorities as Lender of Last Resort 1, 49 (2014); Bank of Japan, *On Financial Stability* (May 28, 1999), available at https://www.boj.or.jp/en/announcements/release_1999/fss9905a.htm/.

183. BO Bank of Japan Act, Japanese law translation (transl. date: Apr. 1, 2009), Article 44, available at http://www.japaneselawtranslation.go.jp/law/detail/?vm=04&id=92 &re=02.

184. Bank of Japan, On financial stability (May 28, 1999), available at https://www.boj .or.jp/en/announcements/release_1999/fss9905a.htm/.

185. Bank of Japan, *Functions and Operations of the Bank of Japan* 1, 165 (2nd ed. 2011), available at http://www.boj.or.jp/en/about/outline/data/fobojall.pdf.

186. Board of Governors of the Federal Reserve System (2015), Statistical Release Z.1, FinancialAccountsoftheUnitedStates (Mar. 12, 2015).

187. Dodd–Frank §1101(a)(6) revises Section 13(3) of the Federal Reserve Act to require the Federal Reserve Board to "establish procedures to prohibit borrowing from programs and facilities by borrowers that are insolvent. Such procedures may include a certification from the chief executive officer (or other authorized officer) of the borrower, at the time the borrower initially borrows under the program or facility (with a duty by the borrower to update the certification if the information in the certification materially changes), that the borrower is not insolvent. A borrower shall be considered insolvent for purposes of this subparagraph, if the borrower is in bankruptcy, resolution under title II of the Dodd–Frank Wall Street Reform and Consumer Protection Act, or any other Federal or State insolvency proceeding."

188. *U.S. House passes Federal Reserve reform legislation*, Holland Sentinel (Nov. 19, 2015), *available at* http://www.hollandsentinel.com/article/20151119/NEWS/151118963.

189. H.R. 3189, the Federal Reserve Oversight Reform and Modernization (FORM) Act.

190. H.R. 3189, the Federal Reserve Oversight Reform and Modernization (FORM) Act § 11.

191. *See Id.*

192. Letter from Janet Yellen, Chair of the Federal Reserve, to Paul Ryan and Nancy Pelosi (Nov. 16, 2015).

193. Ben Bernanke, *The Courage to Act: A Memoir of a Crisis and Its Aftermath* (New York: Norton, 2015), 572.

194. See generally Henry Paulson, On the brink, *Business Plus* 1 (2011).

195. Dodd–Frank Act §1103(s)(2)(A).

196. Dodd–Frank Act §1103(s)(2)(A).

197. *See* http://researchbriefings.parliament.uk/ResearchBriefing/Summary/SN06171.

198. Jeffrey M. Lacker, The Fed as Lender of Last Resort: Comments on "Rules for a Lender of Last Resort" by Michael Bordo, Federal Reserve Bank of Richmond (May 30, 2014), available at https://www.richmondfed.org/press_room/speeches/president _jeff_lacker/2014/lacker_speech_20140530.

Chapter 11

1. Committee on the Global Financial System, Asset encumbrance, financial reform and the demand for collateral assets, 49 *CGFS Papers* 1 (May 2013).

2. Id.

3. Eric Rosengren, Speech at 22nd Annual Hyman P. Minsky Conference on the State of the U.S. and World Economies (Apr. 17, 2013).

4. See Press Release, European Central Bank, Technical features of outright monetary transactions (Sep. 6, 2012), available at http://www.ecb.europa.eu/press/pr/date/2012/html/pr120906_1.en.html.

5. Sometimes referred to as "constructive ambiguity" as well.

6. Bank for International Settlements, Re-thinking the lender of last resort, BIS Paper 79, 5–7 (Sep. 2014).

7. See Xavier Freixas, Optimal bail-out policy, conditionality and creative ambiguity, CEPR Discussion Paper 2238, Centre for Economic Policy Research 1 (1999) (finding that ambiguity may have its merits in some cases [by reducing moral hazard], but when banks are large, the social cost of their bankruptcy is too high); Haizhou Hang and Charles Goodhart, A model of the lender of last resort (IMF Working Paper 99/399, Mar. 1999) (finding that justifications for ambiguity decrease strongly in bank size due to contagion concerns); Tito Cordella and Eduardo Yeyati, Bank bailouts: Moral hazard vs. value effect, 12.4 *J. Fin. Intermed.* 300 (2003) (finding that the possible moral hazard effect of a lender of last resort is outweighed by an increase in charter value that comes from an unambiguous LLR commitment).

8. Dietrich Domanski and Vladyslav Sushko, *Rethinking the Lender of Last Resort: Workshop Summary*, BIS 1 (2014), *available at* http://www.bis.org/publ/bppdf/bispap79a _rh.pdf.

9. Evangeline Drossos and Spence Hilton, The Federal Reserve's Contingency Financing Plan for the century date change, Fed. Res. Bank of New York, 6.15 *Curr. Issues Econ. Fin.*1 (Dec. 2000).

10. Id.

11. Id.

12. Id.

13. Id. at 6.

14. Bruce Tuckman, Federal liquidity options: Containing runs on deposit-like assets without bailouts and moral hazard, Center for Financial Stability Policy Paper 1 (Jan. 24, 2012).

15. Id.

16. Id.

17. Id.

18. Id.

19. Id.

20. Press Release, Bd. of Governors of the Fed. Res. Sys. (Sep. 19, 2008); Federal Reserve, Asset-Backed Commercial Paper Money Market Mutual Fund Liquidity Facility (2010), available at http://www.federalreserve.gov/monetarypolicy/abcpmmmf.htm.

21. Ben Bernanke, Chairman, Federal Reserve, Speech at the Council on Foreign Relations, Financial reform to address systemic risk (Mar. 10, 2009), available at http://www .federalreserve.gov/newsevents/speech/bernanke20090310a.htm.

22. 1940 Investment Company Act, §18(f).

23. Barbara Novick, Rich Hoerner, and Simon Mendelson, Money market funds: Potential capital solutions, *BlackRock ViewPoint* 1, 4 (Aug. 2011), available at http://www .blackrock.com/corporate/en-se/literature/whitepaper/viewpoint-money-market -funds-potential-capital-solutions.pdf.

24. See Kathryn Judge, The first year: The role of a modern lender of last resort, 17 (Sep. 3, 2015).

Chapter 12

1. Richard Carnell, Jonathan R. Macey, and Geoffrey P. Miller, *The Law of Banking and Financial Institutions* 1, 309 (New York: Aspen, 2009) (describing deposit insurance as the "defining policy issue in US banking regulation").

2. See, for example, Milton Friedman and Anna Schwartz, *The Great Contraction 1929–1933* 1, 434–35 (Princeton: Princeton University Press, 1965) (describing deposit insurance as "the most important structural change in the banking system to result from the 1933 panic, and … the structural change most conducive to monetary stability").

3. See Asli Demirgüç-Kunt, Baybar Karacaovali, and Luc Laeven, Deposit insurance around the world: A comprehensive database 1 (World Bank, Apr. 2005), available at http://siteresources.worldbank.org/INTRES/Resources/DepositInsuranceDatabase Paper_DKL.pdf; see also Hal S. Scott and Anna Gelpern, *Int'l Fin., Trans. Policy, Reg.* University Casebook Series 1, 403–406 (20th ed., 2014) (discussing deposit insurance in the European Union), 504 (20th ed., 2014) (discussing deposit insurance in Japan), 1148–49 (18th ed. 2014) (discussing the implicit deposit insurance regime in China).

4. Douglas Diamond and Philip Dybvig, Bank runs, deposit insurance, and liquidity, 91–3 *J. Polit. Econ.* 401, 413–16 (1983).

5. Richard Carnell, Jonathan R. Macey, and Geoffrey P. Miller, The law of banking and financial institutions 1, 309–11 (New York: Aspen Publishers, 2009).

6. Fed. Deposit Ins. Corp., *A History of the FDIC 1933–1983* 1, 40 (1984).

7. Id. at 40.

8. Id. at 40.

9. Id. at 41.

10. Id. at 41.

11. Id. at 43.

12. Dodd–Frank Act §335(a)(1). During the financial crisis certain non–interest-bearing transaction accounts were subject to a temporary unlimited FDIC guarantee, which was extended until the end of 2012. Fed. Deposit Ins. Corp., Final Rule: Temporary Unlimited Coverage for Noninterest-Bearing Transaction Accounts, 12 CFR §330 (2010).

13. See Peter Wallison's support of this interpretation in FCIC Report. Financial Crisis Inquiry Comission, The Financial Crisis Inquiry Report ix, 445 (2011), available at http://www.gpo.gov/fdsys/pkg/GPO-FCIC/pdf/GPO-FCIC.pdf.

14. For examples of related proposals, see IMF, *Sovereigns, Funding, and Systemic Liquidity* (Washington, DC, Oct. 2010), 57.

15. Such a fund could be raised either ex ante or ex post.

16. Richard Carnell, Jonathan R. Macey, and Geoffrey P. Miller, *The Law of Banking and Financial Institutions* 1, 326–328 (New York: Aspen, 2009).

17. Zoltan Poszar et al., Shadow banking, 458 Federal Reserve Staff Report 1 (2012), *available at* http://www.ny.frb.org/research/staff_reports/sr458.pdf. Scope of "shadow liabilities" described in note 4. Short-term nongovernment liabilities come from the Fed's Flow of Funds Accounts and include money market fund shares (L.121 line 1); open market paper (L.208 line 1); federal funds and repurchase agreements (L.207 line 1); net securities loaned (L.131 line 20).

18. Crane Data, Money Market Fund profile (Mar. 31, 2015).

19. Crane Data, Money Market Fund profile (Mar. 31, 2015).

20. Press Release, Financial Stability Board, Proposed assessment methodologies for identifying non-bank non-insurer global systemically important financial institutions (NBNI G-SIFIs) 1 (Mar. 4, 2015), available at http://www.financialstabilityboard.org/wp-content/uploads/Press-Release-2nd-NBNI-ConDoc.pdf.

21. Inv. Co. Inst., Total net assets of the mutual fund industry by composite investment objective (2014), available at http://www.icifactbook.org/excel/data_tables/section_1/14_fb_table04.xls.

22. The premise that the government should price insurance to cover its expected losses deserves emphasis, since it separates my approach from several other approaches by focusing on covering expected losses to the insurance fund, rather than on using price as a mechanism for optimally deterring behavior that contributes to systemic risk. In this regard it also departs from the approaches to pricing insurance based on systemic risk contribution suggested by the International Monetary Fund. IMF, Global financial stability report 1, 75–110 (Apr. 2011).

23. See Milton Friedman and Anna Schwartz, *The Great Contraction 1929–1933* 1, 436 (Princeton: Princeton University Press, 1965).

24. Id. The idea behind this approach was that assuming anticipated losses to the fund had been correctly estimated, premiums collected in excess of these anticipated losses "overinternalized" the cost of providing the guarantee and accordingly should be returned to covered institutions that had paid them.

25. Id. at 434–42 (discussing the success of federal deposit insurance at "achieving … the prevention of banking panics").

26. 12 USC §1811 (2006).

27. Id. §1817(b)(1)(A), (C); Richard Carnell, Jonathan R. Macey, and Geoffrey P. Miller, *The Law of Banking and Financial Institutions* 1, 30, 316 (New York: Aspen, 2009).

28. For a detailed description of this rating and assessment system (including a definition of the CAMELS rating); see id. at 316–18.

29. Id.

30. Id. at 328–29.

31. Marcia Million Cornett, Hamid Merhan, and Hassan Tehranian, The impact of risk-based premiums on FDIC-insured institutions, 13 *J. Fin. Servs. Res.* 153, 156 (1998). This study finds that under the 1992 initial risk-based pricing system, 92 percent of banks paid one of the lowest two premiums in the nine-tiered system.

32. Andrew Kuritzkes, Til Schuermann, and Scott Weiner, Deposit insurance and risk management of the U.S. banking system: How much? how safe? who pays? *Fin. Inst. Ctr.* 1 (2002).

33. Assessments, Large bank pricing, 76 Fed. Reg. 10,672 (Feb. 25, 2011).

34. Id.

35. Press Release, Fed. Deposit Ins. Corp., FDIC approves final rule of assessments, dividends, assessment base and large bank pricing (Feb. 7, 2011). It also attempts to reduce reliance on credit rating agency ratings in determining insurance assessments. Id.

36. A large institution is one with more than $10 billion in assets, while a highly complex institution is one defined to have more than $50 billion in assets and to be "controlled directly or indirectly by a U.S. parent holding company with $500 billion or more in total assets." Barbara Mendelson and Marc-Alain Galeazzi, Client alert: FDIC approves final rule of assessments, dividends, assessment base and large bank pricing, Morrison Foerster 1, 3 (Feb. 11, 2011).

37. Assessments, Large bank pricing, 76 Fed. Reg. 10,689, 10,695 (Feb. 25, 2011).

38. Barbara Mendelson and Marc-Alain Galeazzi, Client Alert: FDIC approves final rule of assessments, dividends, assessment base and large bank pricing, Morrison Foerster 1, 3 (Feb. 11, 2011).

39. Id.

40. Morgan Ricks, Shadow banking and financial regulation 1 (Columbia Law and Econ., Working Paper 370, Aug. 30, 2010) (discussing the necessity of pricing insurance on the basis of the riskiness of the covered firm's activities as a whole).

41. For an example of this type of analysis (and the analogues of capital regulation to deposit insurance pricing), see Andrew Kuritzkes, Til Schuermann, and Scott Weiner, Deposit insurance and risk management of the U.S. banking system: How much? how safe? who pays? *Fin. Inst. Ctr.* 1, 10–14 (2002).

42. This assumes that the government is not trying to make any profit from its insurance operations, a reasonable assumption. It also, for the moment, neglects the issue of operating costs (assumed to be small in the context of the overall insurance scheme) and any "excess" premium initially required to build sufficient reserves in the new insurance fund. In the jargon of the private property and casualty insurance industry, the following

analysis assumes that the government is operating on a run-rate basis with a loss ratio of 100 percent. Constance Luthardt and Eric Wiening, *Property and Liability Insurance Principles* 3.16 (New York: Insurance Inst. of America, 4th ed. 2005).

43. The decomposition of credit risk into probability of default and loss given default is a common convention. See, for example, Darrell Duffie and Kenneth Singleton, *Credit Risk: Pricing, Measurement, and Management* (Princeton: Princeton University Press, 2003).

44. Argyle Executive Forum, Argyle conversation: Evgueni Ivantsov, head of Portfolio Risk and Strategy, HSBC, *Argyle J.* (Jun. 13, 2011), available at http://www.argylejournal. com/articles/argyle-conversation-evgueni-ivantsov-head-of-portfolio-risk-strategy -hsbc/.

45. Christine Harper, Death of VaR evoked as risk-taking Vim meets Taleb's Black Swan, *Bloomberg* (Jan. 27, 2008). For a much more detailed treatment of these issues see Nassim Taleb, *The Black Swan*, Random House 1 (2007).

46. Presumably, in a credible insurance regime, both the probability of default and the loss given default would be lower (because nondeposit creditors would not have had the incentive to run). This reflects Friedman and Schwartz's insight that liability insurance "tends to reduce the contingency insured against." Milton Friedman and Anna Schwartz, *The Great Contraction 1929–1933* 1, 440 (Princeton: Princeton University Press, 1965).

47. Robert Merton, An analytic derivation of the cost of deposit insurance and loan guarantees: An application of modern option pricing theory, 1 *J. Banking Fin.* 3 (1977).

48. Id.

49. Merton's approach to option pricing for deposit insurance, and several notable extensions to it, require the assumption of log-normal returns. See Alan Marcus and Israel Shaked, The valuation of FDIC deposit insurance using option pricing estimates, 16 *J. Money, Credit Banking* 446 (Nov. 1984).

50. Id. at 457.

51. For a discussion of related policy issues, see Hal S. Scott, *Financial Crisis Responsibility Fee: Issues for Policymakers*, Center for Capital Markets Competitiveness (Fall 2010), available at http://www.centerforcapitalmarkets.com/wp-content/uploads/2013/09/ FinancialCrisisResponsibilityFee2010.pdf .

52. This discussion about the appropriate stakeholders to charge parallels the discussion about which stakeholders should pay for TARP investment shortfalls. See *supra* part II(B) (3)(c)(i).

53. For a discussion of which creditors should be covered, see *supra* part II(B)(2)(ii).

54. Statement, Central Bank of Ireland, *Government Decision to Safeguard Irish Banking System* (Sep. 30, 2008) (declaring "a guarantee arrangement to safeguard all deposits (retail, commercial, institutional and interbank), covered bonds, senior debt and dated subordinated debt (lower tier II), with ... Allied Irish Bank, Bank of Ireland, Anglo Irish Bank, Irish Life and Permanent, Irish Nationwide Building Society and the Educational Building Society"); John Murray-Brown and Neil Dennis, Ireland guarantees six banks' deposits, *Fin. Times* (Sep. 30, 2008).

55. Gonzalo Vina and Caroline Binham, Brown lifts deposit guarantee as cash goes to Ireland, *Bloomberg* (Oct. 3, 2008).

Chapter 13

1. Inv. Co. Inst., Research & statistics, money market mutual fund assets (2015), available at http://www.ici.org/research/stats.

2. Bd. of Governors of the Fed. Res. Sys., Assets and liabilities of commercial banks in the United States (Weekly)—H.8 line 46 (2015), available at http://www.federalreserve .gov/releases/h8/current.

3. See Perspectives on money market mutual fund reforms (David Scharfstein testimony before the S. Comm. on Banking, Hous. & Urban Affairs) (Jun. 21, 2012), available at http://www.banking.senate.gov/public/index.cfm?FuseAction=Files.View &FileStore_id=ca1f8420-b2de-46dd-aee1-9a22d47b198c..

4. Inv. Co. Inst., Research & statistics, money market mutual fund assets (2015), available at http://www.ici.org/research/stats.

5. President's Working Group on Financial Markets, Money market fund reform Options 1, 26–28 (Oct. 2010), available at http://www.treasury.gov/press-center/press-releases/ Documents/10.21%20PWG%20Report%20Final.pdf.

6. Inv. Co. Inst., Research & statistics, money market mutual fund assets (2015), available at http://www.ici.org/research/stats.

7. Patrick McCabe, Bd. of Governors of the Fed. Res. Sys., The cross section of money market fund risks and financial crises 1, 4 (Sep. 12, 2010), citing Inv. Co. Inst. Weekly Data as of Sep. 10, 2008.

8. Inv. Co. Inst., Research & statistics, money market mutual fund assets (2015), available at http://www.ici.org/research/stats.

9. Daisy Maxey, Advisers prepare for changes to money-market funds, *Wall St. J.* (Feb. 18, 2015).

10. The Reserve Primary Fund broke the buck on September 16, 2008, as a result of its exposure to Lehman. On September 19, 2008, the Treasury Department announced its intention to guarantee money market fund holdings established by September 19. The program was retroactively implemented on September 29, 2008. On September 22, 2008, the SEC temporarily permitted the Reserve Primary Fund to suspend redemptions. See Sec. & Exch. Comm'n, Responses to frequently asked questions about the reserve fund and money market funds (Oct. 1, 2008), available at https://www.sec.gov/divisions/ investment/guidance/reservefundmmffaq.htm; *see also* Press Release, US Treasury Dept., Treasury announces temporary guarantee program for money market funds (Sep. 29, 2008), available at http://www.treasury.gov/press-center/press-releases/Pages/ hp1161.aspx.

11. William Birdthistle, Breaking bucks in money market funds, *Wisc. Law Rev.* 1155, 1197–99 (2010).

12. See Inv. Co. Inst. comment letter to the Sec. & Exch. Comm'n regarding the President's Working Group Report on Money Market Fund Reform Options (File No. 4–619) 1, 49 (Jan. 10, 2011), available at http://ici.org/pdf/11_sec_pwg_com.pdf (noting that "[w]ithout a federal backstop, private insurance companies would consider unlimited guarantees on money market funds' NAVs uninsurable because of the possibility of contagion").

13. Id. at 46–50.

14. Id. at 47.

15. Id. at 47–48.

16. See President's Working Group on Financial Markets, Money market fund reform options 1 (Oct. 2010), available at http://www.treasury.gov/press-center/press-releases/Documents/10.21%20PWG%20Report%20Final.pdf.

17. Id. at 28.

18. See Inv. Co. Inst. comment letter to the Sec. & Exch. Comm'n regarding the President's Working Group Report on Money Market Fund Reform Options (File No. 4–619) 1 (Jan. 10, 2011), available at http://ici.org/pdf/11_sec_pwg_com.pdf.

19. See Terrorism Risk Insurance Act §106 (2002).

20. Id. at §11 (as reported by the House, Nov. 19, 2001).

21. See Id.

22. Id. However, the PWG does acknowledge that an insurance cap would "do little to reduce their incentive to run should MMF risks become salient." President's Working Group on Financial Markets, Money market fund reform options 1, 28 (Oct. 2010), available at http://www.treasury.gov/press-center/press-releases/Documents/10.21%20PWG%20Report%20Final.pdf.

23. Edward Johnson III and F. William McNabb III, Your money market funds are safe, *Wall St. J.* (May 16, 2011).

24. Samuel Hanson, David S. Scharfstein, and Adi Sundaram, An evaluation of money market fund proposals 1 (Working Paper, May 2014), available at http://www.people.hbs.edu/dscharfstein/MMF_Reform_20140521.pdf

25. US Treasury Dept., Office of Financial Research, Asset management and financial stability 1 (Sep. 2013), available at http://financialresearch.gov/reports/files/ofr_asset_management_and_financial_stability.pdf; Chris Flood, Asset managers under fire, *Fin. Times* (Dec. 15, 2013).

26. US Treasury Dept., Office of Financial Research, Asset management and financial stability 1, 13, 22 (Sep. 2013), available at http://financialresearch.gov/reports/files/ofr_asset_management_and_financial_stability.pdf.

27. *See* Andrew J. Jalil, A new history of banking panics in the United States, 1825–1929: Construction and implications, 7 (3) *Am. Econ. J.: Macroecon.* 295, 312 (2015).

28. Sam Fleming, Stanley Fischer defends Fed's role as lender of last resort, *Financial Times* (Jul. 17, 2015), available at http://www.ft.com/intl/cms/s/0/fe83a13a-2c93-11e5-8613-e7aedbb7bdb7.html#axzz3gFlaHpvx.

29. Id.

Chapter 14

1. Viral Acharya, Hamid Mehra, Til Schuermann, and Anjan Thakor, Robust capital regulation (Ctr. for Econ. Policy Res., Discussion Paper Series 8792, Jan. 2012).

2. Martin Hellwig, Capital regulation after the crisis: Business as usual? Max Planck Institute for Research on Collective Goods (Jul. 2010).

3. Id.

4. See Samuel Hanson, Anil K. Kashyap, and Jeremy C. Stein, A macroprudential approach to financial regulation, *J. Econ. Persp.* (forthcoming).

5. Martin Hellwig, Capital regulation after the crisis: Business as usual? Max Planck Institute for Research on Collective Goods (July 2010).

6. Basel Comm. on Banking Supervision, Strengthening the resilience of the banking sector: Consultative document (Dec. 2009), available at http://www.bis.org/publ/bcbs164.htm; Press Release, Basel Comm. on Banking Supervision, Group of Governors and Heads of Supervision announces higher global minimum capital standards (Sep. 12, 2010), available at http://www.bis.org/press/p100912.pdf; Jaime Caruana, Gen. Manager, Bank for Int'l Settlements, Speech at the 3rd Santander International Banking Conference: Basel III: Toward a Safer Financial System (Sep. 15, 2010), available at http://www.bis.org/speeches/sp100921.pdf; Basel Committee on Banking Supervision, Bank for Int'l Settlements, Annex (Jul. 26, 2010), available at http://www.bis.org/press/p100726/annex.pdf.

7. Joint Press Release, Bd. of Governors of the Fed. Res. Sys., Fed. Deposit Ins. Corp., OCC, Agencies Seek Comment on Regulatory Capital Rules and Finalize Market Risk Rule (Jun. 12, 2012), available at http://www.federalreserve.gov/newsevents/press/bcreg/20120612a.htm; see Dodd–Frank Act Hearing Before the S. Comm. on Banking, Housing & Urban Affairs, 112th Cong. (Jul. 21, 2011) (statement of Ben Bernanke, Chairman, Bd. of Governors of the Fed. Res. Sys.) (noting that "the Federal Reserve ... working with other banking agencies, is on schedule to implement Basel III"). For final rule, see Regulatory Capital Rules: Regulatory Capital, Implementation of Basel III, Capital Adequacy, Transition Provisions, Prompt Corrective Action, Standardized Approach for Risk-Weighted Assets, Market Discipline and Disclosure Requirements, Advanced Approaches Risk-Based Capital Rule, and Market Risk Capital Rule. 78 *Fed. Reg.* 62017 (Oct. 11, 2013). Though Basel II was published in June 2004, it has not been fully implemented in the United States, although eight BHCs exited their parallel runs in February 2014. (The parallel run is essentially a trial run during which supervisors oversee a bank's implementation of the standards, although they are not yet mandatory.) In June 2011, the FDIC approved a rule implementing the Dodd–Frank Act's "Collins Amendment," which mandates that banks with over $250 billion in assets (those eligible under Basel II to use internal risk models) calculate regulatory capital requirements based on the Basel I standard used by smaller banks, and adhere to whichever capital requirement is higher. Federal Deposit Insurance Corporation, FIL-48–2011 (Jun. 17, 2011), available at http://www.gao.gov/assets/670/667112.pdf.

8. See Basel Comm. on Banking Supervision, International convergence of capital measurement and capital standards 1, 3 (1998), available at http://www.bis.org/publ/bcbsc111.pdf.

9. For introductory discussion to the concept of risk-weighting, see Richard Carnell, Jonathan R. Macey, and Geoffrey P. Miller, *The Law of Banking and Financial Institutions* 1, 257–63, 272 (New York: Aspen, 2009).

10. See Basel Comm. on Banking Supervision, International convergence of capital measurement and capital standards 1, 3 (1998), available at http://www.bis.org/publ/bcbsc111.pdf.

11. See Basel Comm. on Banking Supervision, International Convergence of Capital Measurement and Capital Standards 1, 3 (1998); Jaime Caruana, Gen. Manager, Bank for

Int'l Settlements, Speech at the 3rd Santander International Banking Conference: Basel III: Toward a Safer Financial System (Sep. 15, 2010).

12. Basel Comm. on Banking Supervision, International Convergence of Capital measurement and capital standards 1, 3 (1998).

13. See Basel Comm. on Banking Supervision, Basel III: A global regulatory framework for more resilient banks and banking systems 58 (Jun. 2011).

14. Ernest Patrikis, Higher minimum capital standards: Basel Committee on Banking Supervision crowns common equity king, *BNA Insights* (Nov. 30, 2010).

15. 12 CFR Part 208, 217, and 225; 78 *Fed. Reg.* 198 (Oct. 11, 2013), 75473; Davis Polk & Wardwell, U.S. Basel III final rule: An introduction, available at http://www.usbasel3 .com/tool/images/generalInfo.htm. The rule will apply to all banks, regardless of size. Small bank holding companies (generally those with under $500 million in consolidated assets) and certain savings and loan holding companies that are substantially engaged in insurance underwriting or commercial activities are excluded from the requirements.

16. Basel Comm. on Banking Supervision, Global systemically important banks: Assessment methodology and the additional loss absorbency requirement (Jul. 2011), available at http://www.bis.org/publ/bcbs201.pdf. In November 2011, the FSB released its first list of G-SIBs, which included the following 29 banks: Bank of America, Bank of China, Bank of New York Mellon, Banque Populaire CdE, Barclays, BNP Paribas, Citigroup, Commerzbank, Credit Suisse, Deutsche Bank, Dexia, Goldman Sachs, Group Crédit Agricole, HSBC, ING Bank, JP Morgan Chase, Lloyds Banking Group, Mitsubishi UFJ FG, Mizuho FG, Morgan Stanley, Nordea, Royal Bank of Scotland, Santander, Société Générale, State Street, Sumitomo Mitsui FG, UBS, Unicredit Group, and Wells Fargo. Fin. Stability Board, Policy measures to address systemically important financial institutions (Nov. 4, 2011), available at http://www.financialstabilityboard.org/publications/ r_111104bb.pdf.

17. Financial Stability Board, 2013 update of group of global systematically important banks (G-SIBs) (Nov. 11, 2013), available at http://www.financialstabilityboard.org/ wp-content/uploads/r_131111.pdf. The four banks from the 2011 list that were not included in 2013 were Banque Populaire CdE, Commerzbank, Dexia, and Lloyds Banking Group. The four banks included on the 2013 list but not the 2011 list were BBVA, Group BPCE, Industrial and Commercial Bank of China Limited, and Standard Chartered.

18. Financial Stablity Board, 2014 update of list of global systematically important banks (G-SIBs) (Nov. 6, 2014), available at http://www.financialstabilityboard.org/wp-con tent/uploads/r_141106b.pdf. The additional bank is the Agricultural Bank of China.

19. See Fin. Stability Board, Policy measures to address systemically important financial institutions (Nov. 4, 2011), available at http://www.financialstabilityboard.org/ publications/r_111104bb.pdf.

20. Bd. of Governors of Fed. Res. Sys., Risk-based capital guidelines: Implementation of capital requirements for global systemically important bank holding companies, 12 CFR Part 217; 79 *Fed. Reg.* 243 (Dec. 18, 2014), 75473.

21. Proposed rule, *Fed. Reg.* 75479.

22. Proposed rule, *Fed. Reg.* 75474.

23. Proposed rule, *Fed. Reg.* 75475.

24. This is consistent with the Federal Reserve Staff's internal memo on the G-SIB capital surcharge.

25. Table 2 surcharge estimates, multiplied by Basel III RWA as indicated on Q3 2014 FFIEC 101 Schedule A item 60.

26. Federal Reserve Board, Calibrating the GSBI Surcharge (Jul. 20, 2015), available at http://www.federalreserve.gov/aboutthefed/boardmeetings/gsib-methodology-paper-20150720.pdf; see also Final rule: Implementation of risk-based capital surcharges for global systemically important bank holding companies, 80 *Fed. Reg.* 157 (Aug. 14, 2015) (codified as 12 CFR Parts 208 and 217).

27. See generally Michael Crouhy, Dan Galai, and Robert Mark, The use of internal models: Comparison of the new Basel credit proposals with available internal models for credit risk, in *Capital Adequacy beyond Basel* (Hal Scott, ed.) (New York: Oxford University Press, 2005), 197ff.

28. Id.

29. Id.

30. Press Release, Basel Comm. on Banking Supervision, Group of Governors and Heads of Supervision announces higher global minimum capital standards (Sep. 12, 2010), available at http://www.bis.org/press/p100912.pdf.

31. 12 USC §5371 (2012).

32. Id.

33. Id.

34. The proposed rule would apply to US BHCs with at least $700 billion in total consolidated assets or at least $10 trillion in assets under custody. See Regulatory capital rules: Regulatory capital, enhanced supplementary leverage ratio standards for certain bank holding companies and their subsidiary insured depository institutions, 78 *Fed. Reg.* 51,101, 51,104 (Aug. 20, 2013).

35. See Andrew Haldane, Constraining discretion in bank regulation, Speech given at the Federal Reserve Bank of Atlanta 1, 3 (Apr. 9, 2013), available at http://www.bankofengland.co.uk/publications/Documents/speeches/2013/speech657.pdf.

36. Id.

37. Testimony before the S. Comm. on Banking, Housing & Urban Affairs, 112th Cong. 18 (Jul. 21, 2011) (statement of Hal S. Scott, Director, Comm. on Capital Mkts. Reg.), available at http://www.capmktsreg.org/pdfs/2011.07.21_Senate_Statement.pdf.

38. Press Release, Morgan Stanley, Oliver Wyman wholesale and investment banking outlook: Liquidity conundrum: Shifting risks, what it means (Mar. 19, 2015).

39. Id.; see also Press Release, Basel Comm. on Banking Supervision, Basel II capital framework enhancements announced by the Basel Committee (Jul. 13, 2009), available at http://www.bis.org/press/p090713.htm.

40. Basel Comm. on Banking Supervision, Basel III: A global regulatory framework for more resilient banks and banking systems 1 (Jun. 2011), available at http://www.bis.org/publ/bcbs189.pdf.

41. Id. at 21–27.

42. Basel Comm. on Banking Supervision, Principles for sound stress testing practices and supervision (May 2009), available at http://www.bis.org/publ/bcbs147.pdf.

43. Id.

44. See Press Release, Bd. of Governors of the Fed. Res. Sys. (Nov. 22, 2011), available at http://www.federalreserve.gov/newsevents/press/bcreg/20111122a.htm.

45. Id.

46. Bd. of Governors of the Fed. Res. Sys., Comprehensive capital analysis and review 2012: Methodology and results for stress scenario projections 2 (Mar. 13, 2012).

47. Id.

48. US Department of Treasury, 2012 Office of Financial Research, Annual Report to Congress (Jul. 20, 2012), available at http://www.treasury.gov/initiatives/wsr/ofr/Pages/2012annual_rpt.aspx.

49. See, for example, Martin Wolf, Basel: The mouse that did not roar, *Fin. Times* (Sep. 14, 2010), available at http://www.ft.com/cms/s/0/966b5e88-c034-11df-b77d-00144 feab49a.html.

50. See Press Release, Bd. of Governors of the Fed. Res. Sys. (Apr. 8, 2014), available at http://www.federalreserve.gov/newsevents/press/bcreg/20140408a.htm.

51. Hal S. Scott, Reducing systemic risk through the reform of capital regulation, 13 J. *Int'l Econ. L.*763, 773 (2010).

52. Source: Bloomberg and Company 10Ks; as of 12/31/07. Tier I common equity is calculated by adding Accumulated Other Comprehensive Income to Tangible Common Equity. Each capital ratio is calculated based on Basel I risk-weights.

53. 17 CFR §§200.30–3, 240.3a4–2 to -6, 240.3a5–1, 240.3b-17 to -18, 240.15a-7 to -9 (2004).

54. IMF, Global Financial Stability Report (Apr. 2009), available at www.imf.org/exter nal/pubs/ft/gfsr/2009/01/pdf/text.pdf.

55. Laura Chiaramonte and Barbara Casu, Are CDS spreads a good proxy of bank risk? Evidence from the financial crisis 30 (2011), available at http://papers.ssrn.com/sol3/papers.cfm?abstract_id=1666793.

56. Terminating Bailouts for Taxpayer Fairness Act of 2013, SLC, 113th Cong. §2 (2013).

57. Id.

58. Id.

59. Id.

60. H.R. 3189, the Federal Reserve Oversight Reform and Modernization (FORM) Act.

61. In the United States, implementation of the Basel III framework must also be compliant with the floors established under Section 171 of the Dodd–Frank Act (the "Collins Amendment"). The Collins Amendment requires that the minimum leverage requirements and capital requirements for nonbank financial companies regulated by the Fed as SIFIs must not be less than the requirements that apply to insured depository institutions under the Federal Deposit Insurance Act and must also not be less than the requirements in effect for insured depository institutions when Dodd–Frank was enacted in 2010, which were the Basel I requirements. On December 18, 2014, the Insurance Capital

Standards Clarification Act of 2014 was enacted, clarifying that a regulated insurance company would be exempt from these requirements "to the extent such person acts in its capacity as a regulated insurance entity." See Public Law 113–279 [S. 2270], available at http://www.gpo.gov/fdsys/pkg/PLAW-113publ279/pdf/PLAW-113publ279.pdf

62. David Miles, Jing Yang, and Gilberto Marcheggiano, Bank of England, Optimal bank capital (Discussion Paper 31, Apr. 2011), available at http://www.econstor.eu/obit stream/10419/50643/1/656641770.pdf; Brooke Masters and Patrick Jenkins, Bank researchers call for doubling equity safety net, *Fin. Times* (Jan. 27, 2011), available at http://www.ft.com/cms/s/0/1f4841ea-2a0b-11e0-997c-00144feab49a. html#axzz1CNpz1rPk.

63. Neil Maclucas and Katharina Bart, UBS, Credit Suisse face tough new capital rules, *Wall St. J.* (Oct. 4, 2010), available at http://online.wsj.com/article/SB100014240527487 04631504575531222507779044.html.

64. Klaus Wille, Swiss lawmakers approve curbing risks at UBS, Credit Suisse, *Bloomberg* (Sep. 30, 2011), available at http://mobile.bloomberg.com/news/2011-09-30/swiss -lawmakers-approve-curbing-risks-at-ubs-credit-suisse.

65. Swiss Nat'l Bank, 2012 Financial Stability Report (Jun. 2012), available at http:// www.snb.ch/n/mmr/reference/stabrep_2012/source/stabrep_2012.en.pdf.

66. Andy Winkler and Douglas Holtz-Eakin, Regulatory reform and housing finance: Putting the "cost" back in benefit–cost 1 (Oct. 25, 2012), available at http://americanac- tionforum.org/research/regulatory-reform-and-housing-finance-putting-the-cost-back -in-benefit-cost

67. Inst. of Int'l Fin., The net cumulative economic impact of banking sector regulation: Some new perspectives (Oct. 2010), available at http://www.iif.com/download. php?id=/0eTxourA+A=; MAG, Bank for Int'l Settlements, Final Report: Assessing The macroeconomic impact of the transition to stronger capital and liquidity requirements (Dec. 2010), available at http://www.bis.org/publ/othp12.pdf; Paolo Angelini et al., Basel III: Long-term impact on economic performance and fluctuations (Bank of Int'l Settlements, Working Paper 338, Feb. 2011); Scott Roger and Jan Vlcek, Macroeconomic costs of higher bank capital and liquidity requirements (Int'l Monetary Fund, Working Paper 11/103, May 2011), available at http://www.imf.org/external/pubs/ft/wp/2011/ wp11103.pdf; Patrick Slovik and Boris Cournède, Macroeconomic Impact of Basel III (Org. for Econ. Co-Operation and Dev., Econ. Dep't Working Paper 844, 2011), available at http://dx.doi.org/10.1787/5kghwnhkkjs8-en; US Government Accountability Office, Bank capital reforms: Initial effects of Basel III on capital, credit, and international com- petitiveness (Nov. 2014), available at http://www.gao.gov/assets/670/667112.pdf.

68. Phil Suttle, Inst. of Int'l Fin., The cumulative impact on the global economy of changes in the financial regulatory framework (Sep. 6, 2011), available at http://www .iif.com/emr/resources+1359.php.

69. Fin. Stability Bd., Identifying the effects of regulatory reforms on emerging market and developing economies: A review of potential unintended consequences (Jun. 19, 2012), available at www.financialstabilityboard.org/publications/r_120619e.pdf. Input for this study was received from national authorities in 35 EMDEs that are members of the FSB or an FSB Regional Consultative Group. The FSB additionally caveats that "[w] hile it is too early to be able to fully assess the materiality and persistence of the effects of regulatory reforms on EMDEs, it would be useful to monitor them on an ongoing basis as well as to share experiences and implementation lessons." Id. at 4.

70. See Comm. on Capital Mkts. Regulation, Capital study report: Use of market discipline (2014), available at http://capmktsreg.org/app/uploads/2014/07/CCMR-Capital-Study-Report-2014.pdf.

Chapter 15

1. Ernest Patrikis, Higher minimum capital standards: Basel Committee on Banking Supervision crowns common equity king, *BNA Insights* (Nov. 30, 2010).

2. Basel Comm. on Banking Supervision, International framework for liquidity risk measurement, standards and monitoring: Consultative document (Dec. 2009), available at http://www.bis.org/publ/bcbs165.pdf.

3. Press Release, Basel Comm. on Banking Supervision, Report to the G20 on response to the financial crisis released by the Basel Committee (Oct. 2010), available at http://www.bis.org/press/p101019.htm; Basel Comm. on Banking Supervision, The Basel Committee's response to the financial crisis: Report to the G20 (Oct. 2010), available at http://www.bis.org/publ/bcbs179.pdf.

4. Basel Comm. on Banking Supervision, International framework 1, 5–19 (Dec. 2009), available at http://www.bis.org/publ/bcbs165.pdf.

5. Id. at 5.

6. Id.

7. Id. at 7.

8. Id.

9. Id. at 9. Under Basel II's standardized approach for calculating regulatory capital, EU member states' sovereign debt in domestic currency is assigned a risk weight of 0 percent. Under this regime, even the sovereign debt of an EU state facing a major fiscal crisis (for example, Greece in 2011) would receive a 0 percent weighting. This type of misleading risk-weight may call into question the efficacy of an LCR metric based on a definition of high-quality asset derived from Basel II. Basel II's weighting of EU sovereign debt points to a broader potential regulatory conflict, which is also highlighted by US regulators' bullish rhetoric in the wake of S&P's recent downgrade of the country's credit. While regulators are tasked with developing rules to accurately risk-weight assets (including their own governments' debt), they must contend with their potentially conflicting interest in avoiding rapid sell-offs of their own sovereign debt in the case of a downgrade or other negative indicator.

10. See Basel Comm. on Banking Supervision, Basel III: The liquidity coverage ratio and liquidity risk monitoring tools (Jan. 2013), available at http://www.bis.org/publ/bcbs238.pdf.

11. See Basel Comm. on Banking Supervision, Revisions to Basel III: The liquidity coverage ratio and liquidity risk monitoring tools (Jan. 2014), available at http://www.bis.org/publ/bcbs274.pdf

12. See Basel Comm. on Banking Supervision, Guidance for supervisors on market-based indicators of liquidity (Jan. 2014), available at http://www.bis.org/publ/bcbs273.pdf.

13. Id. at 6.

14. Id. Indeed, in its consultative document on liquidity risk measurement, the Basel Committee has outlined runoff rates for various funding sources (e.g., minimum 7.5 percent for stable deposits, minimum 15 percent for less stable deposits, 100 percent for funding from repo of illiquid assets), but does not explain the methodology used to derive these rates.

15. Basel Comm. on Banking Supervision, Basel III framework: The net stable funding ratio (Oct. 2014), available at http://www.bis.org/bcbs/publ/d295.pdf.

16. Defined as "equity and liability financing expected to be reliable sources of funds over a one-year time horizon under conditions of extended stress." Id. at 20.

17. Id. at 20–22.

18. See id. at 21–22, tbl.1.

19. Id. at 22–24.

20. Basel Comm. on Banking Supervision, Basel III framework: The net stable funding ratio (Oct. 2014), available at http://www.bis.org/bcbs/publ/d295.pdf.

21. Id.

22. See id.

23. Basel Comm. on Banking Supervision, International framework 1, 5–19 (Dec. 2009), available at http://www.bis.org/publ/bcbs165.pdf.

24. Liquidity coverage ratio: Liquidity risk measurement, standards, and monitoring, 78 *Fed. Reg.* 71,818 (proposed Nov. 29, 2013); Liquidity coverage ratio: Liquidity risk measurement standards, 79 *Fed. Reg.* 197, 61440 (Oct. 10, 2014).

25. Id.

26. Liquidity coverage ratio: Liquidity risk measurement, standards, and monitoring, 78 *Fed. Reg.* 71,818, 71,833 (proposed Nov. 29, 2013). Id. at 71,822.

27. Id.

28. Id.

29. Id. at 71,833.

30. Id. at 71,824.

31. Id. at 71,833.

32. Id. at 71,822.

33. See Basel Comm. on Banking Supervision, Revisions to Basel III: The liquidity coverage ratio and liquidity risk monitoring tools (Jan. 2014), available at http://www.bis.org/publ/bcbs238.pdf.

34. Id.

35. See Basel Comm. on Banking Supervision, *Results of the Basel III Monitoring Exercise as of June 30, 2011* 1, 22 (Apr. 2012).

36. See Dominic Hobson, Collateral Makes the World Go Around …, *Fin. News* (Sep. 3, 2012).

37. Governor Daniel Tarullo, Liquidity regulation , Speech at the Clearing House 2014 Annual Conference, New York, New York (Nov. 20, 2014), available at http://www .federalreserve.gov/newsevents/speech/tarullo20141120a%20.htm.

38. See Ryan N. Benerjee and Hitoshi Mio, The impact of liquidity regulation on banks, (Bank of England Staff Working Paper 536, Jul. 2015), available at http://www.bankofeng-land.co.uk/research/Documents/workingpapers/2015/swp536.pdf.

39. See *Mobile Collateral v. Immobile Collateral*, Gary Gorton and Tyler Muir, Apr. 27, 2015, https://www.stern.nyu.edu/sites/default/files/assets/documents/Mobile%20Collat-eral%20versus%20Immobile%20Collateral.pdf. See also Ronald W. Anderson and Karin Joeveer, The economics of collateral (Apr. 21, 2014), available at: http://ssrn.com/abstract=2427231.

40. See William C. Dudley, Regulation and liquidity provision, Remarks at the SIFMA Liquidity Forum, Sep. 30, 2015.

41. See Mark Carlson, Burcu Duygan-Bump, and William Nelson, Whydoweneedbothli-quidityregulationsandalenderoflastresort?AperspectivefromFederalReservelendingduri ngthe2007-09U.S.FinancialCrisis (FEDSWorkingPaperFEDGFE2015-11).

Chapter 16

1. Ass'n for Fin. Mkts. in Eur., The systemic safety net: Pulling failing firms back from the edge 7 (Aug. 2010), available at http://www.afme.eu/WorkArea/DownloadAsset. aspx?id=197.

2. Id.

3. Id.

4. Id.; see, for example, Christopher Culp, Contingent capital: Integrating corporate financing and risk management decisions, 15 *J. Appl. Corp. Fin.* 46 (Spring 2002), available at http://www.rmcsinc.com/articles/JACF151.pdf (surveying forms of contingent capital); Russ Banham, Just-in-case capital, *CFO Magazine*, (Jun. 1, 2001), available at http://www.cfo.com/article.cfm/2996186/c_2984346/?f=archives; Gallagher Polyn, Swiss re strikes $150 million contingent capital deal, Risk.net (Mar. 1, 2002), available at http://www.risk.net/risk-magazine/news/1503664/swiss-re-strikes-usd150-million-contingent-capital-deal.

5. See LaSalle re-signs $100 million contingent capital program, *Business Wire* (Aug. 5, 1997), available at http://findarticles.com/p/articles/mi_m0EIN/is_1997_August_5/ai_19650965; Joe Niedzielski, Aon-LaSalle re-post $100M package, *Nat'l Underwriter Prop. Casualty* (Aug. 6, 1997), available at http://www.propertycasualty360.com/1997/08/06/aonlasalle-re-post-100m-package.

6. See, for example, Mark Flannery, No pain, no gain: Effecting market discipline via reverse convertible debentures, in *Capital Adequacy Beyond Basel: Banking, Securities and Insurance* (Hal S. Scott, ed., 2005) (proposing reverse convertible debentures for large financial institutions convertible based on pre-established market capital ratios as a miti-gant against the costs of financial distress); John Coffee Jr., Bail-ins versus bail-outs: Using contingent capital to mitigate systemic risk (Columbia Univ. Center for Law Econ. Studies, Working Paper 380, Oct. 2010), available at http://papers.ssrn.com/sol3/papers.cfm?abstract_id=1675015 (proposing contingent capital convertible into senior preferred stock).

7. See Christopher Thompson, Chinese banks issue most coco bonds, *Fin. Times* (Feb. 11, 2015), available at http://www.ft.com/intl/cms/s/0/5a99b804-b135-11e4-9331-00144fe ab7de.html#axzz3Xt778fnQ.

8. Id.

9. Id.

10. Lynn Strongin Dodds, Hybrid securities revolution is here to stay, *Investment & Pensions Europe* (Apr. 2015), available at http://www.ipe.com/reports/hybrid-securities -revolution-is-here-to-stay/10007298.fullarticle.

11. See *supra* Part II.B.1.a.

12. Simpson Thatcher, Federal Reserve adopts final U.S. bank capital standards under Basel III 8 (Jul. 8, 2013), available at http://www.simpsonthacher.com/google_file.cfm ?TrackedFile=4B46116601DDE2D896B179&TrackedFolder=585C1D235281AED9B6A07D 5F9F9478AB5A90188899.

13. Fin. Stability Oversight Council, Report to Congress on Study of a Contingent Capital Requirement for Certain Nonbank Financial Companies and Bank Holding Companies 19 (Jul. 2012).

14. Daniel Tarullo, Governor, Fed. Res. Bd. of Governors, Speech at the Peterson Institute for International Economics: Evaluating progress in regulatory reforms to promote financial stability (May 2013), available at http://www.federalreserve.gov/newsevents/ speech/tarullo20130503a.htm.

15. Swiss Fin. Mkt. Supervisory Auth., Addressing "too big to fail": The Swiss SIFI policy 12 (Jun. 23, 2011), available at http://www.finma.ch/e/finma/publikationen/Docu ments/be-swiss-SIFI-policy-june-2011-summary-20110624-e.pdf.

16. Id. FINMA's planned "Swiss finish" effectively amounts to a tier I common ratio of 10 percent of RWA, 3 percent of RWA in high trigger CoCos, and 6 percent of RWA in low trigger CoCos.

17. Basel Comm. on Banking Supervision, Proposal to ensure the loss absorbency of regulatory capital at the point of non-viability 1 (Aug. 2010), available at http://www .bis.org/publ/bcbs174.pdf.

18. *Id.* at 9.

19. William Dudley, President and CEO, Fed. Res. Bank of New York, Remarks at the Institute of International Bankers Membership Luncheon: Some lessons from the crisis (Oct. 13, 2009), available at http://www.newyorkfed.org/newsevents/speeches/2009/ dud091013.html; see also Ass'n for Fin. Mkts. in Eur., The systemic safety net: Pulling failing firms back from the edge 5 (Aug. 2010), available at http://www.afme.eu/Work-Area/DownloadAsset.aspx?id=197 (noting that contingent capital "could serve as a bridge between the prudential benefits of higher capital levels and the negative growth consequences of increased capital requirements").

20. Basel Comm. on Banking Supervision, Proposal to ensure the loss absorbency of regulatory capital at the point of non-viability 1, 9 (Aug. 2010), available at http://www .bis.org/publ/bcbs174.pdf.

21. Ass'n for Fin. Mkts. in Eur., The systemic safety net: Pulling failing firms back From the edge 7 (Aug. 2010), available at http://www.afme.eu/WorkArea/DownloadAsset .aspx?id=197.

22A. T. Berg and C. Kaserer, Does Contingent Capital Induce Excessive Risk Taking, 24 J. of Financial Intermediation 356 (2015).

22. Id.

23. Jennifer Hughes, Rabobank warns of "dangerous" bail-ins, *Fin. Times* (Nov. 8, 2010).

24. Helene Durand, After-market mars UBS bank capital first, *Reuters* (Feb. 17, 2012), available at http://www.reuters.com/article/2012/02/17/ubs-tier-idUSL5E8DG50 E20120217.

25. See Basel Comm. on Banking Supervision, International convergence of capital measurement and capital Sstandards 4–7, 14–16 (1998) (defining tier II capital as undisclosed reserves, asset revaluation reserves, general loan-loss reserves, hybrid capital instruments, and subordinated debt).

26. Simon Nixon, Lloyds banking on contingent capital for escape, *Wall St. J.* (Nov. 2, 2009), available at http://online.wsj.com/article/SB125713423970322203.html; Basel Comm. on Banking Supervision, Proposal to ensure the loss absorbency of regulatory capital at the point of non-viability 1, 11–12 (Aug. 2010), available at http://www.bis .org/publ/bcbs174.pdf.

27. Simon Nixon, Lloyds banking on contingent capital for escape, *Wall St. J.* (Nov. 2, 2009), available at http://online.wsj.com/article/SB125713423970322203.html; Basel Comm. on Banking Supervision, Proposal to ensure the loss absorbency of regulatory capital at the point of non-viability 1, 11–12 (Aug. 2010), available at http://www.bis .org/publ/bcbs174.pdf.; see also Alex Monro, New Basel proposals threaten bank sub debt, investors warn, Risk.net (Aug. 26, 2010), available at http://www.risk.net/credit/ news/1729774/new-basel-proposals-threaten-bank-sub-debt-investors-warn.

28. See, for example, Tracy Alloway, Adventures in hybrid debt, fixed income fund edition, FT.com/Alphaville (Sep. 9, 2009), available at http://ftalphaville.ft.com/ blog/2009/09/09/70851/adventures-in-hybrid-debt-fixed-income-fund-edition/.

29. Basel Comm. on Banking Supervision, Proposal to ensure the loss absorbency of regulatory capital at the point of non-viability 1, 5–6 (Aug. 2010), available at http:// www.bis.org/publ/bcbs174.pdf.

30. Id. at 12.

31. Ass'n for Fin. Mkts. in Eur., The systemic safety net: Pulling failing firms back from the edge 8 (Aug. 2010), available at http://www.afme.eu/WorkArea/DownloadAsset .aspx?id=197.

32. Ass'n for Fin. Mkts. in Eur., The systemic safety net: Pulling failing firms back From the edge 9 (Aug. 2010), available at http://www.afme.eu/WorkArea/DownloadAsset. aspx?id=197.; Basel Comm. on Banking Supervision, Proposal to ensure the loss absorbency of regulatory capital at the point of non-viability 1, 12 (Aug. 2010), available at http://www.bis.org/publ/bcbs174.pdf.

33. Oliver Hart and Luigi Zingales, Curbing risk on Wall Street 20, 26 *Nat'l Aff.* (Spring 2010), available at http://www.nationalaffairs.com/publications/detail/curbing-risk-on-wall-street (outlining a framework for protecting systemically relevant debt through the use of a cushion of loss-absorbing subordinated debt). Hart and Zingales propose using the CDS pricing on this subordinated debt as a proxy for measuring the market's estimate of the risk of the issuer and a signal to regulators for when intervention is necessary. *See also* Barbara Rehm, A shot at redemption for credit–default swaps, *Am. Banker*

(Jan. 20, 2011); Laura Chiaramonte and Barbara Casu, Are CDS Sspreads a good proxy of bank risk? Evidence from the financial crisis 29 (2011), available at http://papers.ssrn.com/sol3/papers.cfm?abstract_id=1666793 (concluding that CDS spreads provide good evidence of bank riskiness based on their strong relationship with bank balance sheet ratios through the financial crisis of 2007–2009).

34. Ass'n for Fin. Mkts. in Eur., The systemic safety net: Pulling failing firms back From the edge 9 (Aug. 2010), available at http://www.afme.eu/WorkArea/DownloadAsset.aspx?id=197.

35. See generally Nicholas Beale, David G. Rand, Heather Battey, Karen Croxson, Robert M. May, and Martin A. Nowak, Individual versus systemic risk and the regulator's dilemma, *Proc. Nat'l Acad. Sci. USA* (2011), available at www.pnas.org/cgi/doi/10.1073/pnas.1105882108 ("[T]he regulator faces a dilemma: should she allow banks to maximize individual stability, or should she require some specified degree of differentiation for the sake of greater system stability? In banking, as in many other settings, choices that may be optimal for the individual actors may be costly for the system as a whole, creating excessive systemic fragility.").

36. Kathryn Chen, Michael Fleming, John Jackson, Ada Li, and Asani Sarkar, An analysis of CDS transactions: Implications for public reporting 3 (Fed. Res. Bank of New York, Staff Report 517, Sep. 2011), available at http://newyorkfed.org/research/staff_reports/sr517.pdf.

37. Ass'n for Fin. Mkts. in Eur., The systemic safety net: Pulling failing firms back from the edge 6 (Aug. 2010), available at http://www.afme.eu/WorkArea/DownloadAsset.aspx?id=197.

38. See, for example, id. at 12–15 (comparing bail-ins to a "pre-pack recapitalisation"); Adam Bradbery, Bondholders face a push to impose bank bail-ins, *Wall St. J.* (Aug. 25, 2010), available at http://online.wsj.com/article/SB10001424052748703447004575449440499780022.html.

39. See Chris Bates and Simon Gleeson, Legal aspects of bank bail-ins 5–6 (May 2011), available at http://www.cliffordchance.com/publicationviews/publications/2011/05/legal_aspects_ofbankbail-ins.html (comparing and distinguishing creditor bail-in with contingent capital).

40. Ass'n for Fin. Mkts. in Eur., The systemic safety net: Pulling failing firms back from the edge 5, 11 (Aug. 2010), available at http://www.afme.eu/WorkArea/DownloadAsset.aspx?id=197; see also Chris Bates and Simon Gleeson, Legal aspects of bank bail-ins 5–6 (May 2011), available at http://www.cliffordchance.com/publicationviews/publications/2011/05/legal_aspects_ofbankbail-ins.html (comparing and distinguishing creditor bail-in with contingent capital).

41. Ass'n for Fin. Mkts. in Eur., The systemic safety net: Pulling failing firms back from the edge 5 (Aug. 2010) (distinguishing contingent capital from creditor bail-in, noting that the former is "a recovery (rather than resolution) tool that serves to replenish a firm's capital by converting a [specific class of] debt instrument to equity … well before a firm becomes distressed"); *see also* Wilson Ervin, Presentation at Harvard Europe–US Symposium, Cross Border Resolution Panel 11 (Mar. 2011), *available at* http://www.law.harvard.edu/programs/about/pifs/symposia/europe/2011-europe/panelist-presentations/ervin.pdf.

42. Ass'n for Fin. Mkts. in Eur., The systemic safety net: Pulling failing firms back from the edge 12–14 (Aug. 2010); Thomas Huertas, Vice Chairman, Comm. of Eur. Banking

Supervisor and Director, Banking Sector, Fin. Servs. Auth. (UK), Routes to resolution: Bridge Bank and bail-ins 4–9 (draft for discussion) (describing two related methods of bail-in, by write-down or conversion).

43. Paul Lee, The source-of-strength doctrine: Revered and revisited—Part I, 129 *Bank. Law J.* 771, 771–772 (2012).

44. 11 USC §362 (2006).

45. See 11 USC §362(a)(4)-(7) (2006) (staying, *inter alia*, creation and enforcement of liens against debtor, collections of claims against debtor, and "setoff[s] of any debt owing to debtor" against other claims); id. at §§555, 556, 559, and 560 (exempting securities and commodities contracts and swap and repurchase agreements from the coverage of Section 362).

46. Inst. of Int'l Fin., *The Net Cumulative Economic Impact of Banking Sector Regulation: Some New Perspectives* (Washington, DC, 2010).

47. See also OLA discussion in Part II.B.2.

48. Jennifer Hughes and Brooke Masters, The debt net, *Fin. Times* (Feb. 21, 2011).

49. Id.

50. Christopher Thompson, Senior bank debt issues slump to decade low, *Fin. Times* (Jun. 16, 2013).

51. Alice Gledhill, Bail-in of senior European bank debt not fully priced in, *Reuters* (Oct. 31, 2014), available at http://www.reuters.com/article/2014/10/31/banks-debt-idUSL6 N0SF34W20141031.

52. Jennifer Hughes, Junior debt in line for Moody's downgrade, *Fin. Times* (Feb. 14, 2011), available at http://www.ft.com/cms/s/0/b4edd888-386e-11e0-959c-00144fe abdc0.html#axzz1EnpiUy3Y.

53. Martin Arnold, S&P warns of higher risk in bank bail-in bonds, *Fin. Times* (Feb. 6, 2014).

54. Edward Taylor (ed. David Goodman), Update 1-S&P downgrades three Austrian banks on bail-in uncertainty, *Reuters* (Aug. 13, 2014), available at http://www.reuters .com/article/2014/08/13/austrianbanks-ratings-idUSL6N0QJ4P020140813.

55. Ass'n for Fin. Mkts. in Eur., The systemic safety net: Pulling failing firms back From the edge 11–13 (Aug. 2010).

56. See, for example, Paul Calello and Wilson Ervin, From bail-out to bail-in, *The Economist* (Jan. 28, 2010). Calello and Ervin of Credit Suisse would have applied a bail-in to enable Lehman Brothers to circumvent bankruptcy, while others would restrict use of the policy to situations in which a federal bailout was unnecessary.

57. Ass'n for Fin. Mkts. in Eur., The systemic safety net: Pulling failing firms back From the edge 21 (Aug. 2010); Wilson Ervin, Presentation at Harvard Europe–US Symposium, Cross Border Resolution Panel 9 (Mar. 2011), available at http://www.law.harvard.edu/ programs/about/pifs/symposia/europe/2011-europe/panelist-presentations/ervin. pdf.

58. See Huw Jones, Regulators sound caution on bank bail-in proposal, *Reuters* (Oct. 18, 2010), available at http://www.reuters.com/article/idUSTRE69H28X20101018.

59. Adam Bradbery, Bondholders face a push to impose bank bail-ins, *Wall St. J.* (Aug. 25, 2010), available at http://online.wsj.com/article/SB10001424052748703447004575449440499780022.html.

60. Basel Comm. on Banking Supervision, Proposal to ensure the loss absorbency of regulatory capital at the point of non-viability 2, 6, 10 (Aug. 2010), available at http://www.bis.org/publ/bcbs174.pdf; Chris Bates and Simon Gleeson, Legal aspects of bank bail-Ins 3, 13 (May 2011), available at http://www.cliffordchance.com/publication-views/publications/2011/05/legal_aspects_ofbankbail-ins.html.

61. Id. at 13.

62. George Kaufman, Living wills: Putting the caboose before the engine and designing a better engine 2 (Working Paper, 2010), available at http://ssrn.com/abstract=1599787.

63. As recommended by the 2012 IMF staff note, an effective bail-in regime must provide the resolution authority with the authority to restructure the balance sheet of all entities within a group, not merely the entity subject to the bail-in. IMF Staff Note, *supra* note 733.

Chapter 17

1. Dodd–Frank Act §203.

2. Statement of James R. Wigand, "Improving Cross Border Resolution to Better Protect Taxpayers and the Economy," Subcommittee on National Security and International Trade and Finance, U.S Senate, May 15, 2013.

3. Id. at §§102, 201.

4. Resolving globally active, systemically important, financial institutions, Joint paper by the FDIC and the Bank of England (Dec. 10, 2012), available at https://www.fdic.gov/about/srac/2012/gsifi.pdf.

5. Certain commentators seem to have overlooked this extra Dodd–Frank source of legal authority, see, for example, Paul Kupiec and Peter Wallison, The FDIC's bank holding company heist, *Wall St. J.* (Dec. 22, 2014).

6. Resolution of systemically important financial institutions: The single point of entry strategy, 78 *Fed. Reg.* 76,614 (released Dec. 18, 2013).

7. Id. at 76,620.

8. Id.

9. Id. at 76,617.

10. See Emmanuel Alanis, Hamid Beladi and Margot Quijano, Uninsured deposits as a monitoring device: Their impact on bond yields of banks, 52 *J. Bank. Fin.* 77 (2015).

11. Id. §1106(b).

12. Id. §210(h)(12).

13. Id. §210(n)(6).

14. Financial Stability Board, Adequacy of loss-absorbing capacity of global systemically important banks in resolution 1 (Nov. 10, 2014), available at http://www.financialstabilityboard.org/wp-content/uploads/TLAC-Condoc-6-Nov-2014-FINAL.pdf.

15. Term sheet items 2 and 4.

16. Term sheet item 4.

17. Term sheet item 4.

18. Term sheet item 18.

19. Total Loss-Absorbing Capacity, Long-Term Debt, and Clean Holding Company Requirements for Systemically Important U.S. Bank Holding Companies and Intermediate Holding Companies of Systemically Important Foreign Banking Organizations; Regulatory Capital Deduction for Investments in Certain Unsecured Debt of Systemically Important U.S. Bank Holding Companies, 80 Fed. Reg. 229 (proposed October 30, 2015).

20. Term sheet item 10.

21. Term sheet item 11.

22. Term sheet item 13.

23. Term sheet item 12.

24. Term sheet item 7.

25. Term sheet item 7.

26. Letter from Comm. on Cap. Mkts. Reg. to Bank for International Settlements 1, 4–5 (Feb. 2, 2015).

27. Id. at 4–5.

28. The Clearing House, Quantifying the impact of macroprudential regulation on the largest U.S. banks 1 (Working Paper 4, 2014).

29. Standard and Poor's, U.S. banking sector: Same old song and dance 19 (2014).

30. 12 USC 371c.

31. JPMorgan Chase & Co. (holding company) has an aggregate amount of loans to its bank subsidiaries of $40.809 billion. This represents loans to all of its bank subsidiaries and not necessarily entirely to JPMorgan Chase Bank, NA. However, an assumption that the entire aggregate amount is a loan to JPMorgan Chase Bank, NA, provides an upper bound on the potential debt available as a transmission channel for a capital injection into JPMorgan Chase Bank, NA, from JPMorgan Chase & Co.

32. See JPMorgan Chase & Co., Resolution plan (Jul. 1, 2012), available at https://www.fdic.gov/regulations/reform/resplans/plans/jpmchase-1207.pdf (stating "The preferred Title II strategy would ... recapitalize these businesses by contributing some or all of such intercompany claims to the capital of such subsidiaries ....").

33. See 11 USC §362(a)(4)-(7).

34. Mark J. Roe, The derivative market's payment priorities, 63 *Stan. L. Rev.* 539, 553 (2011).

35. Michael Fleming and Asani Sarkar, The failure and resolution of Lehman Brothers (2014), available at http://www.ny.frb.org/research/epr/2014/1412flem.pdf.

36. Governor Daniel K. Tarullo, Dodd–Frank implementation, at Committee on Banking, Housing, and Urban Affairs, US Senate, Washington, DC (Sep. 9, 2014), *available at* http://www.federalreserve.gov/newsevents/testimony/tarullo20140909a.htm.

37. International Swaps and Derivatives Association, Major banks agree to sign ISDA Resolution Stay Protocol (Oct. 11, 2014), available at http://www2.isda.org/news/ major-banks-agree-to-sign-isda-resolution-stay-protocol. International Swaps and Derivatives Association, ISDA 2014 Resolution Stay Protocol (Nov. 12, 2014), available at https://www2.isda.org/functional-areas/protocol-management/faq/20; FDIC, ISDA Resolution Stay Protocol (Dec. 10, 2014), available at https://www.fdic.gov/about/ srac/2014/2014_12_10_presentation_isda.pdf.

38. See, for example, Bank of England Prudential Regulatory Authority Consultation Paper CP19/15, Contractual stays in financial contracts governed by third-country law (May 2015), available at http://www.bankofengland.co.uk/pra/Documents/publica tions/cp/2015/cp1915.pdf.

39. http://www2.isda.org/functional-areas/protocol-management/protocol -adherence/20.

40. See Financial Stability Board, Recovery and resolution planning for systemically important financial institutions: Guidance on developing effective resolution strategies (Jul. 16, 2013).

41. See id.

42. See id.

43. Hal Scott, Supervision of international banking post-BCCI, 8 *Georgia State Univ. L. Rev.* 487 (1992).

44. Press Release, Federal Reserve Board (Dec. 14, 2012), available athttp://www.feder alreserve.gov/newsevents/press/bcreg/20121214a.htm; Press Release, Federal Reserve Board (Feb. 18, 2014), available at http://www.federalreserve.gov/newsevents/press/ bcreg/20140218a.htm.

45. See Financial Stability Board, Recovery and resolution planning for systemically important financial institutions: Guidance on developing effective resolution strategies (Jul. 16, 2013).

46. See Charles Goodhart and Emilios Avgouleas, A critical evaluation of bail-ins as bank recapitalisation mechanisms, (CEPR Discussion Paper 1, Jul. 2014).

47. Id. at 11.

48. Id.

49. Id. at 32.

Chapter 18

1. The DoddFrank Wall Street Reform and Consumer Protection Act requires that certain bank and nonbank institutions submit resolutions plans, colloquially referred to as "living wills," for their "rapid and orderly resolution in the event of material financial distress or failure." Implicated institutions and requirements are discussed in greater detail in the text. See, for example, Federal Reserve, Resolution plans (2015), available at http://www.federalreserve.gov/bankinforeg/resolution-plans.htm.

2. Gregg L. Rozanksy, Ned S. Schodek, and Shriram Bhashyam, *Living Will Requirements for Financial Institutions* (Shearman & Sterling LLP with PLC Finance, 2012), 2.

3. Id. at 3.

4. Id.

5. Id. at 13.

6. Michael Moore, et al., Biggest global banks shrink under pressure from regulations, *Bloomberg* (Feb. 27, 2015).

7. Id.

8. Hal Scott, The mystery of "living wills" rules for banks, *Wall St. J.* (Sep. 3, 2014).

9. Ryan Tracy and Victoria McGrane, Big U.S. banks refile "living wills" after regulatory rebuke, *Wall St. J.* (Jul. 6, 2015).

Chapter 19

1. Financial Stability Oversight Council, Proposed recommendation regarding money market mutual fund reform (Nov. 2012); and money market fund reform; Amendments to Form PF; Proposed Rule, 78 *Fed. Reg.* 36,834, 36,844 (Jun. 19, 2013).

2. Money Market Fund Reform; Amendments to Form PF; Final Rule, 17 CFR 230, 239, 270, 274, 279 (Oct. 14, 2014) (File S7-03-13).

3. Press Release, Bd. of Governors of the Fed. Res. Sys. (Sep. 19, 2008), available at http://www.federalreserve.gov/newsevents/press/monetary/20080919a.htm; Bd. of Governors of the Fed. Res. Sys., Asset-backed commercial paper money market mutual fund liquidity facility, available at http://www.federalreserve.gov/monetarypolicy/abcpMMMF.htm.

4. Press Release, Bd. of Governors of the Fed. Res. Sys. (Oct. 7, 2008), available at http://www.federalreserve.gov/newsevents/press/monetary/20081007c.htm.

5. Press Release, Bd. of Governors of the Fed. Res. Sys. (Oct. 21, 2008), available at http://www.federalreserve.gov/newsevents/press/monetary/20081021a.htm.

6. Press Release: Treasury announces temporary guarantee program for money market funds, US Dept. of Treas. (Sep. 29, 2008), available at http://www.treasury.gov/press-center/press-releases/Pages/hp1161.aspx.

7. Dodd–Frank Act §1101(a)(2), (6) (requiring lending facilities to be structured with "broad-based eligibility" with "the purpose of providing liquidity to the financial *system*, and not to aid a failing financial *company*" and stating that a "program or facility that is structured to remove assets from the balance sheet of a *single and specific company* ... shall not be considered a program or facility with broad-based eligibility") (emphasis added).

8. See 12 USC §5236(b) (2006).

9. Inv. Co. Inst., Money market mutual fund assets (Dec. 31, 2013), available at http://www.ici.org/research/stats/mmf/mm_01_02_14.

10. Money Market Funds, 17 CFR §270.2a-7 (2010).

11. James Angel, Money market mutual fund reform: The dangers of acting now, Ctr. for Capital Mkt. Competitiveness 8 (2012), available at http://www.centerforcapitalmarkets.com/wp-content/uploads/2013/08/Angel-Costs-and-Costs-of-MMMF-Reforms-draft-6.18.2012-FINAL.pdf.

12. SEC Money Market Reform Memo, Responses to questions posed by Commissioners Aquilar, Paredes, and Gallagher (Nov. 30, 2012).

13. Id.

14. iMoneyNet, Retail money funds, available at http://www.imoneynet.com/retail -money-funds/money-fund-basics.aspx#three.

15. Id.

16. Inv. Co. Inst., Report of the money market working group 1, 62 (Mar. 17, 2009), available at http://www.ici.org/pdf/ppr_09_mmwg.pdf.

17. Money Market Fund Reform; Amendments to form PF; Final Rule, 17 CFR 230, 239, 270, 274, 279 (Oct. 14, 2014) (File No. S7-03-13).

18. Id.

19. Money Market Fund Reform; Amendments to form PF; Final Rule, 17 CFR 230, 239, 270, 274, 279 (Oct. 14, 2014) (File No. S7-03-13).

20. 17 CFR 270.2a-7(a)(2) (2010).

21. 17 CFR 270.2a-7(a)(20) (2010).

22. Money Market Fund Reform; Amendments to form PF; Final Rule, 17 CFR 230, 239, 270, 274, 279 (Oct. 14, 2014) (File No. S7-03-13) at 36,834.

23. See Inv. Co. Inst. comment letter to the Sec. & Exch. Comm'n regarding the President's Working Group report on money market fund reform options 1, 34 (File 4–619) (Jan. 10, 2011), available at http://ici.org/pdf/11_sec_pwg_com.pdf

24. Presentation by David S. Scharfstein to Harvard Law School Class on capital markets regulation (Apr. 1, 2015).

25. Money Market Fund Reform; Amendments to form PF; Final Rule, 17 CFR 230, 239, 270, 274, 279 (Oct. 14, 2014) (File S7-03-13).

26. Id.

27. Id.

28. Letter from Fidelity Invs. to Elizabeth M. Murphy, Secretary, Sec. & Exch. Comm'n (Mar. 1, 2012), available at http://www.sec.gov/comments/4-619/4619-125.pdf.

29. Inv. Co. Inst., Taxable money market fund portfolio data, Report: Monthly Taxable Money Market Fund Portfolio Summary, December 2013, Table 5 (Jan. 21, 2014), available at https://www.ici.org/info/mmf_summary_131231.xls.

30. Sec. & Exch. Comm'n, Statement of Commissioner Kara M. Stein (Jul. 23, 2014).

31. Money Market Fund Reform; Amendments to form PF; Proposed Rule, 78 *Fed. Reg.* 36,914 (Jun. 19, 2013).

32. Id.

33. Id.

34. See, for example, William L. Silber, Why Did FDR's Bank Holiday Succeed? *Fed. Res. Bank of New York Econ. Pol. Rev.* 19, 21–23, (Jul. 2009), available at http://www.newyor kfed.org/research/epr/09v15n1/0907silb.pdf.

35. Adam L. Aiken, Christopher P. Clifford, and Jesse L. Ellis, Hedge funds and discretionary liquidity restrictions 116 *J. Fin. Econ.* 197 (2015).

36. See Financial Stability Oversight Council, Proposed recommendation regarding money market mutual fund reform (Nov. 2012), available at http://www.treasury.gov/initiatives/fsoc/Documents/Proposed%20Recommendations%20Regarding%20Money%20Market%20Mutual%20Fund%20Reform%20-%20November%2013,%202012.pdf.

37. European Commission, Proposal for a regulation of the European Parliament and of the Council on Money Market Funds (Sep. 4, 2013), available at http://eur-lex.europa.eu/legal-content/EN/TXT/PDF/?uri=CELEX:52013PC0615&from=EN.

38. Money-market funds face capital buffer rules in EU plan, *Bloomberg* (Sep. 4, 2013), available at http://www.bloomberg.com/news/articles/2013-09-04/money-market-funds-face-capital-buffer-rules-in-eu-plan.

39. See Samuel Hanson, David S. Scharfstein, and Adi Sunderam, An evaluation of money market fund reform proposals (2014), available at http://www.people.hbs.edu/dscharfstein/MMF_Reform_20140521.pdf.

40. Mary Schapiro, Chairman, Sec. & Exch. Comm'n, Testimony before the Comm. on Banking, Housing & Urban Affairs of the US Senate: Perspectives on Money Market Mutual Fund Reforms (Jun. 21, 2012), available at http://sec.gov/news/testimony/2012/ts062112mls.htm.

41. President's Working Group on Financial Markets, Money market fund reform options 26–28 (Oct. 2010), available at http://www.treasury.gov/press-center/press-releases/Documents/10.21%20PWG%20Report%20Final.pdf.

42. Id.

43. Id.

44. Inv. Co. Inst. comment letter to the Sec. & Exch. Comm'n regarding the President's Working Group report on money market fund reform options (File 4-619) 1, 49 (Jan. 10, 2011), available at http://ici.org/pdf/11_sec_pwg_com.pdf.

45. Daisey Maxey, Advisors weigh impact of new money fund rules, *Wall St. J.* (Aug. 1, 2014).

46. Schwab going all retail, converting Inst Shares; MMP switches to Govt, CraneData.com (Oct. 13, 2015), available at http://cranedata.com/archives/all-articles/5795/.

47. Sabrina Willmer, Federated, Blackrock mull private money funds amid rules, *Bloomberg* (Mar. 15, 2015).

Chapter 20

1. See generally Daniel K. Tarullo, Governor, Fed. Res. Bank of San Francisco Conference on Challenges in Global Finance: The Role of Asia, San Francisco, California (Jun. 12, 2012), available at http://www.federalreserve.gov/newsevents/speech/tarullo20120612a.htm.

2. See Jack Bao, Josh David, and Song Han, The runnables, *Fed Notes* (Sep. 3, 2015), available at http://www.federalreserve.gov/econresdata/notes/feds-notes/2015/the-runnables-20150903.html.

3. Data derived from unpublished manuscript of Morgan Ricks, Fed. Res., Credit market debt outstanding (Mar. 12, 2015), available at http://www.federalreserve.gov/releases/z1/current/accessible/l1.htm.

4. See http://www.federalreserve.gov/releases/cp/volumestats.htm (accessed Jun. 2, 2015); and see Fed. Res. Flow of Funds L.4 line 2. From this we assume an even distribution of maturity between 21 and 40 days, giving 84.68 percent of weekly issuance with a maturity of 30 days or less. At the end of 2014, there was $930.4 billion in commercial paper outstanding, giving an estimate of $787.9 billion = 84.68% × $930.4 billion of runnable commercial paper.

5. US Dept. of Treas. Office of Financial Research, Repo and securities lending: Improving transparency with better data 1 (Apr. 23, 2015), available at http://financialresearch.gov/briefs/files/OFRbr-2015-03-repo-sec-lending.pdf.

6. According to the flow of funds, there was $3,699.8 billion in repo at the end of 2014, see Fed Flow of Funds Z.1 L.207 line 1; The Fed had $509.8 billion in repo liabilities at the end of 2014, see Fed Flow of Funds Z.1 L.207 line 2.

7. The Treasury-backed repo portion was (0.244 * 0.977) * 3,190.0 billion = 760.5 billion.

8. See Copeland, Martin, and Walker, Repo runs: Evidence from the tri-party repo market, J. Fin. (2014) 69–6.

9. Total domestic deposits of $10,367.9 billion less $6,131.9 billion of insured deposits less $1,699 of time deposits. See FDIC Quarterly Banking Profile Balance Sheet Spreadsheet line 50 available at https://www2.fdic.gov/qbp/index.asp for total domestic deposits; FDIC Quarterly Banking Profile at 25 Table III-C available at https://www.fdic.gov/bank/analytical/quarterly/2014_vol8_4/FDIC_Quarterly_Vol8No4.pdf for insured deposits; and FDIC QBP Balance Sheet Spreadsheet line 56 for time deposits.

10. Fed Flow of Funds Z.1 L.131 line 20.

11. See Tobias Adrian, Brian Begalle, Adam Copeland, and Antoine Martin, Repo and securities lending, Fed. Res. Bank of NY Staff Report No. 529 (February 2013).

12. http://www.ici.org/research/stats (accessed Jun. 3, 2015).

13. As discussed in the body of the text, we adjust the $10.6 trillion by subtracting non-runnable components. $1.7 trillion of time deposits is removed, $100 billion of commercial paper with a maturity longer than 40 days is removed, $500 billion of reverse repo with the Federal Reserve is removed, and $230 billion of reverse repo with a maturity greater than 30 days is removed.

14. This represents $1,565.5 of net repo lending from large cash investors less $393.8 billion of Fed RRP. See Flow of Funds Z.1 L.121 line 5 for MMMF repo; Flow of Funds Z.1 L.122 line 2 for mutual fund repo; Risk Management Association Quarterly aggregate composite for securities lender repo; Flow of Funds Z.1 L.124 lines 4, 26 for GSE repo; and Flow of Funds L.100 line 7 for domestic nonfinancial sector repo. See http://www.newyorkfed.org/markets/omo/dmm/temp.cfm

15. The Treasury-backed repo portion was (0.244 * 0.977) * 1,171.7 billion = 279.3 billion.

16. Treasury Direct, Historical debt outstanding—Annual 2000–2014, available at http://www.treasurydirect.gov/govt/reports/pd/histdebt/histdebt_histo5.htm; TreasuryDirect.com, The debt to the penny and who holds it (2015), available at http://treasurydirect.gov/NP/debt/current.

17. At the end of 2014 there was $2.935 trillion US government debt with a maturity less than one year. At the end of 2013 there was $1.523 trillion US government debt with a maturity between one and two years. The debt with a maturity of one-to-two years in 2013 transitions to a maturity of zero-to-one years in 2014. Hence $1.412 trillion of the $2.935 trillion with a maturity of less than one year was issued with a maturity of less than one year. Office of Debt Management, *Fiscal Year 2015 Q1 Report* 1, 26, 28 (2015), available at http://www.treasury.gov/resource-center/data-chart-center/quarterly-refunding/Documents/February2015CombinedChargesforArchives.pdf.

18. Federal Reserve, Credit and liquidity programs and the balance sheet (2015), available at http://www.federalreserve.gov/monetarypolicy/bst_recenttrends.htm.

19. International Monetary Fund, Global Financial Stability Report 80–81 (Oct. 2014).

20. Id. at 5.

21. Cardiff Garcia, Cash Pools, Fed rev-repos, and the stagnationist future, part 1, *Fin. Times*, Alphaville (Jul. 3, 2014), available at http://ftalphaville.ft.com/2014/07/03/1890002/cash-pools-fed-rev-repos-and-the-stagnationist-future-part-1/.

22. International Monetary Fund, *Global Financial Stability Report* 80 (Oct. 2014).

23. See, for example, Robin Greenwood, Samuel G. Hanson, and Jeremy C. Stein, A comparative-advantage approach to government debt maturity, *J. Fin.* (forthcoming) (2015); see also Mark Carlson, Burcu Duygan-Bump, Fabio Natalucci, William R. Nelson, Marcelo Ochoa, Jeremy Stein, and Skander Van de Heuvel, The demand for short-term, safe assets and financial stability: Some evidence and implications for central bank policies (Fed Working Paper 2014), available at http://papers.ssrn.com/sol3/papers.cfm?abstract_id=2534578.

24. See, for example, Jeremy Stein, Monetary policy as financial-stability regulation, 127 *Q. J. Econ.* (1): 57–95 (2012).

25. Financial Stability Oversight Council, 2013 Annual Report, Chart 5.2.3 (2013), available at http://www.treasury.gov/initiatives/fsoc/Documents/FSOC%202013%20Annual%20Report.pdf.

26. Daniel Tarullo, Industry structure and systemic risk regulation, Remarks at the Brookings Institution Conference on Structuring the Financial Industry to Enhance Economic Growth and Stability (Dec. 4, 2012).

27. Id. at 10.

28. Id.

29. Id.

30. Financial Services (Banking Reform) Act of 2013, Section 142Y(1).

31. See, for example, Asli Demirgüç-Kunt and Harry Huizinga, Bank activity and funding strategies: The impact on risk and returns, 98 *J. Fin. Econ.* 626 (Dec. 2010) (finding short-term nondeposit funding increases certain measures of bank fragility); Lev Ratnovski and Rocco Huang, Why are Canadian banks more resilient? (IMF Working Paper 09/152, Jul. 2009) (finding that the ratio of depository funding to total assets was an "important predictor of bank resilience during the turmoil").

32. IMF, Global Financial Stability Report (Apr. 2009).

33. See German López-Espinosa, Antonio Moreno, Antonio Rubia, and Laura Valderrama, Short-term wholesale funding and systemic risk: A Global CoVaR approach, 36 *J. Bank. Fin.* (2012).

34. Thomas Hoenig and Charles Morris, Restructuring the banking system to improve safety and soundness (May 2011), available at https://www.fdic.gov/about/learn/board/restructuring-the-banking-system-05-24-11.pdf.

35. Id.

36. Edward Morrison, Mark J. Roe, and Christopher S. Sontchi, Rolling back the Repo safe harbors, *Business Lawyer* 1, 14–15 (Jul. 3, 2014), available at http://www.newyorkfed.org/research/conference/2014/wholesalefunding/RollingBacktheRepoSafeHarbors_Roe.pdf.

37. Id.

38. Gary Gorton and Andrew Metrick, Regulating the shadow banking system, 41 *Brookings Papers on Econ. Activity* 261 (2010).

39. Arvind Krishnamurthy, Stefan Nagel, and Dmitry Orlov, Sizing up repo (NBER Working Paper 17768, Jan. 2012).

40. Fin. Stability Bd., Shadow banking: Strengthening oversight and regulation 23 (Oct. 27, 2011), available at http://www.financialstabilityboard.org/wp-content/uploads/r_111027a.pdf?page_moved=1. See also John Geanakoplos, The leverage cycle (Cowles Found., Discussion Paper 1304, 2010), available at http://cowles.econ.yale.edu/~gean/art/p1304.pdf.

41. Ryan Tracy, Fed eyes margin rules to bolster oversight, *Wall St. J* (Jan. 10, 2016).

42. Id.

43. Id.

Chapter 21

1. Treasury Direct, Historical debt outstanding—Annual 2000–2014, available at http://www.treasurydirect.gov/govt/reports/pd/histdebt/histdebt_histo5.htm; Treasury Direct, The debt to the penny and who holds it (Mar. 2015), available at http://treasurydirect.gov/NP/debt/current.

2. See Treasury Direct, Historical debt outstanding—Annual 2000–2014, available at http://www.treasurydirect.gov/govt/reports/pd/histdebt/histdebt_histo5.htm

3. Treasury Direct, Treasury bills (2015), available at https://www.treasurydirect.gov/indiv/products/prod_tbills_glance.htm.

4. See Robin Greenwood, Samuel G. Hanson, and Jeremy C. Stein, A comparative-advantage approach to government debt maturity, *J. Fin.* 6; figure 1, panel A at 44 (forthcoming) (2015).

5. Id. at 38.

6. US Treas. Dept., Major foreign holders of Treasury securities (2015), available at http://www.treasury.gov/ticdata/Publish/mfh.txt.

7. Id.

8. http://www.treasury.gov/ticdata/Publish/mfhhis01.txt.

9. Assumes that all maturing debt is re-issued in T-Bills and that projected future deficits are also financed through T-bill issuance. Current maturity profile and deficit projections obtained from Office of Debt Management, Treasury Presentation to TBAC 1, 26 (2015), available at http://www.treasury.gov/resource-center/data-chart-center/quarterly-refunding/Documents/February2015CombinedChargesforArchives.pdf.

10. See Robin Greenwood, Samuel G. Hanson, and Jeremy C. Stein, A comparative-advantage approach to government debt maturity, *J. Fin.* 1 (forthcoming) (2015).

11. Id. at 1.

12. US Treas. Dept., Resource Center: Historical Treasury rates, 30-year nominal rates from 1990–2015 (Mar. 7, 2015), available at http://www.treasury.gov/resource-center/data-chart-center/interest-rates/Pages/Historic-LongTerm-Rate-Data-Visualization.aspx.

13. Robin Greenwood, Samuel G. Hanson, and Jeremy C. Stein, A comparative-advantage approach to government debt maturity, *J. Fin.* 6 (forthcoming) (2015).

14. This presents a greatly simplified synopsis of George Kahn, Monetary policy under a corridor operating framework, Kansas City Fed. Res. Rep. 1 (2012), available at http://www.kc.frb.org/publicat/econrev/pdf/10q4Kahn.pdf.

15. Josh Frost et al., Overnight RRP operations as a monetary policy tool: Some design considerations (Fed Working Paper 2015–010), available at http://www.federalreserve.gov/econresdata/feds/2015/files/2015010pap.pdf.

16. Federal Reserve Bank of New York, Federal funds data (2015), available at http://newyorkfed.org/markets/omo/dmm/fedfundsdata.cfm.

17. George Kahn, Monetary policy under a corridor operating framework, Kansas City Fed. Res. Rep. 1 (2012), available at http://www.kc.frb.org/publicat/econrev/pdf/10q4Kahn.pdf.

18. Id.

19. Federal Reserve, Aggregate reserves of depository institutions and the monetary base—H.3 (2015), available at http://www.federalreserve.gov/releases/h3/current/.

20. Josh Frost, Lorie Logan, Antoine Martin, Patrick McCabe, Fabio Natalucci, and Julie Remache, Overnight RRP operations as a monetary policy tool: Some design considerations (Fed Working Paper 2015–010), available at http://www.federalreserve.gov/econresdata/feds/2015/files/2015010pap.pdf.

21. Id.

22. See Benjamin Friedman and Kenneth Kuttner, Implementation of monetary policy: How do central banks set interest rates? *Handbook of Monetary Economics*, vol. 3B, 2011.

23 Todd Keister and James McAndrews, Why are banks holding so many excess reserves? Fed. Res. Bank of New York (Jul. 2009), available at http://www.newyorkfed.org/research/staff_reports/sr380.pdf.

24. "While changes in bank lending behavior may lead to small changes in the level of required reserves, the vast majority of the newly-created reserves will end up being held as excess reserves almost no matter how banks react." Id. at 2.

25. Id. at 7.

26. Fed. Res. Bank of New York, RRP counterparty eligibility criteria (Nov. 12, 2014), available at http://www.newyorkfed.org/markets/RRP-Counterparty-Eligibility-Criteria.html.

27. Id; see also list of 164 RRP counterparties at Federal Reserve Bank of New York, Reverse repo counterparties list (2015), available at http://www.ny.frb.org/markets/expanded_counterparties.html.

28. Federal Reserve Bank of New York, FAQs: Overnight reverse repurchase agreement operational exercise (Jan. 14, 2015), available at http://www.newyorkfed.org/markets/rrp_faq.html.

29. Josh Frost et al., Overnight RRP operations as a monetary policy tool: Some design considerations 5 (Fed Working Paper 2015–010), available at http://www.federalreserve.gov/econresdata/feds/2015/files/2015010pap.pdf.

30. This would convert "excess" reserves to required reserves. Todd Keister and James McAndrews, Why are banks holding so many excess reserves? Fed. Res. Bank of New York (Jul. 2009), available at http://www.newyorkfed.org/research/staff_reports/sr380.pdf.

31. Fed. Res. Bank of New York, Temporary open market operations (2015), available at http://www.newyorkfed.org/markets/omo/dmm/temp.cfm?SHOWMORE=TRUE.

32. Mark Carlson, Burcu Duygan-Bump, Fabio Natalucci, William R. Nelson, Marcelo Ochoa, Jeremy Stein, and Skander Van den Heuvel, The demand for short-term, safe assets and financial stability: Some evidence and implications for central bank policies (Fed Working Paper 2014), available at http://papers.ssrn.com/sol3/papers.cfm?abstract_id=2534578 (finding that "reverse repo agreements with the central bank are very similar to Treasury bills as a form of public supply of [short-term debt] and can … lower the incentives to issue [short-term debt]")

33. Josh Frost et al., Overnight RRP operations as a monetary policy tool: Some design considerations 1 (Fed Working Paper 2015–010), available at http://www.federalreserve.gov/econresdata/feds/2015/files/2015010pap.pdf.

34. Id.

35. Id. at 12.

36. Id. at chart 4.

37. Id. at 1.

38. Id. at 12.

39. Id. at 7.

40. Liz McCormick and Matthew Boesler, The Fed still needs to figure out how to raise rates, *Bloomberg* (Mar. 25, 2015).

41. Friedman, *supra* note 1350.

42. Josh Frost et al., Overnight RRP operations as a monetary policy tool: Some design considerations, chart 4 (Fed Working Paper 2015–010), available at http://www.federalreserve.gov/econresdata/feds/2015/files/2015010pap.pdf.

43. Id. at 12.

44. Id. at 14.

45. In theory, "borrowers who rely on funding from lenders that are more likely to run because of access to an ON RRP facility could reduce this risk by increasing the term of their funding." Id. at 15.

46. Carlson et al. (2014) discuss options to crowd-out short-term funding without greatly expanding the size of the balance sheet.

47. US Dept. of Defense, Overview (Mar. 2014), available at http://comptroller.defense.gov/Portals/45/Documents/defbudget/fy2015/fy2015_Budget_Request_Overview_Book.pdf.

Chapter 22

1. See Antonio Bernardo, Eric Talley, and Ivo Welch, A model of optimal government bailouts 2 (May 2011), available at http://www.law.berkeley.edu/files/bclbe/Model_of_Optimal_Bailouts_0503.pdf.

2. Id. at 3.

3. Ben Bernanke, Chairman, Bd. of Governors of the Fed. Res. Sys., Current economic and financial conditions (Oct. 7, 2008), available at http://www.federalreserve.gov/newsevents/speech/bernanke20081007a.htm.

4. Press Release, US Dept. of the Treasury, Statement by Secretary Henry M. Paulson, Jr. on Actions to Protect the US Economy (Oct. 14, 2008), available at http://www.treasury.gov/press-center/press-releases/Pages/hp1205.aspx.

5. European Stability Mechanism, About (2015), available at http://www.esm.europa.eu/index.htm.

6. Peter Spiegel, Eurozone bailout fund given power to "directly recapitalize" banks, *Fin. Times* (Jun. 21, 2013), available at http://www.ft.com/cms/s/0/f910151a-d9f9-11e2-98fa-00144feab7de.html#ixzz2rqmH5H87.

7. Dick Nanto. The US financial crisis: Lessons from Japan, CRS Report for Congress (Sep. 29, 2008), available at http://fpc.state.gov/documents/organization/110816.pdf.

8. Id.

9. Deposit Insurance Corporation of Japan, Operations of DIJC (2015), available at http://www.dic.go.jp/english/e_kikotoha/e_gyomu/index.html.

10. See Alex Pollock, TARP on a businesslike basis, Statement before the Congressional Oversight Panel of the Troubled Asset Program (Nov. 19, 2009), available at http://cybercemetery.unt.edu/archive/cop/20110401231809/http://cop.senate.gov/documents/testimony-111909-pollock.pdf.

11. 12 CFR pt. 208.

12. See Brookings Institute, Transcript of "The man in the middle of the TARP: A discussion with Treasury's Neel Kashkari" (Jan. 8, 2009), available at http://www.brookings.edu/~/media/events/2009/1/08-kashkari/20090108_kashkari.pdf.

13. See HM Treasury, Royal Bank of Scotland placing and open offer agreement (Oct. 13, 2008); see also Press Release, Royal Bank of Scotland, Trading update and capital restructuring (Jan. 19, 2009).

14. See Press Release, US Dept, of Treas., Treasury announces participation in Citigroup's exchange offering (Feb. 27, 2009), available at http://www.treasury.gov/press-center/press-releases/Pages/tg41.aspx; see also

AIG, Current report on Form 8-K (filed Jan. 14, 2011), available at http://sec.gov/Archives/edgar/data/5272/000095012311003061/y88987e8vk.htm.

15. In January 2011, the US Treasury exchanged the preferred stock it purchased in November 2008 for AIG common stock. As highlighted in the related Form 8-K, this 2011 recapitalization diluted the holdings of existing AIG shareholders: "the issuance of AIG Common Stock in connection with the exchange for [preferred stock] will significantly affect the determination of net income attributable to common shareholders and the weighted average shares outstanding, both of which are used to compute earnings per share." Press Release, US Dept, of Treas., Treasury announces participation in Citigroup's exchange offering (Feb. 27, 2009), available at http://www.treasury.gov/press-center/press-releases/Pages/tg41.aspx; see also AIG, Current report on Form 8-K (filed Jan. 14, 2011), available at http://sec.gov/Archives/edgar/data/5272/000095012311003061/y88987e8vk.htm. See also US Dept. of Treas., Treasury sells its final shares of AIG common stock, available at http://www.treasury.gov/initiatives/financial-stability/TARP-Programs/aig/Documents/20121212_AIG_v8.jpg.

16. See Press Release, Citigroup, Citi to exchange preferred securities for common, increasing tangible common equity to as much as $81 billion (Feb. 27, 2009), available at http://www.citigroup.com/citi/press/2009/090227a.htm.

17. See Press Release, US Treas. Dept., Treasury converts nearly half of its ally preferred shares to common stock (Dec. 30, 2010), available at http://www.treasury.gov/press-center/press-releases/Pages/tg1014.aspx.

18. See Alex Pollock, TARP on a businesslike basis, Statement before the Congressional Oversight Panel of the Troubled Asset Program 2 (Nov. 19, 2009), available at http://cybercemetery.unt.edu/archive/cop/20110401231809/http://cop.senate.gov/documents/testimony-111909-pollock.pdf.

19. See Id; see also Charles Calomiris, Bank failures in theory and history: The Great Depression and other "contagious" events 9–10 (NBER, Working Paper 13597, Nov. 2007), available at http://www.nber.org/papers/w13597; Hearing before the Congressional Oversight Panel Hearing to Examine Government Responses to Major Banking Crises of the 20th Century 4–5 (Statement of Eugene White, Mar. 2009), http://cybercemetery.unt.edu/archive/cop/20110401231927/http://cop.senate.gov/documents/testimony-031909-white.pdf.

20. See Charles Calomiris, Bank failures in theory and history: The Great Depression and other "contagious" events 9–10 (NBER, Working Paper 13597, Nov. 2007), available at http://www.nber.org/papers/w13597.

21. See Susanne Craig, Matthew Karnitschnig, and Aaron Lucchetti, Buffet to invest $5 billion in Goldman, *Wall St. J.* (Sep. 24, 2008).

22. See Charles Calomiris, Bank failures in theory and history: The Great Depression and other "contagious" events 4 (NBER, Working Paper 13597, Nov. 2007), available at

http://www.nber.org/papers/w13597; see also Dinara Bayazitova and Anil Shivdasani, Assessing TARP, 25 *Rev. Fin. Stud.* 377, 378 (2012).

23. See Pietro Veronesi and Luigi Zingales, Paulson's gift 5 (Oct. 2009), available at http://faculty.chicagobooth.edu/brian.barry/igm/P_gift.pdf. The concept of debt over-hang was first formalized in Stewart C. Myers, The Determinants of Corporate Borrow-ing, 5 *J. Fin. Econ.* 147 (1977).

24. See Douglas Diamond and Raghuram Rajan, Fear of fire sales and the credit freeze 1 (BIS Working Paper 305, Mar. 2010), available at http://www.bis.org/publ/work305.pdf.

25. Robin Greenwood, Samuel G. Hanson, and Jeremy C. Stein, A comparative-advan-tage approach to government debt maturity, *J. Fin.* 3 (forthcoming) (2015).

26. *See* Financial Crisis Inquiry Comission, The financial crisis inquiry report ix, 339 (2011), available at http://www.gpo.gov/fdsys/pkg/GPO-FCIC/pdf/GPO-FCIC.pdf.

27. Edmund Andrews and Michael Merced, Fed's $85 billion loan rescues insurer, *NY Times* (Sep. 16, 2008).

28. See Mark Landler and Steven Lee Myers, Congress grills Paulson and Bernanke on rescue plan, *NY Times* (Sep. 23, 2008).

29. See Carl Hulse and David M. Herszenhorn, House rejects bailout package, 228–205; stocks plunge, *NY Times* (Sep. 29, 2008).

30. On September 29, 2008 the S&P500 opened at 1209.07 and closed at 1106.42, an 8.48 percent decline. Yahoo! Finance.

31. See David Herszenhorn, Bailout plan wins approval; Democrats vow tighter rules, *NY Times* (Oct. 3, 2008).

32. Emergency Economic Stabilization Act of 2008, Pub. L. No. 110–343, 122 Stat. 3765. For a general discussion on how TARP could have been improved, see Charles Calomiris and Urooj Khan, An assessment of TARP assistance to financial institutions, *J. Econ. Perspect.*, 29 Spring 2015.

33. See Office of the Special Inspector General for the Troubled Asset Relief Program, Quarterly Report to Congress 76 (Jul. 28, 2011), available at https://www.sigtarp.gov/Quarterly%20Reports/July2011_Quarterly_Report_to_Congress.pdf.

34. See Mark Landler and Eric Dash, Drama behind a $250 billion banking deal, *NY Times* (Oct. 14, 2008).

35. Office of the Special Inspector General for the Troubled Asset Relief Program, Quar-terly Report to Congress 76 (Jul. 28, 2011), available at https://www.sigtarp.gov/Quarterly%20Reports/July2011_Quarterly_Report_to_Congress.pdf.

36. See Oversight of Implementation of the Emergency Economic Stabilization Act of 2008 and of Government Lending and Insurance Facilities; Impact on Economy and Credit Availability before the H. Comm. on Fin. Servs., 110th Cong. 7 (2008) (statement of Alan S. Blinder, Professor of Economics and Co-director of the Center for Economic Policy Studies, Princeton University).

37. *See* Elizabeth Williamson, Rescue cash lures thousands of banks, *Wall St. J.* (Nov. 3, 2008).

38. See Office of the Special Inspector General for the Troubled Asset Relief Program, Quarterly Report to Congress 76 (Jul. 28, 2011), available at https://www.sigtarp.gov/Quarterly%20Reports/July2011_Quarterly_Report_to_Congress.pdf.

39. One of the initial nine institutions, Merrill Lynch, was acquired by Bank of America and the $10 billion investment for Merrill Lynch was later provided to Bank of America after the acquisition.

40. See Office of the Special Inspector General for the Troubled Asset Relief Program, Quarterly Report to Congress 77 (Jul. 28, 2011), available at https://www.sigtarp.gov/Quarterly%20Reports/July2011_Quarterly_Report_to_Congress.pdf.

41. Id.

42. See Capital Purchase Program, US Dept. of Treas., available at http://www.treasury.gov/initiatives/financial-stability/programs/investment-programs/cpp/Pages/capitalpurchaseprogram.aspx.

43. Id.

44. For a list of banks issuing subordinated debts to the Treasury, see Transactions Report-Investment Programs, US Dept. of Treas., available at http://www.treasury.gov/initiatives/financial-stability/briefing-room/reports/tarp-transactions/DocumentsTARPTransactions/11-10-11%20Transactions%20Report%20as%20of%2011-09-11_INVESTMENT.pdf.

45. See Timothy Massad, Report to Congressional Oversight Panel for Economic Stabilization: Legal Analysis of the Investments by the US Department of the Treasury in Financial Institutions under the Troubled Asset Relief Program 3 (Jan. 27, 2009), available at http://cybercemetery.unt.edu/archive/cop/20110402034824/http://cop.senate.gov/documents/cop-020609-report-dpvaluation-legal.pdf.

46. As of March 6, 2015, two additional institutions had exited, bringing the tally of remaining institutions to 32. US Government Accountability Office, Troubled asset relief program: Winding down the Capital Purchase Program, GAO 15–367 2 (Mar. 6, 2015), available at http://www.gao.gov/assets/670/668904.pdf.

47. Id. at 4.

48. See Id. at 4; See also Office of the Special Inspector General for the Troubled Asset Relief Program, Quarterly Report to Congress 162 (Jan. 28, 2015), available at http://www.sigtarp.gov/Quarterly%20Reports/January_28_2015_Report_to_Congress.pdf.

49. US Government Accountability Office, Troubled asset relief program: Winding down the Capital Purchase Program, GAO 15–367 4 (Mar. 6, 2015), *available at:* http://www.gao.gov/assets/670/668904.pdf.

50. Emergency Economic Stabilization Act of 2008 ("EESA"), Pub L No 110–343, 122 Stat 3765 §120.

51. US Government Accountability Office, Troubled asset relief program: Treasury's framework for deciding to extend TARP was sufficient but could be strengthened for future decisions, GAO 10–531 (Jun. 2010), available at http://www.gao.gov/new.items/d10531.pdf .

52. Dodd–Frank Wall Street Reform and Consumer Protection Act, Pub. L. No. 111–203, 124 Stat. 1376 (2010) Section 1302(1).

53. Id. at 1302(2).

54. Emergency Economic Stabilization Act of 2008 ("EESA"), Pub L No 110–343, 122 Stat 3765 §106(d).

55. Dodd–Frank Wall Street Reform and Consumer Protection Act, Pub. L. No. 111–203, 124 Stat. 1376 (2010) Section 1302(1)(B) and (2).

56. Emergency Economic Stabilization Act of 2008 ("EESA"), Pub L No 110–343, 122 Stat 3765 §106(e).

57. US Dept. of Treas., Financial stability, bank investment programs, available at http://www.treasury.gov/initiatives/financial-stability/TARP-Programs/bank-investment-programs/Pages/default.aspx: "No more taxpayer money is being invested in banks under TARP"; see also, US Dept. of Treas., Troubled asset relief program, Monthly Report to Congress, May 2015 (Jun. 10, 2015); See also Adam Hodge, US Dept. of Treas., Treasury notes "The wind down of TARP is almost complete" (Dec. 30, 2013), available at http://www.treasury.gov/connect/blog/Pages/The-Wind-Down-of-TARP-is-Almost-Complete.aspx

58. US Government Accountability Office, Troubled asset relief program 1, 4 (Jan. 2015), available at http://www.gao.gov/assets/670/667833.pdf.

59. Charles Calomiris and Urooj Khan, An assessment of TARP assistance to financial institutions, *J. Econ. Perspect.*, 29 Spring 2015, at 58.

60. Congressional Budget Office, Report on the troubled asset relief program 1, 6 (May 2013), available at http://www.cbo.gov/sites/default/files/cbofiles/attachments/44256_TARP.pdf.

61. Id. at 6.

62. Id.

63. US Treas. Dept., AIG WRAP-UP: Treasury sells final shares of AIG common stock, positive return on overall $182 billion AIG commitment is now $22.7 billion (Dec. 12, 2012), available at http://www.treasury.gov/connect/blog/Pages/AIG-wrapup.aspx.

64. US Government Accountability Office, Troubled asset relief program 1, 5 (Jan. 2015), available at http://www.gao.gov/assets/670/667833.pdf.

65. Id. at 5.

66. Id. at 5.

67. Id. at 5.

68. Id. at 5.

69. Id. at 4.

70. Calomiris, *supra* note 1419 at 59.

71. USGAO TARP report, *supra* note 1424 at 4.

72. Id. at 10; Office of the Management and Budget, Budget of the U.S. Government, Fiscal Year 2015, https://www.whitehouse.gov/sites/default/files/omb/budget/fy2015/assets/budget.pdf.

73. US Department of the Treasury, TARP Tracker, (accessed Oct. 9, 2015), available at: http://www.treasury.gov/initiatives/financial-stability/reports/Pages/TARP-Tracker .aspx.

74. CNN, Mortgage bailout now profitable for taxpayers (2014), available at http://money.cnn.com/2014/02/21/news/economy/fannie-profit-bailout/.

75. US Government Accountability Office, Troubled asset relief program 1, 26 (Jan. 2015), available at http://www.gao.gov/assets/670/667833.pdf.

76. Id. at 6.

77. Id. at 7–8.

78. Id. at 8.

79. Id. at 26.

80. Id. at 33.

81. Id. at 33–34.

Chapter 23

1. See Alex Pollock, TARP on a businesslike basis, Statement before the Congressional Oversight Panel of the Troubled Asset Program 6 (Nov. 19, 2009), available at http://cybercemetery.unt.edu/archive/cop/20110401231809/http://cop.senate.gov/documents/testimony-111909-pollock.pdf.

2. See Fed. Deposit Ins. Corp., Managing the crisis: The FDIC and RTC experience 558 (1998), available at http://www.fdic.gov/bank/historical/managing/history2-04.pdf.

3. See Timothy Curry and Lynn Shibut, The cost of the savings and loan crisis: Truth and consequences, 13 *FDIC Banking Rev.* 26, 33 (2000), available at http://www.fdic.gov/bank/analytical/banking/2000dec/brv13n2_2.pdf.

4. See Timothy Massad, Report to Congressional Oversight Panel for Economic Stabilization: Legal Analysis of the Investments by the US Department of the Treasury in Financial Institutions under the Troubled Asset Relief Program 2 (Jan. 27, 2009), available at http://cybercemetery.unt.edu/archive/cop/20110402034824/http://cop.senate.gov/documents/cop-020609-report-dpvaluation-legal.pdf.

5. Pub. L. 110–343, §134, 122 Stat. 3765, 3798.

6. See Office of Mgmt. and Budget, Fiscal Year 2014 Budget of the US Gov't 18–19 (Apr. 10, 2013), available at http://www.whitehouse.gov/sites/default/files/omb/budget/fy2014/assets/budget.pdf..

7. See Id.

8. See IMF, A fair and substantial contribution by the financial sector: Final Report for the G-20 (Jun. 2010), available at http://www.imf.org/external/np/g20/pdf/062710b .pdf.

9. See Hal Scott, Financial crisis responsibility fee: Issues for policy makers (2010), available at http://www.uschamber.com/sites/default/files/reports/FinancialCrisis ResponsibilityFee2010.pdf.

10. See Press Release, Eur. Comm'n, Financial transaction tax: Making the financial sector pay its fair share (Sep. 28, 2011), available at http://europa.eu/rapid/pressReleas esAction.do?reference=IP/11/1085&format=HTML&aged=0&language=EN&guiLangu age=en.

11. MEPs back financial transaction tax, *EuroNews* (May 23, 2012), available at http:// www.euronews.com/2012/05/23/meps-back-financial-transaction-tax/.

12. EU approves financial transactions tax, *Reuters* (Jan. 22, 2013), available at http:// www.cnbc.com/id/100395362.

13. Leigh Thomas, EU's Moscovici sees financial transaction tax in place early 2017, Reuters (July 8, 2015), available at http://www.reuters.com/article/2015/07/08/ eu-tax-idUSL8N0ZO1YC20150708.

14. George Parker and Quentin Peel, Germany rebukes UK over Tobin tax opposition, *Fin. Times* (Nov. 15, 2011).

15. Press Release, Eur. Comm'n, Financial transaction tax: Making the financial sector pay its fair share (Sep. 28, 2011), available at http://europa.eu/rapid/pressReleases Action.do?reference=IP/11/1085&format=HTML&aged=0&language=EN&guiLanguag e=en.

16. John Vella, Clemens Fuest, and Tim Schmidt-Eisenlohr, The EU Commission's proposal for a financial transactions tax 8–9 (Draft prepared for Brit. Tax Rev., Nov. 8, 2011), available at http://www.sbs.ox.ac.uk/sites/default/files/Business_Taxation/Docs/ Publications/Working_Papers/Series_11/WP1117.pdf.

17. Id.

18. Jackie Calmes, Obama weighs tax on banks to cut deficit, *NY Times* (Jan. 11, 2010).

19. *See* Hal Scott, Financial crisis responsibility fee: Issues for policy makers 9 (2010), available at http://www.uschamber.com/sites/default/files/reports/FinancialCrisis ResponsibilityFee2010.pdf.

20. See Alex Pollock, TARP on a businesslike basis, Statement before the Congressional Oversight Panel of the Troubled Asset Program 7 (Nov. 19, 2009), available at http:// cybercemetery.unt.edu/archive/cop/20110401231809/http://cop.senate.gov/docu ments/testimony-111909-pollock.pdf.

21. See Bo Lundgren, Testimony of Bo Lundgren, Director General, Swedish National Debt Office before the Congressional Oversight Panel (Mar. 19, 2009), available at http:// cybercemetery.unt.edu/archive/cop/20110401231927/http://cop.senate.gov/docu ments/testimony-031909-lundgren.pdf.

22. See Hal S. Scott and Anna Gelpern, *International Finance, Transactions, Policy, and Regulation,* University Casebook Series 1, 476–478 (New York: Foundation Press, 20th ed. 2014).

23. Id. at 483–489.

24. See Cong. Oversight Panel, April Oversight report 56–59 (Apr. 7, 2009), http:// cybercemetery.unt.edu/archive/cop/20110401232137/http://cop.senate.gov/docu ments/cop-040709-report.pdf.

25. Id.

26. See Japan lender Resona plans to repay public funds in 5 yrs, *Reuters* (May 8, 2013), available at http://www.reuters.com/article/2013/05/08/resona-funds-idUSL3N0DP4 VI20130508.

27. Resona says to repay $1.1 bln govt bailout after June meeting, *Reuters* (Feb. 27, 2015), available at http://www.reuters.com/article/2015/02/27/resona-bailout-idUSL4N0W 135520150227.

28. Hal S. Scott and Anna Gelpern, *International Finance, Transactions, Policy, and Regulation*, University Casebook Series 1, 500–502 (20th ed. 2014).

29. See Cong. Oversight Panel, April Oversight Report 11 (Apr. 7, 2009), http://cyber cemetery.unt.edu/archive/cop/20110401232137/http://cop.senate.gov/documents/ cop-040709-report.pdf.

30. See Charles Calomiris, Bank failures in theory and history: The Great Depression and other "contagious" events 3 (NBER, Working Paper 13597, Nov. 2007), available at http://www.nber.org/papers/w13597.

31. See Joseph Stiglitz, Witness testimony of Joseph Stiglitz, Congressional Oversight Panel Hearing on Impact of the TARP on Financial Stability 4 (Mar. 2011), available at http://cybercemetery.unt.edu/archive/cop/20110401223036/http://cop.senate.gov/ documents/testimony-030411-stiglitz.pdf.

32. See Lawrence Summers, Beware moral hazard fundamentalists, *Fin. Times* (Sep. 23, 2007).

33. See, for example, Kenneth Ayotte and David Skeel, Bankrupcty or bailouts? 35 *J. Corp. Law* 469, 486 (2010).

34. Hibah Yousuf, S&P downgrades 15 banks, CNN (Nov. 30, 2011).

35. Moody's, Moody's downgrades Citigroup Inc to P-2; Citibank Prime-1 affirmed; all long-term senior ratings confirmed (Sept. 21, 2011), available at http://www.moodys .com/research/Moodys-downgrades-Citigroup-Inc-to-P-2-Citibank-Prime-1 --PR_226520; Moody's, Moody's downgrades Wells Fargo & Company rating (Sept. 21, 2011), available at http://www.moodys.com/research/Moodys-downgrades-Wells -Fargo-Company-rating-sr-to-A2-P--PR_226518; Moody's, Moody's downgrades Bank of America Corp. to Baa1/P-2; Bank of America N.A. to A2, P-1 Affirmed (Sept. 21, 2011), available at http://www.moodys.com/research/Moodys-downgrades-Bank-of -America-Corp-to-Baa1P-2-Bank--PR_226511.

36. Id.

37. Moody's, Moody's downgrades firms with global capital markets operations (Jun. 21, 2012), available at http://www.moodys.com/research/Moodys-downgrades-firms -with-global-capital-markets-operations--PR_248989.

38. Moody's, Moody's Concludes Review of Eight Large US Banks (Nov. 14, 2013), available at http://www.moodys.com/research/Moodys-concludes-review-of-eight-large -US-banks--PR_286790.

39. Laura Marcinek, Moody's lowers ratings of four US banks after review, *Bloomberg* (Nov. 15, 2013).

40. See Antonio Bernardo, Eric Talley, and Ivo Welch, A model of optimal government bailouts 4–5 (May 2011), available at http://www.law.berkeley.edu/files/bclbe/Mode l_of_Optimal_Bailouts_0503.pdf.

41. Charles Goodhart and Emilios Avgouleas, Critical reflections on bank bail-ins (2015), available at http://www.bis.org/bcbs/events/bartnf/avgouleasgoodhart.pdf.

42. Id.

43. See Joseph Stiglitz, Witness testimony of Joseph Stiglitz, Congressional Oversight Panel Hearing on Impact of the TARP on Financial Stability 3 (Mar. 2011), available at http://cybercemetery.unt.edu/archive/cop/20110401223036/http://cop.senate.gov/documents/testimony-030411-stiglitz.pdf.

44. See Charles Calomiris, Bank failures in theory and history: The Great Depression and other "contagious" events 5 (NBER, Working Paper 13597, Nov. 2007), available at http://www.nber.org/papers/w13597.

45. See Simon Johnson, Testimony submitted to the Congressional Oversight Panel 3 (Nov. 2009), available at http://cybercemetery.unt.edu/archive/cop/20110401231809/http://cop.senate.gov/documents/testimony-111909-johnson.pdf.

46. See Charles Calomiris, Bank failures in theory and history: The Great Depression and other "contagious" events 16 (NBER, Working Paper 13597, Nov. 2007), available at http://www.nber.org/papers/w13597.

47. See Simon Johnson, Testimony submitted to the Congressional Oversight Panel 6 (Nov. 2009), available athttp://cybercemetery.unt.edu/archive/cop/20110401231809/http://cop.senate.gov/documents/testimony-111909-johnson.pdf.

48. See, for example, Royal Bank of Scotland Group plc, Capital raising (Oct. 13, 2008), available at http://www.investors.rbs.com/~/media/Files/R/RBS-IR/corporate-actions/placing-and-open-offer-october-2008/rbs-news-2008-10-13-general-announcements.pdf.

49. Fed. Deposit Ins. Corp., *Financial Institution Letters, Monitoring the Use of Funding from Federal Financial Stability and Guaranty Programs, FIL-1–2009* (Jan. 12, 2009), available at http://www.fdic.gov/news/news/financial/2009/fil09001.html.

50. Press Release, Bd. of Governors of the Fed. Reserve Sys., Federal Deposit Ins. Corporation, OCC and Office of Thrift Supervision, Interagency Statement on meeting the needs of creditworthy borrowers (Nov. 12, 2008), available at http://www.federalreserve.gov/newsevents/press/bcreg/20081112a.htm.

51. See Cong. Oversight Panel, December Oversight report 114 (Dec. 2009), available at http://cybercemetery.unt.edu/archive/cop/20110401233008/http://cop.senate.gov/documents/cop-120909-report.pdf.

52. Id. at 109.

53. Id.

54. Id. at 110–11.

Chapter 24

1. See Cong. Oversight Panel, February Oversight report 27 (Feb. 6, 2009), available at http://cybercemetery.unt.edu/archive/cop/20110401232131/http://cop.senate.gov/documents/cop-020609-report.pdf.

2. See Cong. Budget Office, The troubled asset relief program: Report on transactions through December 31, 2008 1 (Jan. 2009), available at https://www.cbo.gov/sites/default/files/111th-congress-2009-2010/reports/01-16-tarp.pdf(finding a subsidy of $64 billion for transactions through Dec. 31, 2008).

3. See Cong. Oversight Panel, July Oversight report 26–27 (Jul. 10, 2009), available at http://cybercemetery.unt.edu/archive/cop/20110401232134/http://cop.senate.gov/documents/cop-071009-report.pdf.

4. See Cong. Oversight Panel, December Oversight report 10 (Dec. 2009), available at http://cybercemetery.unt.edu/archive/cop/20110401233008/http://cop.senate.gov/documents/cop-120909-report.pdf.

5. See SIGTARP, Assessing Treasury's process to sell warrants received from TARP recipients 1 (May 10, 2010), available at https://www.sigtarp.gov/Audit%20Reports/Assessing%20Treasury's%20Process%20to%20Sell%20Warrants%20Received%20From%20TARP%20Recipients_May_11_2010.pdf.

6. See Mark Landler and Eric Dash, Drama behind a $250 billion banking deal, NY Times (Oct. 15, 2008).

7. See Hal Scott and Maxwell Jenkins, The U.S. Treasury is a public, not a private, investor, Fin. Times (Mar. 2, 2009), available at http://www.ft.com/cms/s/0/a57eaa72-073c-11de-9294-000077b07658.html.

8. Tom Braithwaite and Francesco Guerrera, U.S. Treasury sells remaining Citi shares, Fin. Times (Dec. 7, 2010), available at http://www.ft.com/intl/cms/s/0/f8d42e04-0181-11e0-9b29-00144feab49a.html#axzz1zpar28rW.

9. US Dept. of Treas., Investment in AIG (Dec. 11, 2013), available at http://www.treasury.gov/initiatives/financial-stability/TARP-Programs/aig/Pages/status.aspx.

10. See Herbert Allison, Written testimony for Domestic Policy Subcommittee of the Oversight and Government Reform Committee 18–21 (Dec. 17, 2009), available at http://www.gpo.gov/fdsys/pkg/CHRG-111hhrg65131/pdf/CHRG-111hhrg65131.pdf.

11. See, for example, Rep. Jim Jordan, Hearing of Committee on Oversight and Government Reform 8 (Dec. 16, 2009), available at http://www.gpo.gov/fdsys/pkg/CHRG-111hhrg65130/pdf/CHRG-111hhrg65130.pdf.

12. Alan Zibel, Watchdog says Treasury let GM, Ally give executives big raises during TARP, Wall St. J. (Sep. 24, 2014).

13. See Alex Pollock, TARP on a businesslike basis, Statement before the Congressional Oversight Panel of the Troubled Asset Program 3 (Nov. 19, 2009), available at http://cybercemetery.unt.edu/archive/cop/20110401231809/http://cop.senate.gov/documents/testimony-111909-pollock.pdf.

14. Id.

15. Id. at 4.

16. Id.

17. See UK Fin. Investments Ltd., UKFI Shareholder relationship framework document (Jan. 2010), available at http://www.ukfi.co.uk/releases/UKFI_FD_180110v2.pdf.

18. Id.

19. Government Accountability Office, Troubled asset relief program: Winding down the capital purchase program, GAO 15–367 4 (Mar. 6, 2015), available at http://www.gao.gov/assets/670/668904.pdf.

20. Id. at 7, 12.

21. See also Office of the Special Inspector General for the Troubled Asset Relief Program, Quarterly report to Congress 230 (Jan. 28, 2015), available at http://www.sigtarp.gov/Quarterly%20Reports/January_28_2015_Report_to_Congress.pdf.

22. Id. at 230.

23. Id.

24. For a comprehensive list of recapitalization programs, see Da Lin, Lessons for TARP from abroad: A survey of recent recapitalization programs, appendix I (May 2, 2012), available at http://www.law.harvard.edu/programs/about/pifs/education/llm/2011--2012/da-lin.pdf.

25. Id. at 19.

26. Id. at 20.

27. Id. at 21.

28. Id. at table 2. For a summary of nonprice conditions for recapitalization programs, see id. at table 2.

Chapter 25

1. Id.

2. SRM Article 2(b),(c), available at http://eur-lex.europa.eu/legal-content/EN/TXT/?uri=CELEX:32014R0806.

3. Rosalind Wiggins, Michael Wedow, and Andrew Metrick, The Single Resolution Mechanism 1, 11 (2015), available at http://som.yale.edu/sites/default/files/001-2014-5B-V1-EuropeanBanking-B-REVA.pdf.

4. George Zavvos and Stella Kaltsouni, The Single Resolution Mechanism in the European Banking Union 1, 39 (2014), available at http://papers.ssrn.com/sol3/papers.cfm?abstract_id=2531907.

5. SRM Regulation Article 27.7, available at http://eur-lex.europa.eu/legal-content/EN/TXT/?uri=CELEX:32014R0806 (stating that the Single Resolution Fund "may make a contribution ... only where a contribution to loss absorption and recapitalization equal to an amount not less than 8 percent of the total liabilities ... has been made by shareholders, the holders of relevant capital instruments, and other eligible liabilities through write-down, conversion, or otherwise.").

6. See, for example, Yasuyuki Fuchita, Richard Herring, and Robert E. Litan, Rock times: New perspectives on financial stability 1, 15 (2012) (noting that before Dodd–Frank "[s]ection 13(c)(4)(G) of the Federal Deposit Insurance Act had allowed, in the event of systemic risk, for capital injections, debt guarantees, and other support for insured depository institutions that go beyond the principles of least-cost resolution." However, "Section 1106(b) of Dodd–Frank modifies that section of the Federal Deposit Insurance Act ... to require that assistance in the event of systemic risk be provided 'for the purpose

of winding up the insured depository institution ...' thus disallowing open bank assistance transactions.").

7. See, for example, SRM Regulation Article 27.6(b), available at http://eur-lex.europa.eu/legal-content/EN/TXT/?uri=CELEX:32014R0806 (stating that under certain circumstances, when certain liabilities are excluded from bail-in measures, the Single Resolution Fund may be used to "purchase instruments of ownership or capital instruments in the institution under resolution, in order to recapitalize the institution").

8. ESM, Frequently asked questions on the European Stability Mechanism (ESM), Mar. 2, 2015, http://www.esm.europa.eu/publications/index.htm (accessed Mar. 21, 2015) (henceforth "ESM FAQ").

9. European Stability Mechanism, ESM reaches target level of 80 billion in paid-in-capital (May 1, 2014), available at http://www.esm.europa.eu/press/releases/esm-reaches-target-level-of-80-billion-in-paid-in-capital1.htm.

10. European Stability Mechanism, ESM direct bank recapitalisation instrument adopted (Dec. 2014), available at http://www.esm.europa.eu/press/releases/esm-direct-bank-recapitalisation-instrument-adopted.htm.

11. *ESM Guideline on Financial Assistance for the Recapitalization of Financial Institutions*, Articles 3.2 and 4.3, available at http://www.esm.europa.eu/pdf/ESM%20Guideline%20on%20recapitalisation%20of%20financial%20institutions.pdf.

12. *ESM Guideline on Financial Assistance for the Recapitalization of Financial Institutions*, Article 4.3.

13. European Council, ESM direct bank recapitalisation instrument (Jun. 20, 2013), available at http://www.consilium.europa.eu/council-eu/eurogroup/pdf/20130620-ESM-direct-bank-recapitalisation-instrument/.

14. European Stability Mechanism, ESM direct bank recapitalisation instrument adopted (Dec. 2014), available at http://www.esm.europa.eu/press/releases/esm-direct-bank-recapitalisation-instrument-adopted.htm.

15. European Banking Authority, EBA consults on criteria for determining the minimum requirement for own funds and eligible liabilities (Nov. 2014), available at https://www.eba.europa.eu/-/eba-consults-on-criteria-for-determining-the-minimum-requirement-for-own-funds-and-eligible-liabilities-mrel-.

16. See, generally, Articles 102 through 126.1.

17. Article 102–1.

18. Hideyuki Sakai, Overview of the Japanese legal framework to resolve a systemically important financial institution in insolvency, *Proceedings in Japan* 1 (2012), available at http://www.law.harvard.edu/programs/about/pifs/symposia/japan/2012-japan/bingham-h-sakai-paper.pdf.

19. Kei Kodachi, Japan's orderly resolution regime for the financial firm, Nomura Institute of Capital Markets Research 1 (2014), available at http://papers.ssrn.com/sol3/papers.cfm?abstract_id=2379907; Article 98.

20. Article 102–1.

21. Kei Kodachi, Japan's orderly resolution regime for the financial firm, Nomura Institute of Capital Markets Research 1 (2014), available at http://papers.ssrn.com/sol3/papers.cfm?abstract_id=2379907.

22. Article 105.

23. Kei Kodachi, Japan's orderly resolution regime for the financial firm, Nomura Institute of Capital Markets Research 1 (2014), available at http://papers.ssrn.com/sol3/papers.cfm?abstract_id=2379907 (noting that the original systemic risk exception did not permit the use of public funds to underwrite a holding company's share issuance).

24. Financial Services Agency, Determination on the recapitalization of the Resona Bank, Ltd (2003), available at http://www.fsa.go.jp/news/newse/e20030610-1.html.

25. Kei Kodachi, Japan's orderly resolution regime for the financial firm, Nomura Institute of Capital Markets Research 1 (2014), available at http://papers.ssrn.com/sol3/papers.cfm?abstract_id=2379907.

26. Deposit Insurance Corporation of Japan, Bank nationalization and re-privatization of Japan (2010), available at http://www.dic.go.jp/katsudo/kokusai/roundtable/5th/2010.3.18f.pdf.

27. Ashikaga applies for TSE listing, *Japan Times* (2015), available at http://www.japan times.co.jp/news/2013/07/31/business/financial-markets/ashikaga-applies-for-tse -listing/#.VRr6oeFLOT8 .

28. Article 126–2(2)(i)-(iv).

29. Kei Kodachi, Japan's orderly resolution regime for the financial firm, Nomura Institute of Capital Markets Research 1 (2014), available at http://papers.ssrn.com/sol3/papers.cfm?abstract_id=2379907.

30. Article 126–19(1).

31. Article 126–22(1).

32. Article 126–2(1)(i)-(ii).

33. Article 126–39(1).

34. Article 125(1).

35. Masahiro Kawai, Asian monetary integration: A Japanese perspective (ADBI Working Paper Series, 2014), available at http://saber.eaber.org/sites/default/files/docu ments/2014.04.18.wp475.asian_.monetary.integration.japan_.pdf.

36. Id.

Appendix

1. Andrew Haldane, Speech delivered at the Financial Student Association, Amsterdam, pp. 9–10 (Apr. 28, 2009), available at http://www.bankofengland.co.uk/archive/Docu ments/historicpubs/speeches/2009/speech386.pdf.

2. Daron Acemoglu, Asuman Ozdaglar, and Alireza Tahbaz-Salehi, Systemic risk and stability in financial networks, 105(2) *Am. Econ. Rev.* 564 (2015).

3. Id. at 574.

4. Id. at 578.

5. Id. at 574.
6. Id. at 569, 572, 574. The threshold is defined as $n \cdot (a - v)$, where n is the number of banks, a is the payoff banks receive on their investments in "the business as usual regime," and v is the level of external liabilities.

7. Matthew Elliott, Benjamin Golub, and Matthew Jackson, Financial networks and contagion, 104(10) *Am. Econ. Rev.* 3115 (2014).

8. Id. at 3122.

9. See id. at 3115–53.

10. Christian Upper, Simulation methods to assess the danger of contagion in interbank markets, 7 (3) *J. Fin. Stability* (2011) at 111–25 (indicating an absence of such events, while noting that this scenario almost unfolded when Herstatt failed in 1974).

11. Id. at 118.

12. Id. at 121.

13. Franklin Allen and Douglas Gale, Financial contagion, 108(1) *J. Pol. Econ.* 1 (2000).

14. Haldane, *supra* note 1, at 10.

15. Prasanna Gai and Sujit Kapadia, Presentation at the CFAP Conference on Interconnections in Financial Markets: Liquidity Hoarding, Network Externalities, and Interbank Market Collapse (Mar. 27, 2010), available at http://www.cfap.jbs.cam.ac.uk/news/downloads/20100327_liquidity.pdf.

16. Prasanna Gai, Andrew Haldane, and Sujit Kapadia, Complexity, concentration and contagion, 58 *J. Mon. Econ.* 453, 463–64 (2011).

17. Haldane, *supra* note 1, at 9–10.

18. Gai et al., *supra* note 16, at 464.

19. Id.

20. Id. at 462.

21. Haldane, *supra* note 1, at 12.

22. Id.

23. Id.

24. See Prasanna Gai and Sujit Kapadia, Contagion in financial networks, 466 *Proceed. Roy. Soc.A* 2401 (2010); see also Teruyoshi Kobayashi, Diversity among banks may increase systemic risk (Working paper, Aug. 2012).

25. Gai and Kapadia, *supra* note 24, at 2403.

26. Haldane, *supra* note 1, at 10.

27. Yakov Amihud, Illiquidity and stock returns: Cross-section and time-series effects, 5(1) *J. Fin. Markets* 31 (2002); Tarun Chordia, Richard Roll, and Avanidhar Subrahmanyam, Order imbalance, liquidity, and market returns, 65(1) *J. Fin. Econ.* 111 (2002); C. M. Jones, A century of stock market liquidity and trading costs, Columbia University Graduate School of Business (Working paper, 2001); Geert Bekaert, Campbell R. Harvey and

Christian Lundblad, Liquidity and expected returns: Lessons from emerging markets, 20(6) *Rev. Fin. Stud.* 1783, 1784 (2007).

28. Yakov Amihud and Haim Mendelson, Asset pricing and the bid—ask spread, 17(2) *J. Fin. Econ.* 223 (1986); Lubos Pastor and Robert F. Stambaugh, Liquidity risk and expected stock returns, 111(3) *J. Polit. Econ.* 642 (2003).

29. See Zijun Liu, Banking sector interconnectedness: What is it, how can we measure it and why does it matter? *Bank of England Q. Bull.* 2015 Q2.

30. See Tobias Adrian and Markus K. Brunnermeier, CoVaR (Working Paper, 2010).

31. See Viral Acharya, Lasse H. Pedersen, Thomas Philippon, and Matthew Richardson, Measuring systemic risk (Working Paper 2010).

32. See Monica Billio, Andrew W. Lo, Mila Getmansky, and Loriana Pelizzon, Econometric measures of connectedness and systemic risk in the finance and insurance sectors, 104 (3) *J. Fin. Econ.* 535 (2012).

33. David Scharfstein and Jeremy Stein, Herd behavior and investment, 80 (3) *Am. Econ. Rev.* 465 (1990).

34. Carmen Reinhart and Kenneth Rogoff, This time is different: A panoramic view of eight centuries of financial crisis (NBER Working Paper 13882, Mar. 2008).

35. Franklin Allen and Elena Carletti, Systemic risk and macroprudential regulation (Jun. 2011), available at http://www.iea-world.org/docs/1043.pdf.

36. Helmut Elsinger, Alfred Lehar, and Martin Summer, Using market information for banking system risk assessment, 2 (1) *Int. J. Centr. Bank.* 137 (2006).

37. Id.

Index